WORLDLY
GOODS

BY LISA JARDINE

Francis Bacon: Discovery and the Art of Discourse

*Still Harping on Daughters: Women and Drama
in the Age of Shakespeare*

*From Humanism to the Humanities: Education and the Liberal Arts
in Fifteenth- and Sixteenth-Century Europe (with A. T. Grafton)*

*What's Left? Women in Culture and the Labour Movement
(with Julia Swindells)*

Erasmus, Man of Letters: The Construction of Charisma in Print

Worldly Goods: A New History of the Renaissance

WORLDLY GOODS

A NEW HISTORY OF THE RENAISSANCE

LISA JARDINE

NAN A TALESE

DOUBLEDAY

NEW YORK LONDON TORONTO SYDNEY AUCKLAND

PUBLISHED BY NAN A. TALESE

an imprint of Doubleday
A division of Bantam Doubleday Dell Publishing Group, Inc.
1540 Broadway, New York, New York 10036

Doubleday is a trademark of Doubleday, a division of
Bantam Doubleday Dell Publishing Group, Inc.

First Published in the United Kingdom by Macmillan, London

Library of Congress Cataloging-in-Publication Data
Jardine, Lisa
Worldly Goods: a new history of the Renaissance/Lisa Jardine.
p. cm.
Includes bibliographical references and index.
ISBN 0-385-47684-1 (alk. paper)
1. Renaissance.   2. Economic history—15th century.   3. Economic history—16th century.
I. Title.
CB361.J35   1996
940.2'1—dc20
96-8710
CIP

1 3 5 7 9 10 8 6 4 2

FOR MY MOTHER

RITA BRONOWSKI

· CONTENTS ·

LIST OF ILLUSTRATIONS

TWO THE PRICE OF MAGNIFICENCE

THREE THE TRIUMPH OF THE BOOK

FOUR LEARNING TO BE CIVILIZED

SEVEN MAPPING THE HEAVENS

EIGHT CONSPICUOUS CONSUMPTION

EPILOGUE

PLATE SECTION ONE

1. Jan Van Eyck, *Arnolfini Marriage*, 1434. London, National Gallery.

2. Carlo Crivelli, detail from *The Annunciation with St Emidius*, showing peacock and rug, 1486. London, National Gallery.

3. Carlo Crivelli, detail from *The Annunciation with St Emidius*, showing plates and vases on a shelf, 1486. London, National Gallery.

4. Sinan Bey, *Portrait of Mehmed II*. Istanbul, Topkapı Palace Museum. Photo: Sonia Halliday.

5. Detail from *The Taking of Constantinople by the Turks, 22 April 1453*, from Bertrand de la Broquière, *Voyage d'Outremer*. Ms Fr. 9087, fol. 207. Paris, Bibliothèque Nationale de France. Photo: Sonia Halliday.

6. Fra Angelico, detail from the altarpiece of St Nicholas of Bari. Rome, Pinacoteca, Vatican. Photo: Scala.

7. Benozzo Gozzoli, detail from *Procession of the Magi*, 1459. Florence, Chapel of the Palazzo Medici Riccardi. Photo: Scala.

8. Ottoman caftan. Istanbul, Topkapı Museum.

9. Niclaus Manuel, detail from *St Eligius at Work*, 1515. Bern, Kunstmuseum.

10. Venetian majolica dish, c. 1495, showing the export of bullion from Venice, with the Doge in the foreground. Cambridge, Fitzwilliam Museum, Cambridge University.

11. Matthaus of Kuttenberg, detail from the frontispiece of the *Kuttenberger Kanzional*, Ms Cod. 15.501, f.lv, c. 1490. Vienna, Österreichische Nationalbibliothek.

12. *The Mint*, from Aristotle's *Ethics, Politics, Economics*, from a French translation. Ms 927, f.145r. Detail showing shelves bearing plates. Rouen, Bibliothèque Municipale. Photo: Giraudon/Bridgeman Art Library.

13. Vittore Carpaccio, *Vision of St Augustine*. Detail showing books and music scores. Venice, Scuola di San Giorgio degli Schiavoni. Photo: Bridgeman Art Library.

Plate Section Two

PREFACE

THE RENAISSANCE was a time of creative energy, enthusiasm, expanding horizons, collaborative enterprises, bravura entrepreneurialism and intellectual excitement. One of the unexpected outcomes of writing the present book has been the way in which those around me, who have given me so much support and encouragement, have replicated the exhilarating sense of discovery which the period, for me, represents. Each and every friend and acquaintance who has been subjected over the past two years to an over-excited deluge of detail from me on the topic of the moment – from the trade in bloodstock horses to pigments, from art thefts to currency fluctuation – has responded with some crucial insight which has contributed to the shape of my final argument. There are, therefore, more people I need to thank than there could possibly be space for in a preface. To all those people I can only say that if you recognize your salient comment somewhere in the text, then accept my most fulsome thanks for your invaluable insight.

There are, however, some who have inevitably listened patiently, and responded enthusiastically, far beyond the call of friendship or duty. Above all, my family has supported me with the unswerving conviction that this is the best book I have ever written (just as my husband always assures me that the last meal I cooked was the best he ever ate). My husband John and my children Daniel, Rachel and Sam have been with *Worldly Goods* every step of the way – including two summers trawling European bookshops, museums and galleries instead of sitting in the sun. John, Daniel and Rachel have read every word (in many drafts), and have argued through almost every point; Sam has calmly sorted out my computer each time it has let me down, and has uncomplainingly made his own tea when I could not be dislodged from my seat in front of the screen. All of them deserve much gratitude for their practical and intellectual help; yet more for their calm, unwavering confidence in me.

Among my colleagues, no prefatory acknowledgement could ever do justice to Jerry Brotton's contribution to *Worldly Goods*. He has helped me assemble research materials throughout, and has been an assiduous and invaluable picture researcher. But, beyond that, he has enlarged the horizons of the enterprise, constantly pressing me to open my mind to avenues of research which without him I would never have seen, let alone pursued. Anthony Pagden, Pat Rubin and Bill Sherman read the manuscript in draft, and each made important suggestions for correction or modification. My agent, Maggie Pearlstine, and my editors in London and New York, Georgina Morley and Nan Talese have consistently given me the benefit of their expertise and encouragement, as well as a sense that the project was an important one.

Since this book brings together in accessible form scholarly work on the Renaissance from a wide range of disciplines, it owes a considerable debt to scholars who have worked in the field over the past twenty years. I have included in my bibliography every work upon which I have drawn, down to the source for the tiniest detail. The bibliography is therefore an eccentric one – a compilation of disparate routes down which the curious reader may choose to go in pursuit of more detailed and specialist research in the areas covered by the book. A small group of scholars whose work has yielded startlingly fresh material and insights deserves special acknowledgement: Martin Lowry and Elizabeth Eisenstein on the history of the book; David Chambers on the Gonzagas; Gülru Necipoğlu and Julian Raby on the Ottomans. Both Jerry Brotton and Alan Stewart allowed me access to unpublished work of theirs; their place in the bibliography will have to wait for a second edition.

There is little consistency in the spelling of proper names in my period. I have tried to use the most familiar forms, generally in the appropriate vernacular. Occasionally, however, an individual has customarily been referred to by the Latin form of their name, in which case I too have preferred that form. For popes, emperors, queens and kings I have used English forms, unless the secondary literature prefers another: Matthias Corvinus, King of Hungary, is an appropriate example, since he is almost invariably known by this, the Latin form of his name.

The Renaissance I explore in this book is one in which money plays a large part. Sums of money crop up throughout my story, in the form of (among others) payments for bulk commodities like pepper, massive debts incurred by European princes, papal taxes, dowries, inheritances or simply cash amounts handed over for small purchases. For the purposes of this book the reader may assume that all the gold coins referred to are of equivalent weight and value – the Florentine and Rhine florin, the Venetian and Hungarian ducat and the Habsburg Philipp are roughly interchangeable, the French écu and English half-noble worth slightly less. Because these coins held their value, bequests and large debts tend in the period to be expressed in terms of one of these standard coins. Commercially, however, sums are expressed in pounds, livres or lire, and these, unfortunately, are quite another matter. This is money of account – the standard, almost European-wide system of calculating value for trading purposes. Established by Charlemagne around AD 800, the livre was originally equal to one pound weight of silver. By the fifteenth century, however, any equivalence with silver weight had long ago been lost, and the value of a local 'pound' varied considerably, depending upon the current economic circumstances. Furthermore, the price of silver fluctuated dramatically, further affecting the value of silver coin in circulation. No wonder Europeans who could not use paper bills (promises to pay, at agreed rates of exchange) to transact their business always preferred to settle all their accounts in gold coin.

LISA JARDINE
London, February 1996

WORLDLY
GOODS

PROLOGUE

In London, as in every other European capital, springtime heralds the arrival of its cultural pilgrims, who throng Trafalgar Square and its surroundings, following trails well laid by the international tourist industry to lead us to the supposed roots of our Western intellectual and artistic heritage. Cameras at the ready, we trawl the museums and galleries ready to record all relevant items from our guidebook inventory of important vestiges of Europe's collective history. High on our list are the treasures of the period which formed what is broadly known as the Western tradition in art and learning – the European Renaissance.

London boasts one of the world's great temples to that cultural moment: the National Gallery. Its new Sainsbury Wing, designed by architect Robert Venturi (imported from North America for the task) and built under the patronage of the Sainsbury family (millionaire merchants, whose wealth was accumulated in super-market trading), was purpose-built to house the early Renaissance collection. It is now possible for the first time to confront the spirit of the Renaissance head on – to encounter the paintings from the period grouped together chronologically and geographically, and physically to come upon them fresh, through the Sainsbury Wing's own imposing entrance to the west of the old National Gallery.

'DUCCIO · MASACCIO · VAN EYCK · PIERO · MANTEGNA · BELLINI · LEONARDO · RAPHAEL' runs the inscription deeply incised in the stone facing, for the length of the impressively grand staircase. These are the names of great masters of Renaissance painting; a roll-call of painters whose works for many people symbolize its artistic achievement and, indeed, define it. The image this assembly of artists conjures up is one of luminous canvases, sumptuous in their glowing depiction of sacred and secular figures, rich with the colour and splendour of an idealized and idealistic Renaissance world. As we ascend the staircase, we anticipate the glories of their subject matter – a familiar range of scenes from the lives of mythic heroes of antiquity, moments from the life of Christ and arrestingly realistic portraits of major political figures and their retinues from across Europe – popes and potentates, court beauties, princes' favourites and the influential rich.

The term 'Renaissance' prompts a litany of names of famous artists; it also evokes a particular kind of timeless achievement. This golden era bathed in perpetual Mediterranean sunlight was, we know, a period of rebirth (sublime, classical culture born again), a return to the glories of the age of political and cultural supremacy of Greece and Rome, after the diversionary interlude of the (local and parochial) middle ages. We tie in such a Renaissance with the recovery of the ancient languages, and our accounts of its reflowering inevitably centre on standards of achievement established early in the period at the symbolic geographical centre of classical art and learning, Italy. Hence we conventionally represent it as a 'golden age restored', an age in which the characteristic mood was a kind of lofty self-confidence, spiritual arrogance and an associated antique ideal of Aryan virtue or manliness. The paintings which we come determined to admire here are indisputably 'Renaissance'.

Why, then, do these paintings fail to live up to our expectations? Why does the vivid account of emerging art and culture shine so much brighter than the works of art we cultural votaries actually encounter on our London pilgrimage? In a book whose goal is to understand the Renaissance afresh this is an appropriate place to begin. For visual representations like those in the National Gallery have shaped our understanding of the Renaissance itself, have indeed come to stand pre-eminently for its cultural achievement.

Through the heavy, smoked-glass doors, passing between pilasters which pay homage to the classical orders, we turn sharply to our right and mount the self-consciously classical stone stairs, flanked by those deeply incised inscriptions in stone. Turn to our left at the top of the staircase and we enter the early Renaissance galleries. Like all the other visitors around us, we brace ourselves expectantly for the assault on the senses of shimmering expanses of pink-tinted human flesh or allegorical representations of antique gods and goddesses from the brushes of Titian and Raphaël, the visionary canvases of Leonardo da Vinci. They are nowhere to be found; they are housed elsewhere, and belong later on in our story.

Instead, the echoing stone-trimmed rooms house densely detailed paintings on wooden panels, indecipherable from any distance, unimposing in their evident aesthetic reluctance to dominate the spaces. The scale throughout is unpretentious, and the most modest of the works are the size of a sheet of typing paper. Art devised for intimacy struggles to assert itself in spaces designed for ostentatiously public communication. On any day we choose we will find the gallery's visitors moving tentatively from work to work, straining to grasp the significance of the lovingly rendered physicality of surfaces which the paintings seem to share. We can, however, make a virtue of that need for close attention. For what we have around us is an assemblage of precious objects whose characteristics we can use to begin to define the age which gave rise to them.

Inside the galleries themselves, turn left and we are confronted by a vista of framing doorways which carries the eye to the nine panels of Carlo Crivelli's *Demidoff Altarpiece*, painted in 1476 and displayed in an ornate gilded Victorian–gothic frame. As we direct our steps towards the altarpiece, Crivelli's Virgin meets our gaze from the central panel, her naked Christ-child leaning across her arm in a pose which is temptingly modern – a mother and child like any we might encounter today. A reminder (so a catalogue might tell us) that the humanity of the Renaissance, its idealized traditions of life and thought, have been passed down to us undisturbed.

Turn around, though, and the impression is more complicated. The *Demidoff Altarpiece* is flanked by sacred images painted by fifteenth-century Italian artists, of a less serenely familiar kind. Striking among these (and at almost 5 feet by 8 feet one of the larger works) is Crivelli's *Annunciation with St Emidius* (1486).

Crivelli's Madonna is a slip of a girl, bent dutifully over an open book. Our eye is directed to her via a shaft of golden light which emerges from the heavens, enters the Virgin's chamber through a tiny, convenient window in the wall above her head, and comes to rest on her temple. A symbolic dove, hovering along the path of the ray, tells us that this is the light of the Holy Spirit. But the rest of the composition makes it hard to countenance the idea that this Virgin is truly meant to be the central subject and focus of all our attention in the painting. The sacred subject is almost crowded out of the picture by the profusion of the painting's physical, secular detail.

Mary is housed in an architecturally ornate Italianate building, on which Crivelli has lovingly inscribed the crafted ornamentation of revived Greek and Roman antiquity. The doorway through which we glimpse her is flanked by antique-style pilasters with Corinthian capitols; a classical frieze runs around the building at first-storey level; on the upper level, columns and arches frame an open loggia with an ornate geometrical ceiling; contrasting colours (gilt, terracotta, ochre and slate) and textures (brick, marble and stone) add to the richness of the exterior. Within the room, panelled in precious wood, the clutter of prosperous living is as lovingly represented as the stitched and embroidered cloth of the Virgin's green cloak and russet gown. A red tapestry hanging is drawn across the doorway; the Virgin's open book rests on a carved reading desk; behind her the table is covered with a green embroidered velvet cloth edged in gold, a pure white cloth is thrown across this, and a pile of embroidered and tasselled cushions is stacked upon that. The rear wall of the room carries a gilded frieze, with, high on it, a shelf loaded with belongings – a brass candlestick, boxes and pots, a pile

1. Carlo Crivelli, *The Annunciation with St Emidius*

of deep porcelain dishes, leather-bound books with clasps, a crystal vase with a stopper. In the window stands a small bush growing in a decorated majolica pot.

The profusion of lovingly depicted objects spills over outside the house. More plants in distinctive stone and earthenware pots stand on the loggia parapet, across which is thrown an oriental rug partly obscuring a terracotta carving set into the low outer wall. Alongside the rug stands an exotic peacock. A birdcage hangs from a rail, on which perches a dove. Beyond the building which encloses the Virgin is a further ornate arch, faced with terracotta carvings, marble and stone. Another oriental rug hangs from its parapet, on which rests a large open book or ledger. A well-dressed man reads a message which has apparently just been received by carrier pigeon (a visual joke about messages from afar and doves). Alongside the cage which houses the pigeon is another bush in an earthenware pot. The commercial transaction on the bridge – possibly a trading communication with a factor or emissary in a foreign land – mirrors and echoes the spiritual transaction between God and his chosen handmaiden in the foreground.

Outside the Virgin's window, the angel Gabriel greets the Virgin, while at the same time apparently conversing with St Emidius, patron saint of Ascoli Piceno (Crivelli's home town, by which the panel was commissioned), who holds a meticulously detailed model of the town he guards spiritually. The client discusses his ambitious town-planning project with his architect – or so it appears. They kneel together on a patterned marble floor, at the base of which is inscribed, in a print reminiscent of the great Italian Aldine printing press, 'LIBERTAS · ECCLESIASTICA' ('Freedom from the Church'). These are the words (we are told) at the start of the papal declaration which gave limited rights of self-government to the people of Ascoli Piceno on the Feast of the Annunciation, 1482.

This virtuoso painting is every bit as much a visual celebration of conspicuous consumption and of trade as it is a tribute to the chastity of Christ's mother. Masonry, marble, fabric and household goods are as carefully documented and as lovingly rendered as are the figures from the Christian story.

The imported carpets from Turkey might have been painted from life, hanging outside a rug-merchant's shop. Indeed, they were probably copied from carpets loaned by an obliging local dealer, or by a wealthy patron. Paintings like Crivelli's are used today by historians of Turkish carpets as documentation for the development in their designs during the fifteenth century. The carpet, in other words, is made 'real' with as much care as is the skilfully modelled flesh of the Virgin's arms and hands.

We do not need to have a specialist interest to find that the triumphantly realistic material objects, surfaces and decoration almost entirely absorb our attention. The thing depicted may in fact be a symbolic attribute of the Virgin: the stoppered crystal bottle, for instance, represents the purity of Mary's conception – as light passes through a glass vessel without its ray being diminished, so the Virgin conceived a child without losing her purity. Nevertheless, so precise are the representations that we would recognize such an object immediately if we saw it today. We could treat the painting like a modern mail-order catalogue, and order our own reproduction door-jamb carvings by the yard; we could comb the antiques markets, using the painting as our wish list for glass and porcelain, curtains, cushions and tapestries.

This meticulous visual inventory of consumer goods is not merely a record of acquisitiveness limited to Italy. The Virgin Mary's surroundings gather together desirable material possessions from across the globe. They announce with pride Italian access to markets from northern France to the Ottoman Empire. Here is a world which assembles with delight rugs from Istanbul, tapestry hangings from Arras, delicate glass from Venice, metalwork from Islamic Spain, porcelain and silk from China, broadcloth from London. The artist has represented with loving care the covetable commodities which by the mid-fifteenth century could be procured for ready money. His own work belongs to this exotic world of desirable possessions;

2. Robert Campin, *Virgin and Child before a Firescreen*

celebrating global mercantilism is part and parcel of what is, after all, for him a commercial project – the entrepreneurial and the spiritual rub shoulders in this early Renaissance world.

Crivelli's *Annunciation with St Emidius* is breathtaking in the virtuosity of its physical detail. It does not take us long to verify that among the paintings of this period it is by no means unusual. In the room next to the Crivellis, for instance, hangs Robert Campin's *Virgin and Child before a Firescreen* (early fifteenth century). Once again we notice the care the artist has taken with the rich fabrics, the meticulous precision of detailing of the bench with carved lions, draped with green velvet, on which the Virgin and Child are seated; the beautifully illuminated book with its minutely observed jewelled clasps, resting on a red and green velvet cushion; the ornate chest and elaborate gilded chalice (repainted in the nineteenth century). The hem of the Virgin's lavender gown is patterned in gems and gold thread, and trimmed with fur at the wrist. Aside from the single

3. Master of Liesborn, *Liesborn Altarpiece: The Annunciation*

central area which encloses the Virgin's face, breast and hands, and the reclining Child, the rest of the oak panel is dedicated to celebrating belongings – the possessions which advertise an individual's purchasing power.

One room further on along the eastern side of the wing, the Master of Liesborn's *Annunciation* meticulously records a burnished brass platter, an ornate candlestick, a small stoppered bottle and an oriental-style metal pitcher, a carved chest with metal hinges and locks, an elaborately tiled floor, an ornate desk and settle, a canopied bed with red brocade hangings, and embroidered cushions.

It is not surprising if this cataloguing of detail has the ring of a household inventory about it, for I think that that is what we are being asked to respond to as we gaze in admiration. The visual impact of these Virgins is enhanced by our understanding that they inhabit a fifteenth-century life-world crowded with desirable consumer objects. But, beyond that, the celebration of belongings transmutes the spiritual awe of beholding the mother of God into a secular frisson of desire at the lavishness of her surroundings. Was the Renaissance admirer of these paintings being encouraged to want to be in the Virgin's spiritual likeness, or was he or she expected to be seduced by all that lavishness to want to inhabit her surroundings, wonderfully cluttered as these are with the booty of international trade? Did the onlooker long for the touch and the smell of the luxuries which fill these panels? Was his or her spirit elevated by the very aspiration to have the things she is represented as owning?

To ask such questions is to suggest that those impulses which today we disparage as 'consumerism' might occupy a respectable place in the characterization of the new Renaissance mind. It is curious how reluctant we are to include acquisitiveness among the defining characteristics of the age which formed our aesthetic heritage.

A competitive urge to acquire was a precondition for the growth in production of lavishly expensive works of art. A painter's reputation rested on his ability to arouse commercial interest in his works of art, not on some intrinsic criteria of intellectual worth. Titian's canvases of statuesque naked women in recumbent poses were regarded as learnedly symbolic by nineteenth-century art historians – it was claimed they were visual explorations of allegories drawn from classical Latin literature. Only recently did contemporary correspondence come to light which showed that these works of art were painted to meet a vigorous demand for bedroom paintings depicting erotic nudes in salacious poses. When Guidobaldo, Duke of Urbino, was negotiating to buy the painting now known as *The Venus of Urbino* from Titian in 1538 he referred to it simply as a painting of 'a naked woman' (and tried to borrow money from his mother Eleonora Gonzaga to pay for it). In 1542 the churchman Cardinal Farnese saw the painting at Guidobaldo's summer residence and rushed off to commission a similarly erotic nude of his own from Titian in Venice. Reporting back on the progress of the painting some time later, the Papal Nuncio in Venice expressed the view that the Cardinal's nude, now completed and ready for shipment, made *The Venus of Urbino* look like a frigid nun. In 1600, in response to a request from an admirer of *The Venus of Urbino* to acquire a copy, the then Duke agreed, on condition that the identity of the owner of the original be kept a secret – he did not wish it to be widely known that he was the owner of that kind of painting.

If this seems a somewhat banal train of thought as we stand in admiration in front of an early-Renaissance Annunciation, let us pursue it a little further in the secular domain. Retracing our steps and crossing to the galleries on the west side of the Sainsbury Wing, we find ourselves in the more intimate space which houses the paintings of Jan van Eyck. The painting known as *The Arnolfini Marriage* (1434) is a deservedly famous example of early-Renaissance Flemish painting. What is striking, after our intense study of those Annunciations, is how closely the attention which has been paid by van Eyck here to the detailing of commodities resembles that which we identified in the sacred works.

Jan van Eyck's double portrait – probably a commission from the Italian merchant Giovanni Arnolfini to commemorate his betrothal or marriage to Giovanna Cenami – is packed with details of acquisitiveness in fifteenth-century Bruges. It invites the viewer's eye to dwell on the oriental rug, the settle and high-backed chair with their carved pommels, and the red-canopied bed, whose hangings echo the cloth and cushions on the chairs. Our eye is irresistibly drawn to the lovingly painted, heavily worked fabrics of the bride's sumptuous green gown with its fur-lined sleeves heavy with tucking and stitching, the crimping of her lavishly layered headdress, the rich velvet, fur-edged over-garment of the bridegroom. The strongly illuminated, discarded pattens or clogs indicate that their wearers were above stepping in the muddy Flanders streets. Behind the sitters hang the much described convex Venetian mirror, its frame inset with enamelling and decorated with painted miniature scenes from Christ's Passion, and an ornate brass chandelier with a single flaming

4. Jan van Eyck, detail from *Arnolfini Marriage*: a secular portrait packed with details of the acquisitiveness of fifteenth-century Bruges

candle. At the feet of the couple the miniature lap-dog looks out at us with kitsch curiosity.

This is not a record of a pair of individuals; it is a celebration of ownership – of pride in possessions from wife to pet, to bed-hangings and brasswork. Such paintings have been called 'realistic portraiture', but surely this misses the point. Only the face of the male subject is (possibly) real – really a portrait. The woman's figure is a perfect stereotype, virtually identical to other female figures in other paintings, down to the details of her face and expression. She is as much a model of womanhood (owned with pride by her wealthy spouse) as the carved saint on the pommel of the chair. Both can be matched in contemporary pattern-books – ledgers of commodities for future design and circulation. We are expected to take an interest in all this profusion of detail as a guarantee of the importance of the sitter, not as a record of a particular Flemish interior.

The composition is a tribute to the mental landscape of the successful merchant – his urge to have and to hold. What is surely striking is how the possessions crammed in here exactly match those laid out behind the Master of Liesborn's Virgin. This is even more apparent if we register that the green of Giovanna's gown is the coded colour of chastity in the secular sphere, just as indigo or deep blue is the equivalent code in the sacred. And, indeed, in support of such a view, we may acknowledge the way the passive content-ment on the face of Mary, surrounded by the trappings of affluence, precisely echoes the dutiful satisfaction of Giovanna Cenami.

Here are the beginnings of a sense that paintings like these celebrate the culture's new access to a superfluity of material posses-sions. We can find the clues to such unashamed enthusiasm for belongings on the walls of every gallery. And not just as detail in the paintings. Hung alongside the painted panels designed to be admired for their own sake are fragments of painted objects which have become separated from their original function. Painted panels from oak storage chests and cupboards, the lids of decorated boxes,

5. Filippo Lippi, *Seven Saints* and *The Annunciation*: painted wooden panels from domestic furniture hung as paintings in the National Gallery

decorative panelling from domestic interiors, are hung as art-works. Even more than the paintings, these bits of artefacts which have lost their original usefulness remind us that the art around us is part and parcel of the Renaissance consumer's accumulation of goods.

There were comparatively few items of furniture even in an affluent Renaissance home – chests for storage, tables and a few chairs and settles. All might be decorated, and the most lavishly decorated item was likely to be the family bed. In the room next to the van Eycks hang two painted panels by Filippo Lippi, *The Annunciation and Seven Saints*. These two companion pieces originally formed part of some article or articles of domestic furniture. Here the painted panel itself formed part of the coveted object – turning the everyday functional possession into something to be admired and valued for itself.

Jacometto Veneziano's *Portrait of a man* (*c.* 1480–90) also reminds us that the painting itself was a 'moveable', a portable possession, and that it was designed to be seen in the round, touched and held, rather than seen at a distance, permanently secured to the wall of a gallery. The tabletop-sized portrait is framed richly in gilded wood; on its reverse is decoration in the form of crossed sprays of myrtle and an inscription from the classical poet Horace in Latin: 'they are three times happy and more, who keep their troth unbroken'. Here is an object that was made to mark a union (a betrothal or a marriage), and was intended to be handled, caressed, admired, passed around. Paintings of this kind were kept wrapped in cloth, or in a purpose-made box (which might itself also be decoratively painted), to be unwrapped and displayed on suitable occasions. Some of these

6. Jacometto Veneziano, *Portrait of a man*: a painting was a portable possession, designed to be seen in the round

portraits still have attached to them the metal ring from which the painting was suspended when its owner, on his or her travels, made a residence their own by unpacking and installing around them their modest quantities of moveables.

Giovanni Bellini's portrait of Doge Leonardo Loredan presents us arrestingly with both these aspects of early Renaissance art – the painting as itself a luxury commodity, and its role in confirming the identity and importance of its owner. A portrait object of considerable magnificence, testifying to the wealth and absolute power of the sitter, it is also luminously eloquent as a record of an opulence we want to reach out and touch. Bellini has captured the texture and intricate patterning of the damask of Loredan's official doge's robes and cap with *trompe-l'oeil* effectiveness. We hardly need to be told that the use of damask for these ceremonial articles of clothing was an innovation, introduced by Loredan when he became the elected ruler of Venice in 1501. The imported fabric

7. Giovanni Bellini, *Doge Leonardo Loredan*: the imported damask of the robe symbolized Venetian access to wealth and goods in the East

(from the Levant) symbolized Venetian access to wealth and goods in the East through its historic position as dominating maritime power in the Mediterranean. The bell-like buttons on Loredan's robe are an invitation to be copied by a theatrical costumier. (This is the painting which inspired the figure of Prospero in Peter Greenaway's film, *Prospero's Books*.) To be this powerful a man, the portrait still says to us, is to be able to robe yourself thus sumptuously to awe the populace. It comes as no surprise to be told that Loredan was renowned for his sartorial vanity.

EARLY RENAISSANCE works of art which today we admire for their sheer representational virtuosity were part of a vigorously developing worldwide market in luxury commodities. They were at once sources of aesthetic delight and properties in commercial transactions between purchasers, seeking ostentatiously to advertise their power and wealth, and skilled craftsmen with the expertise to guarantee that the object so acquired would make an impact.

Take those Annunciations, for example, with which we began. These sacred works are fragments of the altarpieces which dominated the interiors of fifteenth-century chapels and churches. Those who commissioned them demonstrated thereby to the congregation at large their prominent position in the community, and the awe and respect to which they were entitled by birth or office.

Altarpieces were not self-sufficient works, but were conceived to complement or complete a larger decorative enterprise. In our contemporary terms they formed part of a combined project in inter-active media – component panels with distinct subjects artfully juxtaposed, combined in elaborately ornate frames, the separate panels hinged to be opened and shut so that the altarpiece could be viewed in different states according to the dates in the Christian calendar, the whole creation set off by soaring predellas or canopies. The altarpiece might incorporate and enfold an existing religious treasure – a shrine or a statue.

8. Michael Pacher,
St Wolfgang Altarpiece:
a source of amazement
for the humble
congregation

Strikingly positioned in its chapel, an altarpiece was the focal point in the activities of Christian worship, which altar cloth, stained-glass window, chapel furniture, statuary and relics surrounded and enhanced. Even the *Demidoff Altarpiece* gives us little sense of the overwhelming impact of the original artefact of which it formed a part. The attribution of a surviving panel from an altarpiece to a named artist in our catalogue conceals from us the fact that he was also job contractor and site manager for the project.

In 1471, Michael Pacher contracted to accompany his *St Wolfgang Altarpiece* from the location at which it had been executed to Braunau, and thence at the patrons' expense and risk to the pilgrimage church of St Wolfgang near Salzburg. If it was damaged *en route* Pacher agreed to make good the damage. In addition to transport costs, the

patrons also agreed to pay Pacher's keep, and to supply any iron-
work necessary for fixing the altar in place on arrival. The structure
for an altarpiece might have been the separate responsibility of a
carpenter, and was certainly the most costly and prestigious part of
the commission; but the painter was responsible for assembling and
finishing the completed work. The final impact of the altarpiece, in
place, in the location for which it was conceived and designed, was
in the hands of the artist as project manager and impresario.

From within such a controlling context the altarpiece addressed
its audience with compelling authority. Its function was twofold:
to arrest the worshipper in awe before it, in contemplation of the
mystery of Christ's Incarnation; and to advertise the prosperity and
self-confidence of the patron, or the community, the brotherhood
or guild which had commissioned the work. Even in its nineteenth-
century reproduction frame, these are still sentiments to which we
can respond when faced with the *Demidoff Altarpiece*. What is
harder to appreciate is how overwhelmingly physical the original
impact of Crivelli's art must have been, how it awed by its very
grandeur and opulence. The chapel was a treasure-house, a source
of amazement for the humble congregation.

There are other aspects of the message the altarpiece conveys
which are lost to gallery-goers with the passage of time, but for
which the physical evidence is still richly before us. Colour itself
announced the value and importance of the original commission. We
may be alert to the signal which large expanses of gold and gold-
leaf detailing give in a painting: they continue to tell us that the
painter's brief was a lavish one, allowing for the use of expensive
materials. We are no longer attuned, however, to the comparative expense of colour pigments. Paint hues were not perceived as
equal, and the fifteenth-century viewer's eye would undoubtedly
have registered the differences. An important figure in a narrative
painting, or an important gesture might have been coloured with
an ostentatiously costly pigment by the artist precisely in order to
attract the viewer's attention.

Most striking of these colours is ultramarine blue, widely used in sacred works, and abundantly present around us. Ultramarine is a pigment made by grinding the semi-precious stone lapis lazuli – imported from the East – and soaking the powder several times to draw off the colour. The first soaking produced the most intense violet-blue and was the most expensive. For those unable to afford ultramarine, an approximation could be made with 'german blue' – a simple carbonate of copper. Graded use of ultramarines advertised the value of a work of art, and issued instructions on how the painting was to be interpreted. If the Virgin Mary's robe was painted with ultramarine of the quality of two florins to the ounce, then one florin to the ounce ultramarine might do for the robes of the saints who supported her, and this would also ensure that no mistake was made over who is the most important figure in the composition (the blue of their robes would be less intense and eye-catching). Red pigments made from silver and sulphur were similarly to be admired for their expense, and were to be contrasted with the humbler (cheaper) ochres and umbers made from local earths.

Clients commissioning important and ostentatiously expensive works would stipulate particularly high-grade ultramarine in their contract with the chosen painter. When the Florentine painter Domenico Ghirlandaio was commissioned to paint an *Adoration of the Magi* by the Prior of the Spedale degli Innocenti the contract which they both signed specified the materials meticulously:

> That this day 23 October 1485 the reverend Messer Francesco di Giovanni Tesori, presently Prior of the Spedale degli Innocenti at Florence, commits and entrusts to Domenico di Tomaso di Ghirlandaio the painting of a panel which the said Francesco has had made and has provided; the which panel the said Domenico is to make good, that is, pay for; and he is to colour and paint the said panel all with his own hand in the manner shown in a drawing on paper with those figures and in that manner shown in it, in every particular according to what I, Fra Bernardo, think

best; not departing from the manner and composition of the said drawing; and he must colour the panel at his own expense with good colours and with powdered gold on such ornaments as demand it, with any other expense incurred on the same panel, and the blue must be ultramarine of the value about four florins the ounce; and he must have made and delivered complete the said panel within thirty months from today; and he must receive as the price of the panel as here described (made at his, that is, the said Domenico's expense throughout) 115 large florins if it seems to me, the abovesaid Fra Bernardo, that it is worth it.

This painting was duly completed according to contract in 1488 and still hangs in the Spedale.

Ghirlandaio's contract reminds us that works of art from the Renaissance, as from any other period, were the product of a shared undertaking between a purchaser and a skilled artist, where costs, risks and profits were an intrinsic part of the bargain struck. The ordering of Filippo Lippi's *Annunciation and Seven Saints* panels for the Medici Palace formed part of a private commercial transaction of a kind familiar today: the buyer identified an artist whose work he liked; his agent sought him out and arranged the terms. Probably the artist had to put the money up front to buy his materials, and his completed handiwork certainly had to content his client before the work changed hands and he received his final payment. Where the commission was a less obviously domestic one, the arrangements were closely similar. In 1457, when Lippi was at work on a triptych for Cosimo de' Medici's son Giovanni to give as a gift to Alfonso of Aragon, King of Naples, he wrote to his client for an advance on the agreed price, for the gold needed to complete the armour of the figure of St Michael:

If you agree ... to give me sixty florins to include materials, gold, gilding and painting, with Bartolomeo Martelli acting as I suggest, I will for my part, so as to cause you less trouble, have the picture finished completely by 20 August ... And to keep you informed, I send a drawing of how the triptych is made of wood, and with its height and breadth. Out of friendship to you I do not want to take more than the labour costs of 100 florins for this: I ask no more. I beg you to reply, because I am languishing here and want to leave Florence when I am finished.

As this letter makes clear, the purchaser was unambiguously the one with the power in such arrangements. An expensive and ostentatiously lavish work of art was part of a prominent family's attempt to broadcast its power and importance during the patron's lifetime, and to try to ensure the enduring memory of the line for posterity. As such, the work was carefully orchestrated by the patron, and its expense might form a comparatively small part of an overall programme of family commemoration in which, clearly, the artist himself played a minor role.

In 1436 Francesco di Antonio Maringhi, the chaplain of Sant'Ambrogio in Florence and patron of its high altar, left 800 florins in his will to finance the upkeep of his private chapel, and to cover the costs of an elaborate annual celebration of the feast of his patron saint (including a meal for the participants). Yearly on his saint's day a mass was to be said in which Maringhi's name was to be remembered for all time as a person who had been a notable benefactor to his community, and afterwards prominent members of that community would sit down to a dinner in honour of his memory. Compared to this generous bequest, the 240 florins Maringhi spent on an exceptionally expensive altarpiece (by the standards of the day), *The Coronation of the Virgin*, by Filippo Lippi, was a relatively small sum. It was, after all, the benefactor who was to be remembered, not the artist, and to that end an annual feast might be more effective in the long term than an altarpiece.

The composition of *The Coronation of the Virgin* incorporates over fifty figures using conspicuously expensive pigments, and is

9. Filippo Lippi, *Coronation of the Virgin*: there is no ambiguity about whom the worshipper was to regard as 'the creator' of the painting. The figure at whom the angel points is the patron and donor

set off by an elaborately gilded frame. Such ostentatious expense advertised to the worshipper in the chapel that the donor was a man of wealth and generosity. At the same time it provided him with an opportunity to make atonement publicly and permanently for any sins of concupiscence implied by his success in public life – the worldly pleasure he had taken in his prosperity during his lifetime.

So although it is Filippo Lippi, the artist, whom we remember and admire, it was the patron whose renown as the artistic impresario and generous public donor was at issue at the time the altarpiece was painted. In the case of Lippi's *Coronation of the Virgin* the painting itself bears eloquent testimony to this ranking of contemporary public importance. An angel indicates a praying figure in the painting, and carries a scroll with the inscription 'is[te] perfecit opus' ('This man carried out the work'). There is no ambiguity, then, about who the worshipper was to regard as the 'creator' of the painting. The figure at whom the angel points is a painted portrait of the patron and donor, Maringhi. The artist Lippi had merely executed his commission.

The image of the artist as an individual of genius, transferring his own unique imagination to panel or canvas, is a modern one. The Renaissance artist was a craftsman in the service of the powerful. Painting was an inexpensive form of luxury decoration, compared with tapestry, or decoration in gold leaf and ultramarine applied directly to the surface stone and marble of costly buildings. The artists who produced the magnificently individualised works housed in our galleries might equally well be called upon to supply off-the-peg decoration for a patron's palace. Among the drawings which survive from Hans Holbein's period as artist at the English Court of Henry VIII are sketches for ornate pieces of royal table-ware. A woodcut of the Emperor Maximilian in a painter's workshop

10. Hans Burgkmair, *Weisskunig in a Painter's Workshop*: the Emperor Maximilian commenting on designs for pieces of armour and heraldic devices

shows him commenting on designs on the artist's easel for pieces of armour and heraldic devices.

Venice's head of state was the Doge, a prominent member of one of the old families of the city, elected for life by a special government committee. The Doge's Palace on the Piazza San Marco remains a grand statement of the power of the civic ruler whom the Venetians regarded as the heir to Constantine the Great, and who held both temporal and spiritual power over the city's citizens. The ambitious architectural extensions to the Doge's Palace undertaken in the fifteenth century were embarked on in order to advertise to an international audience the Venetian state's power and prestige. The new Byzantine-style entrance was designed to represent Venice as the major land power between Christendom and Byzantium, at a time when Venice was being driven back by the Ottoman Empire from her command over the eastern Mediterranean and its key trade routes.

As part of this programme of propaganda public works, the Venetians decided to embark on a further conspicuously expensive project for the Doge's Palace – the repainting of the twenty-two frescos which decorated the Great Council Chamber. In September 1474 Venice's governing body voted overwhelmingly (by 126 out of 134 votes cast) to commission the distinguished painter Gentile Bellini to oversee the job. For this design commission of major civic significance Gentile Bellini negotiated a contract with suitably long-term benefits: all materials and colours were to be provided, and he was to receive the next state-owned sinecure to become vacant (in other words, to receive a pension for life). By 1495 nine painters were at work, including two apprentices. The most highly paid of these painters (60 ducats a year, compared with the 6 ducats earned by the apprentices) was Gentile's brother Giovanni.

In 1479 Giovanni took over from his brother Gentile as overseer of the entire works for a year, while Gentile was sent on loan to Sultan Mehmed II by the then Doge as part of the terms of the peace treaty signed between Venice and the Ottoman Empire. In

1488 Giovanni Bellini painted a votive painting, which included a portrait of the Doge currently in office, Agostino Barbarigo. A number of his other commissions were directly associated with his post at the Palace.

So when Giovanni Bellini painted the compelling portrait of Leonardo Loredan, Doge of Venice, which we admired earlier, he had been employed as a contracted decorator on the Doge's Palace refurbishment project over a considerable number of years. His 1501 portrait of Loredan, then, for all its luminous intensity, was a piece of work done under contract as part of his artisanal commitments to the Doge-in-office.

What is the significance of this? What kind of difference does it make to our view of the Renaissance to understand that a master-piece like Giovanni Bellini's portrait of Doge Leonardo Loredan was a strictly commercial piece of work, produced in accordance with a whole network of social obligations and power relations in fifteenth-century Venice? To answer that question it is instructive to compare a portrait by his brother Gentile – a portrait of Mehmed II executed as part of that 'loan' of the Doge's painter to the Ottoman Court in 1479. The crafted detailing of this portrait is strongly in the European tradition. We may assume that Mehmed II was impressed by such virtuoso craftsmanship when he asked for a suitable painter to be thrown in as part of the terms of the treaty under negotiation. What he wanted, as part of his generally cosmopolitan outlook, was access to the services of a European artist with the distinctive skills of that artistic culture.

Gentile Bellini's surviving painting suggests that the Sultan was probably a well-satisfied customer. The decorated pillars recall the door-jambs of the Crivelli *Annunciation*; the jewelled cloth in the foreground resembles the hem of the Virgin's gown in the Campin *Virgin and Child Before a Firescreen*. The painting's technique bears tribute to the skill of the Venetian artistic tradition.

The composition and the portrait figure, however, are Ottoman: there is no mistaking the fact that this is a distinctively 'oriental'

11. Gentile Bellini, *Sultan Mehmet II*: a distinctively 'oriental' painting in a
tradition other than our own

painting in a tradition other than our own. Although the artist was Venetian, the commissioner of this work of art, and therefore the ultimate arbiter of its aesthetic taste, was Ottoman. Ultimately it was the taste of the patron or purchaser which had to be respected. Gentile Bellini's portrait of Sultan Mehmed II is as Ottoman as his brother's portrait of Doge Loredan is Venetian. During the period of his stay in Istanbul, Gentile executed informal portrait sketches of local people for his own portfolio which (without the intervention of a local patron) are wholeheartedly in the Venetian style.

The fact that we find these drawings, or the portrait of Doge Loredan, so compellingly attractive owes a great deal to our own position as consumers of a culture whose taste is in a direct line of descent from the Renaissance. The precious artistic commodities preserved in our Western museums and galleries have shaped our enduring idea of aesthetic desirability. The blue background of the Loredan portrait is a marker of splendour for us, not because we naturally respond to the hue, but because of its relationship to the expensive ultramarines of innumerable celestial surrounds and Virgin's gowns in fifteenth-century Christian altarpieces. The impression of opulence of the Doge's robe and curious horn-shaped hat is strengthened by the conjunction of the closely worked detail of the imported damask and the illusion of gold thread throughout, which proclaimed the material wealth of the sitter. Both are Venetian – accurately a reflection of the hierarchy of values of a particular moment in the history of the city. Both continue to connote for us costliness and exoticism – as desirable today as they were almost 500 years ago.

Since we are looking here with admiration at the very texture of damask as a costly fabric, let us end this preliminary exploration of another Renaissance waiting to be discovered with a closer look at the messages being conveyed by some of the other fabrics lovingly represented around us. The fabrics to which our eye is drawn with pleasure in Renaissance paintings are often those which, like the

Doge's damask, announced with enthusiasm the sitter's access to foreign goods and overseas markets.

In Robert Campin's *A Man* and Jan van Eyck's *Portrait of a Man in a Red Turban* the sitters wear virtually identical costumes. The fur-lined robe of sober, heavy-duty cloth suggests a merchant. So too does the exotic turban, both for its form and, especially, for its colour. The intense crimson dye 'in the grain' of the cloth is that achieved with Indian lac – a dye made from ground-up cochineal beetles, or from the bark of the trees within which the beetles lay their eggs. Such crimson cloth might be acquired in Venice or Amsterdam, but because the dye which produced its coveted colour had to be imported it was inevitably costly. The red turban advertised the individual's status as a cosmopolitan man of means with access to an international trading centre as clearly as Doge Loredan's own distinctive headgear advertised his prominent civic role. If, as some believe, the van Eyck is a portrait of the artist himself, then

12. Robert Campin, *Portrait of a Man*: the fur-lined robe suggests a merchant, as does the exotic turban, both for its form and its intense crimson colour

13. Jan van Eyck, *Man in a
Turban*: like the Campin portrait,
the costly crimson of the sitter's
turban advertises him as a
cosmopolitan man of means

van Eyck chose to depict his reputation and prestige in terms of features recognizable as those of a mercantile rather than an artistic life and lifestyle.

When the powerful book publisher Johann Amerbach decided to join a guild (a professional union) to protect his interests, he was entitled to apply for membership of a craft guild such as the goldsmiths. But it was the guild of merchants – men of trade rather than skilled artisans – that he chose to join. And when the distinguished humanist teacher and writer Desiderius Erasmus commissioned a portrait of himself from the Flemish painter Quentin Metsys in 1515 he too instructed the artist to give his sitter a mercantile persona. Erasmus' own trade was in knowledge and learning, producing and disseminating throughout Europe a stream of learned works and innovative textbooks in the liberal arts. These are the works of the classical revival which modern scholars consider to have nurtured the flowering of intellectual achievement across Europe in

14. Quentin Metsys,
Portrait of Erasmus:
the sitter's fur-lined
broadcloth gown and
a merchant's purse
around his neck
identify him with
the world of commerce

the second half of the sixteenth century. In the Metsys portrait, however, Erasmus is shown in a fur-lined broadcloth gown with a merchant's capacious purse prominently suspended round his neck. Here a man acutely aware of his 'image' allies himself visually with those who traffic in worldly goods and who inhabit a world of cash transactions, commodities and dealing. To be a man of distinction and reputation in the Renaissance evidently meant, for Erasmus and his contemporaries, confidently to inhabit the world of commerce.

As we embark on this project of redefining the achievements of the European Renaissance, let us take to heart the fierce pride in mercantilism and the acquisitiveness which fuelled its enterprises. The Renaissance proclaimed by the paintings in the Sainsbury Wing – its particular kind of rebirth, reawakening and renewal – was a celebration of the urge to own, the curiosity to possess the treasures of other cultures, and pride in a new craftsmanship which can make the most humdrum commodities desirable. The portable images and painted panels, indeed, are all that survives of a deluge of exotic goods and covetable commodities with which entrepreneurial businessmen flooded the Renaissance market – we begin with those surviving painted traces, but will find ourselves before long among the more varied Renaissance treasures of gems, brocade fabrics, tapestries and fine books. It is this entreprenurial spirit which I shall be pursuing in the chapters that follow, in order to sustain my claim that the seeds of our own exuberant multiculturalism and bravura consumerism were planted in the European Renaissance.

ONE

CONDITIONS FOR CHANGE: GOODS IN PROFUSION

CONSTANTINOPLE (now Istanbul) stands on a peninsula at the mouth of the Bosphorus, dominating the route from the Black Sea via the Sea of Marmora into the eastern Mediterranean. Its position on the grid of fifteenth-century international trade-routes gave it critical strategic and commercial importance: it functioned as a kind of valve through which goods flowed to and from the oriental markets in the East and European markets in the West. At the point of intersection between the more or less entirely Christian territories to the north and west of the Mediterranean and those to the east and south increasingly under Islamic rule, the city had acquired symbolic importance in the urgently fought power struggle between the earthly leaders of two of the great monotheistic religions – the Ottoman Sultan on behalf of Islam, the Pope on behalf of Christendom.

Constantinople also had an international reputation as a city of intellectual riches. The Byzantine Empire, of which Constantinople was the capital, was the last, much diminished remnant of the Roman Empire. Scholars at Constantinople continued the ancient traditions of rigorous and meticulous textual study of texts in the classical languages of that Empire – Latin and Greek. According to the humanist Aeneas Sylvius Piccolomini (later Pope Pius II), any young man with pretensions to classical learning in the early decades of the fifteenth century went to Constantinople to complete his education. The fall of Constantinople to the Ottomans in 1453 was thus a symbolic watershed between the intellectual infancy of western Europe and the flowering of the Renaissance. The centre of Western scholarly erudition and artistic accomplishment shifted

Nach der gepurt Cristi vnsers haylands.M.cccc.xc.iar am.xij.tag des monats Julij kome in der königclichē
statt Constantinopel ein grosses vormals vngehörts vngewitter.vnnd als sich das fewr der öbern dreyer
gestirne(das man den fallenden fewystral nēt)in vermischung der feüchtigkeit vnd der hitze beweget vn die ver
samelt feüchtigkeit in dem trüben lust vberhannd genomen het.vnd der wind oder tunst sich in dem gewülcke ar
baytet do warden erstlich grosse thonyslege gehört vnd darnach prinnend wetterplitzen mit langē fewystraln ge
sehen. vnd wiewol die vnglawbigen maynten das sölchs von dem gistirne des planeten Saturni herköme(als
dan ettwe in tuscia ein reiche statt võ dē gestirne des planetē martis mit dē plitze gātz verprēt ward)yedoch schrei
bē die cristē solchs õ götliche fürsichtigkeit vñ rachsale zu.dañ õ thonyslag plitze vñ vngestüme wetter hat nicht al
lain einē teil õ sewln des pilds des kaiser Cōstantini ernder gewoiffen:sunder auch(als dañ glawbwirdig Vene
digisch vnd andere kawslewt gesagt haben)bey achthundert hewßen verprent.vnd bey dreytawsent menschen
ertödt in einem zirckel.wie dañ die hernachgesetzt figur zeergennen gibt.

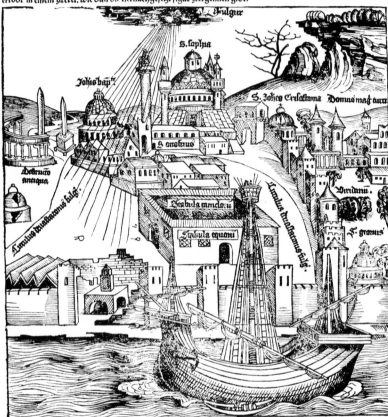

Als hieuor an mäche endē võ vil vñ mancherlay seltsamen
dingē die sich am himel ereigt habē gemeldt wordē ist vñ
sundlich dz ein stayn mit eim creutz gezaichnet zu dē zeiten kaiser
Friderichs des andern võ obē herab gefallē sey also ist zu dē zei
tē kaiser Friderichs des dritte in dē iar cristi.M.cccc.xcij.am.vij.
tag des monats nouēbris in mytte tag ein grosser stayn bey eim
zentner schwer.ein wenig kleiner dañ ein saltzscheyb.gestalt wie
ein kriechisch D.vnd dreyegket von oben herab auß dē lüfte bey
Ensißheim in dē Suntgew nider gefallen vnnd zu anzaigung
seltsamer geschihten noch vorhanden.

Iser zeit sind zwischē Maximiliano dē römischē könig vñ
dē könig zu Fräckreich võ õ herzogin zu brittania wegen
vil kriegischer aufrür entstandē vñ gewest vñ doch durch wil
heln beschossen zu Aystet vñ andere darnach mit güetlichē ver
trag hingelegt.

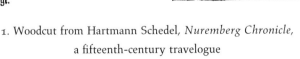

1. Woodcut from Hartmann Schedel, *Nuremberg Chronicle*,
a fifteenth-century travelogue

permanently away from the Byzantine Empire, with its continuous command of the classical tradition, to western Europe – first to Italy, and then northwards to Germany and the Low Countries.

In 1452 a Hungarian engineer and gun-manufacturer named Urban presented himself to the Emperor of the Greek Byzantines at Constantinople and offered to build him a super-gun of such size and might that it would hold back the armies of the Turkish Ottomans from the city's walls. The Emperor Constantine XI could not raise the money necessary to pay for the technician's services, nor could he provide the large quantities of metal and the men skilled in new metalworking technologies required for the project. Urban was no particular supporter of the Byzantine Empire; his was strictly a business proposition. Accordingly, once his offer had been turned down by Constantine, he went on to the Court of the new Ottoman Sultan, Mehmed II, at Adrianople. There he met with a much warmer reception, and a better-informed one, based on a keener assessment of the political benefits to be gained from the outlay of money and the possible riskiness of the venture. He was offered a salary four times greater than he had proposed to the Byzantines, and was promised all the technical assistance he needed for the gun's production.

In the first half of the fifteenth century Hungary had developed mining techniques which greatly increased output and made them one of the major producers and marketers of iron and copper. The availability of plentiful amounts of refined metal contributed to their growing expertise in weaponry and gun-manufacture (activities notoriously high in consumption of metals as their basic raw material). In a politically unstable Europe, demand for the services of Hungarian engineers was heavy; by the 1450s, the desirability of having ready access to both metals and technology had for some time encouraged the Ottomans to negotiate mutually advantageous trade agreements with the Hungarians. The positive response Urban met with at Adrianople was a direct result of this conjunction of pragmatic and commercial factors.

2. Mehmed II's 'Karaküle
(Black Tower) ' fortress
provocatively located

Urban was as good as his word. Just three months later, in November 1452, Mehmed II installed the huge cannon the Hungarian had built for him on the ramparts of his newly built fortress Karaküle (the Black Tower), a fortress strategically (and provocatively) located on the Bosphorus ten miles up the coast from Constantinople so as to blockade European commercial traffic coming from the Black Sea. When the cannon sank a passing Venetian merchant ship which had failed to stop for inspection of its cargo, the Mediterranean mercantile states woke up suddenly to the danger posed by the Turks' possession of this vital piece of new military technology.

In spite of Mehmed II's deliberately threatening displays of Islamic military might, the trading nations of Europe, whose commercial relations with the Ottomans were on the whole cordial and profitable, were not keen to enter into open hostilities. Venice and Genoa, Rhodes and Dubrovnik (Ragusa) had all been well pleased when their trade treaties with the Ottomans were successfully renewed in the flurry of diplomatic activity which followed Mehmed's accession to the sultanate in 1451. Furthermore, the loudest voice calling for a military task-force to prevent Mehmed's attacking the coveted capital of the Byzantine Empire, Constantinople, was inevitably that of the Pope, Nicholas V, who, as the members of the Venetian Council reminded one another as they went into a series of emergency sessions, still owed Venice substantial sums of money for the last joint military venture they had been reluctantly drawn into (also contrary to their commercial interests) against the Turks in 1444. Not for the first time, the urging of the Catholic Church to attack the infidel was perceived to be strikingly at odds with the everyday realities of states which for business and economic purposes preferred to remain on cordial terms with the 'great Turk'. Paralysed by an indecision born largely of commercial self-interest, the maritime powers of Europe sat and watched as the Ottomans closed in on Constantinople.

The fact that Christendom failed to come to Constantinople's rescue probably caused no surprise to any of the politicians involved. For at least fifteen years repeated attempts had been made by successive Byzantine emperors to enlist the help of the Vatican and of the states of Europe to hold together the remnants of their Empire. Each attempt was made in the name of shared Christianity; each rebuff or procrastination used doctrinal uncertainties and difficulties as the excuse for doing nothing. In private, however, individual states admitted that they were reluctant to impede the healthy flow of goods across the Ottoman Empire to and from the markets of the West. Venice, whose commercial activities, prosperity and power were (after Genoa) most closely enmeshed with those of the Ottoman Empire, tended to be in the forefront of those prepared to tolerate the growing power of the Islamic Empire rather than show open hostility to a lucrative trading partner.

3. Leonardo da Vinci,
sketch of a super-gun
under construction

On 2 April 1453, the Turkish army arrived outside the walls on
the landward side of Constantinople; an armada of Turkish ships
had already set up a blockade of the two seaward sides of the city
in late March. Urban's new monster-cannon – twice the size of the
one which had so astounded the Western powers six months earlier
– was moved into position facing the walls where they crossed the
River Lycus, together with an extensive armoury of other state-of-
the-art batteries of guns of various sizes, also developed with the
help of German and Hungarian technology.

Urban's newest gun had been cast in Adrianople the previous
January. Its bronze barrel was more than twenty-six feet long, eight
inches thick and thirty inches across; the cannon-balls it fired were
800 pounds in weight. The cannon was dragged from Adrianople to
the walls of Constantinople by sixty oxen, while 200 men marched
alongside it to keep the gun-carriage steady; another 200 men

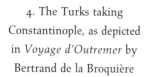

4. The Turks taking
Constantinople, as depicted
in *Voyage d'Outremer* by
Bertrand de la Broquière

went ahead to make good the road along which the gun would travel, and to strengthen the bridges. Once in place on 11 April, the unwieldiness of the Sultan's great guns meant they could only be fired seven times a day; but each of those seven shots caused devastating damage to the triple walls which the Byzantines had proudly believed would withstand the fiercest attack.

Constantinople fell to the Turks on 28 May. In the end it was the Sultan's gun power and his deployment of the new technology of warfare which tipped the balance against the traditional military techniques, tight organization, determination and naval acumen of the Byzantines and their remaining allies. Although the allied fleet largely outmanoeuvred the Turks on the seaward sides of the city, the constant bombardment of the triple wall weakened the city's defences against land attack. Those guns and their technology were in Turkish hands predominantly for calculatedly commercial reasons

5. Mehmed II's 1453 trade agreement with the Genoese in Galata

of a kind entirely familiar to us today. The power which would negotiate with and pay those exploiting the international arms race by marketing military know-how, the power which had the foresight to understand the political advantage to be gained by being ahead in new technology, carried the day.

The commercial vested interests which had fatally held up any international agreement to send ships to the aid of Constantinople resurfaced within days of the cessation of the siege. Across the mouth of the Golden Horn from Constantinople itself the inhabitants of Pera (Galata), a thriving colony of merchants from Genoa, had remained elaborately neutral during the conflict even when Mehmed's guns firing from the Turkish fleet destroyed parts of their own city. The livelihood of this trading community depended on remaining on good terms with the aggressor. These were hard-headed businessmen whose refusal to become involved reflected the considered view of non-Greeks locally that the Byzantine Empire could not survive; it made little difference to them whether the ruler of Constantinople was Greek or Turk. They would comfortably deal with anyone who allowed them to pursue their trading interests in the East, and regarded the sums which had to be paid into the Pope's coffers in 'indulgences' (papal exoneration) for associating with the infidel as money well spent. For these men also Constantinople's reputation as a centre of esoteric learning was of little interest. What mattered was that it was a crucial staging post in the traffic of goods from India and the spice islands to Genoa, Antwerp and all points north. What characterized the city for them was its extraordinarily heterogeneous and exotic population – a multicultural mix facilitating exchanges of every kind of goods and influence. Above all, for them Constantinople was already the city of market bustle and bazaars, rather than a serene site of idealized and unworldly learning. For these merchants, the Constantinople of the 1450s was already in spirit the hub of the new mercantile order, Istanbul.

Within days of Constantinople's fall to the Ottomans the Genoese had sent two ambassadors, Babalino Pallavicino and Marco de Franchi, with an interpreter, to renegotiate their own peaceful coexistence with the new power in the land. Their neutrality during the siege and the alacrity with which they showed their willingness to submit to Ottoman rule paid off. They were granted an imperial *firman*, a solemn undertaking, which gave them the right to trade within the Ottoman Empire, and freedom to continue to practise the Catholic faith. Their sons were not to be subject to the *devshirme* (the forced recruitment of boys from Christian families for the Janissary corps or the Ottoman civil service), nor were any Muslims to be settled within the Christian colony. Within a remarkably short time it was business as usual for the expatriate Italians shipping their cargoes of oriental goods from Galata via Genoa to destinations throughout western Europe and vice versa.

Venetian trade through the city was likewise barely interrupted. Venetian merchants began negotiating for renewed commercial privileges almost immediately, and by early 1454 the Venetian Republic had signed a treaty of peace and friendship with the Turks, binding her not to support hostilities against them in any way, thereby enabling Venetian merchants to renew trading under attractive terms within the city. The Doge of Venice instructed the Ambassador to the Sultan on 15 January 1454: 'it is our intention to live in peace and friendship with the Turkish emperor'. Under the terms of the agreement, Venetians would pay only 2 per cent customs duty on goods entering and leaving Ottoman territories, and had the right to keep a commercial agent in Istanbul, in return for an annual tribute of 200,000 gold ducats.

To understand the determination of Genoese and Venetian merchants not to let their carefully nurtured involvement with Ottoman trade be destroyed by power politics we need only consider how structured and indeed institutionalized this international trade was by the middle of the fifteenth century. The Turks were vigorous traders themselves with longstanding and sophisticated arrangements for accommodating foreign commerce, and the luxury merchandise passing through Constantinople went both from East to West and from West to East. The accounts kept by the Venetian merchant Giacomo Badoer, trading in Constantinople between 1436 and 1440, show velvets, damasks and satins arriving from Italy *en route* eastwards, as well as silks and spices moving west. In general terms the commercial world in which these men operated was one of tolerance, in which all three 'religions of the book' (Christianity, Islam, Judaism) could coexist and thrive. In this climate it was the Venetians as well as the Turks who benefited from mutual tolerance, growing rich and powerful as a result.

The relationship between successful Western merchants like the Venetians and their oriental trading partners was, moreover, by convention an intimate one. The customary way for members of the caste of noble Venetian families who conducted import–export businesses to run their affairs was entirely 'hands on'. While some members of a given family fronted the business on the Rialto (the trading area in Venice), others were stationed abroad to conduct the negotiations required to set prices, check the quality of goods and ultimately take the decisions on buying and selling. If we look

6. Venetian merchants exchanging cloth for spices in the East, from Marco Polo,
Livre des Merveilles

at some of the activities of the Contarini, Barbarigo, Cappello and Mosto families in the middle of the fifteenth century (all famous names in Venetian commerce):

> Lorenzo Contarini was in Damascus in 1437, in Beirut in 1440, and domiciled in Syria on behalf of the family business from 1451 to 1455.
>
> Andrea Barbarigo was actively trading in Crete, then in London during the 1430s, and finally in Valencia (then under Islamic rule).
>
> Andrea Cappello was Venetian consul (official overseer of Venetian trading activities locally on behalf of the Venetian government) at Trebizond in 1417, then for several years in Cyprus.

7. Fra Angelico, *Altarpiece of St Nicholas of Bari*, which shows European
merchants exporting grain overseas

Andrea da Mosto was consul at Tunis from 1465 to 1467, and
stayed on until 1473, encouraging his family to lease ships from
Barbary to extend their trade in the region. He owned a house
and a shop in the Venetian enclave in Tunis.

These men spoke the languages of their overseas trading bases,
and were on close terms with local businessmen and dignitaries in
the town where they operated. Their involvement with a city like
Constantinople was thus a more personal affair than the political
manoeuvrings of officers of the state at home. In fact, in spite of
the indecision shown by the Venetian state over whether they
should send forces, some of the Venetian merchants who found
themselves trapped within the city at the onset of Mehmed's siege
had personally shown great courage in helping to defend it, as their
sense of honour towards their longstanding commercial partners
required. An eye-witness account of the siege by a fellow Venetian
records members of the Cornaro, Mocenigo and Contarini merchant
families offering their ships to help protect the harbour.

In spite of the pragmatic indifference shown by the merchants *in situ* once Constantinople fell into Turkish hands, back in Italy the response to Mehmed II's expansionist activities was more predictably ideological and sectarian. Two groups there reacted vigorously and negatively to the loss to the Ottomans of the great figurehead city of the West. The first of these was the clergy, who for twenty years had been struggling to reunite their Catholic Church with the Greek Orthodox Church as a bulwark against Islam. The second was the expatriate Byzantines who had been drawn to Italy in the course of the ensuing doctrinal negotiations and had settled there into lucrative university professorships for which their superior command of the classical tradition qualified them over their Italian counterparts. To both groups the fall of Constantinople represented a disaster for the Christian world.

What is more difficult to determine is the extent to which this sense of disaster was sincerely felt as a spiritual catastrophe for the Christian Church, rather than merely a way of voicing secular political concern at the expanding power bloc of the Ottoman Empire encroaching westwards. Indeed, confusion over whether the grounds for intervention in Byzantium were political or religious may have contributed to the international indecision and paralysis of will. The series of events following the last ecclesiastical council to be held before Mehmed's siege of Constantinople, called by Pope Eugenius IV in 1437, encapsulates the tensions between secular and spiritual papal ambitions for East–West dominion.

In the autumn of 1437 an ecclesiastical and diplomatic mission from the Pope arrived in Constantinople and was solemnly greeted by the leader of the Greek Orthodox Church, Patriarch Joseph II, and representatives of the imperial government. The mission included the famous German cardinal Nicholas of Cusa, who arrived in the Greek capital at the beginning of October, a little later than most of the other members. He brought with him 300 archers recruited in Crete, as directed by Pope Eugenius IV, for the defence of Constantinople. Here, already, the signals were confused: Nicholas of Cusa arrived as an ambassador of the Catholic Church; the gift he brought as pledge of good faith was a contribution to the military strength of the beleaguered city. He came apparently to make overtures of union on behalf of the Pope towards that part of the Holy Roman Church which had separated from papal authority centuries earlier; he did so in the form of a symbol of military alliance and support not entirely in keeping with the celestial aspirations of the Father of the Church. Fifteen years later, in November 1452, Cardinal Isidore of Kiev with a company of 200 archers similarly arrived in a Constantinople on the brink of war. This time they were offered as a pledge that Pope Nicholas V stood by the somewhat nebulous union of the two churches achieved on that earlier occasion (but never actually acknowledged publicly either by Rome or by the inhabitants of Constantinople at large). On this second occasion also it was deemed that the Pope's gesture meant that he would provide military strength to back up his protestations of support for the threatened Emperor Constantine – a promise the Pope did not in the end fulfil.

Nicholas of Cusa and Isidore of Kiev both believed fervently in a shared intellectual heritage between the Italian 'Latin' Church and the Byzantine 'Greek' one. Like the great Greek scholar Bessarion they were passionately committed to holding together what they saw as two complementary traditions in Christian philosophy. Their political leaders, however (both churchmen and secular politicians), were more interested in alliances which would provide a power base against the combined threats of Islam and Ottoman imperial might.

On 8 February 1438, the Byzantine Emperor John VIII and the Patriarch Joseph II, head of the Church in Constantinople, arrived in Florence (where the papal Court was currently based), together with about twenty Byzantine bishops and a large advisory body of other Greek prelates, monks and learned laymen – about 700 Greeks in all. The bill for the event was footed by the Italians; years later successive popes were still paying off debts incurred by the massive

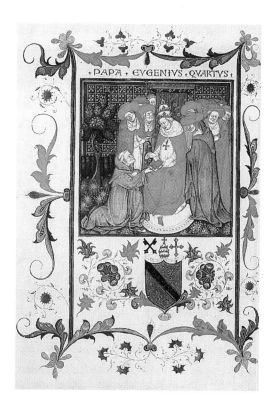

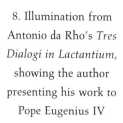
8. Illumination from Antonio da Rho's *Tres Dialogi in Lactantium*, showing the author presenting his work to Pope Eugenius IV

cost of transporting and entertaining an embassy of this size. In theory the negotiations which followed were concerned with issues of the Christian faith, and the possibilities of reconciling papal doctrine with the practices of the Eastern Church. In practice this was a piece of power-brokering, symbolized by the fact that the most heated moments in the discussions were those where issues of precedent arose: should the Emperor preside over the proceedings? Was the Patriarch of the Greek Church equal to or subordinate to the Latin Pope? Which dignitaries of which Church got to take precedence in the many ceremonial processions which formed part of the highly public proceedings?

Twenty years later Benozzo Gozzoli commemorated this great Florentine public occasion for the powerful Medici banking family in a series of frescos for their Florentine *palazzo*. Here Florentines and Byzantines vie with one another for opulence and the splendour of their entourages. The central scene is entitled *The Procession of the Magi* – John VIII, the Patriarch Joseph II and Lorenzo de' Medici (aged twelve at the time) have become the three Magi, travelling with sumptuous retinues to the Orient. It is an elaborately celebratory work – a piece of retrospective romantic fiction in which the inconclusive events of the Council have become the triumph of the boy-heir to the Medici fortunes in a moment of ceremonial splendour. The costumes of the Byzantines are lovingly represented in all their oriental exoticism and magnificence (picked out in gold leaf). The narrative version of the Council may be a piece of retrospective political propaganda; the meticulous attention to every gorgeous detail of apparel, gems, weaponry, horses and their accoutrements is, however, a faithful record of the real basis for the international summit meeting. In the 1430s the growing power of the Medicis was linked to their position as the Pope's bankers and to Cosimo's close personal friendship with Eugenius IV; their wealth was directly related to the trade in luxury goods of the kind which adorn the figures in Gozzoli's procession, exchanged via Constantinople.

The frescos remind us that as far as the inhabitants of Florence were concerned the impact of the Council was not doctrinal but cultural and ceremonial. It exposed them to an influx of visitors – a veritable crowd – from an utterly different yet highly sophisticated and exotic civilization. A delightful incident is recorded by an Italian called Giovanni di Jacopo di Latino de' Pigli of Peretola. He found himself unexpectedly giving hospitality to John VIII's travelling party when a midday resting-place was needed as the visitors returned to Florence after a morning's sightseeing trip to Pistoia. Giovanni made his house available to the Emperor and his retinue, and was astonished by the Byzantines' culinary arrangements. For a start, the Emperor appeared to regard salad as a delicacy – to the Italians, greenstuff was food for peasants:

The first food the Emperor ate was a salad of purslain and parsley, with some onions, which he himself wished to clean. After that there were chickens and pigeons, boiled, and then chickens and pigeons quartered and fried in the frying pan with lard. As the dishes came, they were placed before him, and he took what he wanted, and sent them along to the others. His last dish was eggs thrown on hot bricks where the other things were cooked. And they set them before him in a plate with many spices; I cannot imagine how they were done, but such is the fact.

Spices represented the fascinating and the outlandish to Giovanni. At the same time, it was the growing, acquired Western European taste for ginger, pepper, cloves and nutmeg which fuelled expanding trade with the Orient. Pepper was the merchant's 'black gold' – the commodity which held its value most securely, and whose transport and sale guaranteed the seller reliable profit. In the early fifteenth century, Italy (above all the thriving seaboard cities of Genoa and Venice) was the first port of call for ships returning from the eastern Mediterranean and beyond carrying spices; from there, consignments were dispatched by navigable river transport to Germany, where there was a thriving and rapidly increasing demand for them.

Writing to a trading associate from Nuremberg in 1392 the Venetian merchant Francesco Amadi specifies the going rate for pepper – information which will enable the German to set an appropriate commercial price at the point of sale: 'Pepper is worth 227 lire. Spices are at the same rate as when you left. There is no other news.' Three weeks later he wrote again, with more information about spice prices:

Today, 4 October, at dawn, the three vessels arrived from La Tana, heavily laden. I enclose with this letter a sealed inventory of the cargoes of these ships so that you can be precisely informed on what they contain. Know that today also three ships arrived from Syria, from whose crew we are reliably informed that our Venetians have bought large amounts of spices there, above all pepper and ginger. It is true that the ginger has been bought at a rather high price, as has the sugar and the dyeing pigment (gall). For the rest of the merchandise, however, the prices were more reasonable. As a result of this news we all feel that there will be adequate supplies of spices on offer this year in Venice, as far as we can tell. It is not, however, possible to fix the conditions of sale in writing yet, because we await the arrival about the 7 or 8 of October of the vessels from Beirut (God guide them to safe harbour). Then we will have accurate prices.

Commodities like pepper and sugar were to become an index of commercial power over the international markets in the sixteenth century. When the Portuguese King commissioned a series of

9. Pepper-gathering in the kingdom of Quilon, from Marco Polo, *Livre des Merveilles*

10. A customer choosing from an increased diversity of goods in a
Renaissance shop

expensive tapestries from a renowned firm of Flemish tapestry-
makers in the 1530s, it was stipulated that they would be paid for
in pepper. The Queen of Portugal's charitable donations to convents
across Portugal, and even into Italy, were made in the form of mule-
loads of sugar, sold on by the nuns to furnish them with ready
money for less luxurious commodities. But the cost of spices to the
individual probably meant that in the 1430s they were beyond the
means of someone of comparatively modest means like Giovanni
di Jacopo di Latino de' Pigli. Even the most humble of tables had
to have salt on it – and the fortunes of the Venetians had originally
been made in sea salt (for which in the 1430s they still held a virtual
European monopoly, both for home production and for imported

salt from Cyprus and Ibiza). Pepper, ginger, cloves and nutmeg were in the process of becoming equally indispensable to the European palate, with some heavy marketing encouragement from those who imported it.

The surviving records of visitations like the 1438 Florentine Council remind us that East and West were in constant – if sometimes tense – dialogue, and that the very instability of the Mediterranean political scene led to percolation from one culture into the other. In 1490, ambassadors from the Sultan of Cairo brought Doge Barbarigo of Venice fine Chinese porcelain. Diplomats bargaining for territorial advantages and trading missions negotiating safe passages for goods and men were exposed to the lavish splendour of the Court of the Ottomans. In the early years of the sixteenth century, Suleiman the Magnificent presented visiting dignitaries at his imperial palace, the Topkapı Saray, in Istanbul with 'robes of honour' to take home to the sovereign or head of state they represented. The most lavish of these were brocades woven with gold and silver thread, occasionally even bordered with sable. Such trophies, brought back by ambassadors to doges and princes provided tangible evidence of a ceremonial opulence beyond anything the West knew, and set the fashion for oriental fabrics and oriental-style garments reflected in the garments worn in official portraits of Western rulers of the same period.

As with other types of exchange between the Venetians and the Turks, such gifts were invariably reciprocated. In August 1518, Marino Sanuto recorded in his diary the list of gifts given to the Sultan and eminent members of his entourage by two Venetian emissaries:

> 8 robes of the heaviest cloth of gold
> 1 length of crimson velvet, of double height pile
> 1 length of paonaz [purplish red] velvet, double height pile
> 2 lengths of multicoloured velvet, double height pile
> 1 length of crimson velvet

1 length of paonaz velvet
2 lengths of multicoloured velvet
2 lengths of damask
2 lengths of crimson satin
8 lengths of multicoloured satin
20 scarlet wool sheets
20 paonaz wool sheets

By this date the Venetians had become one of the leading producers of fine silk fabrics in Europe – directly emulating the Ottoman silk-weaving which they had admired for so long (and, indeed, substantially building both their techniques and their designs on Ottoman prototypes).

A further cultural impact made on the Italians by the 1438 delegation from Constantinople was that produced by the impressive baggage of books and learned texts with which they travelled. The intricacies of the doctrinal negotiations meant that on either side the prelates had assembled their best intellects to help with the proceedings. On the Italian Catholic side this group included Ambrogio Traversari, a learned humanist and patristic translator and commentator. In March or early April 1438, Traversari wrote to his friend Filippo dei Pieruzzi, from Ferrara, that he had already seen some of the Emperor John's books: a beautiful Plato, a Plutarch, Aristotle, Diodorus, Dionysius of Halicarnassus, and looked forward presently to seeing many more. Subsequently Traversari met the young Greek scholar Bessarion (who in the course of the negotiations was raised by the Patriarch to the clerical status of Metropolitan of Nicaea), whose books he made no secret of coveting. Bessarion told Traversari he had brought only a small part of his library of books with him 'but had left a big pile at Modon':

I proceeded, however [writes Traversari], to ask questions, and he stated that he had left there two big volumes of Strabo. These are not accessible here, but there are several others not unknown to us. How ill I took it that he had not brought the volumes along! But I had to conceal the fact. I am led to hope, nevertheless, that they are to be brought. . . . He has Cyril's big book against Julian the Apostate which we shall take care to copy if we can find the parchment. . . . I came across a number of mathematical works among his stuff, a Euclid and a Ptolemy, written in his own hand with the appropriate figures.

What is telling in this exchange is the interests which the scholars from the two cultures share, while the masters they serve struggle to reconcile insuperable differences between their religious ideologies and their political outlooks. While Byzantine and Roman doctrines and temperaments collide, the intellectual experts on hand to facilitate the negotiations continue to collaborate, with apparent disregard for the tenseness of the prevailing political situation. They are unhampered in exchanging views and expert opinion on mathematical texts, just as their mercantile compatriots continue unimpeded to transact their exchange of silks and spices. There are apparently only permeable boundaries where a traffic in goods – intellectual or material – is concerned.

It was books written in Greek which most impressed the scholars in Florence. The inability of monastic copyists to transcribe the unfamiliar alphabet of Greek script, and the difficulty in learning classical Greek anywhere in the West had, for instance, cut the intellectual tradition off from the work of the great Greek mathematicians and geometers – Euclid, Apollonius, Pappus, Ptolemy. By the middle of the fifteenth century shipbuilders in the Levant had grasped the need for a proper understanding of geometry to produce seaworthy vessels capable of withstanding marine and military onslaught, and were using the Greek (and Arabic) texts of Euclid's three-dimensional geometry of solids and Apollonius' treatise on conic sections to construct the blueprints for their warships. European designers, however, had to wait a good deal longer for the texts to be translated into Latin.

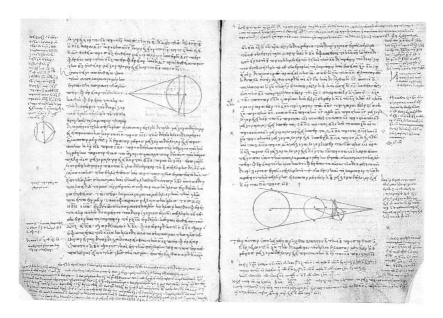

11. A rare Greek astronomical manuscript from the Vatican Library

The percolation of the Greek studies, in which Byzantium (a territory with a significant presence of native Greek-speakers) excelled, into the world of Italian humanism in these decades was part of a continuous process of cross-cultural fertilization. Although the outcome would be the intellectual vigour and scholarly expertise of European humanism, the transmission of culture and exchange of ideas began here as a shared heritage and a set of academic interests in common, rather than a 'movement' with conscious ambitions and intellectual goals. The steadily increasing vogue for classical Greek learning in Italy during the early decades of the fifteenth century started from the casual and largely unplanned encounter of interests directly associated with small groups of partisan individuals like those who accompanied the union-seeking churchmen to Florence.

It was, predictably, the scholars from Constantinople in John VIII's retinue who argued most vigorously in favour of a union between the two churches. For them the scholarly benefits promised if cordial and close relations could be established between the intellectuals of the two surviving wings of the classical tradition were a strong inducement to settle doctrinal differences and to unite under the leadership of the Pope. Constantinople, depopulated and commercially in decline, looked like a city without prospects for the talented and ambitious; Florence, on the other hand, a thriving centre of commerce, and the home of the ambitious and cultivated merchant-banking Medici family, actively welcomed and encouraged the intellectual pursuit of the new and arcane.

A striking example of the way the Florence Council impinged on re-emerging classical studies is Cosimo de' Medici's so-called Platonic Academy (a research institute for the esoteric arts financed by a cultivated millionaire – the fifteenth-century equivalent of the Getty Centre in California). Of the advisers accompanying the 1438 delegation from Constantinople, George Gemistus Plethon had been most uncooperative towards all proposals for union. Plethon was an academic and a specialist in the works of the ancient Greek philosopher Plato. He believed passionately that in Plato's pagan philosophy lay the secret of a tolerant and humane Christian Church. At the time of the Florence Council he had already withdrawn from Constantinople, which he regarded as intellectually impoverished and in decline, to Mistra, where, under the patronage of the most cultivated of Emperor John VIII's sons, he had founded a Platonic Academy, devoted to the study of Plato's philosophy, and was planning a reorganized enlightened order based upon it.

Intransigent as Plethon was in matters of faith during the Florence Council, the series of lectures he gave on Platonism to an invited audience of fellow scholars during his stay aroused an enormous amount of interest. The Medici decision to invest in a research initiative devoted to the recovery and study of Platonism in the West was made as a direct response to the excitement aroused in intellectual circles in Florence by the lectures. Plethon never visited Italy again, but Cosimo's Platonic Academy, and the lavish funding given for the work of the gifted Greek specialist (son of Cosimo's

12. Marsilio Ficino's translation
of Plato's *Dialogues*

personal physician) Marsilio Ficino, had lasting consequences for later developments in Greek studies. To Plethon belongs responsibility for introducing to Europe the mystical bent in interpretation of Plato's writings, and his association of Plato with the so-called 'prisca theologia' or original world religion.

Unlike Plethon, the scholar Bessarion had enthusiastically supported John VIII's attempts to persuade the inhabitants of Constantinople to accept the terms of the proposed union on their return. When they were met with a largely negative response (the union was never in effect implemented) he soon returned to Italy, and settled permanently in the land which had welcomed and appreciated him and where his scholarly skills were considered to be extremely valuable. There he continued to campaign on behalf of the Byzantines whenever the slightest possibility arose of a 'crusade' to rescue his compatriots from the Turks. As that hope receded he invested his emotional energies in assembling a personal library of rare books, particularly Greek works, so that the Byzantine intellectual heritage should not be lost:

> I tried, to the best of my ability, to collect books for their quality rather than their quantity, and to find single volumes of single works; and so I assembled almost all the works of the wise men of Greece, especially those which were rare and difficult to find. ... They must be preserved in a place that is both safe and accessible, for the general good of all readers, be they Greek or Latin.

Bessarion's energies for the remainder of his life were devoted to the secular scholarly task of rebuilding a classical learning built from a fusion of the Byzantine Greek and Italian Latin surviving traditions. Two other learned members of the delegation did likewise – Isidore, Metropolitan of Kiev (like Bessarion, raised from

13. Cardinal Bessarion's personal copy of Simplicius, *Commentary on Aristotle, De caelo*

the status of monk to bishop for the purposes of the Council), and George of Trebizond.

Scholar–theologians like these prominent members of the mission to unite the Eastern and Western Christian churches were fundamental influences on the intellectual development of the European Renaissance. Pope Nicholas V was himself a scholar, who conceived the idea of founding the great public library of the Vatican in the late 1440s. While Bessarion was pressing him to back an expedition to rescue Constantinople from the infidels, another great Greek specialist, Francesco Filelfo, who had married the daughter of the Byzantine professor Johannes Chrysoloras, was urging the French King to do likewise. Neither of the great rulers responded positively on the military front, but both backed the new Greek studies in Europe in the years that followed the loss of Constantinople.

In 1468 Cardinal Bessarion gave his own magnificent collection of books and manuscripts not to Florence but to Venice. His choice was, as he explained in his deed of donation, determined by the very cosmopolitan and commercially lively ambience which made Venice the contemporary hub of the mercantile Mediterranean:

> I could not select a place more suitable and convenient to men of my own Greek background. Though nations from almost all over the earth flock in vast numbers to your city, the Greeks are most numerous of all: as they sail in from their own regions they make their first landfall in Venice, and have such a tie with you that when they put into your city they feel they are entering another Byzantium. . . . So I have given and granted all my books, both in Latin and Greek, to the most holy shrine of the Blessed Mark in your glorious city, sure in the knowledge that this is a duty owed to your generosity, to my gratitude, and to the country which you wanted me to share.

In an environment coloured by mercantile interests, a profusion of luxury possessions of all kinds was the readiest way of conveying

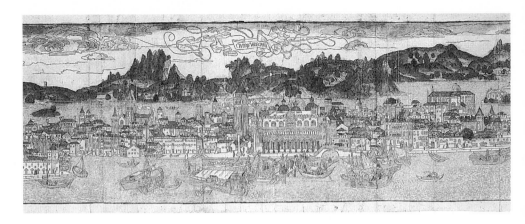

14. Reeuwich, woodcut of fifteenth-century Venice

the impression of power. The material consequences of this can be seen particularly clearly in the interactions during the first half of the fifteenth century between the Venetian Republic – a largely secular state, operating on behalf of its commercial and civic interests – and the Vatican – representing the Christian Church on earth, but clearly also power-brokers and international investors. After the fall of Constantinople friction between religious and secular interests noticeably produced an investment (psychological and material) in competing versions of 'splendour' (conspicuous consumption of all kinds) on the understanding that this would be interpreted by competitors as correlating with 'power' in the international arena.

In 1459 another pope attempted to raise an army and launch a crusade against the Turks. This time the Ecumenical Council which Pope Pius II called met at Mantua, and the prominent individual who lavishly hosted the gathering of diginitaries was Ludovico Gonzaga, Marquis of Mantua. Ludovico Gonzaga had been educated by the leading humanist Vittorino da Feltre and was soon to be widely known for his erudition and his patronage of scholars, artists and architects. On the occasion of the Council, Ludovico planned meticulously the supplying of food, a good clean water supply and appropriate lodgings for the visiting dignitaries. The Pope was provided with private apartments in the Gonzaga Palace, and a large audience chamber was made available to him within the palace precincts. Bessarion, who once again led those pleading passionately for intervention to retrieve his native Constantinople for Christendom, had written ahead to the Marquis reminding him that his accommodation in Rome was extremely comfortable – he was housed in Mantua's Franciscan convent.

The Council was in effect a showpiece political summit of the kind made familiar to us today by regular congregations of the members of the Group of Seven (the world's wealthiest nations). A great deal of eloquent speaking went on, orchestrated as today by professional speech-writers from among the leading classical scholars of the day (most of the speeches were in Latin). The Pope himself, a scholar of some distinction, pronounced himself in his private memoirs well pleased with his own performances, which he prided himself out-shone those of the renowned scholar Cardinal Bessarion. He may, however, be something of a biased witness. According to members of foreign delegations who were present, some of the Pope's oratorical *tours de force* took three hours to deliver.

From the political point of view the occasion was an extravagant failure. The moral and religious imperative which Pius II tried to use to rally the nations of Europe against the infidel proved weaker than the local political interests of the several power blocs assembled. For Ludovico Gonzaga, the leading role he had played in the occasion produced an acceptable reward. In 1461 his younger son Francesco, barely seventeen years old, was named cardinal by Pius II (to account for his extreme youth the rather weak justification was produced that Francesco 'looked old for his age'). In 1462 he arrived in Rome in great splendour, with an entourage of eighty-two persons (fifty-four on horseback) wearing Gonzaga livery, to take up residence in the papal Court.

Francesco never became much of a churchman. Chanting the office in the papal chapel on Christmas Day 1464 he evidently forgot the chant part-way through, and had to make up his own – causing the new Pope, Paul II, enough amusement for him to repeat the

15. Andrea Mantegna's
portrait of *Cardinal
Francesco Gonzaga
as a boy*

story several times in company. The story of his appointment
reminds us that by the mid-fifteenth century major offices in the
Catholic Church were political plums, to be filled by members of
prominent and powerful families like the Gonzagas as recompense
for services rendered. The power wielded by the Papacy was worldly
as well as spiritual, and if they were to give their continued
support to the Church the nobility of Europe expected to be part of
the action.

Here, however, it is one particular aspect of Cardinal Francesco
Gonzaga's affluent lifestyle which concerns us. Francesco was a
notable collector. Throughout his life he spent lavish sums of money
in acquiring a range of precious belongings, ranging from gems
and tapestries to rare books and manuscripts. He owned a fabulous
collection of cameos, which he had housed in a series of specially
manufactured display trays, twenty of them of silver bearing the
Cardinal's coat of arms, two made of jasper, into which were set

twenty-four and sixteen cameos respectively , one of prasma (green quartz). The inventory of Francesco's belongings taken for probate purposes in 1483 lists 500 gems, intaglios and cameos. Two hundred and seventy-two of the gems were unset, including a 'very ancient' cornelian cameo bearing the head of Julius Caesar (which Francesco left in his will to the Duke of Calabria). Among the mounted cameos were fourteen on gold rings and eight on a square silver mirror.

The Cardinal's tapestries astonished contemporaries during his lifetime for their opulence, the splendour and variety of their design, and the compelling nature of the scenes chosen for depiction. They gained him a considerable reputation as a connoisseur at the papal Court. Pius II was impressed by a display of Francesco's hangings and tapestries at Viterbo in 1462 and wrote in his personal reminiscences that 'the Mantuan cardinal almost entirely covered the expanse with tapestry and adorned them with opulent hangings into which the weavers had woven the most outstanding stories'. During the Habsburg Emperor Frederick III's visit to Rome for his coronation by the Pope in 1469, Francesco's tapestries were singled out for praise, together with the rest of his household furnishings. The amazement occasioned by the scale and splendour of the Cardinal's retinue and possessions when he arrived in Bologna is recorded in a local chronicle of the time:

> Cardinal Francesco Gonzaga entered Bologna on the 21 of July at noon. He came with a fine entourage of retainers and priests, there were around eighty horses in his retinue. He had with him more than 300 lire worth of ornate silverware and large numbers of hangings of arras-style fine tapestry, worked in silk and gold, estimated at a value of more than 10 thousand ducats. All his rooms were decorated with these hangings. Among them was one at the entrance which carried the story of Alexander the Great's campaign against the King Porto of India, with soldiers in armour on horseback and on foot, and elephants with 'castles' on their backs and the men fighting. The scene was executed

with such skill that many of the figures seemed alive, both men and horses, they were worked so naturally. To see so many beautiful works of gold and silk was wonderful and lifted the beholder's heart.

The tapestries depicting the life of Alexander are to be found among a substantial collection of hangings and tapestries in the probate inventory of the Cardinal's possessions. Some of these finely woven pieces are identified there as being of oriental provenance, others as having been made in the great European centres for tapestry-weaving, Tournai, Bruges and Siena. Some were evidently commissioned; others were purchased ready-made, sometimes from other prominent collectors (four 'antique hangings of arras quality tapestry of gold and silk' are specified in the inventory as having

16. Niclaus Manuel, *St Eligius at work*, which shows him hammering a silver chalice on an anvil

belonged to Alfonso of Aragon, King of Naples, who had died in 1458).

The inventory of the Cardinal's belongings also itemizes sumptuous articles of clothing – 'turkish style' floor-length robes of damask (crimson or green, some of it 'moorish'), several kinds of velvet and various woven silks, some lined with ermine. There are silks and brocades in panels and lengths, and quantities of damask, velvet and brocade cushions (some of these, again, specified as 'from Alexandria'). And there is silver and gold tableware, of elaborate design, including a large silver-gilt candlestick in the form of a tree with Adam and Eve, and goblets decorated with animals and nymphs.

This is a collection of treasures – all kinds of what today might be called 'collectibles' – whose magnificence established the reputation of its owner as a cultured man of discerning taste. Cardinal Gonzaga 'may in truth have had rather a mediocre mind', according to the historian who has worked most closely on his life. Yet his collection was the height of contemporary taste, admired by his contemporaries and coveted by other collectors. It also had the advantage of giving him informal access to a circle of other collectors who were prominent political figures inside and outside the Vatican. Pope Paul II – a notoriously difficult character politically – nevertheless seems to have been on cordial antiquarian terms with Francesco Gonzaga. A cameo in a ruby setting in the Cardinal's collection with the head of Pope Paul on it evidently came from the Pope's own collection. The Cardinal's correspondence also contains details of negotiations to sell a particularly valuable item from his own collection to Pope Paul in 1467 (the deal fell through).

In all of this the Cardinal had expert professional help. Cardinal Gonzaga's cultivation and connoisseurship were carefully nurtured by his family in just the same way as they had lobbied assiduously to secure his appointment to high clerical office. When the youthful Cardinal was sent off from Mantua to Rome he was accompanied by able and highly qualified staff who supplied him with the

17. Cameo seal imprint of Francesco Gonzaga's 'Felix Gem' – one of the treasures of his collection

cultivation and maturity he lacked. Foremost among these was his personal secretary Giovanni Pietro Arrivabene, whose father and brother were in turn chancellors back in Mantua. Throughout his life Arrivabene ensured that the Cardinal's public image as a man of letters was a distinguished one. He appears to have been responsible for almost every letter in the extensive correspondence the Cardinal was required to conduct with eminent members of the clergy and nobility, and even with his family. Every aspect of the fifteenth-century art of letter-writing except the signature was orchestrated by the highly educated Arrivabene – the elegant script, the composition, the construction and the content.

Arrivabene was also probably responsible for the presence of richly illuminated Greek manuscripts in the Cardinal's book collection. Francesco Gonzaga's library was full of expensive and beautiful works produced by renowned copyists and illuminators; among these are visually exquisite items like his copy of the Greek gospels. Such a work would have been admired and highly prized by contemporaries as a fine art-object; there is, however, no evidence that the Cardinal had either the inclination or the requisite linguistic skills to read it, and after his death it passed into the possession of the man who had overseen its excecution, Arrivabene (the Cardinal also owned illuminated manuscripts in Arabic).

It was the highly trained and educated members of the Cardinal's household who saw to it that the *objets d'art* acquired for his collections were of the highest calibre, that he was informed whenever a desirable item came on to the market and advised on the quality of the piece and a suitable price to offer for it. Arrivabene was evidently something of a connoisseur of gems (he had two signet rings made for himself out of ancient intaglios). Francesco Maffei, another member of his household, supplied the Cardinal with semi-precious stones. He also organized loans of substantial sums of money to the Cardinal from the Maffei family funds. Indeed, gems and borrowing went together. As well as being an object of rare beauty a fine gem could be used as security against a cash loan and was therefore treated as a capital investment (just as diamonds still are today).

Francesco was particularly reliant apparently on his specialist advisers on the comparatively few occasions when he ordered contemporary pieces, as opposed to acquiring various kinds of rarities of antiquarian interest. Shortly after the Cardinal's death, one of his employees, Gaspare da Padova, wrote to Francesco's brother, the Marquis of Mantua, asking to be paid an outstanding amount of 22 ducats for services to Francesco in his capacity as adviser in the commissioning and procuring of fine *objets d'art*: 'He gave me instructions to commission a porphyry pepper-mill to be made by one Juliano de Scipio; and I was instructed to search out medals and other antique coins and to order them.' When the goldsmith fell behind schedule in completing the pepper-mill, Gaspare stayed on to wait for it, and to check that it had been executed as requested. In a subsequent letter we learn that he had difficulty putting pressure on Juliano because (as was usual with the Cardinal, apparently) no written contract had been drawn up. Responsibility was left entirely with the specialist artistic adviser to see to it that the work was satisfactory and that the price matched the quality of the goods.

By the mid-fifteenth century, being the possessor of such a collection is a mark of magnificence and an indication of individual worth in the civic sphere. Cardinal Gonzaga may not have been a person of intellectual pursuits or a man of highly educated taste, but his collection bestowed upon him a reputation for splendour which contributed to the esteem in which he was held in Rome. Ostentation and authority went hand in hand; to be ostentatious was an important part of being considered a figure of civic worth. In the speech made at Cardinal Gonzaga's funeral this esteem was converted, just as the Gonzaga family would have wished, into a version of his life (nowhere to be matched by surviving records of his actual conduct) as one of virtue, piety and weighty learning, the life of a wise and discriminating man, a true father of the Church.

The presence of oriental and oriental-influenced objects among Cardinal Gonzaga's treasures is a reminder that the flow of goods along the trade routes to and from the East did not stop with the fall of Constantinople in 1453. Sultan Mehmed II's first moves to establish the city as the appropriate capital for his expanding empire were deliberately aimed at improving its attractiveness as a crossroads for the international world of trade. In 1455 he began to build the grand bazaar, or covered market – the centre of Istanbul's commercial life down to the present day. He repopulated the city with skilled artisans in the key luxury industries – silk-weaving and cotton-weaving, glass-making, porcelain- and ceramics-making, and enamelled tile-making – forcibly relocating them where necessary from other recently conquered areas in the Empire. And he embarked on a programme of building mosques and palaces which rivalled the equivalent construction programme of the same period in Venice in the consciously ostentatious state-ment it made about the wealth and power of the Ottomans. The contemporary Greek-speaking historian Kritovoulos of Imbros (who dedicated his *History of Mehmed the Conqueror* to the Sultan) described how by 1460 Mehmed had turned his attention to building:

When the Sultan had reached Constantinople, and had rested a bit, he gave attention to the situation in his realm and to arranging and renovating things everywhere, especially what was connected with his own palace. . . . He zealously directed operations on the buildings he was erecting on his own account – that is the mosque and the palace. For he was constructing great edifices which were to be worth seeing and should in every respect vie with the greatest and best of the past. For this reason he needed to give the most careful oversight as to workmen and materials of many kinds and the best quality, and he also was personally concerned with the very many and great expenses and outlays. Not only so, but he himself also made frequent inspection and watched over the work, doing everything very ambitiously and with excellent taste, altogether in the regal manner.

By 1465 Kritovoulos describes the interior decorations of the Sultan's palace as of breathtaking splendour, striking awe into the onlooker:

The walls shine and scintillate with an abundance of gold and silver, within and without and with precious stones and marble with various ornaments and colours, all applied with a brilliance and smoothness and lightness both attractive and worked out with the finest and most complete skill, most ambitiously. Both in sculpture and plastic work, as well as painting, they were the finest and best of all. . . . And the whole was beautiful and adorned with myriads of other brilliant and graceful articles.

It is possible that one of the projects Gentile Bellini undertook during his stay in Istanbul in 1479–80 was that of planning frescos for a pavilion in the palace gardens.

By the 1480s Istanbul was an international centre of about 100,000 people, of whom approximately half were Muslims, one-quarter Byzantine Greeks and the remainder Europeans, Jews and Armenians. By the 1480s the Ottoman centre for ceramics-production at Iznik

18. Fifteenth-century
Iznik ceramic jar

was producing work of a quality unmatched anywhere in the world, whose fine decoration would exert a strong influence on European design in tiles, textiles and marquetry (inlaid wood decoration), while the reputed 1000 silk looms in the town of Bursa were pro-ducing fine fabrics of a richness and complexity of design which the whole of Europe strove to emulate. In the panorama we are sur-veying of emerging influences on European culture, the cultural as well as the political might of the Ottomans plays a vital part.

The network of agents and merchant communities from the Adriatic ports into the heart of Ottoman territories meant that the extremely rich and powerful in Europe could make personal approaches to the Turks to supply expensive goods from the East to their own specifications. In the 1490s Francesco Gonzaga, Marquis of Mantua (Cardinal Francesco Gonzaga's nephew), sustained an amicable correspondence with Mehmed II's successor, the Ottoman Emperor Bayezid II, over a period of years. The reason for this correspondence was the Gonzaga family's passion for breeding horses – the very best horses were Arab, and the very best source of

Arab horses was the Sultan. In 1492 Francesco sent Alexis Becagut to Istanbul bearing lavish gifts and authorized to negotiate the purchase of purebred horses. In his letters home Becagut describes entering the Chamber of Petitions in the inner sanctum of the Sultan's palace, and being escorted into a small, unornamented vaulted chamber where the Sultan was seated cross-legged on a dais lavishly fur-nished with carpets, brocades and awnings. There he was granted the exceptional honour of kissing the Sultan's hand.

Thirty years later, Francesco's son Federico II also attempted to establish a relationship with the Ottoman Sultan. He sent his personal chamberlain Marcelli Anconitano to Istanbul with gifts for the Sultan, and a request to buy a significant number of bloodstock

19. One of Marquis
Francesco Gonzaga's
favourite horses, from
Andrea Mantegna's
fresco in the Ducal
palace in Mantua

Arab mares. He left Ancona on 15 November 1525, but took twenty-three days to reach Ragusa (where an Italian agent reported his safe arrival) because of violent storms. An Italian agent in Istanbul reported Anconitano's arrival there on 6 March 1526: 'An emissary from the Marquis of Mantua has arrived here. He has brought presents for the Sultan of armaments for footsoldiers and for cavalry, saddles, falconets [small artillery pieces] and other things. He wants to negotiate for some horses.' On 14 March Suleiman responded to Anconitano's approach with a cordial letter to Federico in Turkish, sent with an accompanying Italian translation (although three years later the household of the Gonzagas boasted a Turkish 'interpreter'). But Suleiman was preoccupied with impending hostilities against Hungary, and three months later Anconitano was still waiting for a final decision; on 18 July he wrote to Federico from Ragusa to say that he had failed to acquire any horses from the Sultan, but describing in minute detail the seventeen horses he had managed to buy from other sources.

Demand from an increasingly discerning clientele for goods traditionally produced in exotic locations (including, as the century went on, the north coast of Africa, India and China, Guinea and Russia) inevitably encouraged enterprising merchants and bankers to develop more readily controlled manufacturing bases inside Europe. The promoters of these new industries were helped by regular influxes of refugees – mostly skilled artisans – fleeing the results of political upheaval. When political disturbance drove the tiny elite of silk-weavers out of Lucca, the Medicis welcomed them into Florence, which became a leading centre for the production of ornate brocades and silk velvets. In Marseille, skilled Jewish workers, probably displaced from Spain via Sicily, did fine work on the coral fished from the waters along the coast, or round Naples and Sicily. The coral beads they produced were not just for the home market, they were particularly sought after in Egypt and Syria, and are recorded as part of cargoes carried by ships going east from Marseille, to return with consignments of silk and spices.

In the face of such diversity, the idea of consumer choice emerges in this period with remarkable vigour. Those who made their purchases with pride, because the distinctiveness of their possessions was a marker of their social prestige, knew exactly what they wanted, and they were prepared to look beyond the immediately available for the style of product most to their taste. While the painter and engraver Albrecht Dürer was in Venice, various of his friends in Nuremberg, including his patron Willibald Pirckheimer, asked him to make purchases on their behalf. Dürer's letters home reveal him embroiled with the precise requirements of the purchasers. Will the fifty cornelian stones he has bought Stefan Paumgartner be the right size? He can find only white feathers, not green ones; will these do for Pirckheimer? Pirckheimer wants a square rug; he can find only long thin ones, does he want one of these?

The extension of trading ventures from well-recognized and reliable routes to 'discovery' has to be set against this backdrop of pressing consumer demand, commercial ferment and the urge to expand markets. Merchants' wealthy customers were prepared to pay large sums for particularly rare and unusual goods; they could even be asked to put up money to finance speculative ventures to explore import–export possibilities in territories not already staked out by the agents of the powerful trading nations. As the horizons of possibility expanded with improved navigational technology and ships, speculative voyages to locate new trading bases and new ports where ships could take on fresh supplies in the course of long journeys were part of an energetic programme of investment and exploration of business opportunities in the mid- to late fifteenth century. In the 1480s merchants from Bristol made a number of attempts to locate the 'Island of Brasil' to their west. From the 1420s Portuguese entrepreneurs backed a series of initiatives heading south from Lisbon along the west coast of Africa in search of alternative access to central Africa's reputedly rich gold supplies; they discovered the Azores, Madeiras and Canaries by 1432, reached Cape

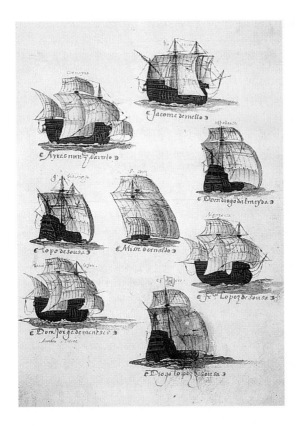

20. The Portuguese
fleet embarked for
the Indies

Verde by 1444, and by 1460 had arrived at Sierra Leone and the Guinea coast.

The Madeiras and the Azores were uninhabited when the Portuguese arrived, and thus offered a distinctive kind of trading opportunity: privileged settlement by the ship-captain to exploit its natural resources, under licence from the King. Sugar plantations on these islands produced lucrative crops, using as labour the slaves who formed a significant part of the trade in exotic 'goods' on the African continent. A Venetian, Alvise da Cadamosto, who travelled to west Africa in 1454, described the tight control Portuguese interests exerted over trade from the fortified island of Arguim, just off the north-west coast of Africa:

You should know that the said King of Portugal has leased this island to Christians for ten years, so that no one can enter the bay to trade with the Arabs save those who hold the licence. These have dwellings on the island and factories where they buy and sell with the said Arabs who come to the coast to trade for merchandise of various kinds, such as woollen cloths, cotton, silver, and 'alchezeli' [coarse cloth], that is, cloaks, carpets, and similar articles and above all, corn, for they are always short of food. They give in exchange slaves whom the Arabs bring from the land of the Blacks, and gold dust. The King therefore caused a castle to be built on the island to protect this trade forever. For this reason, Portuguese caravels come and go all year long to this island. . . . These Arabs also have many Berber horses, which they trade, and take to the land of the Blacks, exchanging them with the rulers for slaves. Ten or fifteen slaves are given for one of these horses, according to their quality.

The documents promoting alternative routes eastwards almost invariably use the lure of possible sources for gold as the major incentive for potential patrons. The increasingly fierce contest for access to new sources of gold was part and parcel of the expanding horizons of international trade in a growing range of commodities. It was a state's reserves of gold (whose value was regarded as reliably fixed, while that of silver fluctuated) which fostered confidence in its capacity to honour trading debts: the gold coins minted in Venice, Florence, Genoa and Lisbon were treated as international currency. John II of Portugal was prepared to invest heavily in exploring possible routes for obtaining Sudanese gold directly from the producers, rather than via the middlemen in the Berber Kingdom (the Mahgreb) who sold it to merchants in the Mediterranean ports along the north coast of Africa; that funding resulted in Bartolomeu Dias rounding the Cape of Good Hope in 1488. In July 1497 Vasco da Gama followed up Dias's success with a voyage which would take him to India and back, encouraged by the belief (correct, as it turned out) that there must be a direct route to the spice and gem markets, thus avoiding the high transport costs along Ottoman-dominated routes, with their high tax or duty charges on goods in transit. His own account of the journey up the east coast of Africa makes clear its single-mindedly mercantile motivation:

> The people of Mozambique are of a ruddy complexion and well made. They are Muslims, and their language is the same as that of the Moors. . . . They are merchants, and have transactions with white Moors, four of whose vessels were at the time in port, laden with gold, silver, cloves, pepper, ginger, and silver rings, as also with quantities of pearls, jewels, and rubies, all of which articles are used by the people of this country. We understand them to say that all these things, with the exception of the gold, were brought thither by these Moors; that further on [towards India] where we were going to, they abounded, and that precious stones, pearls and spices were so plentiful that there was no need to purchase them as they could be collected in baskets.

Three years later, in 1500, a major expedition funded by King Manuel of Portugal to capitalize on da Gama's direct overtures to the Indian mercantile community, and led by an inexperienced young Portuguese nobleman by the name of Pedro Alvarez Cabral, ran off course and accidentally discovered the coast of Brazil. In the eyes of his sponsor Manuel, however, the significance of that discovery was slight compared to his satisfaction with Cabral's successful delivery of lavish gifts once he reached India, in order to establish a factor and trading privileges in the Indian port of Calicut for the Portuguese Crown ('a rich saddle, a pair of enamelled bridles for a horse, a pair of stirrups and their spurs, all of silver, enamelled and gilded, a breast strap and cords of the proper kind for the said saddle, and furnishings of very rich crimson, and a halter worked in gold thread for the aforesaid horse, and two cushions of brocade and two other cushions of crimson velvet, and a fine carpet,

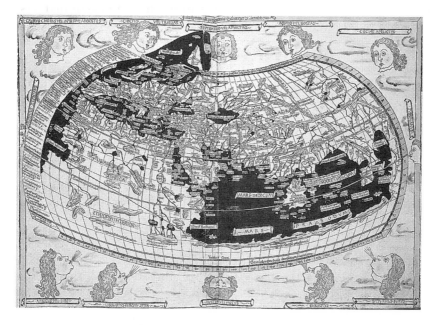

21. A 1486 map of the world based on the calculations of distance in
Ptolemy's *Geography*

and a piece of tapestry, and two pieces of scarlet cloth – worth more
than a thousand ducats in Portugal – and also a length of crimson
satin and a piece of crimson taffetta').

Against such a background the conviction with which Columbus
set off west in search of an alternative route to the Indies is easy to
understand. The Portuguese successes in navigating eastwards via the
Cape of Good Hope created intense commercial pressure to find an
equivalent route which also cut out the Ottoman middlemen essential
to overland traffic from India to the West. Columbus' conviction that
such a route lay westwards round the globe to the eastern edge of
India was encouraged by an accident of the scholarly literature in
which he immersed himself in preparation for his venture: the ancient
scholar Ptolemy had significantly underestimated the circumference
of the earth in his *Geography*. While today we remember Columbus

for having 'discovered' America, he himself died believing that he had successfully arrived on the doorstep of the familiar Indian spice markets.

Columbus was a native of Genoa, with all the mercantile sea-faring know-how of the Genoese, and their historical commitment to command of the pepper trade as the yardstick of mercantile success. He made his first attempt to interest the King of Portugal in a speculative voyage westwards in 1485, an attempt which probably failed because John II's financial efforts were already heavily invested in explorations pressing onwards around the coast of Africa. So, in the same spirit of entrepreneurism as the skilled cannon-builder who forty years earlier had marketed his apparently wild idea for a super-gun to Mehmed II, Columbus went on to Spain, to try to interest Isabella of Castile and Ferdinand of Aragon in his project. As Urban the armaments-maker had done with the Sultan, he found in the Spanish monarchs rulers with a shrewd grasp of business opportunities and a strong sense of the driving forces in contemporary power politics.

The Spanish monarchs were not convinced immediately. They ordered a copy of Ptolemy's *Geography* for themselves from a Valencian bookseller, and they organized an investigative commission which met in Salamanca to consider whether the considerable outlay of money, and the association of the Crown of Spain with the project, would be advisable. For the next five years Columbus was retained in the service of Ferdinand and Isabella, employed in a whole range of Castilian commercial projects. Finally, in April 1492 it was agreed to put up the 2500 ducats needed to finance Columbus' voyage: ships were fitted out, Columbus' titles and offices were confirmed, and he was provided with a letter of recommendation to be delivered to the Grand Khan and all the kings and lords of India when he arrived there. Significantly, the person who finally persuaded Ferdinand and Isabella that the venture was financially sound was a banker and papal tax-gatherer from Valencia (one of Valencia's many converted Jews), who had been responsible for raising a number of substantial loans for them, some from his own personal funds – a shrewd and wealthy businessman, with wide experience in trade.

Acute shortage of currency (especially gold) figured largely among the reasons for the Spanish decision to back Columbus. Expenditure on a sequence of military campaigns – against the Portuguese for control of the Canary Islands and against the Iberian Muslims for southern Spain – had entirely emptied the coffers of Aragon and Castile. For all the flamboyant magnificence of Ferdinand and Isabella's public appearances, vital in order to convince the rest of Europe of their combined political might, they were living largely on credit. Columbus was proposing a venture with the possibility of enormous profits if it succeeded; the opinion of the royal couple's financial advisers after lengthy consideration was that it was worth the risk.

In January 1492 the military forces of Ferdinand and Isabella had finally conquered the small province of Granada, in the extreme south of the Iberian peninsula, Spain's one remaining Islamic state, with an almost entirely Muslim, Arabic-speaking population. Here was one more pragmatic and mercenary reason for backing Columbus; it was becoming crucial for Spain to gain access to the luxury-goods markets without the need to use Muslim middlemen.

Like the fall of Constantinople to the Ottomans, the fall of Granada was in many ways more symbolic than strategic. It marked the end of a Spanish culture in which Islamic, Spanish and, indeed, Judaic strands had been inseparably intermingled for centuries, with a corresponding permeation of the cultural practices of each community into the others. The presence of the crafts and skills of the Islamic nations is readily identifiable in fifteenth-century Spain in its decorative ivory- and metalwork, ornate weaponry, leather-working (particularly in connection with equipment relating to horses), fine tapestry- and carpet-weaving, and damask and brocade silks. When the marriage of the heir to Aragon and the heir to Castile led to a unified power bloc under Catholic rulers in 1479,

22. Felipe de Bigarny, The Catholic monarchs, Ferdinand and Isabella, entering
Granada in triumph in 1492

23. Niccolò degli Agostini, *The siege of Padua*, a woodcut showing cannon breaching the city walls

the power-struggle at the political level between Christian and Islamic rulers in the Iberian peninsula was resolved almost fortuitously. Their combined resources finally allowed the possibility of mounting a military campaign capable of clinching the long-running contest to dominate the peninsula.

Once again in the military campaign which followed it was cannon-power which proved decisive, and this time the strength was on the side of Ferdinand's army. The Granadans' strategy was to retreat into highly fortified city strongholds, to withstand assaults from the Aragonese army. In the campaigns begun in 1484, however, Ferdinand systematically picked off the Granadan strongholds one by one, using heavy cannons to batter down walls which the citizens had believed were impregnable; Alora, Setenil and Ronda fell in turn, and Marbella surrendered before the big guns were even in position. The Spanish administrator Fernando del Pulgar described the effect of the heavy bombardment on the citizens of Ronda as follows:

> The bombardment was so heavy and so continuous that the Moors on sentry duty could only hear one another with great difficulty: they did not have the opportunity to sleep, nor did they know which sector most needed support, for in one place the cannon knocked down the wall, in another the siege engines destroyed the houses, and if they tried to repair the damage wrought by the cannon they could not, for the continuous hail of fire from the smaller weapons killed anybody on the wall. . . . The inhabitants of the city had felt safe and confident because of their massive fortifications, but now their confidence was suddenly converted into terrified disarray.

In spite of assurances given to the Granadan Muslims that they would be allowed to continue with their faith and their way of life unhindered under the new Christian regime, the fall of Granada marked the affirmation of a unified Christian state in Spain, with an aggressively homogeneous culture. Two events of the same year underline this: one was the expulsion of the Jewish community from the whole of Spain in April 1492; the other was the decision to give Spanish financial backing to Columbus' voyage westwards.

By turning their backs on the peninsula's multicultural heritage, in order to consolidate political power and stabilize the united territories into a single Spanish state, Ferdinand and Isabella effectively proclaimed a non-reliance on that colourful traffic in goods and commodities which we have seen animating the cultural life of Europe in the second half of the fifteenth century. Instead they announced an official policy of homogeneity of cultural practices, dress and religion, and the ruthless suppression of local custom, ritual and belief. In spite of the fact that the growing prosperity of Spain, as of the other European nations, depended on vigorous

24. Michael Sittow (attributed to), *Virgin of the Catholic Monarchs*: Ferdinand
and Isabella as the defenders of Christendom

and heterogeneous trade throughout the known world, and in spite
of the fact that the artisanal skills which supported lucrative industries like carpet manufacture, ceramics or brocade-weaving were
tightly associated with specific ethnic and religious groupings, the
victorious Spanish regime declared ethnic and doctrinal purity as
the foundations of the stability of the new state. By sponsoring

a daring and improbable attempt to forge an entirely new set of trading routes westwards and thereby arrive at the same desirable commodities and sustain the same vigorous trade without recourse to the existing network of Christian, Jewish and Islamic agents, merchants and middlemen, Ferdinand and Isabella ostentatiously set their sights on an ethnically cleansed 'new world' – one in which Spanish might would be unhampered by other interests, and one in which the Christian faith would inevitably dominate.

At the beginning of his account (as preserved for us by Las Casas) of that first voyage Columbus himself (by backdating the royal decision) makes explicit the connection between the 'cleansing' of the Iberian peninsula of its exotic elements and his own enterprise:

> On 2 January in the year 1492, when your Highnesses had concluded their war with the Moors who reigned in Europe, I saw your Highnesses' banners victoriously raised on the towers of the Alhambra, the citadel of that city, and the Moorish king come out of the city gates and kiss the hands of your Highnesses, and the prince, my Lord. And later in that same month . . . your Highnesses . . . decided to send me, Christopher Columbus, to see those parts of India and the princes and peoples of these lands, and consider the best means for their conversion, and your Highnesses ordered that I should not travel overland to the east, as is customary, but rather by way of the west, whither to this day, as far as we can know for certain, no man has ever gone before. Therefore having expelled all the Jews from your domains in that same month of January, your Highnesses commanded me to go with an adequate fleet to these parts of India. . . . I departed from the city of Granada on Saturday 12 May and went to the port of Palos, where I prepared three ships.

From Palos, Columbus sailed to the Canary Islands to revictual and begin his planned expedition. The Spanish had finally wrested control of the Canaries from the Portuguese in 1481, at last establishing

25. Pedro Berruguete, *St Thomas presiding over the burning of Heretics*:
Ferdinand and Isabella ostentatiously set their sights on an ethnically
cleansed 'new world'

a Spanish possession off the coast of west Africa, vital if Spain were to compete with Portugal for African commodities (including gold). Had Columbus sailed directly from Palos he would probably never have found a following wind, and thus never have reached land westwards. The imperatives of trade, and the practicalities of the pursuit of commodities, shape the beginnings of the world we recognize.

· TWO ·

THE PRICE OF MAGNIFICENCE

DEBT WAS AS MUCH A FEATURE of the day-to-day life of the wealthy in the early-fifteenth century as was the accumulation of belongings. Indeed, the two go hand in hand. To be 'magnificent' was to be someone with the means to acquire all those coveted possessions which expanding trade made available, someone who proclaimed that purchasing power by the public ostentation of his or her apparel and furnishings. To be magnificent was also to be someone with a credit rating high enough to put together the significant amounts of gold and silver which enabled the purchase of expensive goods at will. In order to be lent significant sums, too, there had to be something in it for the lender, who was generally a prominent merchant with extensive trading interests and ready access to large amounts of gold and silver, looking increasingly like what we would call a merchant banker. Where great named individuals were concerned – popes, cardinals and heads of state – the incentive to lend to them was likely to be some lucrative franchise or trade concession offered in lieu of interest on the loan.

The inventory of Cardinal Francesco Gonzaga's worldly goods, from his priceless gems to his exquisite manuscripts, makes breath-taking reading, but its sumptuous splendour is a dazzling illusion. At the time of his death the Cardinal was massively in debt, to the tune of something like 20,000 ducats – in contemporary terms a small fortune. He owed the Medici bank in Florence 3500 ducats, and around 1000 ducats to a Milanese merchant operating out of Rome. The twenty silver trays set with rare cameos, the two jasper trays and the quartz tray were not in fact in any of the Cardinal's residences, but were lodged as pledges against the debts – the

1. Quentin Metsys, *The Debt Collectors*: debt was as much a feature of the
day-to-day life as was the accumulation of belongings

silver trays with Lorenzo de' Medici's uncle, Giovanni Tornabuoni, the Medici bank's agent in Rome, the remaining three with the merchant from Milan. In spite of lengthy negotiations neither pledge was apparently ever redeemed; in other words, the cameos became the property of the cardinal's creditors.

Those with the capacity to borrow (those whose reputation for wealth gave them a suitably high credit rating) could take advantage of it to run up bills with a whole array of creditors, resulting in large amounts owing. It was quite usual for such debts to remain unsettled until an individual's death. When Sixtus IV was elected pope in 1471 he found himself dealing with staggering debts which had been run up by his predecessor Paul II, and appointed a team of Cardinals to settle them by selling off Paul's personal assets, including the embarrassingly fine collection of precious gems and art-objects on which much of the money had been spent.

Among the members of ruling houses and prominent public bodies of Europe, position and reputation were usually enough to ensure that large sums could be borrowed from suitably placed merchants or bankers when needed; the lender might nevertheless require valuable belongings to be deposited as surety against the loan. At the end of the century the Venetian government lodged jewels from the Cathedral of San Marco with the papal bankers in Rome to secure a loan of 20,000 ducats for pressing military expenditure. For the weddings of two of her children in 1495 Queen Isabella of Castile had to retrieve her crown of gold and diamonds from Valencia, where it had been held since 1489 as a pledge against a loan of 35,000 florins, one of three sums advanced as part of a total loan of 60,000 florins raised to support the war against Granada. A ruby and pearl necklace which had been a gift to her at her own wedding served as a pledge for a further 20,000 florins.

The financial crisis in which Ferdinand and Isabella found themselves in the 1480s as a result of their Portuguese and Granadan wars, and the city of Venice's escalating debts caused by conflict with neighbouring Italian states, were characteristic situations at the end of the fifteenth century. Because of the escalating costs of armaments and weaponry, military adventures figure alongside a taste for expensive imported goods as the most costly items of expenditure for fifteenth-century princes. There was in any case a kind of symmetry in all of this: both military aggression and ostentatious expenditure on luxury goods could serve as part of a strategy of establishing 'worth' in the political arena.

Political and social success were increasingly inseparable from the raising of sums of money so huge as to be inconceivable without elaborate credit facilities. In 1491 the Augsburg merchant Jakob Fugger lent the future Emperor Maximilian (currently Duke of Tyrol) more than 200,000 florins to finance his wars consolidating the Habsburg territories. In return Maximilian gave Fugger exclusive rights to the profitable Tyrolean copper and silver mines. Large injections of Fugger capital into the mines to install all the most up-to-the-minute mining technology significantly increased productivity. When Maximilian became emperor in 1493 his financial needs increased, and necessitated his renegotiating his bank-loan arrangements with Fugger; this time Jakob Fugger got the additional rights to the Habsburg mines in Hungary. During the ten years from 1495 to 1504 about 100,000 tons of copper from the Hungarian mines were sold on the open market, almost three-quarters of the proceeds going to the Fugger account. Meanwhile the silver was separated off from the copper using a recently developed smelting process, once again assisted by the German merchant's investment capital. Under the agreement with Maximilian, Jakob Fugger paid 8 Rhine florins in advance for every 280 grams of refined silver to be extracted: of this 5 florins went to the operator of the mine and 3 florins to the Habsburg coffers as a tax or duty. Fugger was then entitled to sell on the silver at any of the locations where he had an agent and a trading branch. If he resold the silver for 9 florins, this represented a return of 12.5 per cent on the money advanced, against the minor risk that the price of silver might drop – an unlikely prospect when silver was in high demand both for fine

2. Mining for metals in
Renaissance Hungary

ornament and as the second negotiable currency after gold, though
it was always in short supply. Fugger's almost total monopoly
of the European silver mines meant in any case that he had a
considerable measure of control over its market value.

Jakob Fugger's shrewd financial arrangements with a prominent
figure destined to become one of the most powerful men in Europe
ensured him the role of Habsburg 'banker'. Yet Fugger's decision-
making was always based on the financial implications for the firm,
and not on the promotion of considered policies or large-scale plans
concerning the balance of European political interests. In 1493 the
Fugger company (or 'bank') paid the costs of the Habsburg embassy
to Senlis, where Maximilian renegotiated control of Artois, and
took advantage of the occasion to consolidate their own dominant
business position in northern Europe by opening an import–export
supply depot at Antwerp. During the period of expansion of
Portuguese trade with Africa via the Guinea coast, the Fuggers were

the chief arms suppliers, contributing largely to the possibilities for aggressive confrontation on the African continent.

Huge loan agreements like those arranged by the Fuggers have an air of grave seriousness about them, because they could result in significant alterations in the power balance between princely houses (depending on who could raise the biggest loan), and because they clearly establish particular merchant-banking families as the power-brokers of Europe. But here too princely extravagance provides the banker with ample opportunity to render indispensable financial service in return for commercial advantages. Like all his European counterparts Emperor Maximilian had expensive tastes in leisure pursuits, whose costs were met out of the funds raised by deals like the granting of the Fuggers' mining option. These included a passion for hunting, for which activity he supported a kennel of 2000 hounds.

The habit of indebtedness (whether in the interests of luxury or of conquest) developed naturally alongside an elaborate collection of arrangements made necessary by the vigour of fifteenth-century international trade and commerce. The rise of paper transactions for financial expenditure of all kinds, in other words, encouraged the concept of 'notional' expenditure, on which heavy borrowing depends.

Currency exchange is an area in which it is clear that paper accounting simplifies an otherwise onerous task of physically trans-porting different currency and coin from one geographical location to another. An inhabitant of any European town could make do with the local coin to buy his bread or cloth; a merchant dealing with a number of outside suppliers, however, needed to render payment in the currency of the locality of the producer. International tax collection likewise resulted in the accumulation of cash in more than one currency. This problem arose early in relation to the taxes due to the Pope from the Christian faithful right across Europe. In 1362 the keeper of accounts for the papal treasury reported that the sums collected included 15,653 florins and 299 écus:

Of the florins 4222 are florins 'of the Chamber', 3869 florins 'of the Sentence', 7438 heavy florins, 16 Venetian ducats, 5 Genoese florins, 31 Aragon florins, 7 French florins, 59 light-weight florins, 6 Cambrai florins.

Of the écus 271 are ancient écus of good weight, 1 English écu, one Bavarian écu, 2 ancient écus, not of true weight, 17 counterfeit ancient écus, 8 Philipp écus.

A century later, between 1476 and 1480 sales of a papal indulgence in the Burgundian states netted around 18,000 gold pieces in seventy different currencies from the fifty-five churches, from Groningen to Mâcon, in which it had been sold.

For travellers the proliferation of European currencies added to the hazards of the journey, and provided easy opportunities for extortionate demands and short-changing. During Albrecht Dürer's year-long journey around the Low Countries, from Bruges to Cologne and northwards to Nijmegen, he had to deal with the following currencies:

pfennigs (silver);
heller;
stuivers (stüber);
weisspfennigs (2 heller 20 weisspfennigs = 24 stuivers = 2.53 g.
    gold);
blanke (2 stuivers);
pfund (30 pfennigs);
orrt (¼ gulden);
Rhenish gulden (8 pfund 12 pfennigs);
'schlechter' gulden (12 stuivers);
Hornish gulden (issued by the Count of Horn);
Portuguese gulden;
Philipps gulden (Netherlandish: 25 stuivers);
crona (Sonenkrone: gold pieces worth c. 1 florin 9 stuivers);
anglot (English coins: 2 florins 2 stuivers);

rose nobles;

Flemish nobles;

Hungarian ducats;

gold Carolus gulden (1.71 g. gold = 20 stuivers).

The difficulty and confusion this caused the traveller are brought into focus if we set this diversity of currency against Dürer's own account of his eve-of-departure preparations as he set off for Nuremberg after a month's stay in Antwerp in July 1521:

> Paid the doctor 6 stuivers, again I gave the Steward of the Augustinian convent at Antwerp a Life of Our Lady and 4 stuivers to his servant. I gave Master Jacob an Engraved Passion and a Woodcut Passion and 5 other pieces, and gave 4 stuivers to his servant. I changed 4 florins for expenses. I bought 14 fishskins for 2 Philipps florins. I have made portraits in black chalk of Aert Braun and his wife. I gave the goldsmith who appraised the three rings for me 1 gulden worth of art. Of the three rings which I took in exchange for prints, the two smaller are valued at 15 crona, but the sapphire is worth 25 crona – that makes 54 gulden 8 stuivers. And among other things that the above Frenchman [Jan van de Perre] took are 36 large books: that makes 9 gulden. I bought a screw-knife for 2 stuiver. Item: the man with the rings has cheated me by half – I do not understand it.
>
> I bought a red beret for my god-child for 18 stuiver. Item: I lost 12 stuiver at card play. Drank 2 stuivers. Item: I bought 3 fine little rubies for 11 gulden and 12 stuivers. I changed 1 gulden for expenses. I have eaten one more time with the Augustinians. I paid 5 stuivers for brushes made of wild guinea-pig bristles. I bought 6 more brushes for 3 stuivers.
>
> Item: I made the great Anthony Haunolt's [the new Fugger agent in Antwerp] portrait on a royal sheet of paper carefully with black chalk. I made careful portraits of Aert Braun and his

wife with black chalk on two royal sheets of paper, and I drew him once more with the silverpoint. He gave me an angelot.

Hardly surprisingly (since the list of purchases and payments continues for a further page), Dürer was obliged to borrow cash in order to settle his transactions: 'Item: Alexander Imhoff loaned me 100 gold gulden on 1 July, 1521. I gave him my sealed bond for it to repay the money with thanks on delivery of the bond to me at Nuremberg.' He settled a further outstanding debt before leaving Antwerp: 'I have reckoned up with Jobst, and I owe him 31 more gulden. I have paid it to him, deducting the two portraits painted in oils, for which he paid 5 Netherlandish pounds of borax. . . . And this settlement with Jobst is made on 29 June 1521.'

Dürer's fame meant that he could sometimes pay with his own woodcut prints and with chalk drawings. But his acceptance of a quantity of a material he needed for his work (here borax) in part payment for the portraits he executed is quite typical. Contracts between skilled workmen (including artists) and patrons might be made in a combination of specified currencies (Venetian ducats, or Genoese ducats, or florins, or écus) and payments in kind. Luca Signorelli's contract for frescos in Orvieto Cathedral stipulated a sum of money, gold leaf and azure pigment, lodgings and a bed (after negotiations the offer was raised to include two beds). During the period in which Benozzo Gozzoli was painting the Medici frescos, the Medici bank made some of the rental payments on his house. In other words, calculating what was owed, and settling the account, was often an elaborate business.

Where payment had to be rendered in cash rather than in reci-procated services, it was convenient, and increasingly regarded as preferable, for payment to be tendered as a paper bill, and the rate of exchange calculated by the receiving merchant, to be credited as the appropriate sum in his local currency. When such transactions took place on a regular basis this soon led to notional payment, whereby the receipt was held as a paper credit, to be discharged at such later date when the recipient rendered a service in his turn. As soon as one individual (or one family, or partnership) is receiving substantial sums from a range of clients, it becomes a relatively simple matter for him to act as a central guarantor for transactions conducted among them. He holds their money on 'deposit', they incur financial obligations to one another on paper, and go to him to turn the outcome into cash. In the absence of formal banking in the period, these paper transactions are conducted by individual 'bankers', but the procedures are remarkably close to those of twentieth-century international banking.

Technically, Church law prohibited interest payments on any loan. In practice, however, there was a multitude of arrangements available which allowed interest to be collected. The money lent against a pledge was always less than the 'value' of the object pawned – the value at which the individual would be obliged to retrieve it. The goldsmith Oderigo di Credi pledged a jacket in a public 'presto' or pawnbrokers in Florence in 1412 for a loan of 20 lire. Six months later he retrieved his jacket for 24 lire 13 soldi, which corresponds to an annual rate of interest of 45 per cent. Cardinal Gonzaga's twenty trays of cameos had been used to raise a loan of 3500 ducats with the Medici bank. When his family tried to retrieve them in 1486, however, the asking price was 4100 ducats (effectively 600 ducats interest). And since Lorenzo de' Medici himself was interested in acquiring the cameos the Gonzagas were asked to find something more like 5000 ducats to secure their return.

In the course of the fifteenth century the commercial world developed an elaborate collection of financial arrangements, stimulated by the growth in the exchange of goods and services. Innovations like bills of exchange clarified the merchant's understanding of the financial consequences of all aspects of buying and selling, and the impact on profits of levies, customs duties, bad debts and interest payments. At the most fundamental level such arrangements made possible the purchase of merchandise which was either intrinsically of very high value (like gems) or which had to be purchased in bulk (like alum or salt) without direct recourse to cash, and allowed the calculation of prices in advance, taking into account costs and overheads.

The most striking innovations in the regulation of affairs are in methods for transacting of money and keeping of accounts. Double-entry bookkeeping was in use in Italy by 1400: the 1395 ledgers for the bank of Averardo di Francesco di Bicci which survive in the Florence archives are kept according to all the rules of double-entry. Among the procedures which come into regular use are: arrangements for making substantial sums available in credit, in order to effect the initial outlay at the appropriate moment when the price is competitive; negotiable notes or bills for holding the receipts from the sale of goods in a foreign port, and for transacting them in local currency as expenditure to buy further goods on which profit can be made; forms of underwriting at a premium in case the cargo is lost, destroyed or taken by force.

Putting up the capital to smaller businesses for ventures with the prospect of yielding novel or rare marketable goods allowed already prosperous merchants to increase their wealth. They either made the necessary funds available in the form of a contracted loan, or entered into a commercial partnership with the active trading party and put up the money as investment capital. 'Banking' in this period is thus inseparable from mercantile activities themselves – merchant bankers are entrepreneurial businessmen with surplus cash available for investment or loan.

When we look at the glamour of the goods crowded together in the merchant's shop, what we are seeing is the company showrooms of enterprises whose money-making activities actually extend far beyond the simple buying and selling of desirable commodities. Around 1400 the tycoon merchant Francesco di Marco Datini's sales outlet in Paris was offering silks and velvets from Lucca, silk muslin and cottons from Perugia, embroidered goods and gems from assorted Eastern locations, weapons from Toledo, leather goods from Córdoba, and paintings from Siena and Florence. In the 1460s in Venice Andrea Barbarigo was offering woollen cloth from Florence, spices from India, cotton from Syria, gold thread from the Levant, leatherwork from Italy, and iron and tin from England, as well as slaves from La Tana. In fact, however, Barbarigo had only 10 per cent of his capital tied up in the shop – the rest was used for loans and investments through the Venetian state finance system; and Datini had investments in properties and manufacturing industries in nine separate locations across Europe.

Credit became the mainstay of the world of consumer goods during the fifteenth century. The families of merchants turned bankers who both financed the manufacturing and import–export enterprises and offered the loans were the new aristocracy in a Europe whom trade had made receptive to tastes from every known corner of the globe. Even before they became princes themselves, merchant bankers were prince-makers. Twenty-five years after Jakob Fugger had ensured the success of Maximilian's bid for the imperial throne of the Habsburgs, a similarly massive loan to Maximilian's grandson enabled him also to spend the necessary sums in bribes and backhanders to become the Emperor Charles V, with yet more extensive dominions than his grandfather, and yet more power to assist the Fuggers in their business enterprises. Within another generation members of Jakob Fugger's own family were ennobled. The axis on which the transformation taking place in the culture turned was the 'worth' of the prominent families which drove its new economy – the value in hard-cash terms which they could realize in cases of political or social necessity.

It was the very proliferation of credit arrangements offered as part of their speculative involvement with international trade by the emerging banking companies like the Medicis in Florence and the Fuggers in Augsburg which also made it possible for would-be purchasers of luxury goods to borrow the large sums of money required for their expensive collecting habits. The same kinds of arrangement allowed heads of state without the requisite funds in their coffers to raise the cost of military expeditions. The growing affluence of the new dynastic banking families fed the illusion of

3. Titian, *Equestrian Portrait of Charles V*

magnificence of the princely houses. The immense loans made to them enabled them to display a kind of splendour unmatched in the West (and matching that of the increasingly territorially powerful East). It also allowed them to stockpile expensive modern military equipment so as to make challenges to their authority virtually unthinkable. Behind the great Renaissance rulers, patrons of art, manufacture and learning, stand the new credit mechanisms and the long-term loans which sustained their magnificence.

Since those who lent and those who borrowed needed reliable information on the likely outcome of any financial negotiations in hand, the emerging world of credit depended heavily on improved communications. When considering whether to make a loan, a prudent financier would inform himself of the current prices of marketable commodities at the destination of the voyage he was backing. Similarly, reliable information on the solvency or otherwise of an individual might prove invaluable.

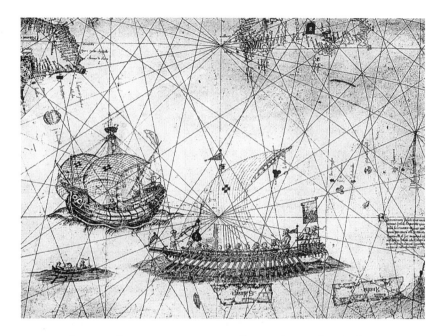

4. Gratiosus Benincasa, Portuguese galleys and caravelles on their way to
explore the Antilles

Written records of a wide variety of kinds form the body of
'intelligence' or knowledge-gathering which supported commercial
endeavours. Account books and records of tax receipts are still an
invaluable source today of comparative information about wealth
and expenditure in the fifteenth century. The Florentine records for
the *catasto* or property tax for the year 1457, for instance, show
that the Medici family were the highest taxpayers in the city, paying
four times as much tax as the next two wealthiest families, the Benci
and the Rucellai.

The new trade which was established as a result of ventures like
the Portuguese exploration of the coast of Africa in the second half
of the fifteenth century meant that maps, besides being sought after
because of their intrinsic interest and beauty, were a vital source of
information on business openings and opportunities for investment.

At the time of Cabral's successful voyage round the Cape of Good Hope to India, Italian interests tried to get hold of copies of new Portuguese maps, showing the latest discoveries. In August 1501 (when news of Cabral's triumph was freshly out), Angelo Trevisan di Bernadino wrote to Domenico Malpiero in Venice, informing him of the progress being made by the Venetian Ambassador to Spain, Domenico Pisani, in using his diplomatic influence to get copies of maps in Lisbon:

> We are daily expecting our doctor from Lisbon, who left our magnificent ambassador Pisani there: who at my request has written a short account of Cabral's voyage from Calicut, of which I will make a copy for Your Magnificence. It is impossible to procure a map of that voyage because the king has placed a death penalty on anyone who gives it out.

Writing three months later, however, Trevisan's 'intelligence' concerning the Cabral route had significantly improved:

> If we return to Venice alive, Your Magnificence will see maps both as far as Calicut and beyond there, less than twice the distance from here to Flanders. I promise you that everything has come in order; but this Your Magnificence may not care to divulge. One thing is certain, that you will learn upon our arrival as many particulars as though you had been at Calicut and farther.

If this makes it sound as though the manner in which Trevisan had come by the maps was not entirely reputable, that is highly likely. In 1502 an Italian secret agent named Alberto Cantino was sent to Lisbon by Ercole d'Este, masquerading as a dealer in purebred horses. For a bribe of 12 ducats he acquired from a Portuguese cartographer the so-called 'Cantino planisphere', showing all the most recent Portuguese discoveries. The stolen map was as up to date as it could possibly have been: the letter from Cantino

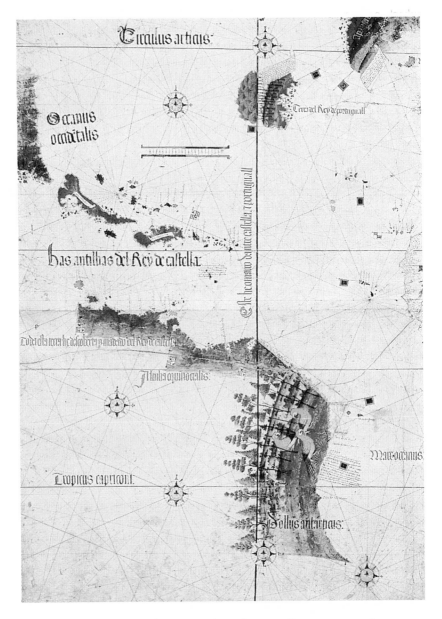

5. A detail, showing North America, from the secret Portuguese map known as the Cantino Planisphere.

which accompanied the map when it was smuggled out was dated November 1502, yet the map shows the position of Ascension Island, news of whose discovery had reached Lisbon only on 13 September.

Short of outright theft, surreptitious copying of documents and maps could be accomplished by using trusted servants sent on 'business'. In 1506 the great patron of learning and the arts, Isabella d'Este, complained in a letter to her husband Francesco, Marquis of Mantua, that the painter she had sent to Venice had been refused permission by Doge Loredan to copy a map ('the Italy', by Antonio di Leonardi), on the ground that 'Your Excellency speaks words in private which are harmful to the Venetian government.' Possibly it was thought that the Marquis might make unfriendly use of information contained in the map; in any case the information concerning his attitude towards the Venetians had presumably been obtained by espionage. In Venice itself, three noblemen made a hole in the roof of the Doge's Palace in order to eavesdrop on the most recent information brought from Istanbul.

In November 1407 the Florentine notary Ser Lapo Mazzei sent this confidential note to Luca del Sera concerning the desirability of advancing money to a client: 'Regarding Cristofano: he is in financial difficulties. According to rumours and certain opinions he is in debt in Florence and elsewhere. I do not think that his eight hundred florins are worth as much as a thousand, as he has no credit.' To the appropriate recipient, such inside information was invaluable, as was intelligence on matters ranging from the layout of a castle's fortifications to the likelihood of a marriage between dynastic houses (when costly fabrics would be at a premium). Reliable informants were vital: in 1458 the merchants of the Hanseatic League in Riga notified their colleagues in Lübeck that Russian buyers preferred light English cloth to heavy Flemish, and were more interested in low prices than in quality. The sooner a merchant could learn how much pepper had been loaded on to a convoy of ships in Alexandria, the earlier he could strike profitable deals with potential purchasers of the cargo in Venice.

Accurate information was also needed to support the new long-distance financial machinery. The negotiating of bills of exchange (Renaissance credit notes), for instance, depended upon the parties being confident that the bills were bona fide documents and not counterfeit. The Medicis authorized only the senior managers in the branches of their bank to write out bills of exchange. A specimen of their handwriting was sent to correspondents, and they were instructed not to honour bills in any other hand. So in 1455 the Rome branch was notified that it was to honour only bills made out in the hand of Giovanni Benci, Francesco Inghirami or Tommaso Lapi, the general manager, manager and assistant manager of the Tavola in Florence. Florence, meanwhile, was to pay only on bills drawn on the Roman branch which were made out in the hand of Robert Martelli, Leonardo Vernacci or Giovanni Tornabuoni.

Smaller operations had to rely on personal contacts. The traditional prominence of Jewish families as merchants and as bankers derived in part from the scattered nature of their communities: as a diaspora they had family members, or at least contacts with some connection or bond of attachment, throughout Europe and the Orient. A Venetian merchant who needed to collect money on a bill of exchange in Tripoli made it out as follows:

> At the end of October I made a sale and consigned 36 pieces of kersey to a Jew named Prospero Romano, whose home is in Damascus, and the price of the said goods was 9 Venetian ducats, and having given him two months (that is, until the end of December) to pay the remainder, which amounts to 170 Venetian ducats. And since the aforesaid Jew lives in Damascus, and I have no plans for the time being to go there, he has given me as guarantor and principal payer Rabbi Samuel Alegre, who resides in Tripoli and has a shop almost opposite Ca' Novo; and he has given me a written record of his debt in the hand of his notary, signed by several witnesses and also by the said Prospero. And knowing no one who would do me such a service more readily than you, I have

decided to take advantage of this arrangement and to beg you to receive the money, for I would do as much for you if you thought me fit to serve you. Hence I beg you, when you have reached Tripoli, to find the above-named Samuel Alegre at once, telling him to make ready to pay the bill when it falls due, and saying you will return him his note in exchange.

Under pressure of the desire to be properly informed, the volume of letters written and sent increased out of all proportion to the amount of business actually being transacted. Between 1364 and 1410 Datini exchanged 125,549 letters with his factors or agents stationed in Barcelona, Valencia, Avignon, Genoa and Pisa. At the height of his business activities he was exchanging around 10,000 letters a year with those in charge of his outlets in other cities. It is hardly surprising that Datini's agent in Avignon complained that 'we spend half our time reading letters or answering them'. The impact of this kind of explosion of written material on literacy and its corresponding influence in producing a potential readership for the new marketable commodity, the mass-produced, printed book, should not be underestimated.

However prolific the correspondence, and however widespread the net of factors, agents, informants and messengers trawling for up-to-the-minute information, fifteenth-century businesses were often obliged to make decisions based on inadequate knowledge. The sheer difficulty and danger of travel, the strong likelihood of letters going astray, cargoes being lost, goods being stolen in transit, impeded the smooth flow of information even within the best-run organizations. One solution was diversification: individuals spread their investments over a variety of operations and a range of commodities. A potent fantasy, however, was that of supernatural control: to be able to gain knowledge at a distance before your competitors might mean the difference between the success or failure of a venture. Jakob Fugger is said to have retained a personal fortune-teller to predict outcomes of deals currently in process.

The Medici family in Florence are the most lastingly famous of the merchant dynasties who made their fortunes and their reputations through banking and commerce. By 1441 the Medici bank had branches in operation in Rome, Venice, Ancona, Bruges and Geneva, in addition to the parent company in Florence (which included, as well as its other commercial activities, partnership in a company manufacturing silk and two manufacturing wool). In 1442 they opened a branch in Pisa, and in 1446 branches in London and in Avignon (which controlled their financial activities in Marseille, Montpellier and Toulouse). Finally, in 1452 they began operating in Milan, and in 1464 transferred their Geneva branch to Lyon. In the 1450s they were active everywhere in Europe where significant business was transacted; we come across their agents' financial dealings in Lübeck, Barcelona, Antwerp and Bergen-op-Zoom.

Banking, lending and international money-changing were not in themselves strikingly lucrative. Of the company profits in 1451, 25 per cent came from the three cloth-manufacturing companies (as opposed to finance), and 17 per cent from business conducted in Florence itself, where the bank's interests were most diversified. But the Medicis' business activities meant that they had ready access to cash, and this made them indispensable to those whose public offices involved them in large-scale expenditure. When Pope Eugenius IV was planning the 1438 Council of Churches it was Cosimo de' Medici who proposed Florence as the venue, on the ground that it was the only city with the necessary funds available to subsidize the occasion. Although the early sessions at Ferrara were financed by the Papal Chamber, it was Medici loans which provided the cash, and when the Council moved to Florence the Florentine Commune (heavily subsidised by the Medici) paid for the Byzantine delegation's accommodation and living expenses; the Medici bank also underwrote the whole cost of the return journey to Constantinople. The dependence on Medici financial support for the success of the entire expensive operation is summed up in a begging letter sent to Cosimo de' Medici by Cardinal Giuliano Cesarini, who was in charge

6. Benozzo Gozzoli, detail from the *Procession of the Magi*, showing members
of the Medici family

of arrangements to transfer the Council from Ferrara to Florence.
He had run out of money *en route* at Faenza and urgently needed
200 horses and mules to complete the journey: 'For the honour of
our Latin Church which is in question, and so that we can keep our
promises firmly made to the Byzantines, I beseech you to take all
possible steps to send the horses and mules.' Without Medici backing
the Council of Florence would probably have collapsed. No wonder
Gozzoli's fresco in the Palazzo Medici portrays the Medici family
in the midst of the popes, patriarchs and heads of state, in imperial
splendour.

Financial favours of this crucial kind, performed for those with power and influence, put the Medicis within reach of the real high-return investment opportunities. The staggering wealth accumulated by the Medici family, and the meteoric rise to international prestige and power of contemporary finance-house successes like the Fuggers, came from individual pieces of brilliant financial wheeler-dealing conducted as a result of inside information, or in exchange for further financial favours to princes, at precisely the right market moment. In the case of the Medicis, that opportunity came with the discovery of alum at Tolfa.

In the production process for dyeing cloth, alum is the chemical mordant which makes dye colours bite into the fabric, bonding them so as to intensify the hues and make the fabric colour-fast. The major source of alum for the European cloth industry was Phocaea in Anatolia, on the edge of the Ottoman Empire. In the early fifteenth century Genoa had possession of Phocaea and held a

7. Dyeing cloth with alum,
from Joost Amman's *Book
of Trades*

114

virtual monopoly on the importing of alum into Europe, loading it on to its bulk-carrying ships on the neighbouring island of Chios, which was also a Genoese territory. Just as Venice's wealth depended upon a virtual monopoly of sea salt, the indispensable bulk product for food preservation, Genoa's mercantile affluence derived from her control over the commodity equally indispensable for cloth production. In the mid-fifteenth century, as the Ottoman Empire under Mehmed II conquered increasing areas of Anatolia, and threatened the offshore islands where the Genoese and Venetians took on their cargoes, both groups of merchants were prepared to pay substantial sums to the Turks in order to cement trade agreements which allowed them to continue their lucrative importing of alum and salt.

Salt and alum were vital commodities in themselves, with a predictable and widespread demand which guaranteed the importer his profit (and the rulers who held the tax monopoly on them their steady income). They were also essential as inexpensive bulk cargoes which could ballast the large-bottomed Italian trading ships returning from the eastern Mediterranean. Silks, gems and spices were valuable but light; the ships whose holds had been full of grain or bales of woollen cloth on the outward journey replaced these with salt and alum to complete their profit-making traffic from the Levant to Italian ports.

In 1460 Giovanni da Castro, a godson of Pope Pius II, returned to Italy from the Levant, where he had run up substantial debts in trade. Protected from his creditors by his godfather, he turned his attention to scientific study, above all geology and the detection of minerals. He noticed physical similarities between the landscape round Phocaea and that at Tolfa in the papal territories. In his memoirs, Pius II himself describes what happened:

> While Giovanni was walking through the forested mountains he came on a strange kind of herb. He was surprised, and noted that similar herbs grew on the mountains of Asia which enrich

the Turkish treasury with alum. He also observed white stones which appeared to have mineral in them. He bit one of them and found them salt. He smelted them, experimented, produced alum.

Then he went to the Pope and said, 'Today I bring you victory over the Turk. Every year they wring from the Christians more than 300,000 ducats for the alum with which we dye wool various colours. For alum is not found in Italy except a very small quantity in the island of Ischia near Puteoli, and this supply was depleted by the Romans in ancient times and is almost exhausted. But I have found seven mountains so rich in this material that they could supply seven worlds. If you will give orders to engage workmen, build furnaces, and smelt the ore, you will provide all Europe with alum and the Turk will lose all his profits. Instead they will accrue to you and he will suffer a double loss. You have a harbour nearby in Civita Vecchia where ships may be loaded to sail to the east. Now you may equip a war against the Turks. This mine will supply you with the sinews of war, i.e. money, and take them from the Turks'.

The events that followed the speculative discovery of a rich Italian source of alum typify the emerging commercial attitudes of this crucial period in Europe's development. Pius II (more scholar than entrepreneur) immediately claimed the Tolfa alum deposits as Church property. Here was alum providentially discovered on the Italian mainland just as it seemed inevitable that Islam, in the form of the Ottomans, would have permanent control over this vital commodity. God had provided the raw materials, and his minister on earth would mine and distribute them.

A significant level of investment was needed, however, in order to extract, process and sell the alum. Unlike his predecessor Pius, Paul II, who became pope in 1464, came from a business background himself and quickly recognized that the Tolfa alum deposits were a potential money-spinner for the papal coffers. He turned to the

Medici bank, as the business organization most obviously qualified to pursue the matter speculatively. In 1465 the Medici signed a contract with the papacy, which thereby handed over to the bank the entire operation of investment in the mines and the distribution and sale of the alum. They would pay to the papacy 2 florins 'tax' on every fifty kilos of alum extracted, retaining all additional profit for themselves. Within a remarkably short space of time the Tolfa mines were supplying alum as far afield as London and Bruges and producing extraordinary profits for both parties to the original deal.

Matters were helped, once again, by using the Pope's political muscle to enhance the profitability of Tolfa alum on the market. The most dangerous competition in the alum market came from the Ischia mines, controlled by Ferdinand I, King of Naples. In 1470 the Rome branch of the Medici bank was able to exploit the friendly relationship between Ferdinand and Paul II to negotiate an agreement with Angelo Perotto, manager of the Ischia mines, under which the two parties divided the alum market between them, and agreed to sell only at a price agreed by the cartel. Papal interests were well served by the agreement, but so also was Medici business.

As a major centre for fine cloth manufacture Venice was Italy's biggest customer for alum, and throughout the latter half of the fifteenth century a succession of popes tried without success to force the Venetians to abandon their continuing trade in alum with Phocaea and the Ottomans, and to turn instead to the local Italian source. At the end of the century, however, when the Venetians were financially embarrassed, they applied to the current banker in charge of papal interests at Tolfa, Agostino Chigi, for a large cash loan. Purchase of papal alum at a prearranged price was part of the ensuing agreement, and Venice was forced to comply. There is a final irony here in the fact that by this time the fortunes of the Medici were on the wane. When Piero de' Medici in his turn applied to Agostino Chigi for a loan in 1496 he gave as security 'twenty silver trays . . . each engraved with the arms of Cardinal Francesco Gonzaga of Mantua' – the twenty trays of cameos which the Medici bank had acquired in settlement of Francesco Gonzaga's debts twenty years earlier.

The fortune made by the Medici family in Florence in the mid-fifteenth century is almost unimaginable. It brought with it elevation to the new aristocracy, and power and prestige of legendary magnitude. In two generations the Medici family rose in Florence from the position of prominent local businessmen to that of ruling princes and, as their social standing grew, so did the family's investment in representing that status as securely established and of long standing. When the Byzantine Emperor John VIII and the Patriarch of the Byzantine Church had come to Florence in 1438 the Medicis were simply a prominent and powerful business family in the Florentine community, Cosimo de' Medici its foremost citizen. By the time Piero de' Medici commissioned Benozzo Gozzoli's celebratory fresco alluding to that occasion, his own son Lorenzo – soon to become Lorenzo the Magnificent, greatest of all the Medici leaders of Florence – takes pride of place, as if even then the Medicis were a ruling dynasty. Giovanni Tornabuoni, who as manager with Lorenzo of the Rome branch of the Medici bank had negotiated the fundamentally important deal with the Pope to administer the Tolfa alum mines, also subsequently became an important patron of the fine arts. For both men business success meant the possibility of establishing a dynasty which would continue to dominate Florentine affairs: both men commissioned works of art in which their families are represented in splendour for posterity, including major pieces from the most prominent and sought-after artists of their day – Ghirlandaio and Botticelli.

Communities also used the production of fine artworks to advertise their success and prosperity. In 1482 the town of Ascoli Piceno was given special religious exemptions by Pope Sixtus IV. The news was received on 25 March and it was immediately agreed that the event should be commemorated with an annual procession. In addition, two major paintings were commissioned (one for the municipal chapel from Pietro Alamanno (1484), the other for the

8. Duccio, *Maestà: Virgin Taking Leave of the Disciples,* commissioned by the commune of Siena

Church of the Annunciation from Crivelli (1486)), each bearing the inscription 'Libertas ecclesiastica' – the opening words of the papal document they had received. Duccio's *Maestà* was commissioned by the commune of Siena, and artisan guilds in Venice commissioned works from Gentile Bellini and Carpaccio.

In the last quarter of the fifteenth century, when Venice ceased to dominate Mediterranean trade, the Senate poured huge quantities of its wealth into ostentatious expenditure on the physical fabric of the city, as if to demonstrate by its architectural grandeur that it remained in a strong position in the internal power politics of Europe. In the same period Venetian artists were commissioned to execute civic paintings which record the splendour of the ceremonial occasions on which the members of Venice's leading houses processed across the Piazza San Marco – works whose propaganda impact matches that of the painter's artistic skill.

Ceremonial sumptuousness could also be used to show pride in the very sources of a ruling elite's affluence. Around 1500 Doge Leonardo Loredan's introduction of ornately designed and richly

9. Gentile Bellini, *Procession in the Piazza San Marco*: members of Venice's leading families process across the piazza

threaded damask and velvet as fabrics for the Doge's formal costume was consciously part of the programme advertising Venice's silk industry. Such fabrics had long been produced by the Ottomans, and had become much sought-after in Europe when imported by Venetian merchants. In the latter half of the fifteenth century Venice had developed a luxury silk-weaving industry of her own (using silk imported from the orient), and her own brocades, damasks and velvets were coveted all over Europe. The portraits in which the exotic fabric of Doge Loredan's robe and bonnet are rendered by the painter in the minutest and most lovingly realistic detail thus both amaze the onlooker with their visual magnificence and serve as reminders of Venice's wealth and prestige. In 1467 Pope Paul II (Francesco Gonzaga's fellow antiquarian collector, and a man with expensive tastes) adopted the scarlet produced by the use of imported kermes or galls as the official colour for cardinals' robes. The visible expense of the cloth worn by the cardinals – the Pope's represen-tatives across Europe – created an effect of power and opulence; it also reminded Christendom of the additional might the Pope had

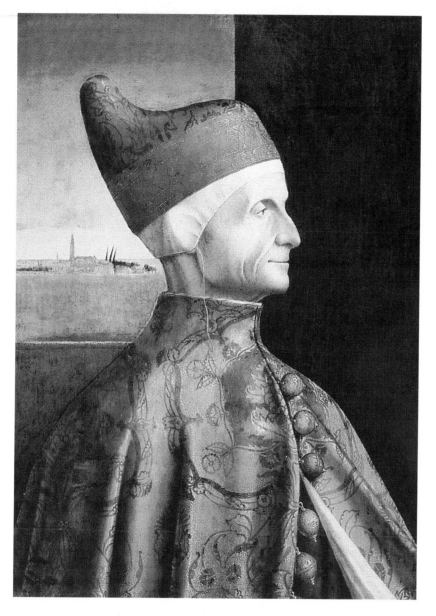

10. Vittore Carpaccio, *Doge Leonardo Loredan* in lovingly
rendered damask

gained by astute investment in alum (the key agent in all cloth-dyeing).

Precious garments and objects of great beauty were the marks of the splendour of a particular noble line or royal office, but they also doubled as surety on vast loans. In the early 1400s Innocent VII gave his 'mitre of great price' as pledge to Giovanni di Bicci de' Medici (Lorenzo's great-grandfather), against a huge loan to try to overturn the claim to the papal throne of his rival Benedict XIII. By the time this bejewelled papal tiara was redeemed in 1409 by Innocent's successor, Gregory XII, its retrieval cost 12,000 florins (which Gregory raised by borrowing elsewhere). The appreciation of that papal tiara's magnificently crafted beauty became a complicated matter as it was passed around and handled lovingly by the Pope's creditors. Aesthetic pleasure was closely associated with a more raw, commercial sense of the worth of the object – its price on the open market.

Men who had made their fortunes from the traffic in precious and exotic objects, exquisite silks and rare gems announced their success to the world by ostentatiously surrounding themselves with just such belongings acquired for themselves. And, once fine workmanship is appreciated in the settings of precious stones or the goldsmith's workmanship, a taste for fine art-objects follows easily from a taste for fine belongings. A visitor to the home of Jacques Duché in Paris early in the fifteenth century described with awe the opulence of his mansion:

> The doorway is carved with marvellous art and there are peacocks and other exotic birds in the courtyard.
>
> The first room you come to is decorated with many paintings and instructive inscriptions, attached to and hanging from the walls. . . . There is a study where the walls are covered in precious stones and spices which give out a delicious odour. There is a room where there are furs of all kinds. There are many further rooms richly furnished with beds and tables ingeniously

carved, and adorned with rich cloths and carpets with gold thread.
. . . And above the pinnacles of the mansion are beautiful gilded
pictures.

Duché also had complete rooms full of different musical instruments,
weaponry (ornamental crossbows, pennants, suits of armour), and a
dining room with a panoramic view, situated so high in the building that the food had to be hauled up from the kitchen on pulleys.

From the mid-fifteenth century important artists are to be found
wherever a major trading centre is located, or wherever an expensive commodity is being produced and exported (tapestry in Tournai,
silk fabric in Lucca) and there are therefore wealthy entrepreneurs
to purchase. The art we value and admire is inextricably bound up
with the financial prosperity through trade of particular regions,
and the business successes of particular individuals and groups of
individuals. In the 1420s the painter Robert Campin was working
in Tournai, to where he was followed by Roger van der Weyden,
who became his apprentice. The most distinguished Flemish painter
of the fifteenth century, Jan van Eyck, produced his major works
from a studio in Bruges (where he was in the entourage of the Duke
of Burgundy, Philip the Good), and he in his turn was followed by
Petrus Christus in the 1440s.

The loving care with which material possessions are represented
in the works of artists like van Eyck and Petrus Christus anticipates
the appreciation these were expected to elicit from the patron whose
expert eye could recognize the texture and design of an expensive
damask, the lustre and intensity of a valuable gem. When the prominent merchant from Lucca, Giovanni Arnolfini, married Giovanna
Cenami, the daughter of another successful merchant in the
same community, the alliance represented a highly advantageous
fusion of powerful financial interests, an occasion of note in the
business community. Jan van Eyck's painting of the happy couple
used a precise realism to record the assured confidence of a family
partnership with a solidly profitable future ahead of them.

Admiration – the aesthetic sense of wonder with which the beholder gazes upon the work of art – becomes here a mental response
in which sensual delight is strenuously linked with an appreciation of the market value of the goods and the urge to acquire. In
the mid-fifteenth century the social rise of the merchant brought
with it an aesthetic of expenditure – a visual mode which gave
delight through the intrinsic desirability of endlessly varied and
exquisitely manufactured belongings, available for purchase. The
eye of the onlooker responded with pleasurable longing to the
fantasy of possession, which was independent of any real possibility
of owning such wonders themselves. The art of Flanders like the
art of Venice celebrated the triumph of worldly goods. Nor was
the printed book far behind in this dawning of a high culture of
commodities: printer's ink – that intensely coloured, adhesive and
fast-drying material essential for the quality of reproduction of the
sumptuous books issuing from the new printing press – was derived
from the new oil-based colours used by northern painters like van
Eyck to produce vivid hues while allowing fine detailing. Printing
made pleasant recreational reading available to the man of business
of more modest means, with smaller sums available to dispose of
on luxury goods. The great works of art and architecture designed
and executed in the centres of international commerce were made
available in mass-produced form for his delight as intricate woodcut
illustrations – produced for the press by men like Albrecht Dürer
who had begun their careers apprenticed to goldsmiths, making
finely detailed one-off worked pieces in precious metal for the very
rich.

By the middle of the fifteenth century the man of means could
reap in abundance the earthly rewards of the fortune he had earned;
there was still, however, his immortal soul to consider. With the
balance-sheet precision of the professional bookkeeper the successful
merchant set aside for God and for good works a carefully judged
portion of his wealth, to ensure his soul a place in heaven. In his
will he left ample amounts to the poor, to charitable institutions

11. Albrecht Dürer,
*The Revelation of St John the
Divine*: a woodcut which in its
fine detail draws on Dürer's
training as a goldsmith

and to convents, as well as a modest amount for masses to be said
for his soul. During his lifetime he matched the ostentation of his
lifestyle by ostentatious benefactions to religious foundations; in
some fifteenth-century contracts a small percentage of the profit
anticipated was earmarked as a donation to a local organization
for the needy. The prominent merchant-banking families who surrounded the Medici in the heady days of financial success in Florence
in the mid-fifteenth century funded the building and restoration of
churches, and lavish decoration in the form of frescos and altarpieces.

Consciously or unconsciously, there is a blurring of boundaries
between piety and vanity in these works paid for by rich and
powerful individuals from the profits of trade. Giovanni Rucellai
paid for the construction of a dramatic new façade for the church
of Santa Maria Novella; the architect, Leon Battista Alberti, included
the emblem of the Rucellai – the full sail of a ship – prominently

12. Façade of Santa Maria
Novella, Florence, showing the
Rucellai emblem

in his design. In the 1480s Giovanni Tornabuoni paid for a series
of frescos by Ghirlandaio for the same church; these include portraits
of his family, including one of Tornabuoni himself in a pose of pious
worship. Francesco Sassetti endowed a burial chapel in the church
of the Holy Trinity in Florence to ensure that his immortal soul
would escape torment, and he commissioned Ghirlandaio to execute
a series of frescos for it depicting scenes from the life of St Francis,
his own patron saint. After Sassetti's death the burial chapel became,
as he had directed, the family mausoleum of the Sassetti family –
the triumph of whose commercial success was already immortalized
in the St Francis sequence of frescos, one of which shows Francesco
and his son alongside Lorenzo de' Medici. In his private diary
Rucellai wrote that the money he spent on financing religious
projects gave him 'the greatest satisfaction and the greatest pleasure, because it serves the glory of God, the honour of Florence,
and my own memory'.

13. Robert Campin, *Mèrode triptych*: the donor and his wife appear to be as awed
by the décor as by the scene they witness

The habits of mind which encouraged the merchant to pay close
attention to every minute detail of the commodity he was considering buying also inform the fine art they commissioned. At the
end of the day the artist relied upon the patron's approval if he was
to be properly rewarded for his efforts: in one of his frescos Benozzo
Gozzoli agreed to overpaint with clouds two angels which had not
pleased Piero de' Medici. Silks, rugs, inlaid furniture, silver- and
goldware, china and glass – the staple of the merchant's everyday
business – are rendered in the paintings of this period with infinite
care.

The religious paintings donated to their local churches and
chapels by the new monied families lavish attention on the same
lovingly executed detail as those which decorated their mansions in
rendering with intense realism the possessions which surround the
Virgin and the Saints. The sacred figures are depicted inhabiting a
world which is recognizably the contemporary material one – the
details of the interiors closely resemble the patron's own environment. The objects which surround them are copied with meticulous
accuracy from examples lent by the patrons themselves, or by other

local merchants: gems, chalices, candlesticks, carpets and hangings, items of furniture, fabrics and porcelain. The Virgin and the Saints enjoy the same luxury level of lifestyle as those who give the artist his instructions; hence there is a suggestion that true sanctity will bring you wealth, comfort and the pleasure of beautiful possessions. In Campin's Mèrode Triptych, Mary has the same look of quiet satisfaction in the midst of great comfort as the Lucca merchant's daughter Giovanna Cenami in van Eyck's painting of the Arnolfini marriage. The donor and his wife who kneel in rapt adoration at the door of the home of Mary and Joseph appear to be as awed by the décor as by the scene they witness.

One of the features of the investment mentality which character- ized Florentine mercantilism and which accompanied the emergence of powerful banking interests elsewhere in Europe was the mer- chant banker's keen eye for suitable new commodities and markets. Hence the extremely shrewd deals struck by individuals like Jakob Fugger and Cosimo de' Medici linking substantial loans to manufac- turing and distribution rights on key commodities. Money-lending and speculative trade were connected by a common prospect of capitalizing on an initial outlay of money not currently in use to produce a significant return over a period of time. The successful businessman–financier of the fifteenth century is the person who is sufficiently well informed and alert to current trends to be prepared to invest heavily with a strong element of risk. The possibility of ruin through an ill-judged investment is mitigated as far as possible by diversification – none of the 'bankers' who rose to power and prominence in the fifteenth century concentrated all their energies in a single direction.

Nowhere is the interrelatedness of cultural innovation and shrewd financial exploitation of a new market opportunity more strikingly illustrated than in the emerging book trade. Although there was neither a local court nor a local university to stimulate a market for the new printed books, there were already printers in Venice by 1469. They began by producing high-quality works, closely simulating manuscript books, printed on vellum and hand illuminated, in runs of 300 or so. These books were apparently aimed at the elite of existing manuscript-collectors, and may have been financed by subscription. They were certainly expensive; an edition of works of Cicero sold for 3 Venetian ducats – the monthly wage for a skilled artisan. The new product failed to take off in this form, and by 1474 nine of the twelve printing houses which had been set up had failed.

Around 1472, however, Venetian printing attracted the attention of the merchant bankers. Here, it seemed, was a field wide open for investment. Two German bankers from Frankfurt, Johann Rauchfas and Peter Ugelheimer, invested in Nicolas Jenson's printing house; Jean de Cologne became a partner in the Windelinus printing house. In 1476 the Florentine bank of Filippo Strozzi financed a series of editions of works in Italian.

The new financial arrangements could have their drawbacks. The printer was committed to producing works which met with his backer's approval, and production was entirely dependent on his providing cash (or paper and ink) at the appropriate moment in the process. A contract drawn up between the German printer Leonardus of Ratisbon and his backer Nicholaus of Frankfurt in 1478 demonstrates the restrictions such arrangements might impose:

> The above-mentioned Lord Nicholaus for his part has promised to give and pay Master Leonardus, for his labour and for the printing of [Bibles], the sum of 243 gold ducats and all the paper needed to print them. Of the 930 books, the aforesaid Lord Nicholaus should have just 910; the others, up to the said total, should be for Master Leonardus.
>
> The said Lord Nicholaus is required and obliged to disburse and pay these funds to the said Master Leonardus in the following manner: as often as the said Master Leonardus has delivered and consigned to the said Lord Nicholaus one complete gathering of all the copies, then the said Lord Nicholaus is bound

to pay 5 ducats, and so he must continue to pay 5 ducats for each successive gathering until the full sum of 243 ducats is paid. There must be no exceptions.

The said Lord Nicholaus is also obliged to give the same Master Leonardus paper for the printing of the books, and at the good pleasure of Master Leonardus. Furthermore, should there be any pages in the printed copies which have not been clearly printed and stamped and are not to the liking of the said Lord Nicholaus, in that case the aforesaid Master Leonardus is obliged to reprint them at his expense though with Lord Nicholaus supplying the paper as above.

Leonardus was also barred from taking on any other work.

In the 1480s, Erhard Radholt began publishing in Venice, in this new climate of commercial realism. His 1482 edition of Euclid's *Geometry* (a text of vital interest to the shipbuilding community) was dedicated to the Doge, and copiously illustrated with 420 woodcuts. The market it was aimed at is indicated by its remarkably low price of 2.5 lire. In 1481 Ottavio Scoto opened another new field of publishing when he printed missals with musical notation included on a four-line stave. By the 1490s Venice led the rest of Europe in music printing; among the legible music scores propped in the foreground of Carpaccio's painting of *Vision of St Augustine* some are surely printed books rather than manuscripts – a tribute to their current commercial success.

In 1498 the enterprising Demotrico Terracina obtained a twenty-year monopoly for the printing of editions in oriental script – unfortunately the outbreak of war between Venice and the Ottomans in the following year put paid to his dream of cornering the Turkish market in printed books. Terracina was, however, on the right track commercially. Mehmed II was an enthusiastic book-collector, employing scribes to produce Latin, Greek and Arabic manuscripts. A fine, handwritten copy of Ptolemy's *Geography* in Greek survives which belonged to Mehmed. The manuscript also contains

14. Vittore Carpaccio, *Vision of St Augustine in his study*: legible music scores are propped in the foreground, some of which are surely printed

excerpts from works on military tactics and Hero of Alexandria's *Pneumatica*, and was probably a gift from his first wife Zulkadiroglu Sitt Hatun on the occasion of their marriage in 1448 (the illuminated frontispiece carries her portrait and that of her brother, Malik Arslan).

It was sound capital financing combined with astute judgement of openings in the market and possible patronage which enabled the printing industry in Venice to stabilize, and established the book there as a desirable commodity alongside other non-essential goods. Without such a commercial climate the great Aldine printing press of Aldus Manutius could never have undertaken its ambitious programme of publication in printed form of first editions of major classical works in both Latin and Greek. The financial backers of the Aldine press were the well-established businessman and bookdealer Andrea Torresani and Pierfrancesco Barbarigo, son of Doge

Marco, of the powerful Venetian dynastic family (Marco's brother Andrea was also doge). In other words, in spite of descriptions of Aldus (by personal friends) as a beleaguered idealist, struggling to bring high culture to the masses, and of his publishing house as a scholarly beacon in a benighted world, the Aldine press was solidly underwritten by a partnership of substantial Venetian business interests. The printed book too was part of the ferment of commercial development and entrepreneurship which led a contemporary visitor to exclaim that 'here, in Venice, absolutely everyone is a merchant'.

THREE

THE TRIUMPH
OF THE BOOK

BETWEEN 1495 AND 1498 the printer Aldus Manutius issued the complete works of the ancient philosopher Aristotle, in Greek, in handsome large-format (folio) volumes. In 1498 the five volumes were offered in Aldus' sales catalogue at a total cost of 11 ducats. Set against the annual salary of a well-paid humanities professor, who might earn as much as 150 ducats a year, this price was high. The important Greek works made widely available to a scholarly readership for the first time by the Aldine press were of a remarkable quality, as regards both their typographical beauty and their accuracy and textual exactness, but they were not cheap. Nor did they sell rapidly. Thirty years later, in 1527, the translator and scholar Erasmus of Rotterdam was still able to order a copy of the complete Greek Aristotle, and, furthermore, the price had not dropped – there was apparently no discounting for slow sales. When Erasmus published his own edition of the Aristotle in 1531 he made a point of telling his readers that his edition was offered at a competitive price, since the cost of the Aldine Aristotle (the only other edition to date) had put it out of the reach of most students.

Competition between the wish to make key ancient works accessible, likely consumer demand, production costs and pricing for sale was already an issue for Aldus Manutius here, when printing was in its infancy. From his first forays into the printing trade, Aldus (who had trained for academic teaching) was publicly frank about the financial risk the book trade involved. In the preface to his second venture into the printing of Greek, in 1495, he exhorted his student readers to buy his edition of the Greek poet Musaeus' erotic love poem 'Hero and Leander': if they did so, he promised to

1. Aldus Manutius's
printed edition of Musaeus,
Hero and Leander

reward them with further treasure of Greek writing; 'without a great deal of money, however, I cannot print'. In the same year, Aldus applied to the Venetian Senate for a privilege which would prevent anyone else reprinting or importing into Venetian territories any of the books (in Greek, or translations from Greek) which he was intending to publish. Aldus' argument for such a privilege (to be held for a period of twenty years) was the labour, expertise and cost of producing his new Greek typeface 'of the utmost beauty', which had used up 'a great part of his wealth', so that he was obliged to recoup the costs over a significant period of time.

Before the arrival of printing, the handwritten book was a treasured artefact, produced by the skilled work of a team of artists and craftsmen and wholly suitable for a wealthy collector's attentions. In both East and West the ornately bound, illuminated manuscript was a precious object, a collector's item on a par with gemstones, tapestries and fine porcelain; manuscripts were individually prized and were bestowed as significant gifts upon favoured recipients on appropriate occasions. Specially commissioned manuscripts might commemorate an event like a bishop's consecration, or a contract; richly ornamented and bound religious works might be given to bride and groom on their marriage. An exquisitely handwritten Books of Hours carrying the arms of the Medici and Salviati families, written in Florence in 1485 by Antonio Simbaldi and illuminated by Francesco Rosselli, was probably a gift to Lorenzo de' Medici's eldest daughter Lucretia on her marriage to Jacopo Salviati in 1488 (matching Books of Hours by the same scribe were probably commissioned at the same time in anticipation of the projected marriages of her sisters).

It is not possible to detect a moment at which the manuscript ceased to be coveted or, indeed, collected. Printed books begin to appear among the handwritten manuscripts in the book collections of the wealthy in the 1470s. There were occasional complaints in the second half of the fifteenth century from book-purchasers that dealers were passing off mass-produced (that is, printed) copies as if they had been handwritten, but that only serves to remind us with what care printers simulated the scribally produced product with their early typefaces and their organization on the page. Perhaps just because early books were so exquisitely produced and presented, book-collectors were apparently prepared to accept a printed copy of a rare or important work if a manuscript version was not available.

Isabella d'Este, Marchioness of Mantua, complained that the elegant little italic-font volumes Aldus Manutius was printing around 1500 were overpriced for their size, but she bought his printed books nonetheless. Federigo da Montefeltro's manuscript-purchasing agent Vespasiano da Bisticci claimed that the Duke would not countenance printed books in his collection, but the Urbino collection quickly acquired a significant holding in mass-produced volumes. Mehmed II's library in Istanbul contained

2. Handwritten Book of Hours bearing the Medici arms

multiple copies of the Greek cartographer Ptolemy's *Geography* – a work whose detailed maps were invaluable for the military tactician with ambitions to conquer the whole of Europe. Alongside a number of manuscript versions, with richly illuminated maps (including the one his first wife had given him as a wedding present), sat printed copies of the same work. The library of Francesco Gonzaga, too, contained printed books alongside his manuscripts, printed books which were decoratively embellished and inscribed in ways directly comparable with the older form, and often employing the same illuminators.

In the case of both handwritten and printed books, Cardinal Francesco Gonzaga and the Ottoman Sultan paid equivalently large sums to bind their volumes lavishly in silk and in leather, on which distinctive patterns, crests and lettering made immediately apparent to whom the book belonged. Matched bindings, often carrying an impressed crest or emblem identifying the owner, ensured that manuscripts and printed books blended together as 'fine' items in a prestigious collection. Federigo da Montefeltro's book-buyer

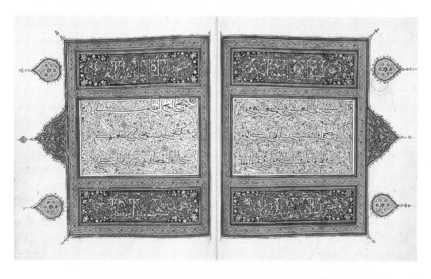

3. Manuscript Koran from the Ottoman Sultan's collection

described how the books he acquired for Federigo's personal library at Urbino were provided with lavish matched bindings:

> The Duke having completed his library at the great cost of thirty thousand ducats determined to give every writer a worthy finish by binding his work in scarlet and silver. Beginning with the Bible, as the cornerstone of his collection, he had it covered with gold brocade, and then he bound in scarlet and silver the Greek and Latin doctors and philosophers, the histories, the books on medicine and the modern doctors, a rich and magnificent sight.

Even when print-production gradually reduced the intrinsic cost of the book itself, bindings continued to be lavish, as a reflection of the perceived value of the texts they protected. Books were customarily sold as unbound sheets, and then 'personalized' for the purchaser

4. Red morocco leather and gold-tooled binding with silver gilt clasps belonging to Cardinal Domenico della Rovere

with a custom-made binding (impoverished students bound them in paper).

The shift from manuscript to print did not produce any particular upheaval in binding conventions. Back and front boards of solid wood continued to be covered with precious fabrics – velvet, silk, cloth of gold, or leather (tanned calf- or sheepskin). Decorative designs were then impressed on the covers using specially designed finishing tools, and the binding might be completed with elaborate metal clasps or ties to hold the work closed when not in use. As the sixteenth century proceeded, bindings became less elaborate, and the tooling tended to be done with tools specially made to produce repeat patterns without too much skill on the part of the binder. Luxury bindings were still provided for printed books for the most affluent buyers, and from the close of the fifteenth century morocco leather and techniques of gold tooling using heated tools applied to thin gold leaf were introduced into Europe from the Islamic world. Morocco from Córdoba was imported into Naples via the Balearics, and Levant morocco came to Venice via Istanbul. Ferdinand of Aragon's books were being bound in this Islamic fashion in Naples in 1475, and by 1500 the Venetians were emulating such bindings. Gold tooling in Eastern motifs was a characteristic of the bindings which Aldus Manutius provided for the copies of editions of his Greek works presented to distinguished patrons of his printing shop.

Hand illumination and fine binding preserved the early printed book's aura of expense and preciousness. At the same time, the mass-manufacturing process of print was itself a response to the pressure of market demand for multiple copies of key written texts, particularly those needed for teaching purposes. Writing in the 1520s, in his brief history of printing, Jacopo Cromberger (a German printing books in Spain) particularly emphasized the fact that printing had solved the problem of shortage of reading matter. He also suggested that one of the merits of the craft was that it had reduced the cost of books; and a Spaniard, García de Santa María,

5. Detail of a hand-finished page from an early printed edition of Aristotle's *Works* decorated with images of precious stones

noted in his will of 1519 that the advent of printing had considerably reduced the value of his library, since previously rare works were now available in mass-produced form.

In the period of transition from manuscript to print the relationships between authors, manufacturers, buyers and backers were shaped by those kinds of accidental opportunities which characterize any innovation in the commercial sphere. The prospect of producing an individual work in print might be the result of a commitment to a particular educational or doctrinal project (the urge to make available a little-known classical work or to circulate a piece of polemical religious writing), but it was above all a business opportunity, suggested by a 'gap in the market' or by a recognized local demand for printed material of a particular kind.

The educated English diplomats John Shirwood, John Russell and John Gunthorpe were all enthusiastic collectors of finely hand-written manuscript books at the beginning of their public political careers in the 1460s. All three of them took a fashionable interest in works written in antiquity by Greek and Roman authors, which in the course of the early fifteenth century had been painstakingly copied by scholars from the few manuscripts surviving in monasteries and convents across Europe, to be recopied and circulated in expensive, customized versions for wealthy clients.

Between 1476 and 1482 these English bibliophiles began to shift their attention from scribally produced, individually commissioned manuscripts to mass-produced printed volumes. In the late 1470s they started to add to their collections the new printed editions of the classics from printer–publishers in Venice. Shirwood acquired Nicolas Jenson's two-volume edition of Plutarch's *Parallel Lives* and his edition of Cristoforo Landino's Italian translation of Pliny's *Natural History*; Russell also owned the Plutarch by 1482; Gunthorpe acquired his Pliny around the same time. On 9 November 1482 Russell recorded in his notebook that he had purchased a six-volume set of another Jenson-published work from a London bookstall. Since neither Russell nor Gunthorpe had left the British Isles during this period the books they were purchasing had evidently all been imported from Venice and sold to them locally.

In the case of Pliny's *Natural History*, it is possible to follow the process by which the printed copies reached their English purchasers. During the summer of 1475 Nicolas Jenson was approached in Venice by Girolamo Strozzi, the local agent for the Strozzi family firm of bankers in Florence, and asked if he could provide multiple copies of Pliny's *Natural History* in Italian, and of similar Italian translations of two Latin histories of Florence, to be sent to London. The request apparently came from Florentine businessmen and diplomats posted to England who were looking for more sophisticated reading matter than was available locally and had approached the London Strozzi agent to import some. Jenson complied, and provided eight copies of the Pliny and five each of the Florentine histories; these were dispatched in late summer 1476, shipped via the fleet of Venetian galleys which set out each year at that time carrying goods bound for Flanders and England. Gunthorpe's copy of the Pliny probably came from this consignment, and the Plutarch (by the same publisher) arrived by the same route two years later. By the 1480s this traffic in books between Venice and London had developed into a flourishing, regular trade, encouraging the setting up of competing English presses to supply the growing demand.

The Strozzi agents were apparently alert from the start to the business possibilities of traffic in printed books. They handled the 1475 'special order' of Italian language books for shipment to London as a speculative commercial venture. Rather than simply commissioning individual copies of the books, the agent in Venice negotiated and organized the financing for an entire printed edition – a venture in which it was the backers rather than the printer who bore the commercial risk. The printing of the Jenson Pliny was carried out as a business partnership between a group of merchant bankers, Cristoforo Landino, the author of the translation (a distinguished humanist) and Nicolas Jenson the printer. Girolamo and Marco Strozzi initiated the venture in response to a perceived 'market opportunity' within the expatriate Florentine community in London. On 2 March 1476 Girolamo Strozzi paid Cristoforo Landino 50 florins for an Italian translation of the Pliny which he had apparently already done for production in handwritten form for King Alfonso of Naples. Alfonso, to whom the text is dedicated, was another aristocratic collector of fine manuscript copies of classical works.

Another Florentine expatriate in Venice (from another merchant-banking family) Giambattista Ridolfi recommended Jenson as the ablest local printer. The Strozzi bank put up the money for a run of 1025. The first thousand of these copies were printed on paper; twenty-five were specially printed on vellum. Vellum – prepared animal skin, otherwise known as parchment – was the material on which fine manuscript books had traditionally been written, and was a particularly good surface for the expensive pigment and gold-leaf illumination used to decorate them. Because of its association with expensive one-off books it also probably had more cachet than paper – printers went on producing a small number of elite copies of their mass-produced books on vellum until the end of the sixteenth century.

A further merchant-banking family, the Agostini, contributed financially to the undertaking by providing the paper (their home town of Fabriano was a centre for paper-making, and they may have been themselves involved in the paper business). On 14 February a transfer of 731 ducats was arranged between the Strozzi and the Agostini bank in Venice 'for 86 bales of paper they provided to print the Italian Pliny'. The Strozzi firm instructed the printer that the resulting edition should be put on the market at 7 ducats a copy, and that no reductions in price were to be allowed unless the bank authorized it. Four years later, in 1480, the Italian Pliny was on sale in Florence for 6 florins, presumably to unload the remainder of the copies.

So the small number of copies of the Italian Pliny sent off to London were in the end 'spin-off' from a large-scale publishing venture, a partnership between the financier who had spotted the opportunity, close associates of his in the business world, and the printer who provided the technology and the skills, but did not have the resources to carry the commercial risk. It may be the printer-publisher's name which has its lasting place in history (Jenson is regarded as an important 'father' of early printing); it was astute investment and commercial manoeuvring by existing merchant-banking interests which made the project possible.

This Jenson–Strozzi export venture did not, however, confidently treat the books produced as market commodities like the bolts of fine fabric, the porcelain and tableware whose manufacture and distribution were also undertaken as partnerships between skilled craftsmen and merchant investors. Jenson and the Strozzis hedged their bets. The Pliny text was printed (in a font closely simulating the modern humanist handwriting in which a manuscript of the work might have been written) with wide margins, without initial capital letters at the

6. Hand-finished page from Nicolas Jenson's *Pliny*, printed in Italian and decorated for the Strozzi family

beginning of chapters, and with its titles isolated in a sea of blank paper on the frontispiece, crying out for illustration and decoration. Those copies which were run off on vellum (already signalling a nostalgia for the preciousness of the manuscript book) were probably sent off immediately to be hand-finished with colour and gold leaf so that they entirely resembled the pre-printing, customized book. It was these decorated, and therefore expensive, copies which were probably shipped to England for aristocratic purchase. Meanwhile the plain text went on the market in Venice for the newer, humbler kind of book-buyer. Such a purchaser might or might not add modest decoration to suit his own taste.

A copy of the Jenson Italian Pliny which belonged to the head of the Strozzi bank, Filippo Strozzi, survives, as does one bearing the Ridolfi coat of arms (there are also two separate copies in existence of the later, two-volume Jenson Plutarch, both with the Agostini crest on their frontispieces). In addition to whatever commercial profits the investors in these editions derived from them, the participants in the deal received a specified number of fine copies of the work they had financed as an immediate recompense upon publication. Each of these personal presentation copies was hand-illuminated by one of the specialist miniaturists and illuminators who had traditionally worked on the ornamentation of customized handwritten books before the advent of print – and who continued in the service of the nobility in the sixteenth century as the in-house producers of another commodity of increasing commercial importance, the hand-coloured map.

On the frontispiece of Filippo Strozzi's copy, the margins of the text are crammed with brilliantly coloured representations on alternating red and blue ground of intricate floral arrangements in gilded classical vases, between which are set gems (rubies set in gold and ringed in pearls) and cameos (carefully copied from those in Lorenzo de' Medici's collection). In the bottom corners are miniature portraits of Ferdinand of Naples, and of Filippo Strozzi with his small son. Within the lavishly decorated initial D of the book's opening is a painting of Pliny as a scholar writing at his desk, in a high red hat, with an armillary sphere in his hand. A central roundel contains the arms of the Strozzi, surmounted by an eagle and surrounded by cheerful putti. In the Ridolfi copy, Pliny appears wearing a brilliant blue robe and red skullcap in an initial E at the beginning of book two, with a bowl of apples on a shelf behind his desk. The text is flanked by Corinthian columns of mottled marble, above which perch two peacocks. In both cases the relatively small block of printed text on the page is little more than a foil for the exuberant and rich decoration which surrounds it. For the banker, it says, it was the cash value of this new product which counted – its financial rather than its intellectual worth.

In the milieu of the influential merchant bankers, the book market was still one associated with exclusivity and ostentatious expenditure. Even as they collaborated in the production of cheap off-the-peg copies of sought-after texts, the bankers assembled their own copies with the same connoisseur habits as those they developed in relation to their collections of priceless gems and antique cameos. Gems, cameos and precious pigments recur in the margins of their customized copies of Cicero and Livy, Pliny and Plutarch – their illuminators frequently using real objects from collections (either of their patron or of his friends and associates) as models for their decoration. Filippo Strozzi paid 60 florins to the firm of Giovanni di Miniato for one of their renowned miniaturists (probably Gherardo di Giovanni di Miniato) to decorate his copy of the Pliny. So the decoration cost 10 florins more than Cristoforo Landino received for his translation of the text, and more than eight times the price set on the plain printed volume for sale on the open market. Peter Ugelheimer from Frankfurt, another business associate of the printer–publisher Jenson, and investor in a number of Venetian printers' projects, employed a team of miniaturists, led by Girolamo of Cremona, at vast expense to decorate a whole series of volumes from the presses he supported, for his own private collection.

In Peter Ugelheimer's case, the triumphant relationship between backer, priceless value and the book was inscribed on the frontispieces of his customized volumes themselves. At the top of the frontispiece to his copy of Pietro d'Abano's Latin commentary on Aristotle's *Problems* (printed in Venice in 1482), above a veritable clutter of meticulously painted cameos, pearls, rubies, emeralds and amethysts, set ornately in gold, is an inscription in gold leaf which reads, 'I give back to you the precious golden things which Peter Ugelheimer gave to you' – in other words, the illuminator's gold restores the outlay of gold with which Ugelheimer had financed the Aristotle edition. Ugelheimer's copy of Jenson's 1477 edition of Justinian's *Digest* (a standard legal text) carries the inscription 'Peter Ugelheimer of Frankfurt, of good birth, bequeaths this book to his posterity.' Ugelheimer's surviving books are bound in elaborate gold-tooled bindings, decorated with patterns of knots and lacings interwoven with one another, and closely resembling Persian bindings of

7. Printed copy of Pietro d'Abano's commentary on Aristotle's *Problems*, illuminated for Peter Ugelheimer: the inscription at the top of the page acknowledges Ugelheimer's investment in the edition

the same period. Jenson's financial partner seems to have found the urge to make his printed book orientally 'exotic' and ostentatiously 'precious' irresistible, in spite of his entrepreneurial commitment to the new machine-manufactured product.

The diplomats in the English court circle who bought Jenson's books from the shrewd banker shipping them to London were making purchases which were prompted both by an urge to obtain fashionable reading matter and by a desire to possess exquisite, collectable art-objects. Printing made it possible to own a portable art-object of great intrinsic beauty at a price considerably less than that necessary to acquire a personally commissioned, handwritten version. At this crucial point in its history the book as art-object and the book as treasured text (important to read and study) were curiously intertwined: was the Pliny a fine purchase because it was a text the English book-collectors wanted to read, produced with the new precision of the printed text and the improved clarity of the fonts cut by the printer? Or was it only 'fine' once it lost its mass-produced features, retrieved its identity as 'treasure' and became once more 'unique' through the attentions of a skilled illuminator?

The opportunity to produce a text for which a demand had been identified in printed form was treated by the new printer–entrepreneurs from the outset as a business opportunity, and the organization of the printing trade developed accordingly as part of an increasingly sophisticated commercial world. Printers tended to have started out as skilled craftsmen (gold- or silversmiths, leather-workers, apothecaries) who had seen a lucrative opening in printed books and invested in a press and type-fonts as a commercial venture. The printing trade grew up in various key commercial locations as a direct response to consumer demand for more, and less expensive, copies of works needed in teaching. The printing press's intrinsic capacity to proliferate copies of sought-after works in its turn encouraged consumer demand. But the locations, and the nature of the text published, were determined above all by commercial pressures: a gap seen in the market; a location where a demand had been recognized for a particular sort of work (religious or secular, vulgar or erudite); or an individual entrepreneur prepared to back, and take the financial risk in, a particular printing venture.

The first printers in Valencia, for instance, had not gone there in the 1470s out of an intellectual desire to spread familiarity with Greek and Latin literature from Italy to Spain: they were summoned there by Jakob Vizlandt, the commercial agent for the largest import–export firm operating in the region, the Great Trading Company of Ravensburg. As in the case of the German merchant initiative in Venice, experienced commercial interests spotted a business opportunity in bringing the printing press and mass-produced books to a promising location; the printer and his associates then decided what were fruitful areas for local publishing. In other words, the printer controlled production, the commercial interests the sales and distribution (and presumably in large part the profits). Time

1. Jan van Eyck, *Arnolfini Marriage*: this is not simply a record of a couple; it is a celebration of ownership – of pride in possessions from wife to pet, to bed-hangings and brasswork

Carlo Crivelli, *The Annunciation with St Emidius.*

2. *Above left:* Detail showing peacock and rug: did the onlooker long for the touch and the smell of these luxuries?

3. *Above right:* Detail showing plates and vases on a shelf: the triumphantly realistic material objects, surfaces and decoration entirely absorb our attention

4. *Below left:* Sinan Bey, *Portrait of Mehmed II*

5. *Below right:* Detail from *The Taking of Constantinople by the Turks*, 22 April 1453

6. Fra Angelico, detail from the altarpiece of St Nicholas of Bari: business being conducted in the thriving seaboard city of Bari

7. Benozzo Gozzoli, detail from the *Procession of the Magi,* showing the young Lorenzo de' Medici

8. Ottoman caftan of oriental woven silk

9. Niclaus Manuel, detail from *St Eligius at Work*, displaying the goldsmith's products

10. Venetian majolica dish, showing the Doge overseeing the export of bullion from Venice

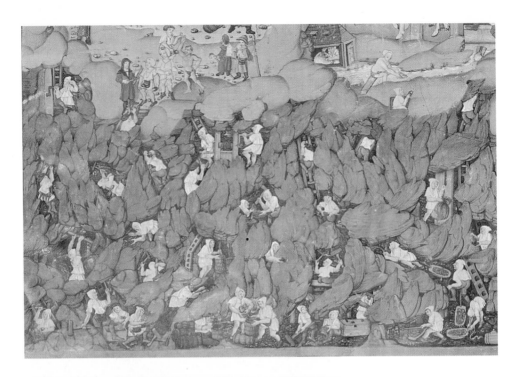

11. *Above:* Matthaus of Kuttenberg, detail from the frontispiece of the *Kuttenberger Kanzional,* showing underground mining for precious metals

12. *Left:* Detail from *The Mint,* from Aristotle's *Ethics, Politics, Economics,* showing precious dishes and jugs displayed on shelves

13. Vittore Carpaccio, detail from *Vision of St Augustine,* showing books and music scores

14. Detail from Aristotle, *Works: Porphyrius, Isagoge*: hand-illumination preserved the early printed book's aura of expense and preciousness

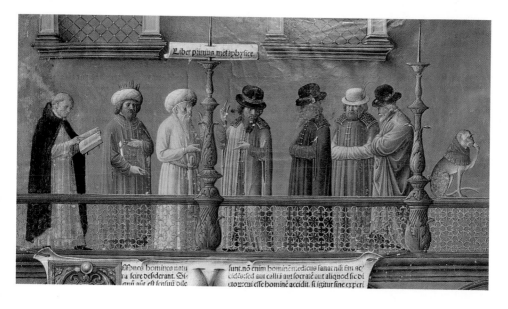

15. *Above:* Detail of illumination from Francesco Gonzaga's copy of the Greek gospels: the inventory of Francesco's worldly goods, from his priceless gems to his exquisite manuscripts, makes breathtaking reading

16. *Left:* Portrait of Cardinal Bessarion. Detail from *Orations and Letters to the Christian Princes against the Turks*

and again in the early days of the printed book, the bankers and financiers showed confidence that a market for books existed, but somewhat less understanding of how these markets were to be tapped (beyond the specific occasions like the Jenson Pliny).

The most prominent printer of early books in Portugal, Valentim Fernandes of Moravia, worked as a broker and interpreter for the German merchant community in Lisbon. The first printer in England, William Caxton, was an important mercer who invested the money he had made as a merchant in his press. The greatest printers in Europe all had to set up business relationships with bankers and merchants in order to launch the new trade. The substantial capital required to equip a printing shop, the high price of paper, the slow return on the initial investment (sometimes it took a printer twenty years or more to unload an expensive edition), and particularly problems of distribution meant that printers tended to establish their presses in important centres of commerce, and to rely on major international banking firms to support their enterprise.

Printing and publishing required an initial investment of large amounts of capital which were generally beyond what could be assembled up-front by any individual printer. In the early days of his printing house Christophe Plantin published works in which he could certainly not have risked his own financial investment, by printing them at the cost of the author, or with the financial backing of third parties with an interest in the work's being published. Sometimes these third parties were secular or ecclesiastical authorities who subsidized the publication of specified editions. When Plantin published Hadrianus Barlandus' *History of the Counts of Holland* in Leiden in 1583 the States of Holland gave him a grant of 100 florins, while the Senate of the University of Leiden added a further 200 florins. Some copies also carry a special dedicatory letter addressed to the States of the Province of Utrecht, a body which had contributed an additional 60 florins for the publication of this celebration of local worth, and which had presumably received a number of customized copies for its pains. Whether they were individuals or organizations, the investments these third parties made were generally recompensed by supplying the backer with a prearranged number of copies of the completed works.

Profitability controlled the strategies individual printers adopted to reduce risk and guarantee sales, and taxed their ingenuity to devise risk-reducing schemes. Sometimes this might involve an astute piece of financial brokering when a particularly advantageous opportunity was spotted. In the 1560s the Council of Trent, responding on behalf of the Catholic Church to the reforming moves in northern Europe, recommended revising various of the books used in church services. On 9 July 1568 Pope Pius V published the details of the reformed breviary, and gave the monopoly for printing them to the foremost printer in Rome, Aldus Manutius' son Paulus. This meant that every breviary in Europe had to be replaced immediately, guaranteeing a huge captive market for the printers involved. Within a month of the Pope's declaration Christophe Plantin had concluded an agreement with Paulus Manutius for the latter to subcontract monopoly rights for publication of the new breviaries in the Low Countries to Plantin – indeed, Manutius and Plantin had been negotiating this deal for the previous nine months, in anticipation of some such decision by the Pope. Plantin contracted to pay Manutius a 10 per cent royalty for the privilege – ten copies of the breviary or their cash value for every hundred printed. He later succeeded in acquiring equivalent monopolies for printing the new missal and Book of Hours of Our Lady. The importance of this kind of large-scale, guaranteed print job in putting a printing house on a secure financial footing cannot be exaggerated – in 1571 four out of Plantin's five presses were in use printing breviaries and missals, the remaining press being devoted to production of his polyglot Bible.

Sometimes litigation might see off a competitor for a lucrative printing opportunity – following his success in obtaining the monopoly for breviaries in the Low Countries, Plantin went to law

8. Jan Stradanus, *Interior of a Printing Shop*

to overthrow a competing claim from another Antwerp printer, Trognesius, who thought he had gained the monopoly through local patronage. Alternatively, it might be possible to buy off the opposition. On another occasion Plantin made an agreement with two Ghent printers, Hendrik van den Keere and Cornelis Manilius, that he would supply them with a hundred free almanacs in German and a hundred in Flemish, in exchange for an undertaking from them not to print a competing almanac.

The comparative speed and efficiency of production of the typeset book meant that new material could be made available to the reading public much more rapidly, and distributed to diverse locations as soon as the public had become aware of a work's availability. Novelty – either fresh and unfamiliar reading matter, or classical works produced in exceptionally clear and accurate editions, often with original commentary – was a key selling-point, to which authors and publishers consistently drew attention in their prefatory material. Printers also quickly understood that buyers were prepared to purchase more than one copy of a work if it was advertised as substantially revised and updated – the promise that the work is 'completely revised, updated and emended by the author himself' becomes a familiar boast on the title page of books designed for a mass market.

The value attributed to a particular printed book by the purchaser's eagerness to own a copy of some currently talked-about item, like the intrinsic value of the commodity itself, was built on foundations already there in the manuscript tradition. Before the fifteenth century, itinerant scholars had travelled from library to library and monastery to monastery in search of copies of rare works, and had corresponded energetically with men and women like themselves elsewhere in Europe, enquiring after the whereabouts of particular (usually ancient) texts rumoured to have been discovered or recovered. Once print allowed for the publication of a newly retrieved work, or of a modern work incorporating the latest in up-to-the-minute thinking on a developing topic, scholars began to write to one another requesting to be sent the latest work by a best-selling author, or asking the correspondent to look out for a work promised in the preface to another work (or about which rumours are circulating in the scholarly community) but which is unobtainable at the location from which the letter was sent. A remarkable amount of fifteenth- and sixteenth-century correspondence between scholars in what was increasingly widely known as the 'republic of letters' (the global village of intellectual pursuits) was taken up with tracking down and obtaining published works hot off the printing press. Indeed, as we shall see in the next chapter, it is hard to disentangle the pan-European network of scholars and intellectuals corresponding over the whereabouts of clean texts of works for which there was a perceived demand within the educated community from the so-called 'scholarly community' of those with a disinterested commitment to enlarging the horizons of knowledge *per se*. Humanists (practitioners of the liberal arts and the study of the Greek and Latin literature of antiquity) were as much international promoters of the print trade as they were individual, contemplative scholars. It is no accident that one of the figures most closely identified within the humanistic revival of learning in northern Europe, Erasmus, was associated throughout his career with the most prominent and successful printing houses in Italy, France, the Low Countries and Germany.

Erasmus was also particularly adept at ensuring that each single work which he edited for the press was made available through a number of printing houses, in a range of European locations. With print came the promise of almost instant gratification once an edition of a work was announced, and an accelerated programme of retrieval and circulation of works of antiquity hidden from sight during the middle ages in private or monastic libraries. With print, too, came the possibility of capitalizing on the investment (intellectual and material) of others. From the beginning of the sixteenth century printers identified a profitable market by watching a printer-colleague's sales of a new item, and then produced an edition of that work themselves. Sometimes this was done with the consent of the original editor–author and his publishing house; more regularly printers unashamedly reissued works from copies acquired on the open market and reset in their own print-shop. This might be with the connivance of the author of the original volume, to increase sales. On several occasions Erasmus connived in, or at least turned a blind eye to, the passing of a printed text of a work that was selling well to a printer in another location, to extend its market distribution. Badius Ascensius in Paris was only one printer to complain to Erasmus that by allowing German printers to reissue his works he was adversely affecting sales of the original edition:

> Dearest Erasmus, I have lately had two letters from you, and with the first a reprint of your *Metaphors*, which I accept as a token of friendship rather than a sop to Cerberus; but even so, since my friend Thierry Martens has printed it such a short time

ago, I dare not trust it to my press for fear of causing him to lose money. I set a much higher value on friendship than the gentleman who reprinted the *On Copiousness* – which you had sent me as a handsome present complete with your preface – and not a little reduced the value of the work I had put into it. Or than that other lot who, having solemnly promised me your *Adages,* sold them off for not less than a Philipp florin each which I had contracted to buy a year and a half before I received one copy (for even now I have not had them all). I had planned to make good my loss by printing the New Testament in the same type, which I had acquired for quite another purpose; but I shall write it off and think no more of it in view of my friendship with you, dearest Erasmus, and our host. Your printers need have no anxiety about their earlier edition at any rate; I shall do them no harm. But I shall take it kindly, if they in their turn consider my intersets.

Such wheeler-dealing on the part of best-selling authors was possible because of a guaranteed steady demand for printed books. The sizes of print-runs in the early sixteenth century (when printers were regularly producing works in editions of a thousand or more) testify to the confidence of the printer–publisher that there existed a sizeable and committed book-buying public, and that they would go on buying more, and more varied, sorts of books. The assiduousness with which early printers responded to the reading requirements of a close circle of patrons and backers suggests that they were less interested in potential, untested mass markets than in interesting a guaranteed and known readership in an ever-more varied selection of goods to purchase. The printed advertising catalogues of stock which printers began to issue from remarkably early in publishing's history (Jenson issued one around 1480) support the view that the selling strategy for books was to tempt those who had bought already into extending their purchases. The stock inventories of booksellers confirm this. The ledger in which the Venetian bookseller Francesco

HOMERVS POETA · SALOMON REX · HESIODVS ·

ARISTIDES DEMOSTH PLATO · ARISTOT EVRIPID · ARISTOPHAN

PLVTARC 9 LVCANVS ·

CICERO · QVINTIL ·

PLINIVS · A: GELLIVS ·

IO. FROBENIVS PO-
litioris literaturæ cultoribus, s·

Adnisi sumus æditione proxima, ut hoc
opus cum primis frugiferū, quàm emen-
datissimū prodiret in lucem, nec arbitror
quenqǝ inficiaturū, id nos infeliciter fuisse
conatos: nunc quicquid in arte mea pos-
sunt promittere curæ, id totū expromptū
est. Accessit & autoris opera, qui multa uel
auxit, uel reddidit meliora. Atqǝ utinā hoc
diu illi liceat, in studiorum lucrum potius
quàm meū. Sed uereor ne hāc recognitio-
nem ab illo simus habituri postremā. Qui
literario gaudet lucro, habent hic lucrū nó
aspernandū: quibus res est angustior do-
mi, quàm ut identidē idem opus mercent,
habēt postremā, ni fallor, autoris recognitione, simul & locupletatione. Bene ualete,
& nostræ industriæ, si promereor, fauete.
BASILEAE, AN. M. D. XXIII.
Ex autoris recognitione postrema.

THEOCRIT· PINDARVS ·

VERGIL · HORATIVS ·

LIVIVS · SALVSTVS ·

9. Frontispiece to Froben's edition of Erasmus's *Adages*

de Madiis kept a record of his sales shows a steady stream of regular customers, who increasingly fell into the habit of buying more than one book at a time. When one customer returned a dictionary eleven days after he had bought it, he didn't get his money back, but instead bought a two-volume work in its place, which was actually 3 lire dearer. Customers also bought work hot off the press – Francesco sold two copies of a book dated 24 December 1485 on 29 December, and six more copies before the end of January. Book-ownership bred a developing interest in reading matter, and (aside from the steady trade in essential liturgical works and text-books for students) that is what printers and booksellers catered for. Over the first fifty or so years of printing the reading public (and thus the book-buying public) probably grew only slowly; but those who could read were the proud possessors of increasingly larger numbers of volumes.

The appetite of book-owners for expanding numbers of titles was enhanced by marketing tactics on the part of both author–editors and printers which encouraged their eagerness to buy. Printers competed with one another (and hence generated an atmosphere of competing demand and comparison shopping by purchasers) to advertise the most up-to-date edition of a work already selling well. Every print-house in Europe seems to have indulged in the relatively low-cost profit opportunity of unauthorized reprinting of works first licensed and published elsewhere. Commented editions of standard educational works by competing scholars from presti-gious universities advertised the superior nature of their text and the particular advantages of the (sometimes extremely lengthy) notes and glosses. The text of Rudolph Agricola's manual of human-istic logic, a standard university text, was issued with commentaries by the German university professor Phrissemius in the 1520s and by the Low Countries scholar Alardus of Amsterdam in the late 1530s. Both editors insisted in their prefatory material that they had used an improved and clarified text of the work; both claimed that their commentary finally made the work accessible to students.

10. Johann Reuchlin triumphing over his detractors

In fact both used the same corrupt text first printed by Martin Dorp in Louvain in 1516.

Print 'controversies' were another reliable way of stimulating book sales. In 1514 the Hebrew scholar and reformer Johann Reuchlin published a volume of his correspondence with major scholars across Europe, as his response to a printed diatribe by Johann Pfefferkorn proposing that all Hebrew publications should be suppressed by the Church authorities. The two works provoked an acrimonious debate, in the course of which Ulrich von Hutten and Crotus Rubeanus masterminded an anonymous volume of parody letters – *Letters of Obscure Men*. Gratius, the translator into Latin of Pfefferkorn's virulent published attack on Hebrew scholarship, became in this volume the butt of a collection of more or less scurrilous and obscene attacks, packaged as letters to him from obscure academics, but including the names of real scholars. Although the scurrility of the *Letters of Obscure Men* upset scholars like Erasmus (who were implicated in the letters), they proved a highly popular selling item: in 1516 the *Letters* were reissued, with an additional seven letters, and in spring 1517 a second section of sixty-two further fictitious, burlesque letters was added. In 1518 Gratius responded with a volume of letters of his own, in part in self-justification, but at least in part cashing in on the sales the controversy had generated.

In 1505 Aldus Manutius entered current prices by hand against the new titles listed in a copy of his catalogue of books for sale. These prices tell us that a buyer could purchase four small-format, italic-type Latin volumes (unbound) for a ducat, or a two-volume edition of Euripides or Homer in Greek for a ducat and a half. A servant at this time earned about 7 ducats a year, a senior administrator around 90 ducats. A master mason might make 50 to 100 ducats a year, and a schoolmaster or lecturer in the humanities earned about the same. So in Venice around 1500 these purchases represented about a week's salary for a teacher or skilled artisan.

In the course of the sixteenth century, speed of production and availability became increasingly crucial parts of print production in the face of vigorous competition between printing houses, and the character of printed books altered. Printers no longer tried to make their books look like the fine manuscripts which continued to be produced for the top of the market. Instead they developed small, compact typefaces and layouts, and exchanged the ornamental beauty of the printed page and even typographical accuracy for low cost and speed of issue. By the middle of the century print was treated everywhere in Europe as a technological convenience, allowing printers to issue staggering numbers of new titles annually, and stimulating intense competition between printers for works by popular authors and those with guaranteed sales.

In the end the number of copies of any particular book to be printed was decided strictly on the grounds of potential market. Just occasionally a printer might produce a book for (and at the expense of) an individual customer. In the 1560s Christophe Plantin's smallest runs were printed to order: twelve copies of a piece of music (Plantin's assistant Moretus pointed out that this job would make a financial loss); fifty of a small, privately circulated memorial work; 120 copies of a volume of Latin verse. Usually, however, Plantin's runs consisted of 1250 copies for ordinary editions and 1000 for black-and-red liturgical books, although for books with a perceived demand (like his 1566 Hebrew Bible) runs between 3000 and 4000 were not unusual. Sometimes the decision to produce a shorter run was itself an astute business move: when Plantin set about printing his breviary in 1569 he considered a run of 2000, but decided that it was preferable to run 1000 (thus getting the copies in circulation more quickly), and to reprint as soon as demand justified:

I have only printed 1000 copies. My intention was to have printed double that number in a single run, which would greatly have enhanced my profit, but the job would have been in press that much longer, to the dissatisfaction of those who were daily awaiting its publication.

Reprinting in successive editions of the same work (sometimes with different printers) was an obvious way of acknowledging a perceived buoyant demand for any work. Books with obvious reading appeal from the outset (like Aldus Manutius' introduction to the erotic Latin poetry of Catullus), and books such as legal commentaries for which steady long-term sales to law students were anticipated, went into initial printings of 3000 copies or more. A book which was known in advance to be likely to have a guaranteed market, like Luther's German Bible, was printed in a run of 4000 even in its first edition. The decision made by individual printers like Aldus Manutius in Venice or Johann Froben in Basle to print books in these kinds of numbers represents a clear commercial understanding of consumer demand.

In the lulls between print-runs for book-length volumes, print-shops turned out other types of product than substantial-sized books. Printers employed significant numbers of trained, skilled and semi-skilled workers; when there was no work on large projects they were kept busy running off single-sheet or single-folding items. In 1528 Jacopo Cromberger's print-shop in Seville contained 50,500 sheets of rhymes, 21,000 sheets of prayers, over 10,000 copies of devotional woodcuts normally of one sheet each, 3000 'Rosaries of Our Lady' (two sheets), and smaller quantities of ABCs and pamphlets setting out the rudiments of plainsong. When his son Juan Cromberger died eleven years later, the shop contained 10,000 ABCs, over 5000 sheets of rhymes, over 3000 copies of a 'Life of Our Lady', and various other broadsheets. Of most of these not a single copy has survived.

In terms of overall costs, whatever the type of material being committed to print the price of acquisition of a text was comparatively modest. So too were the one-off costs of installing the equipment (printing presses and associated technology) to produce the printed text. The real expense was the paper on which the book was printed, representing two-thirds of the total cost of a book's production. The press was a huge consumer of paper, using three reams (1500 sheets) per press, per day. It has been estimated that by the sixteenth century there were between 500 and 1000 presses at work in France alone, so that paper manufacturers had to supply anything from 1500 to 3000 reams a day to keep them in production.

11. Papermaking, from Joost Amman's *Book of Trades*

To commit oneself to a long print-run meant putting up a substantial sum in advance to pay for the stock of paper needed, a sum which could only be retrieved once sales of the book were well under way. Already by the 1480s, printers were in financial partnership with prominent bankers, to provide the advance capital to underwrite an edition – the agreements between the parties regularly included staggered contributions of quires of high-quality paper as well as of cash.

Ensuring a steady supply of paper seems to have been one of the foremost preoccupations of early printing houses. Most of the paper used by the Crombergers in Spain was imported, and it was not until 1520 that they bought direct from the paper-mills rather than from merchant intermediaries. When Jean Crespin set up his press in Geneva he contracted to buy and import the entire annual production of one paper-mill. Robert Estienne had a standing order with a mill, and when he died in 1559 his son Henri strengthened the agreement by purchasing the mill's entire paper stock for eight years at a rate of 1000 reams a year. Both Crespin and Henri Etienne were prepared to go as far as investing capital in their chosen paper-mills in order to guarantee monopoly access to their output.

Printers could enhance their financial stability by acquiring a significant patron. In Italy, as we have seen, Aldus Manutius managed to obtain the backing of the Pope for some of his printing projects. In France Robert Etienne turned to King François I; his son Henri, who ran a press in Calvinist Geneva, obtained the financial backing of the powerful German merchants, the Fuggers. In Spain Arnao de Brocar was subsidized by Cardinal Cisneros, and in Antwerp Christophe Plantin was backed by Cardinal Granvelle and Philip II. In 1571 it was Philip II who gave Plantin the monopoly for the printing of the new post-Tridentine breviaries, missals and other liturgical books destined for Spain and the American colonies. This allowed Plantin to drop his arrangement with Paulus Manutius for a 10 per cent royalty on breviary printing for the Low Countries, at considerable financial saving (Philip, by contrast, simply retained the right to act as sole agent for the Spanish distribution of breviaries, taking a much smaller levy on sales). Plantin subsequently delivered at least 47,000 breviaries and other liturgical works to Spain, to a total value of 9389 florins, thereby significantly cushioning his other printing projects financially (and incidentally ruining a number of Spanish printers).

Indulgences (single-sheet exemptions from punishment for sins, sold by the Church) were another modest but lucrative printing enterprise – Jacopo Cromberger printed over 20,000 for the Spanish diocese of Jaén in 1514 and another 16,000 two years later. Handsome profits could be made by indulgence printers, particularly if they ran off rather more copies than had been ordered and sold the extras for themselves. In Seville in 1514 and again in 1525 printers were interrogated about fraudulent indulgence sales.

By the early sixteenth century books were bought and sold as freely and to as committed a market as loaves of bread. Indeed, in a letter written in the 1520s Albrecht Dürer drew a witty little pen-and-ink drawing of a printer shovelling books into the printing press on a baker's paddle. Dürer himself had benefited from the possibility of producing drawings hot off the press, in multiple batches for eager consumers. His little drawing reflected the fact that by the end of the first quarter of the sixteenth century books were rolling off the printing presses across Europe in such numbers, and at such a speed, that anyone who was minded to purchase one they fancied could confidently do so (just as he could a loaf of bread).

In the context of such a proliferation of perfectly replicated goods, and in the face of a consumer demand which made speed of production of the essence, hand-finishing or custom-decoration of books (by illumination or hand-lettering) before sale was almost out of the question. Only if a copy was being prepared for presentation to its dedicatee and potential patron, or to a dignitary on some official, ceremonial occasion, was it worth the time and expense to the printer of customizing it. The eager purchaser, by the mid-sixteenth century, required his copy of a work to look exactly like the one purchased

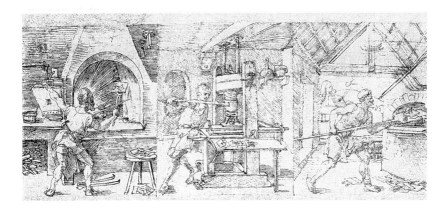

12. Albrecht Dürer's humorous sketch of books being mass-produced like loaves of bread

by his neighbour – they could pore over their personal copy, and compare notes, confident that in every respect the two books matched.

In this respect the book trade, by the 1550s, closely resembled the trade in tulip bulbs at the same date. Once the bulbs of the exotic variegated flowers which the Low Countries Ambassador had originally seen growing in the Ottoman Sultan's garden in Adrianople had been acquired, they could be divided, and the blooms replicated precisely by the skilled bulb-grower. Courtiers, scholars and bankers back in Antwerp, Brussels and Augsburg could be sure that the bulbs they purchased would grow into the identical fashionable flower to that which grew in the gardens of their peers. For just this reliability and replicability they were prepared to pay good money – the owner's thrill of delight derived from its likeness to its fellow tulip rather than from its idiosyncratic distinctiveness.

As if to symbolize the instant commercializing of the trade in printed books, promotion at the annual spring fair at Frankfurt became the standard way of launching new books from the early sixteenth century (as it remains today). In July 1533 Erasmus of Rotterdam apologized to a friend in a letter for not being able to

13. Renaissance woodcut of a
'Turkish' tulip

send him a copy of his recently published commentary on the Lord's Prayer – a book dedicated to Ann Boleyn's father Thomas: 'The book came out at the Frankfurt Fair this spring. I would send you a copy with this courier, if I could lay my hands on one, but I haven't a single one left. Jerome Froben, who published it, says that he sold out entirely at Frankfurt in three hours.' Thomas Boleyn, well pleased with the success of the book, sent Erasmus 50 gold crowns as a sign of his gratitude for receiving the dedication to such a hot best-seller, and the Protestant faction in England (to which the Boleyns belonged) specified Erasmus' little volume by name for compulsory reading in schools in 1547, when Edward VI succeeded to the English throne.

Less than a century after the beginnings of print, book-production itself had lost its glamour and become an almost humdrum affair. The books issuing from the proliferating presses right across Europe were modest in size and format; those who worked on them were similarly modestly regarded and rewarded (*castigatores* or proof-readers were paid in books, and might be provided with board and lodgings while they worked on a volume). Authors, too, received only a modest sum for their manuscript, and were expected to assist with and oversee the technical business of putting the work through the press (they might also proof-correct for other volumes in production at the same time). The print-shop was staffed by a body of trained and technically skilled people, whose working conditions were controlled by organized agreements and overseen by the appropriate guilds. The team-work between compositor (typesetter), inker and press-operator necessitated for the smooth running of a press meant that printworkers developed a sense of group identity and solidarity; they gained a reputation early on for walking out on the job if the agreed house rules governing book-production were not adhered to. At the end of the fifteenth century a group of compositors in Padua staged a walk-out because their beds had not been made (they got the sack).

As printing stabilized into a consistently profitable commercial undertaking, patterns of staffing and management emerged which drew upon a range of skills and types of specialist expertise on the part of its employees. Ex-silversmiths and metalworkers who struck the type and perfected the operation of the presses worked alongside scholars of Latin and Greek, whose textual expertise was needed to establish copy and check proofs. The escalating number of well-educated people needed to staff the whole printing operation – authors, editors of compilations, textual editors of classical works, copy-editors, typesetters, proof-correctors, indexers – drew university graduates of the new European universities into printing and publishing in droves. Publishing houses sprang up wherever there was a centre of learning, to exploit both the local market for textbooks and the expertise of university teachers. Around 1515 Thierry Martens's press at Louvain produced a wide range of small-format, inexpensive books suitable for use in the famous Louvain theology faculty and in the new liberal arts college founded by Jerome Busleyden. Among these was the first edition of the Englishman Thomas More's *Utopia*, which was seen through the press by his Low Countries friend Pieter Gilles, who worked part time for the Martens

14. The frontispiece
of Thomas More's
Utopia, illustrating
the imaginary island

press. Prefaces and epigrams attest to the fact that the editorial work on all these volumes was being carried out for Martens by a group of junior academics from the two institutions.

The vigorous response of the mercantile community to the book as a potentially highly profitable commodity on the open market inevitably led to some people deciding that here was an opportunity to get rich quick (without undue effort). The most obvious way to avoid the risk, time and effort required to transform an author's speculatively selected manuscript into a printed book was forgery – unacknowledged reproduction of entire books issued from someone else's press, and simply reset and run off at another location.

In 1503 the Giunti merchant–publishers in Florence issued an edition of the best-selling poetry of Catullus which used the same text as that printed by Aldus the previous year in Venice. The editor Ricciardini acknowledged his indebtedness to Aldus in the preface, but, in spite of the flattery, this represented direct competition. More worryingly still, the volume was produced in a new cursive type-face which could only be described as a very close imitation of Aldus' compact new italic for which he had received a Venetian patent. The format of three popular Giunti-published texts (Catullus, Horace, Valerius Flaccus) also aped that of Aldine editions: they were in small-format octavo, which Aldus had just begun to use for humanist texts, describing them (in his 1501 Juvenal) as 'more convenient for holding in the hands', and which were significantly cheaper to produce than folio and quarto large-type editions.

In 1528 (during the short-lived Florentine Republic which fol-lowed the sack of Rome in 1527) the Giunti published Castiglione's *Book of the Courtier*, in an edition directly copied from Aldus' edition of the same year. Aldus had been granted sole publishing rights to the work under papal privilege, but that privilege was hardly likely to be recognized by the administration in territories which were at war with the Pope.

Aldus was not the only prominent printer to suffer financially as a result of forgery and plagiarism. In August 1554 Jean Crespin issued the first French edition of his *Martyrology* (*Book of Protes-tant Martyrs*), whose publication had been authorized by the Council at Geneva. The Council had not, however, granted it a specific 'privilege' which would have protected it legally from reprinting by another printer. On 28 September Crespin lodged a complaint concerning a counterfeit edition which was in the process of being printed by Adam and Jean Rivery. Probably in this case there was some kind of out-of-court settlement, since the Rivery edition was completed and published, and Crespin even complimented it in his own second edition. He did, however, apparently succeed in delaying the publication of the Rivery edition until his own first edition of the work had sold out. And he persisted in pursuing a formal 'privilege' or licence for publication, which he succeeded in getting in March 1555. Thereafter only he was permitted to publish the work.

On at least two other occasions printers in Lyon and elsewhere produced religious works with Jean Crespin's name and press device (a serpent wound round an anchor) on the frontispiece. For the Lyon edition Crespin once again appears to have reached some kind of financial agreement with the counterfeiter. What these cases indicate, however, is that even where the printed books were 'controversial' religious works, circulating clandestinely in Catholic territories, they represented a lucrative market for the printer – sufficiently lucrative to tempt maverick printers into imitating the press marks of well-known publishers of such works, in the hope of cashing in on their reputation.

In such cases the printer acquired his copy-text by unscrupulous means, paying neither the author nor the original printer in the first instance. It was in response to this serious threat to earnings on volumes in which individual printers had invested heavily that, long before the introduction of copyright law, an elaborate system of 'privileges' developed in the various European territories: the allocation of sole rights to a printer for a particular published work, with severe penalties within the area of jurisdiction of the issuer of the privilege for any breach of privilege. A typical privilege, granted by François I to the Paris printer Robert Estienne in 1546, and printed on the final leaf of the book, contains this acknowledgement of the need for such restrictive practice:

> François I to his loyal counsellors and his Parlement. We have received the humble supplication of our dear and well-beloved servant Robert Estienne, bookseller, resident of Paris, who wishes to print at his own expense a book addressed to us, entitled 'La Coltivatione', by Luigi Alamanni. The said Estienne fears that after it is printed other unauthorized people will print the same text, or have it printed, and put it on sale competitively,

thus depriving the supplicant of the fruits of his labour, of his expenditure and outlay. Against Estienne's humble petition to us, we provide these letters of ours as a defence and protection.

Attempts to control the circulation and reproduction of printed books in the interests of the printer–booksellers who manufactured them had limited success, since they could not control or penalize pirate editions beyond the boundaries of the individual ruler's jurisdiction. The power to control heretical or seditious material was correspondingly limited. Printed books permanently altered the way information was distributed around Europe. Men of dangerous or dissident ideas could be kept out of areas whose authorities did not approve of them – their books, it quickly became clear, could not. Endlessly reproducible, small, unobtrusive and portable, for every book seized by customs officers and impounded, another ten could be got to their desired location hidden in bales of cloth (as Tyndale's English New Testament was reputedly smuggled into England under the noses of the Henrician authorities), or under the deck floorboards of ships (as prohibited books were smuggled into Spain under the noses of the Inquisition). If we think of the Renaissance as a flowering of new knowledge, then it is fittingly represented by the incredible expansion in numbers of readers and books, in increasingly numerous locations, in the century following the invention of printing in the 1450s.

Attempts to monitor and control the circulation of books and the information they contained, in case it was politically subversive, doctrinally heterodox or damaging of an individual's or an administration's reputation, began almost as early as print itself. Religious reformers were quick to use printed books to disseminate their reforming ideals as widely as possible, and the Church responded with legislation aimed at containing their influence. The Catholic Church introduced book censorship in the mid-sixteenth century as a direct response to the book's perceived influence in broadcasting seditious and heretical doctrine. Starting in the 1540s the Church promulgated lists of heretical books, and books by authors known to hold heretical views. The Index (as this list of prohibited authors and works was called) was issued to the local authorities in every territory under the jurisdiction of the Pope. It was the job of local officials to search out, confiscate and destroy all copies of banned titles.

Sectarian book censorship, however, proved unexpectedly resistant to implementation. Just as the attempts to deter maverick printers from plagiarizing other printers' publications proved of limited force, given the temptation to make a quick financial killing with a pirate edition, so censorship legislation ran up against powerful financial pressures which militated against co-operation, this time on the part of the booksellers and financial backers. By the beginning of the sixteenth century there existed a thriving and powerful network of financial interests for whom the guaranteed profits of the book trade were of greater importance than directives from officials of the Church concerning the reputability of the material they were selling.

In Florence, Duke Cosimo de' Medici was at first apparently happy to co-operate with the Pope's Holy Office (its censoring centre) in Tuscany, even though by implication it gave the Catholic Church powers which interfered with his own. In 1549 Cosimo himself issued a decree against Lutheran works and ordered anyone owning heretical writings to hand them over to the Church authorities within fifteen days, on pain of a 100 ducat fine and ten years' imprisonment.

In 1559, however, Pope Paul IV issued the first list of forbidden books for the entire Catholic Church. It was received in Florence by one of Duke Cosimo's secretaries, who drafted an opinion on it for the Duke. If Cosimo were to comply with the Church's directive, the cost in books lost from private libraries alone would amount to more than 100,000 ducats. He pointed out that what was at issue was not heretical books as such, but a large number of other categories which the Index included: books authored by 'heretics', but not themselves on the subject of religion; books condemned merely because they

15. Jacopo Pontormo, *Portrait of Cosimo de' Medici*

were published in France or Germany; Bibles; books which did not give offence but which were issued by publishing houses which had at another time issued heretical works. In his view there would be no objection to implementing the full Index if the Inquisition were prepared to pay for the value of the books, but failing that, he advised procrastination.

After months of unsatisfactory negotiation Cosimo authorized a token public book-burning – calling in a small number of books limited to 'religion or sacred things, or magic, spells, geomancy, chiromancy, astrology and other similar matters'. The Inquisition's delegate in Florence agreed that books needed by lawyers, physicians and philosophers should be exempted (with special emphasis on the importance of Jewish medical books for intellectual and medical progress), particularly since these professions had become largely dependent on books imported from Lyon and Basle, rather than printed locally. By this token gesture Cosimo expressed the hope that he could satisfy the Church while sparing 'the poor booksellers'.

Throughout these discussions it is clear that the Medici had a strong political position, which involved protecting if at all possible the financial interests of the book trade, even where this conflicted with the wishes of the Catholic Church. To comply with the full list would have ruined the Florentine book trade, in which the Medici family had a considerable financial stake. Over the next ten years the Florentine authorities contrived to be sufficiently dilatory in their efforts to control the print-houses to ensure that prohibited books continued openly to be distributed, and Medici profits, as represented in the sums tied up in existing stocks of such books, were not damaged.

In 1570 Torelli, the ducal secretary, informed the Duke that he had had a meeting with the Florentine booksellers and did not find them to be selling forbidden books. He explained that the booksellers considered the officers of the Inquisition over-zealous and the request that booksellers compile their own lists of prohibited volumes 'impertinent'. Why could not the officers go round the book warehouses and compile their own lists? The further suggestion that the books of deceased persons should not be allowed to be sold until they had been inspected by the Inquisition was, Torelli advised, unfair, since such a restriction did not apply to any other category of second-hand sale, and would hinder the free workings of the book trade. All in all, Torelli's view was clearly that the Medici had too great a stake in the Florentine book trade to countenance any kind of outside interference in its operation.

The first recorded legislation on censorship in France dates from March 1521, and was introduced by the King, François I. François issued a directive to his Parlement forbidding the printing of books on religious questions without prior inspection by the Faculty of Theology of the Sorbonne. As a result the Parlement condemned the writings of Luther (August 1521) and Philip Melanchthon's defence of Luther (November 1521).

16. Jean Clouet, *Portrait of François I*

In late 1523, however, the King heard that the Sorbonne was on the point of condemning the works of Erasmus, whom he himself had recently invited to France. He instructed the Sorbonne to suspend its examination and to await a ruling of his own. By 1526 the King and the religious authorities were entirely at odds over Erasmus: in May the Sorbonne censured his *Colloquies* and authorized the publication of Noël Béda's printed attack on him and on Jacques Lefèvre d'Etaples, for their translations and annotations of scripture. On 17 August 1526 the Parlement read a formal statement of the King's displeasure to the Dean and Doctors of the Sorbonne Faculty of Theology:

> The King has written to the Court that he has been advised that even though he had shown the strong displeasure of himself and his Council at the seizing by the Faculty of Theology of certain commentaries on the Gospels published by Lefèvre d'Etaples, nevertheless the Faculty has authorized the publication of certain books composed by Beda which contain accusations of supposed doctrinal errors in those commentaries. He demands of the Court that all such books printed be seized and inventoried against his arrival in the city. In addition the Court shall summon the deputies of the said Faculty to defend their action in writing, composing and printing in this City or elsewhere, generally and in particular, any books whatsoever which have not been seen and given prior approval by the Court.

Béda, who was present, rashly continued to maintain that Lefèvre d'Etaples and Erasmus were heretics. He was ordered to obtain from the booksellers an exact account of every copy of his book, and to see to it that they were withdrawn from sale. Once again, the King, with financial interests in supporting the mushrooming market in humanistic books of the kind produced generally by Lefèvre d'Etaples and Erasmus, set himself against the hardline religious censors, where their interests clearly interfered with commercial bookselling.

The religious ferment in Europe in the early decades of the sixteenth century thus failed to upset the smooth operation of the printing trade, despite religious resistance to free speech. The free market won out over sectarian controls. Nevertheless, the religious controversies of the period did have a direct impact on the development of printing in other ways. By the 1550s, when religious opinion had become significantly more polarized, the body of active and successful printers sympathetic to the reformed Church took refuge in Protestant Geneva. Jean Crespin, Conrad Badius (son of Badius Ascensius, the prominent Parisian printer) and Robert Estienne all moved their print-houses to the safety of Geneva to avoid persecution. Between 1550 and 1572 a large number of Protestant works issued from these presses, with the editorial help of reformers like Calvin and Theodore Beza, who had also retired there.

The printed book revolutionized the transmission of knowledge, and permanently changed the attitudes of thinking Europe. Print brought with it many of the features of a book-based culture which in our everyday lives we now take entirely for granted. The scribally produced manuscript was unique (the pagination of each copy would be different); the printed book for the first time allowed two readers to discuss a passage in a work they were both reading by referring to the precise page on which it occurred. Consistent pagination also made it possible for author or editor to provide an index, to which anyone collecting data on a particular topic could turn. The comparatively effortless production of multiple copies meant that printed books could disseminate knowledge much more rapidly, widely and accurately than their handwritten antecedents. The dramatically lower price of the printed book also made written material available for the first time to a large, less privileged readership.

The cartographer Abraham Ortelius (author of a much republished, best-selling volume of contemporary maps) was an experienced author in the difficult matter of negotiating payment for work submitted to the press, particularly where it involved both text and illustrations. In 1586 his nephew, who was trying to place his

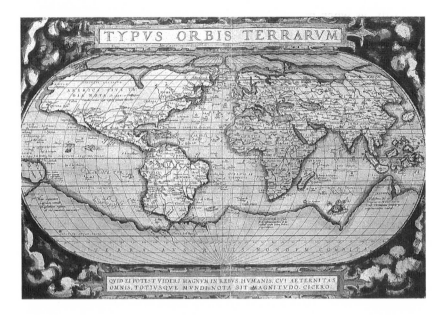

17. Abraham Ortelius's world map

sensational, and thus eminently publishable, history of the revolt in The Netherlands, wrote to ask Ortelius' advice concerning the kind of financial reward he should be asking for from the publishers he was approaching. Here is Ortelius' reply:

> It seems to me that, as far as I have been able to find out in our own days, authors seldom receive money from their books, for they are usually given to the printers, the authors receiving some copies when they are printed. The authors also have some expectation from the work's dedication, through the generosity of a patron, in which they are often and indeed, I believe, mostly disappointed. I have also been present when Plantin received a payment of one hundred daelders from an author who wanted his book printed. This was Adolphus Occo with his book of medallions. It may be that the printer gave him to understand that the work would not sell well. Then again, when books are

costly, as when many pictures have to be made for them, this is commonly charged to the author. Sambucus paid for all the figures in his Emblem book. Plantin has recently accepted a little book that will bring him in 200 guilders. Although it seems to me that authors seldom receive money from the printers, as I have said, they do receive some copies. The greatest number I have heard of (and that was by prior agreement) was 100. When Plantin had printed my book of Synonyms he sent twenty-five copies to my house, for which I thanked him very much. What he will do with my Thesaurus (which he is now printing) time will show. Some authors, having seen that their work was beautifully printed, have presented him with a silver bowl.

As Ortelius here makes explicit, the commercial context of publishing sanctioned a variety of arrangements between author and printer, just as long as the risk-taking publisher ended up with a respectable profit.

Today publishers of books for the academic or intellectual market produce them in print-runs of well under a thousand copies (and reckon to balance their financial books by achieving sales of under half of them). The long print-runs of books issued by early publisher–printers demonstrated their confidence (and that of their backers) in the existence of an educated reading public willing to buy books in large quantities, and to go on buying them. That confidence depended upon their being sure that the financial outlay (the backer's investment) was guaranteed to produce a significant profit over a realistic period of time – if that had not been the case the sources of investment looked to by the book trade would certainly have dried up.

The book was, after all, first and foremost a piece of merchandise, produced to earn its manufacturer a living, even when he was a scholar and intellectual, like Aldus Manutius, or Thierry Martens in Louvain. The impact of book culture on the Renaissance depended upon the fact that the staggering escalation in book production in the course of the sixteenth century was consistently driven by commercial pressures. It was market demand as understood by the printer and his backers which determined choices of texts and strategies for distributing them.

FOUR

LEARNING TO BE CIVILIZED

AROUND 1456, a leading member of the Medici banking family, Piero de' Medici – an enthusiast for ancient political history – commissioned personalized, illuminated copies of the works of the Roman historian Livy and the Greek chronicler Plutarch (in Latin translation) for his personal collection of manuscript books. He already owned fine, richly decorated manuscripts of the ancient historians Josephus and Suetonius and of the contemporary historians Bruni and Palmieri.

Piero housed his library in a purpose-built *studiolo* in the Medici Palace in Florence, designed as a 'cabinet of curiosities' to which important guests might be brought to admire his manuscripts alongside his collections of gems and other precious objects. The room was a compact four by five and a half metres. According to a contemporary description it had a white, porphyry-red and green barrel-vault ceiling into which were set twelve glazed-terracotta roundels of the months. The floor was of glazed-terracotta tiles by Luca della Robbia. Cupboards of decoratively inlaid wood housed the gems and other precious items, while the manuscripts, in their fine velvet and tooled-leather bindings, were displayed on flat, forward-sloping shelves built along the walls. A visitor described his pleasure at the mere sight of row upon row of gorgeously coloured velvet bindings of the books displayed in the *studiolo*. Piero's books, gems and precious objects were a lavish spectacle, to be shown to the awed visitor – a sign of conspicuous consumption, and a source of visual and aesthetic delight.

Federigo da Montefeltro, Duke of Urbino, invested the wealth he had accumulated as a professional soldier, power-broker and diplomatic negotiator in the 1460s and 1470s ostentatiously in palaces,

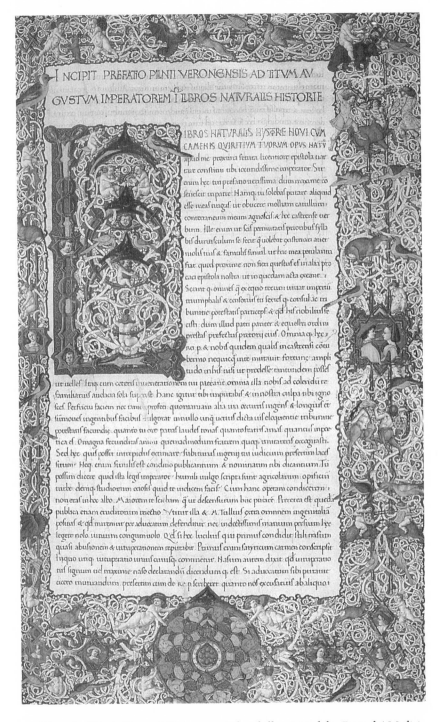

1. Pliny the Elder's *Natural History*, copied and illuminated for Piero de' Medici

2. A glazed terraccotta roundel (one of twelve) by Luca della Robbia, depicting the month of June, from the ceiling of Piero's *studiolo*

art-works, precious objects and a distinguished library. His *studiolo* in the Ducal Palace was built around 1474, its décor carefully programmed to provide a lavish and theatrical space in which to display his prized collection of books. It was sumptuously decorated with *trompe-l'œil* marquetry panels of inlaid wood, and with a series of twenty-eight paintings of 'illustrious men'. For the wall of Federigo's reading room, alongside paintings by Justus of Ghent depicting the Duke and his son kneeling at the feet of the muses of the arts and sciences, he commissioned this inscription:

> In this house you have wealth, golden bowls, abundance of money, crowds of servants, sparkling gems, rich jewels, precious chains and girdles. But here is a treasure that far outshines all these splendours. In these halls you have pillars of snowy marble and gold, painted figures set in deep recesses; within, the walls are hung with the tale of Troy, without, are gardens fragrant with bright flowers and green foliage. Both within and without the house is glorious. But all these things are dumb; only the library is eloquent.

3. Federigo da Montefeltro's *studiolo* in the Palazzo Ducale in Urbino

Federigo's immense wealth had been accumulated as direct payment for his military skills – he was one of the most successful *condottieri* (aristocratic mercenary soldiers) of his generation. By 1467 he was earning 60,000 ducats a year as a peacetime retainer, and 80,000 ducats a year when actually fighting on behalf of his paymaster Francesco Sforza of Milan. Spending lavishly on 'culture' was one way in which Federigo could give himself, and his princely court at Urbino, respectability. By surrounding himself with priceless artistic treasures, discerningly selected, he could establish himself as truly noble, and not simply 'new money'. The two artists responsible for decorating Federigo's library also painted portraits

4. *Federigo da Montefeltro with his son Guidobaldo* by
Pedro Berruguete: here Federigo, still in armour, reads from his prized
collection. The helmet in the top left corner is Persian

of the Duke with his heir, Guidobaldo, at his knee, in which folio books feature prominently as 'accessories'.

Federigo da Montefeltro collected fine books as he did his other works of art – in order to outclass his connoisseur peers and to establish a reputation for cultivation on the basis of the magnificence (or perhaps excessiveness) of his expenditure. Like his purchasing of paintings and *objets d'art*, the library project was embarked upon systematically, and with professional help. The entrepreneur fine-book seller and commissioner of manuscript books, Vespasiano da Bisticci, described in his personal memoirs how Federigo set about building his library:

> Federigo, Duke of Urbino, had a mind to do what no one had done for a thousand years or more; that is, to create the finest library since ancient times. He spared neither cost nor labour, and when he knew of a fine book, whether in Italy or not, he would sent for it. Over a period of fourteen or more years he always employed, in Urbino, in Florence and in other places, thirty or forty scribes in his service.

Vespasiano supervised the commissions and purchases for Federigo's library just as Ottaviano Ubaldini supervised his artistic commissions and oversaw the architectural designs for his ostentatious programme of building. In practice this meant that the bookseller ordered and oversaw the production of individual volumes for Federigo's library, working to a programme whose ambition was to assemble nothing less than the complete extant classical works (Latin, Greek and Biblical Hebrew). Thus Vespasiano tells us Federigo began with 'the Latin poets, with any commentaries on the same which might seem merited; next the orators, with the works of Cicero and all Latin writers and grammarians of merit ... He added all the books written by ancient and modern doctors on all the faculties, all the books known in Greek, also the complete works of Aristotle and Plato (written on the finest vellum).'

A connoisseur like Federigo, for whom prized books formed just one part of an extensive programme of expenditure, nevertheless built his own personal preferences into the brief he gave his agents on the type of written material he wished to acquire, both in manuscript and (later) in print. Like his fellow *condottiere*–prince Ludovico Gonzaga, Federigo was interested in treatises on military tactics and in ancient military history (he liked to have the ancient Roman historian Livy's works read to him at dinner). He was also influenced by the 'modern' and 'liberal' education he had received – as a boy Federigo da Montefeltro had been tutored alongside the Gonzaga children in Mantua, by one of the new specialists in the surviving works of classical Greek and Roman literature, Vittorino da Feltre.

But in order to ensure the worldwide renown of a Renaissance library, the books commissioned or purchased by a wealthy amateur like the Duke of Urbino tended on the whole to be those suggested by specialist advisers retained in the household for the purpose, who could suggest to their patrons what was the current, or most fashionable, area of informed intellectual interest. The unique status aimed at by Vespasiano for Federigo's private collection was the fame which could be established for its completeness. Federigo's expert purchaser (whose role lay somewhere between professional stationer–bookseller and entrepreneur) guaranteed his noble client a library whose spectacular resources would be widely coveted, one which would be strictly comparable with the best in Europe:

> A short time before the Duke went to Ferrara it chanced that I was in Urbino with his Lordship, and I had with me the catalogues of the principal Italian libraries: of the papal library, of those of San Marco at Florence, of Pavia, and even of the University of Oxford, which I had procured from England. On comparing them with that of the Duke I remarked how they all failed in one respect; to wit, they possessed the same work in many examples, but lacked other writings of the author; nor had they works in all the faculties like this library.

A strong element of competitiveness was of the essence in the library-building exercise. Vespasiano da Bisticci had also been called upon to act as agent for Piero de' Medici's father Cosimo when he had decided to enhance the public prestige of the powerful merchant-banking family with a book collection:

> One day, when I was with him, Cosimo said: 'What plan can you suggest for the formation of my library?' I replied that the books could not be bought on the open market, because they were not available. Then he went on, 'Then tell me what you would do in the matter.' I said that it would be necessary to have the books copied to order, whereupon he wanted to know whether I would undertake the task. I said that I would, whereupon he replied that I might begin when I liked, that he left everything to me, and that, as for the money for daily costs, he would order Don Archangelo, the prior, to present the bills to the bank where they would be duly paid. He was anxious that I should use all possible despatch, and, after the library was begun, as there was no lack of money, I engaged forty-five scribes and completed two hundred volumes in twenty-two months, taking as a model the Vatican library of Pope Nicholas V and following directions which Pope Nicholas had given to Cosimo, written in his own hand.

The connoisseur of fine art-objects who purchased books as part of his collection was expected to be as little expert personally in their contents as he was in painting technique or gem-cutting. With the specialist help of his personal secretary Arrivabene, Francesco Gonzaga collected exquisitely copied and illuminated manuscripts just as he did cameos and damasks. His valuable library included a beautifully illuminated copy of the Greek gospels written specially for him in 1478 by the Cretan scribe Johannes Rhosos, even though Francesco did not read Greek (Arrivabene did). At his death a sumptuous and lavishly illustrated Greek Homer remained incomplete,

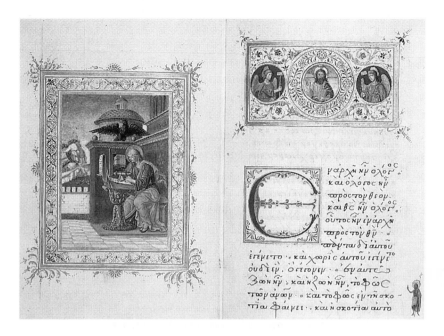

5. Francesco Gonzaga's copy of the Greek Gospels, written and illuminated
for him by Johannes Rhosos – despite the fact that the Cardinal could
not read Greek.

testimony to the extravagant investment of time and skill that such
an object represented (indeed, a significant number of the illuminated manuscripts which survive today were never completed). The
Ottoman Sultan Mehmed II's collection of manuscripts in Istanbul
included valuable illuminated copies of works written in Latin,
although diplomatic documents sent to Istanbul from Venice at the
time were generally translated into Greek from the elegant Latin in
which they had originally been drafted.

The 'great' library thus operated on two levels, that of the status
symbol or ostentatious display of art collectables, and that of a
serious text-bank, a systematically organized repository for recovered and original compositions – a vital resource in the new tradition
of revived classical learning. In the library collections of the great

Renaissance men of power, however, the view of the book as an exquisite rarity took precedence over its scholarly content – rarity either in the sense of artistic and aesthetic uniqueness and quality, or in the sense of an extraordinarily ancient or hitherto unknown exemplar.

An entrepreneur like Vespasiano da Bisticci had a vested interest in encouraging the general view that the value (commercial cost) of an art-object denoted the worth (aesthetic taste and moral esteem) of its purchaser. In the monumental work which Vespasiano himself wrote documenting the lives and works of his most prominent clients, he was careful to suggest that those who spent large sums of money on collecting books had thereby proved themselves to be especially 'humane' – to be men of virtue and integrity. In the case of the Duke of Urbino or the Medici family (the scions of whose houses were better known for their military prowess or for their business acumen than for scholarly pursuits), the patron's claim to commendable studiousness and virtuous seriousness was established not on the basis of the time he spent reading, but on the basis of the visionary grandeur of the project – the sheer size and beauty of the collection. In other cases, however, Vespasiano argued that book-purchasing was consistent with the individual collector's life-time involvement in humane pursuits, study and personal moral rectitude.

Describing the exemplary life of the fifteenth-century Florentine patrician Niccolò Niccoli, Vespasiano explained that he had attached unusual importance to book-collecting. He had made personal sacrifices in order to build his library, and had copied some of his manuscripts in his own hand. He had been responsible for bringing to Florence the first complete text of the Roman author Cicero's *On the Orator*, which had only recently been rediscovered. He had spent all his inheritance on books, taking especial pains to obtain a copy of any manuscript not otherwise available in Florence. According to Vespasiano, Niccolò had from the start made his precious books freely available for study in Florence, and had hoped that his collection would eventually form the basis for a public library after his death (a sentiment which Vespasiano also ascribed to a number of his other connoisseur clients). Vespasiano attributed similarly elevated motives to Niccolò in his equally prominent role as a patron of the arts:

> He not only favoured men of letters but he had an understanding of painting, sculpture and architecture, in all of which he had the most complete knowledge. And he lent the greatest favour to the work of Brunelleschi, Donatello, Luca della Robbia and Lorenzo di Bartoluccio, with all of whom he was very intimate. He had a universal knowledge in all fine things, on account of the universal judgement he possessed of them.

Ostentatious expenditure on fine books guaranteed that the purchaser would be established for posterity as a person of virtue, honour and nobility, regardless of his social origins or the source of his wealth. It did not matter that the librarian in Federigo da Montefeltro's Urbino library was only instructed to point out to visitors the 'beauty, features, lettering, and miniatures' in prized volumes (if the guests were of sufficient 'power and influence' to be taken on a guided tour to admire them). The impressively serious content of the Greek and Latin texts was guaranteed to ensure that reports of the priceless collection would refer approvingly to its owner's standing as a person of cultivation and learning.

Vespasiano's book-commissioning activities on behalf of his private clients had a direct effect on the process of recovery and distribution of the written texts of classical antiquity as it accelerated during the second half of the fifteenth century and at the beginning of the sixteenth. Vespasiano had at his disposal very considerable sums of money, held on behalf of his wealthy clients, in order for him to carry out the ambitious programmes of purchasing he had designed for them. Entrepreneurial booksellers readily responded to his enquiries concerning particular titles or specified authors, and themselves invested in procuring novel and covetable works to be sold on to Vespasiano and his copyists. Rare works of Greek, Latin, Hebrew and Arabic literature, science, mathematics and theology which had hitherto been of interest only to a tiny group of expert individuals in scattered monastic and other institutions across Europe and the East became sought-after items as Vespasiano advised his noble patrons that no library would be complete without them. The new collectors competed openly with each other over who could acquire unusual – if possible, unique – works to display on their *studioli*'s shelves. The high prices which collectors like Federigo and Cosimo were prepared to pay for specified hard-to-obtain texts generated a lively market in rare books and ensured that quantities of unusual items came their way – some of them dubiously procured by unscrupulous speculators, trawling the monasteries of Europe and beyond. Since the patrons concerned had close links with the individuals and finance houses which provided investment in the printed-book trade, decisions taken in relation to private libraries tended to have a further impact by influencing the choices made by the new commercial printers as to which works they should bring out in printed form for their less exclusive clientele.

The purpose-built study area which Federigo da Montefeltro built in his palace at Urbino in the 1470s to house his manuscript and book collection reflected its owner's personal vision of his library in its decorations. When he commissioned a sequence of portrait panels for the library, Federigo chose as their subject the greatest scholars and intellectuals of pagan and Christian antiquity. Alongside the pagan philosophers and poets – Aristotle and Plato, Homer and Virgil – were hung panels depicting the fathers of the Church, Jerome and Augustine. For Federigo, these were the men who had established the tradition in learning which he was endeavouring to follow in assembling his book collection – the works which would make the intellectual holdings of Renaissance Italy a match for the finest scholarly achievements of classical Greece and Rome.

6. Justus of Ghent, *Aristotle*. From the series of *Illustrious Men* painted for the *studiolo* of Federigo da Montefeltro at the Palazzo Ducale in Urbino

One of the figures selected by Federigo for his gallery of fathers of the renaissance of classical learning was Cardinal Bessarion, the fifteenth-century Greek refugee from Byzantium, who had settled in the West following the fall of Constantinople to the Ottomans. As we saw in Chapter 1, Cardinal Bessarion had given his magnificent collection of books and manuscripts to Venice (in 1468) – a collection whose manuscript treasures matched those of the recently founded Vatican Library in Rome. No matter that these books sat in their presentation boxes for nearly a century before the State of Venice could decide what to do with them. For Federigo, Bessarion evidently stood for the whole enterprise of recovery of the precious lost knowledge of the past. The great Byzantine patriarch was the

7. Justus of Ghent, *Plato*. From the same series

conduit through whom the crucial texts of an ancient intellectual world had passed, and thereby been retrieved from the eastern Mediterranean. Since his arrival from Greek Byzantium, Bessarion had indeed earned an international reputation as a superlative Greek scholar and man of personal erudition, who had introduced a younger generation of scholars to the Greek language and its literary treasures. He had done so, above all, by means of his own extraordinary library. He was famous across Europe – like Federigo himself – as a collector of fine books and manuscripts, the building blocks for understanding and reconstructing the Greek and Roman heritage in literature, science and mathematics. The inclusion of the 'modern' Bessarion in Federigo's roll-call of all-time-great contributors to

8. Justus of Ghent, *Cardinal Bessarion*, one of the
few contemporary figures included in Federigo's
pantheon of the illustrious

learning is a major tribute to him – the only other such individuals to figure there are closely associated with the Duke's own introduction to learning, like Vittorino da Feltre (his tutor) and Pope Pius II, the scholar–Pope (himself a notable collector of art-objects and books).

Federigo's pictorial homage recognized that what made Bessarion a peculiarly influential figure – indeed a symbolic figure – for the growth and development of learning in the Renaissance were the resources of his library, reflecting his special access to the Eastern sources of ancient archetypes. Throughout his life, Bessarion worked as a kind of scholarly catalyst, bringing the contents of his book collection to life by connecting them with the right readers, patrons and interpreters. Nor did this only happen across the crucial boundary between the old world of learning in Byzantium and the new world of learning in Italy. As part of the process of assembling his magnificent collection of unknown or little-known ancient Greek works, Bessarion consulted as widely as he could those with the expertise to read and interpret them. His position as a secretary in the Vatican offices meant that he travelled widely on papal business, and could therefore take advantage of Europe-wide advice on his rare manuscripts.

In March 1461, Pius II appointed Bessarion as papal legate to the Diets of Nuremberg and Vienna, at which the Pope hoped to persuade the German Emperor Frederick III to counter the expansionism of the Ottomans by agreeing to provide an imperial crusading army of 10,000 cavalry and 32,000 infantry. The Germans procrastinated, and in the end declined. But the six months Bessarion spent waiting for the decision, first in Nuremberg and then in Vienna, were evidently not wasted.

Scientific works were a particular strength of Bessarion's magnificent collection (as Traversari had already noticed in 1438). Among his more than 600 Greek manuscripts were copies of the ancient mathematical works of Archimedes, Apollonius and Ptolemy. When Bessarion returned to Rome in September 1461 he brought with him

9. Bessarion, *Orations and Letters to Christian Princes against the Turks*,
showing the Cardinal at the presentation of his book to King Edward IV
of England

a talented young German mathematician and astronomer, Regiomontanus (Johann Müller), whose specialist skills the Cardinal had
enlisted to advise him on his Greek mathematical manuscripts.
Bessarion taught Regiomontanus Greek in his own household, and
then set him to work on the texts of the Greek mathematicians which
he had collected or copied in Byzantium. It was Regiomontanus who
made technical sense of these mathematical works, and who began to
develop a modern mathematics based on their principles. It was he
rather than Bessarion who excitedly recognized that the recovery of
the Greek works of Archimedes and Apollonius would be of greater
importance to the modern world than any of the rediscovered Greek
literary works by Homer, Euripides or Plato.

10. A woodcut likeness
of Regiomontanus,
conversing with Ptolemy,
from his *On Triangles*

The treasures of ancient mathematical learning lovingly collected, but not technically understood, by a collector of rare volumes like Bessarion had to wait for expert interpreters before their intellectual importance (as opposed to their aesthetic worth and rarity) could be recognized. It was not enough that Bessarion was able to appreciate the value and importance of the manuscripts he 'rescued', nor that he was master of the necessary linguistic and critical skills to recognize their finer textual points. The impact on learning of Greek mathematics required an expert mathematician to interpret them accurately and to propagate a new mathematics based upon them.

Regiomontanus himself apparently appreciated how crucial the resources of major private manuscript collections were for the

11. Antonio Pisanello, *Matthias Corvinus,* King of Hungary and bibliophile

technician in pursuit of developments in innovative learning. In 1467 he was approached by the King of Hungary, Matthias Corvinus, and invited to Buda, where Corvinus aspired to establish a cultural centre to match those in the Courts of Italy. Corvinus had built up a magnificent library (with the help of his Latin secretary and close adviser János Vitéz), particularly rich in Greek manuscripts, to which Hungary's proximity to the old centres of learning of Byzantium, and to the new ones of Mehmed's Istanbul, gave easy access. Drawn by the potential intellectual opportunities offered by the rich resources of Corvinus' library, Regiomontanus moved from Italy to Hungary. Between 1467 and 1471 he was librarian to Corvinus' collection, helped establish an astronomical observatory at Oradea, and held an appointment at the newly founded University of Bratislava. He used the holdings at Buda to continue his innovative work in astronomy, and dedicated his tables for spherical astronomy to Vitéz and to Matthias Corvinus.

Following the fall from favour of Vitéz, Regiomontanus moved back to Nuremberg in 1471 and set up a printing press, dedicated to mass-producing the original ancient texts which he had so closely studied, as well as the new works, mathematical tables and tables of astronomical observations which he had drawn up. As a prosperous commercial and business centre, committed to new technology in trade and travel, Nuremberg was a shrewd choice of location for such a venture. Regiomontanus appears to have had no trouble getting financial backing from a local businessman with an interest in astronomy. Hartmann Schedel, whose own monument to the new spirit of enquiry and innovation in print – the *Nuremberg Chronicle* – was published in Nuremberg in 1493, corresponded enthusiastically with his older cousin Hermann about the publications from the Regiomontanus press. 'He is extremely secretive,' Hermann wrote to Hartmann in 1473, 'but I am ingratiating myself with his servants, and hope soon to get a sight of what he is producing. When I do, I shall send you a copy immediately.'

The printing press's reliability for reproducing tables of figures

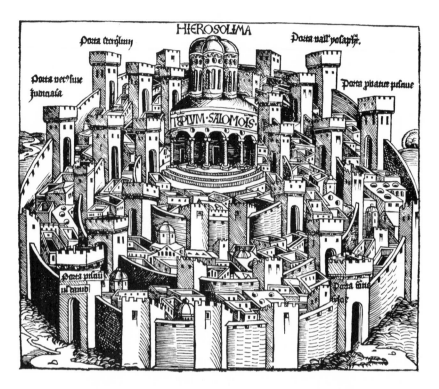

12. Woodcut of Jerusalem from the *Nuremberg Chronicle*
by Hartmann Schedel

(where transcription by hand inevitably tended to introduce errors) made it a particularly attractive tool for the mathematician. As with Schedel's *Nuremberg Chronicle,* a single work could be distributed throughout the known world, bringing instant renown to the author, his work and its place of origin. Regiomontanus dreamed of having the reliably reproduced readings in his astronomical tables verified by independent observers across Europe and beyond – a dream realized in the publications issued from presses all over Europe by the end of the fifteenth century.

The private book-collectors' readily available funds also encouraged the production in quantity of expensive 'coffee-table' items –

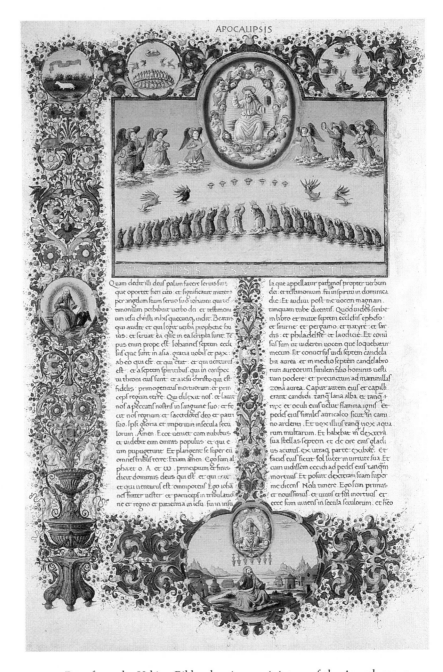

13. Page from the Urbino Bible, showing a miniature of the Apocalypse: a
sumptuous Bible was the centrepiece of any respectably magnificent book
collection

popular works, produced with especial glamour, which lent themselves to being shown off – ostentatiously displayed on important public occasions. When Borso d'Este of Ferrara travelled to Rome in 1471 to be invested with his dukedom by the Pope, he included in his luggage his two-volume, lavishly decorated Bible (total weight, 34 pounds), to be displayed alongside the tapestries and furnishings which also went with him on the trip. Borso's Bible had cost him the enormous sum of 2200 florins and included more than a thousand miniatures by Taddeo Crivelli and Franco dei Rossi. To enhance its beauty further Borso had it specially rebound for his triumphal visit to the Vatican. A sumptuous Bible was the centrepiece of any respectably magnificent collection, and patrons borrowed each other's copies on short-term loan to give their own miniaturists inspiration (Borso d'Este borrowed one which had belonged to the first Marquis of Ferrara, Niccolò III).

Apart from the extravagant Bibles, the ancient scientist and cartographer Ptolemy's *Geography*, complete with coloured and illuminated maps of the known world, took pride of place in a surprisingly large number of great men's libraries. The *Geography*, too, was an extremely expensive purchase, since some copies contained as many as sixty individual maps, each of which had to be accurately drawn and locations precisely marked before the delicate business of colouring and decorating could even be begun. Nicholas Germanus (about whom we know almost nothing) was responsible for more than ten copies of the *Geography* which Vespasiano commissioned. Borso d'Este gave Germanus 100 gold florins for his copy in 1466, after his personal astronomers had checked it for accuracy. When printed editions of Ptolemy's *Geography* began to be produced, their woodcut maps shamelessly plagiarized Germanus', usually without acknowledgement.

The frequency with which printed and handwritten copies of the same or related works shared library space around 1500 suggests that the collector's urge to possess every conceivable variant available of an important work easily overcame any residual inhibitions he

might have had about printed books. When the German printer
Erhard Radholt began printing scientific books in Venice in the late
1470s, Federigo da Montefeltro was one of the patrons to whom he
dedicated his editions.

It was above all the connections between collectors and their
expert advisers which provided the growth point for Renaissance
responses to the textual riches recovered in the book-collecting boom
of the second half of the fifteenth century. It was from this base,
and under the guidance of equivalent advisers to the early presses,
that the directions of development of printed book-production were
established.

Vespasiano's idealized book-collector, the Florentine Niccolò
Niccoli's personal associate in manuscript acquisition, was the erudite Latinist Poggio Bracciolini. While Niccolò organized the copying
of recent acquisitions in Florence (sometimes copying them himself),
Poggio, one of the secretaries with the papal Curia in Rome, pursued
promising leads through contacts all over Europe. In 1428 he wrote
to Niccolò with the news that he had tracked down a complete text
of the Roman historian Livy's *Decades* (known only in a fragmented
version), and urged him to enlist the financial support of Cosimo de'
Medici (as on previous occasions) to follow up the lead:

> A scholar has arrived from Germany; he has travelled over a
> large part of the world and is a man of keen intelligence (though
> somewhat unreliable). He claims that he has seen ten Decades
> of Livy, in two large, rectangular volumes written in Lombard
> script, and that the title on one of the volumes says that it
> contains all ten Decades, and that he has read quite a bit of both
> volumes. I am telling you this so that you may talk it over with
> Cosimo de' Medici and make a real effort to get hold of these
> volumes, for it will be easy for you to do. They are in the
> Cistercian Monastery of Sora, two German miles from Roschild,
> that is, a little more than one day's journey from Lübeck. See
> to it that Cosimo writes as soon as possible to the Medici agent

in Lübeck, and asks him to go to the monastery himself if needs
be. For if this is true we shall have a major triumph.

As Poggio had surmised, the 'scholar' who claimed to have found
a complete version of Livy was mistaken – there was no surviving,
complete manuscript of Livy's *Decades*. But he was evidently
successful in enlisting the financial resources of Cosimo de' Medici
(via Niccolò Niccoli) in the 'treasure hunt' for the lost portions of
Livy's history of Rome. In 1444 Cosimo presented a fine manuscript copy of the *Decades* as a gift to King Alfonso in Naples,
who like himself was an avid collector, with a substantial library.
Alfonso's copy was carefully studied, emended and glossed by
(among others) the wayward thinker and expert Latinist Lorenzo
Valla, who had recently moved to the Court at Naples from Rome.
As part of his own scholarly efforts to establish the best possible
text, Valla managed somehow to acquire and further annotated the
composite manuscript which the distinguished scholar and pioneer
of manuscripts-collecting Francesco Petrarch had put together a
century earlier.

In 1469 the first printed edition of Livy appeared in Rome, dedicated to Pope Paul II. In his prefatory letter the editor, Giovanni
Andrea Bussi, recounted the story of the search for and retrieval of
the almost complete text of Livy, and described how Petrarch had
also engaged in the hunt for ancient archetypes, in order to restore
this key work of Roman history to its ancient glory. From this point
onwards the availability of texts of Livy in multiple copies (in other
words, a printed edition) accelerated the process of reconstruction
of a reliable text of the work.

Printed editions made it possible for scholars at last to compare
more than one version of the same work at a single location (rather
than travelling from one library to another). When Antonio Agustin
was working on the handwritten text of a key legal work from
antiquity – Justinian's *Digest* – in the 1540s, he consulted a very
early manuscript in the library of the Medici family in Florence.

At the same time, however, he also had in front of him the 1529 printed edition of Gregory Haloander, against whose text he compared the manuscript. In his own printed volume of emendations to the text (published in 1543) he explained how each of his own corrections could be entered into the reader's copy of Haloander's edition: 'Since many copies of Haloander's edition are readily available in every library, it will be easy for all to use our emendations.'

Even before 1500 editors themselves were publicly acknowledging printing's role in this process of editorial cleaning-up of the received works of antiquity. In the preface to his early edition of Livy, Marcus Antonius Sabellicus blamed printer–publishers for readers' increasing awareness of disagreements between the various printed texts available. They were issuing so many printed editions of single works that readers could readily see that the different editors were passing off dramatically dissimilar versions as 'authentic'. In his edition, he claimed, he had consciously seen to it that the reader was given the definitive text of Livy, incorporating the most up-to-the-minute revisions of the best scholars:

> The art of printing has with incredible speed crammed not just Italy but almost the whole of Europe full to bursting with a marvellous wealth of books. But it sometimes happens that either through the carelessness or negligence of the printer, the reader encounters a large number of aberrant locutions scattered through the printed text; once these have been tackled it will be altogether easier to attempt zealously to undertake the study of the liberal arts. Therefore, in order to answer the complaints or anxieties of so many readers, I have recently been asked to undertake the reconstruction of the integral text of Livy, using the most rigorous methods.

Although such claims contained a large helping of publishing hype, the final decades of the fifteenth century and the early decades of the sixteenth did see dramatic improvements in the quality of available texts of key classical works, stimulated and assisted by the printing trade itself.

In the case of Livy's *Decades*, by the early years of the sixteenth century the process of working through, emending, adding to and deleting from, commenting on and collating the various fragments had produced a work whose importance had inevitably been magnified by the growing tradition of expertise surrounding it. With the proliferation of printed editions, and the spread of publishing houses all claiming a commitment to accuracy and authenticity in their editions, in the first quarter of the sixteenth century a strong element of intellectual and commercial competition came into play. Who was entitled to claim the most complete and readily usable version of the text of Livy?

Around 1520 the great Aldine press issued an important edition of the Livy by Franciscus Asulanus, which assiduously assembled all the new material retrieved to date. By this time, however, the centre for the intensive pursuit of ancient texts still largely unavailable to the community of scholarly book-buyers and readers had shifted away from Italy and had moved north, to Basle. There a particularly active circle of scholars and educators had gathered around the Froben printing house, guided and encouraged by the Low Countries editor, author and educator Erasmus of Rotterdam. In 1526, Simon Grynaeus, Professor of Greek at Basle University and admirably skilled at locating rare manuscripts, discovered the final five missing books of Livy in a fifth-century manuscript in the library of the Benedictine abbey at Lorsch in Hesse (a spectacular library, whose manuscript-collecting activities had been directly supported in the eighth century by the Emperor Charlemagne). Grynaeus brought the Lorsch manuscript to Basle, where it was used as the copy-text for Froben's 1531 edition of Livy.

In 1535, Erasmus' protégé Beatus Rhenanus produced an annotated edition of Livy for the Froben press which took full advantage of all the scholarly attention the work had received to date. To establish his own definitive text he borrowed two manuscripts from cathedral libraries, to collate and compare textually with Grynaeus' printed text: one from the Cathedral of Worms, the other from the Chapter Library of Speyer. In the course of marking up with corrections and setting the work for print, both these manuscripts were destroyed. It is an irony of the arrival of the printing press that, by the time its power to disseminate ancient knowledge, impeccably restored and edited, to the widest possible readership was understood, enthusiasts for this new technology showed little respect for the physical manuscripts with which they worked as precious in their own right.

Livy's *Decades* became a cornerstone of Renaissance understanding of Roman history and politics, almost ritually referred to and cited by any author writing or commenting on politics and history, ancient or modern. The speeches recorded by Livy (actually rhetorical confections composed by the author to brighten up his narrative history) were used as models for political negotiation by diplomats throughout the sixteenth century. Niccolò Machiavelli's technical handbook of political strategy, *Discourses on the First Decade of Livy*, immortalized the ancient historian's analyses of key moments in Rome's fortunes from its foundation.

Inevitably, the growing band of virtuoso technical linguists working over the treasury of classical works were limited in their endeavours by the restricted body of works which had actually survived. The arbitrariness of that process of survival was not lost on some Renaissance scholars, nor was the irony that a work was likely to be regarded as 'important' simply because it was still available to be read. In the English scholar Thomas More's satirical fiction *Utopia*, the traveller Raphael Hythlodaeus arrives on the island with a trunk full of Greek and Latin books which he has brought with him for light reading on the voyage. This chance collection of texts becomes the Utopians' 'classical heritage', which they quickly mass-produce in printed form:

Before leaving for the voyage I had placed on board a good-sized packet of books. Thus the Utopians received from me most of

Plato's works and many of Aristotle's, as well as Theophrastus's book *On Plants*, though the latter, I'm sorry to say, was somewhat mutilated – during the voyage I had carelessly left it lying around, and a monkey got hold of it and from sheer mischief ripped a few pages here and there. Of the grammarians they have only Lascaris, for I did not take Theodorus with me, nor any dictionary except that of Hesychius; and they have Discorides' work on herbs.

While I was showing them on Aldine editions of various books, we talked about paper-making and type-cutting, and with great sharpness of mind they immediately grasped the basic principles of printing. If they had had the texts of all the Greek authors, they would soon have had no lack of volumes; but as they only had the titles I have mentioned they have had to content themselves with printing these repeatedly in thousands of copies.

The first stages of new intellectual initiatives thus took place almost parenthetically within the great libraries and the Courts and households in which they were located. While Poggio Bracciolini was pursuing lost Roman masterpieces in his spare time, he was also responsible for whole tomes of papal correspondence in exquisite Latin, from the foundation documents for Eton College in England, issued by the Pope to Henry VI, to safe-conducts for foreign diplomats crossing the papal territories. Once the rare archetypes or fine copies had been acquired for the connoisseur's library, however, the scholars retained in noble households (or, in the case of the Vatican Library, in the administrative offices of the Pope at the Vatican) as secretaries and advisers could work on them under almost ideal conditions in terms of materials and resources, heavily subsidized by the day-to-day, functional activities of a secretarial office. There, supported by a patron who aspired to demonstrate his commitment to humane learning, they could work without distraction to produce erudite commentaries and original works of poetry or prose extensively influenced by the learning they contained.

In the late 1480s Lorenzo de' Medici's patronage allowed the outstanding classical linguist Angelo Poliziano to devote himself entirely to scholarly study of ancient texts, using the magnificent collection of ancient manuscripts in the Medici family's library in Florence. There he had access to a fourteenth-century manuscript of the Roman author, and politician Cicero's *Familiar Letters* – a manuscript he showed had been copied from a ninth-century manuscript to which he also had access. Poliziano found that the pages of the manuscript in the Medici library had been wrongly bound – a whole gathering of pages had been inserted in the wrong place in the text. In his miscellaneous remarks on correcting classical texts he explained:

> The manuscript has been bound by a careless bookbinder in such a way that we can see from the numbers of the gatherings that one gathering has clearly been transposed. Now the book is in the library of the Medici family. From this one, then, so far as I can tell all existing manuscripts of these letters have been derived, as if from a spring and fountainhead. And all of them have the text in that ridiculous and confused order which I must now put into proper form and, as it were, restore.

Poliziano concluded that the only text worth taking seriously was the ninth-century one, and he produced his own corrections to the available version of Cicero's familiar letters working from that manuscript.

In Florence, the seal of approval was set on a scholar's original work commenting on or building on the foundations of the revived classical heritage by its being received in a specially inscribed presentation copy into the Medici library. To have a work of scholarship like Poliziano's *Miscellany* accepted into the collection by Lorenzo de' Medici, to sit side by side with the treasures of the past, bestowed the ultimate stamp of approval upon its author. It virtually guaranteed him some kind of financial reward, a regular pension or even a long-term position in the patron's household. Nor was Poliziano alone in putting the expertise he had gleaned during his lengthy perusals of ancient manuscripts back into practice in Greek and Latin poetry of his own, which also took its place among the patron's literary treasures.

A generation before Poliziano, Marsilio Ficino, the son of Cosimo de' Medici's personal physician and a Greek prodigy, had similarly been set to study Cosimo's newly acquired, treasured Greek manuscripts. Beautifully handwritten and illuminated copies of Ficino's semi-mystical works on Plato and the *priscia theologia* (the supposedly original pagan theology from which Christianity had come) took their place permanently alongside the ancient texts that had inspired them in Cosimo's library.

Federigo da Montefeltro's library at Urbino, too, included presentation copies of original contemporary works by humanist scholars

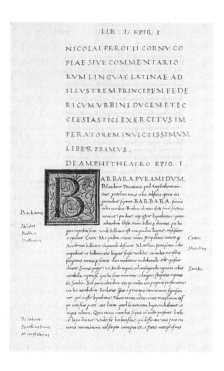

14. Niccolò Perotti, handwritten presentation copy of his *Cornucopia* for Federigo da Montefeltro

and commentators, specially written and dedicated. Niccolò Perotti presented his *Cornucopia* – a commentary on the ancient Roman author Martial's scurrilous *Epigrams* – to Federigo in a specially handwritten and finely illuminated copy on parchment, with a dedication extolling his virtues as a 'soldier of the Church'. The work was a compilation of marginal comments and emendations Perotti had made to an illuminated Martial he himself had copied from an older archetype. A generation later, Perotti's son Pirro used the presentation copy from Federigo da Montefeltro's library as the copy-text for a printed edition of *Cornucopia* issued in Venice. Perotti's work went on to become a standard classroom text in the sixteenth century, running through numerous editions with a variety of publishing houses, and becoming a standard school and university reference work.

Humanist learning developed in the rarefied competitive atmosphere generated among the rulers of the city-states of Italy, and spread from there to princely courts as far afield as London, Moscow, Buda and Krakow. With the rapid proliferation of printed editions of the classical texts made freshly accessibly by their scholarly efforts, a new market opened up in textbooks aimed at the schoolrooms, where the less privileged could acquire the technical skills necessary to study them.

Curriculum demands sometimes took the form of a perceived need for a definitive edition of a standard work, for instance the codified rules of law as expressed in the *Codex* of Justinian, reliably edited and produced for lawyers. But equally what was sometimes eagerly sought out for purchase was a particularly voguish or talked about set of comments by a distinguished teacher, which practitioners in the field were eager to lay their hands on.

In October 1513 the Low Countries printer Thierry Martens published a new commentary on a standard legal text by a distinguished professor of law at the University of Louvain. In a prefatory letter to his student readers Martens explained how the volume had come about:

Professor Nicholas Heems, doctor of humanities and outstanding professor of law, was tutoring a small number of privileged students in private, in his home, dictating to them an introduction to the Institutes of Justinian. By this excellent means he was able to make the whole subject of jurisprudence easier for them. Some of these young people transcribed their master's lectures with great accuracy, and later showed him their notes. When he realized how much they had benefited from his coaching he judged it appropriate to use the art of printing to produce a thousand copies. I, the printer, agreeing that such a book would profit you as students of law, and greatly advance your studies, accepted the handwritten text from your master, and produced a large number of copies in my printing house. Here I offer the fruits of my labour to the Faculty of Law. If you like this little work, in a few months I will produce more printed texts on the same sort of subject.

A year or so later, in a little volume of three assorted best-selling polemical pamphlets which had already been published in Germany, the same printer explained to the same students of Louvain why he had brought out his own edition when there was already one available:

I try to suit your pockets, as well as helping you with your studies, dear students – find me another printer who is so obliging! To that end I have printed these three little works as a separate, cheap volume, because I know that most of you will already have purchased the larger works they come bound with in the German edition, and that you will not want to have to buy those twice, just to get hold of these lightweight works.

Martens was behaving with simple sixteenth-century business acumen when he drew his prospective readers' attention to the way his decision to go into print with particular volumes depended on local circumstances and customer demands: a perceived need on the part of students for specified set texts; the popularity of a professor's lectures as broadcast by his pupils; a scandalous printed topical controversy for which the public is clamouring. Direct references to consumer demand are a regular feature of the prefatory letters and advertisements prominently placed as 'blurbs' on the title pages to Martens' conveniently compact volumes. They tell us that even the most intellectually ambitious publisher was committed to printing precisely what his readers would want to purchase. Equally, they remind us that the broader dissemination of learned material which print brought about was not necessarily governed by explicit and coherent programmes of reform – it might be the accidents of occasion which determined what did and did not get wide circulation.

Textbooks and educational works were regarded by the printing trade (then as now) as reliable earners, in a culture which increasingly saw individual self-improvement by means of a liberal-arts education as the most direct route to employment opportunities and prosperity. The Frenchman Mathurin Cordier was appealing to a recognized set of sympathies which he sent his commented edition of the elementary Latin grammatical work, the *Distichs of Cato*, to the printer Robert Estienne in 1533 with this covering letter:

Mathurin Cordier to Robert Estienne, printer and citizen of Paris, greetings. I dictated last year to my beginners in literary studies certain boyish trifles, to wit, a Latin and French interpretation of the famous *Distichs* attributed to Cato. It seemed to me therefore it would be a great saving of time if once and for all I checked the whole thing through rapidly and had it set down by your art of printing, especially as my pupils seem to desire nothing better. So I am sending you the little book and commit it to you, on this condition: if, when you have talked it over with friends, you think it is going to be some use to boys – and to yourself – print it with your usual care, with your types; if not, suppress it finally . . . But I can really imagine you wrinkling your brows at me for continuing a really rather wordy letter about trifles to hold up your extremely pressing labours. Goodbye then, and ever serve the interests of the present generation and posterity, as you do.

Lobbying his printer for a new edition of his popular legal textbook in 1525, the jurist Zasius appealed directly to his commercial instincts:

> Furthermore, since my collection is entirely attractive, useful and saleable, and will be especially attractive in Spain, Italy, France and the Low Countries, and since I have no doubt that it will also be well received in Germany among learned persons, I believe that if two thousand books were printed they would go quickly, even for half a guilder each. For Parrisius, the professor in Padua, Mercurino Gattinara, grand chancellor in Spain, Jafredus Passerius, chancellor in Savoy, Frosch, chancellor in Würzburg – all doctors – as well as Willibald Pirckheimer in Nuremberg, all doctors in the Chamber and many others have ordered this book in advance, of which I have sure knowledge.

On occasion, the textbook chosen to represent 'modernization' of the curriculum could be a pragmatic matter of availability – the possibility of the booksellers' supplying the necessary copies at short notice. In 1535 the English King, Henry VIII, retaliated against the refusal of the Pope and the canon lawyers of the Catholic Church to sanction his divorce and remarriage to Anne Boleyn by banning all study of canon law at the universities of Oxford and Cambridge. In the revised curriculum stipulated by Thomas Cromwell, all textbooks structured around the foundation texts for canon law were replaced by those of 'Rudolph Agricola, Philip Melanchthon, and George Trapezuntius'. These were indeed textbooks gradually entering a liberal-arts programme focused on classic literary texts in Latin (the educational programme broadly labelled 'humanism').

No explicit commitment to humanism is, however, to be found within the instructions for curriculum reform at Oxford and Cambridge. Rather, the injunctions demand 'that allegiance under the common seal of the university to the statutes concerning royal succession and supremacy be sworn by all', and that everyone attend 'a mass for the King and Lady Anne, his lawful wife, and Queen of the realm'. Dedicating to the Chancellor Stephen Gardiner his elementary textbook in logic adjusted to these new demands, John Seton explained that he had devised the textbook because 'after the royal injunctions there were a great number of outdated logic texts and I had at hand no suitable author whom I might teach to the young students'.

Textbooks, like the one John Seton wrote for his Cambridge students, were generally designed to be used in conjunction with the most readily available primary classical texts. The mid-sixteenth century saw the appearance of numerous competing commentaries and glosses on Latin literary works, like Virgil's *Aeneid* and Horace's *Odes*, and on the key 'moral' works like Cicero's *Orations* and Seneca's essays, which had provided the backbone for the publishing boom twenty years earlier. At the same time, a more advanced body of secondary commentary developed to facilitate the study of the Greek texts which had been the pride of the Venetian printing presses, including a growing body of specialist commentaries on the philosophical and scientific works of Aristotle. Unlike the manuscript commentaries on Aristotle which these works superseded, the Renaissance commentators were able to take advantage of the scrupulous work establishing a reliable text which the Byzantine exiles in Italy had dedicated their time to after 1453.

In an educational context, where the explicit aim of the exercise was the efficient dissemination of knowledge, the exigencies of the market were referred to without embarrassment by printers and authors to justify a particular publishing venture. Printers were, however, generally somewhat more coy where they were responding directly or indirectly to political pressure. In 1555 the Habsburg

15. Titian, *Portrait of Philip II*

Emperor Charles V stepped down as ruler of the Low Countries and handed over his powers there (and in his Spanish territories) to his son Philip II. In January 1556, the Antwerp printer Christophe Plantin produced a handful of copies in his print-shop of a small volume of verse. Composed by Plantin himself, the verses were a somewhat florid celebration of the new King's virtues and talents. They were printed in an elegant italic typeface, with several ornamental initial letters. The eight pages of text were bound in an elaborate morocco-leather binding, the centrepiece of whose intricate tooled front cover was an oval panel with Philip's title incised upon it. The poem inside was addressed to 'the very mighty and most serene Prince Philip II, by the grace of God, King of Spain, of England, of France and of the two Sicilies, Archduke of Austria, Duke of Milan and of Brabant, Count of Habsburg, of Flanders and of the Tyrol'. The thirty or so stanzas of the poem represent Plantin's fortune as that of a ship, destined to be driven hither and thither on the high seas, unless 'your Royal Majesty will deign to accept me as his servant, and unless your liberal bounty will favour me in my hour of need'.

Plantin's celebratory poem, produced as a volume from his printing house designed to show off the quality of his press and his own in-house bindings, is a particularly striking example of something like a trade 'sample'. The presentation copy of this volume which the suitor for preferment delivered to his potential patron proudly displayed its printed qualities – what was on display in this little book were the beauty of the fonts, the clarity of the printed text, the refinement of the layout on the page and, finally, the exquisite, compact desirability of the leather-bound finished product. With it Plantin hoped to attract to his product the attention of the new ruler in the region, and thus to gain his patronage – the financial support necessary to make printing viable as a commercial enterprise.

The bid to demonstrate Plantin's skill as a printer to a potential investor and backer was, it seems, gratifyingly successful. Plantin had no capital of his own, nor any other powerful financial supporters at this time. Within two years of his strategically drawing Philip's attention to the quality of his work (and to the ardour of his professed attachment to his sovereign) he was called upon to print the official tribute to Philip's father with a full state subsidy: a magnificent and sumptuous volume giving the 'Account of the Funeral Ceremonies of Charles V'. Shortly thereafter Plantin became Philip's official publisher (a title he managed to retain, even after 1576, when he also became official printer to the States General in the Netherlands, at the height of the Low Countries' rebellion against Philip's Spanish rule). So when the monopoly for revised service-books, as stipulated by the ordinances of the Catholic Church at the Council of Trent, came up in 1568, Plantin's connections to the royal house of the Netherlands enabled him to corner a large part of that market. In 1571 Philip gave Plantin sole rights to the printing and distribution of all such service-books for his Spanish territories.

By the sixteenth century, close political liaisons between a designated printer and the state were not unusual anywhere in Europe. In 1537, when François I of France was in negotiation with the German Protestant princes to form a political alliance against the Habsburg Emperor Charles V, Robert Estienne published a volume entitled *The texts of letters by which François, Most Christian King of France, is defended against the slanders of his enemies, and by which are explained the causes of the differences through which the present war has arisen between him and the Emperor Charles V* – a piece of pure propaganda, in which various French government officials, including Cardinal du Bellay, ghosted letters purporting to explain François's admirable motives for courting the Germans. After François had signed a controversial treaty with the Ottoman Sultan Suleiman the Magnificent in 1536, Estienne published a series of works on Turkish customs and practices, countering European prejudice against Islam with an account of the Turks' extremely civilized nature, their self-discipline and their courage in battle. In England, Henry VIII's printer Berthelet performed a similar service, publishing a sequence of books vindicating the King's political policies and doctrinal stance, particularly concerning the royal divorce.

Political pressures, then, as well as commercial ones, played a significant part in a printer–bookseller's publishing strategies. An apparently spontaneous publishing project, or one whose motivation appears purely academic or directed at the advancement of learning, might in fact be undertaken for other, far more pragmatic reasons. When Sir Thomas Elyot translated into English two Greek orations on the duties of kingship by the ancient author Plutarch early in the sixteenth century, they were apparently selected because of a purely personal, academic interest in ancient political thought. In fact, in making his choice Elyot was responding to an earlier publication by the Low Countries educator Erasmus.

16. *Portrait of Henry VIII,* showing the king as a patron and benefactor,
artist unknown

In 1516 Erasmus had appended Latin translations of precisely these two speeches, dedicated to Henry VIII, to a pedagogic work dedicated to Charles V, the *Education of a Christian Prince.* Erasmus hoped thereby to attract the attention, and the patronage, of two of the most powerful rulers in Europe, with a book which promoted the idea of a pan-European peace and an era of prosperity fostered by a ruling class educated on the model of ancient Greece and Rome – the so-called 'humanist' programme of learning. In 1522 Charles V recalled the dedication when he invited Erasmus to visit his court: 'You offered your *Education of a Christian Prince* to us, not only for the enhancement of our name but also to the great profit of posterity. We therefore reckon it part of our royal duty to show you all our gratitude as occasion may offer.' Thomas Elyot's publishing project was similarly associated with his sovereign Henry VIII's response to the Erasmus volume. Henry apparently wanted the two orations translated into English for those of his subjects who could not read Latin, so that they would associate with him the glowing tributes to humanely educated princes in the Plutarch.

A range of commercial, political and doctrinal pressures came into play when a publisher entered into an agreement with an author or editor to print and sell his work. We saw in the last chapter what an important factor patronage, and the financial security it represented, was in determining publishing strategy in the early printing houses. The examples of Plantin and Estienne add a further layer of circumstances which underpin the appearance of a particular printed book, in a particular location, at a particular time.

The shift in scholarly humanistic activities out of Italy and into northern Europe in the 1520s was linked to a significant alteration in the goals and aspirations of humanism as an intellectual movement. Italian humanists like Petrarch had had a strong vested interest in retrieving their intellectual 'roots' in the culture of ancient Rome (and their exiled Byzantine colleagues had had an equivalent interest in tracing their cultural heritage to the ancient Greeks). From the very outset, however, both these projects were underwritten by northern European financial backing. For the German merchants and bankers who invested in intellectual undertakings like Nicolas Jenson's printing press in Venice, the new learning was a status symbol and a potentially lucrative commercial undertaking. That a byproduct of printing was valuable technical knowledge in a range of new fields was, at least to begin with, probably incidental.

To the German merchant bankers the potential of the new technology to disseminate knowledge along the same routes they customarily used for other consumer commodities (including perishables like oranges) was immediately attractive. Around 1504 the German Johann Cuno, a friend of Reuchlin, made the journey to Venice to study Greek with the circle of specialists associated with the editions of classical Greek works being produced by the Aldine printing press. In search of expertise in one of the ancient languages fundamental to the study of sacred scripture in the original, Cuno was drawn to Venice by its reputation as an international cosmopolitan trading centre (the same reputation which had encouraged Bessarion to leave his Greek-dominated collection of manuscripts and

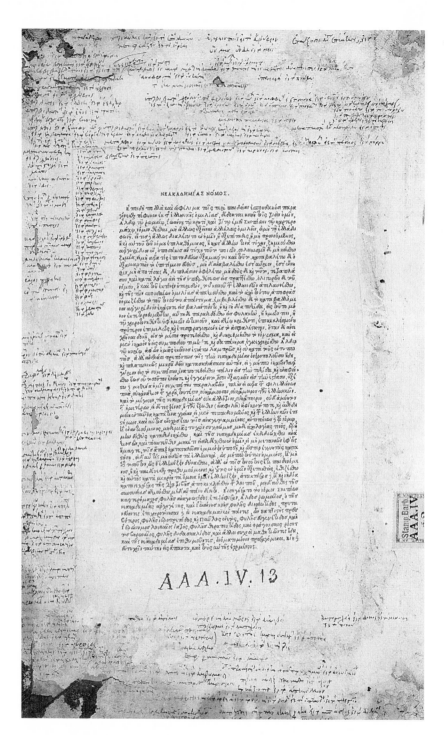

ΑΑΑ·IV.13

17. Aldus Manutius: the rules for his proposed Greek academy

books to Venice). In 1505 Cuno wrote to one of his German backers, Willibald Pirckheimer – a wealthy German and keen purchaser of Greek books – indicating that Aldus was prepared to move his scholarly circle and his printing activities to Germany:

> Aldus is preparing to move to Germany, to found a New Academy under the Holy Roman Emperor, in some place determined by him. With him will be various other men, some highly learned in Greek and some in Hebrew, who, while Aldus prints all the best books, will instruct the youth of Germany not only in sound scholarship, but, as Aldus claims, in military skill and exercises, so that those who are well versed in literature may not be proved unwarlike.

This would have been exciting news for the Nuremberg banker. 'I have every Greek book printed in the whole of Italy,' he had boasted the previous year. One of Cuno's tasks while in Venice was to acquire books for Pirckheimer's collection – a task also undertaken by another Pirckheimer protégé, the painter and engraver Albrecht Dürer, when he too spent time in Venice sponsored by the German financier, learning about Italian artistic techniques. Among the volumes which survive today from Pirckheimer's library, early Aldine editions predominate – thirty Greek editions, as against a handful from other Italian presses.

Nothing, however, came of the proposal to transfer the centre of Greek printing northwards. Instead, in 1510 Cuno settled in Basle, and began to teach Greek there. In 1511 Beatus Rhenanus – later to become Erasmus' most trusted editor of Greek texts – travelled to Basle expressly to study with Cuno, and because the local printing house under Johann Froben had an established reputation for printing scholarly works in Greek and Latin. The Froben press at Basle was already among the most famous in northern Europe for its editions and commentaries of classical Roman and Greek works, supported by the linguistic expertise of figures like Cuno. Rhenanus joined a team of scholars close to his age and interests – students, recent graduates and professors – from the University of Basle, on whom the press drew for advisers, editors, correctors and proof-readers. Following Cuno's transfer of his teaching activities to Basle, four of his pupils (Beatus Rhenanus and the three sons of the printer Johann Amerbach) joined Johann Froben, contributing their expertise to the press which issued Erasmus of Rotterdam's landmark scholarly edition of the complete works of St Jerome. Rhenanus and the Amerbach brothers acted as press assistants, editors, proof-readers and general print-shop personnel. In this way printing and scholarship moved almost literally hand in hand from the economically unstable Italian south to the financially buoyant German north, where printing and scholarship together became altogether less esoteric and elite.

This is how Erasmus' young colleague Beatus Rhenanus described his work for the press on a printed edition of the patristic commentator Gregory of Nyssa, balancing his own expertise, his Greek teacher's specialist input and the inevitable pressures of production in the printing house:

> Scrutinizing Gregory of Nyssa's works, I assessed them for their utility. My master Cuno had previously filled the text I was using with marginal annotations. I was burdened at the time, above all by my intensive Greek studies, but I thought, nevertheless, in spite of everything, that I ought to transcribe the text. This task was made more difficult for me by the fact that the Frankfurt Fair was imminent, and the printers were clamouring for the copytext I had promised them. Truly, although we have done our best to correct everything, we have not been able entirely to rule out barbarisms (that would have meant entirely redoing the translation), but like polishers, we have smoothed out the most troubling roughnesses, leaving other matter still to be shined up. Therefore, venerable master, I beg you to take up the defence of Gregory of Nyssa the moment he is published, even if he is not adorned with an elegant style, you will not despise him, I know, but you will

admire his elevated philosophy, you will recommend him, you will make him widely known. And please be kind about my corrections.

By the 1520s, the partnership between book production and scholarship had become a merger, and in the process both had become less exclusive. The brilliant scholar now devoted his energies to collating variant manuscripts for a publisher rather than for a private patron. While an edition was in process he lived in the printer's house, editing, correcting, proof-reading and seeing the work through the press. He both commented on ancient texts, wrote prefaces and publishing blurbs for the works of others, and (inevitably) wrote minor pieces of his own for typesetting and distribution well beyond the imagination of the old-style private scholar. Meanwhile, the publisher addressed the increasingly apparent commercial opportunities in mass markets like education, rather than catering for the exclusive demands of individual patrons.

Albrecht Dürer recognized the commercial potential in a commodity which could be mass-produced and sold steadily at a realistic price. When he had finally completed a demanding piece of work in Frankfurt – an altarpiece for the wealthy cloth merchant Jakob Heller – he vowed never again to undertake such a commission:

> No one could ever pay me to paint a picture again with so much labour. Herr Georg Tausy himself wanted me to paint him a Madonna in a landscape with the same care and in the same size as this picture, and he would have given me 400 florins for it. I flatly refused to do it, for it would have made a beggar out of me. Of ordinary pictures. I will in a year paint a pile which no one would believe it possible for one man to do in the time. With such things one can earn something. But very careful nicety does not pay. Therefore I shall stick to my engraving, and if I had done so before I should today have been a richer man by 1000 florins.

Single-sheet woodcuts, sold cheaply and widely distributed, represented a better investment of the artist's time and talent than one-off paintings for patrons who watched suspiciously for over-charging and were reluctant to pay until the work precisely matched their specifications.

In 1526, in the midst of preparing the sixth edition of his *Adages*, his best-selling encyclopaedic volume of proverbial sayings, Erasmus broke off from the project to describe the way the new technology of print had been commandeered by unscrupulous entrepreneurs:

> It is provided by law that no man shall sew a shoe together or make a cupboard, unless he has been approved by his trade guild; yet eminent classical authors, to whose works we owe religion itself, are published to the world by men so ill-educated that they cannot so much as read, so idle that they are not prepared to read over what they print, and so mercenary that they would rather see a good book filled with thousands of mistakes than spend a few paltry gold pieces on hiring someone to supervise the proof-correcting. You may say, it is not the seller's business to guarantee the buyer against any and every defect. Perhaps: but at least it should be so here, if the title-page promises diligent accuracy and the book is stuffed with blunders. And some are errors which even good scholars cannot at once detect. It is the innumerable crowd of printers that now throws all into confusion, especially in Germany. The first comer is not allowed to set up as a baker; printing is a source of profit from which no mortal is excluded.

What scandalized the serious scholar Erasmus (as it fascinated Dürer) was the fact that, not much more than half a century after the first appearance of the printed book, demand had turned it into a product beyond the control of the scholars and specialists. The book had taken over as the transmitter of European written culture, before scholars and educators had had time to come to terms with its power and influence.

· FIVE ·

NEW EXPERTISE
FOR SALE

In the spring of 1461, Mehmed II sent letters to Sigismondo Malatesta, Lord of Rimini, via the Venetian agent for the alum trade in Istanbul, Girolamo Michiel, requesting the loan of the services of the painter, architect and portrait medalist Matteo de' Pasti.

According to Mehmed's first biographer, the Ottoman Sultan had decided in 1460 that the time had come to build an entirely new palace at Istanbul (the palace now known as the Topkapı Saray), as a fitting symbol of his imperial dominion and his military conquests

1. Piero della Francesca, *St Sigismund venerated by Sigismondo Malatesta*

extending from the East to the West. The Sultan 'gave orders for the erection of a palace on the point of old Byzantium which stretches out into the sea – a palace that should outshine all and be more marvellous than all preceding palaces in looks, size, cost and gracefulness'. The site was selected after consultation with leading engineers and advisers who had toured Europe inspecting the newly constructed palaces and fortresses of the likes of Sigismondo Malatesta, and it was on the advice of these well-travelled experts that Mehmed set about assembling his own team of architects and builders:

> He was concerned not just to collect carefully the materials necessary for the work, but to choose those that were most expensive and most rare. He also took care to summon the very best workmen from everywhere – masons and stonecutters and carpenters and all sorts of others with experience and skill in such matters. For he was constructing great edifices which were to be worth seeing and should in every respect vie with the greatest and best of the past. For this reason he needed to pay close attention to the choice of workmen and materials of many kinds and the best quality, and he also concerned himself personally with the very many and great expenses and outlays. Furthermore, he had many overseers for these things, men who were exceptionally wise and experienced in such matters.

Mehmed's request for the loan of de' Pasti was thus an informed one, with which Sigismondo Malatesta swiftly complied, since the approach offered an opportunity for some form of political accord with what was more and more clearly the major imperial power in the Mediterranean.

It was not surprising that Matteo de' Pasti's reputation as an outstanding artist and overseer of building works had reached as far as the Ottoman Empire. He had worked as artist-in-residence and cultural adviser to Sigismondo in Rimini since the early 1450s,

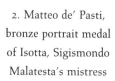

2. Matteo de' Pasti, bronze portrait medal of Isotta, Sigismondo Malatesta's mistress

producing a range of fine art-objects for him, from illuminated manuscripts to portrait medals of Sigismondo's mistress Isotta. Above all, he had been responsible with Agostino di Duccio for the building work on the Tempio Malatestiano – Sigismondo's ambitious monument to his own military glory, begun in 1453 (and left unfinished at his death in 1468). An inscription in Greek along the side walls of the Tempio proclaimed that, 'victorious on account of the deeds he had courageously and successfully accomplished, Sigismondo Malatesta set up this temple with due magnificence and expense to God immortal and to the City of Rimini'.

In contemporary documents, de' Pasti is described as the 'architect' of the Tempio, which was built to the specifications of the reviver of ancient architectural principles, Leon Battista Alberti. Alberti's architectural designs were inspired by the Latin treatise *On Architecture* of Vitruvius (first century BC), rediscovered in 1414. Alberti's own treatise *On Architecture* inspired an entire generation of Renaissance buildings, commissioned by humanist-educated princes like the Gonzagas, encouraging them to adopt the new vocabulary of classical architectural forms. Di Duccio and

3. Façade of
the Tempio
Malatestiano,
at Rimini

de' Pasti were together responsible for the lavish interior decoration of the Tempio Malatestiano, which featured an elaborate programme of themes and designs (one chapel was decorated with planets and signs of the zodiac), including figures of the Holy Fathers, Virtues, Liberal Arts, Sibyls and the Muses.

De' Pasti set out for Istanbul in October 1461. In an elaborately complimentary letter to Mehmed which he carried with him, Sigismondo Malatesta articulated with exquisite rhetorical care his sense of the importance of this cultural transaction between great princes. Cicero reported in his *Letters to Atticus* (he wrote) that Alexander the Great, mindful that for enduring greatness his likeness ought to be preserved for posterity, chose only the greatest painters and sculptors for the task. In just the same way, the incomparable Mehmed the Conqueror had discerningly requested the outstanding artist Matteo de' Pasti to produce a record of his appearance. It gave Sigismondo immeasurable pleasure to be able to respond in friendship to the Sultan by agreeing, exceptionally, to his request – princes from all over Europe had made similar approaches, but had been refused.

By making available to the Ottoman Sultan this 'close companion and gentleman of his house', as a preliminary gesture of friendship, Sigismondo went on, he dared to hope that a bond had been established between himself and Mehmed. Accordingly, he had ventured to add a further gift, one appropriate to the awesome majesty of the recipient:

> The greatness of your majesty is such that its formidable power easily exceeds the capacity not simply of myself, but of the whole human race. It seemed to me, therefore, that if what I should offer was to be of sufficient stature it should be something close to me personally, and unique to me, something which I believed would thereby give you the greatest pleasure. So I have decided to make you companion to my studies and my pleasures, and to share with you a substantial and erudite work on military matters, in which are to be found the great leaders and imperial rulers not simply of our own time, but of preceding ages, all of whom, incontrovertibly, and with one voice you are acknowledged to excel and surpass in merit. I devoutly hope that in your divine humaneness, you will receive the work kindly, with delight and with outstretched arms. We do not presume to offer you gold and gems, for these are of no consequence to us, and interest you still less. Instead we offer this unique work, crammed with the words and deeds of many of the most noble leaders of all time. I bestow upon you this precious work, painstakingly illuminated and illustrated, and which totally and altogether reflects my own heart and mind, and represents my deepest convictions.

The book Sigismondo sent as a personal gift to Mehmed was a handwritten copy of Roberto Valturio's original compilation of military tactics and equipment, *On Military Matters*, lavishly illustrated with diagrams and drawings of military machinery by Matteo de' Pasti himself. In this technical handbook for military leaders, Valturio made the claim that the military engines whose designs the book included had the authority of ancient Roman military science behind them, and that the work as a whole gave the enlightened princely reader access to the ancient secret techniques for wielding imperial power – the *arcana imperii*.

Valturio was also a member of Sigismondo's personal entourage. Indeed, he had drafted the highly wrought Latin letter to Mehmed on Sigismondo's behalf which accompanied the gift-copy of his book. Valturio's *On Military Matters* carried a dedication to Sigismondo, which celebrated him as the exemplary modern prince and general, the only one worthy to be classified among the ancients. The dedication included elaborate praise for Sigismondo's cultural achievements in Rimini, and commended his intellectual discernment in choosing the sophisticated figural reliefs to decorate the interior of the Tempio Malatestiano (reliefs in whose design and execution de' Pasti had participated):

> These representations appeal especially to learned viewers, who are almost entirely different from the common run of people – not least because to appreciate the appearance of the figures it is necessary to have knowledge of characteristics which you (Sigismondo) have derived from the secret depths of philosophy.

Several finely drawn and topographically accurate maps of Italy and the Adriatic were included with the book – further gifts of significant value, appropriate to a ruler with expansionist ambitions towards Europe, and providing further evidence that the donor was a formidably powerful person, exceptionally well-informed in the most modern aspects of strategy and warfare.

This cultivated transaction between Sigismondo and Mehmed depended for its success on the specialist talents of the men who

4. Relief panel of the goddess Diana in the Tempio Malatestiano

served them as advisers and facilitators. Sigismondo's advisers gave him power-broking material to trade with Mehmed; Mehmed in his turn would have had his linguistic experts translate Sigismondo's elegant letter into equally elegant Turkish or Greek, and have given his military experts and cartographers access to the gifts of maps and book. Matteo de' Pasti was to serve Mehmed for a specified period of time, and would have been rewarded with a stipend and lavish gifts (as Mehmed later rewarded the 'loaned' Venetian artist Gentile Bellini).

For the patron, the financial investment in these kinds of service was well worth while. His privileged access to the services of a scholarly expert in Roman military history like Valturio gave him a potential advantage in the political power stakes – this new knowledge was the raw material for rapidly developing modern expertise in new fields like cartography and ballistics. Sigismondo of Rimini effectively owned both Valturio's command of ancient Roman military tactics and Matteo de' Pasti's understanding of Vitruvius' ancient architectural principles (which they applied to works directly tailored to his requirements). The job of the specialists who served the great prince was to transform the pure knowledge of which they were masters into the specific applied projects which would enhance his prestige and renown. The valuable artefacts which they created (or obtained) for their patron were at the same time intrinsically costly commodities and potentially exploitable as the basis for a significant power-broking transaction (like the offer of up-to-the-minute tactical military expertise and precise cartographic data to Mehmed). Even Sigismondo's letter to Mehmed – beautifully crafted so as at once to flatter and to draw the recipient into a mutually advantageous, intimate relationship – was such an object, a piece of scholarly expertise composed by Valturio in his capacity as Sigismondo's Latin secretary and professional persuader (following the codified rules of classical rhetoric).

In the event, this particular attempt at cultural exchange failed. The Venetians, forewarned of Mehmed's request to Sigismondo by the agent who had brought the original message from Istanbul, were on the look-out for de' Pasti, anxious to check that he travelled as an artisan and cultural ambassador rather than as an emissary on a political mission. On the island of Crete he was detained by the Venetian authorities there. After inspection, the letter, maps and book were confiscated (judged, correctly, to be sensitive material militarily) and de' Pasti was sent back to Rimini. But over the period of construction of Mehmed's new palace a number of Italian artists, including Costanzo da Ferrara and Gentile Bellini (temporarily released from his contract repairing the frescos in the Doge's palace in Venice), did successfully make the journey to Istanbul and contribute to the fabric of the building.

Prominent Renaissance artists like Matteo de' Pasti were also officially experts in the practical, construction aspects of the manufacture of works of art. It was these practical skills above all which were in the forefront of demand from those who employed them. In 1482 Ludovico Sforza, Duke of Milan, acquired Leonardo da Vinci's services as a surveyor and military engineer – as a match, in other words, for Sigismondo of Rimini's Valturio. Leonardo had advertised the military and surveying aspects of his talents prominently in a formal letter by which he approached Ludovico for his patronage:

I have perused and studied the works of all those who call themselves inventors of the machinery of war, and I find that their inventions are in no way different from the ones generally in use already. Accordingly, I dare to address myself to your Excellency, and to offer to show you the following:

I am able to build very light, sturdy and portable bridges, to pursue and, when necessary, rout the enemy. I can build others which are more solid, which are fire- and attack-resistant, and easy to raise and take down. And I can equally burn and destroy those of the enemy.

To establish a fortified location, I know how to empty ditches of water, and how to build any number of bridges, battering rams, scaling ladders and other engines used in this sort of engagement.

I can also construct underground tunnels and secret passage-ways, noiselessly, to arrive at a designated location, even if these have to be dug under ditches or rivers.

Where cannon cannot be used, I can build catapults, and other marvellously efficient, little-known machines. In short, according to need I can build an infinite number of diverse engines, both for attack and defence.

Even when he came to inventory his peacetime talents, Leonardo listed his technical skills as a specialist in waterworks and as a caster of large-scale bronzes alongside his aptitude in painting:

In times of peace I believe I can give perfect satisfaction to the equal of any other in architecture and the construction of build-ings both public and private, and in guiding water from one place to another. I can carry out sculpture in marble, bronze, or clay, and also I can do in painting whatever it is possible to do, as well as any other, whoever he may be. Again, the monumental bronze horse you wish for may be taken in hand, which is to be the immortal glory and eternal honour of the prince your father of happy memory, and of the illustrious house of Sforza.

Knowing how to cast in bronze was a skill equally appropriate to the manufacturer of monumental sculpture and to gun tech-nology. Indeed, the casting of a monumental equestrian statue on which Leonardo did embark for Ludovico Sforza had to be post-poned in 1494 when the huge quantity of bronze purchased for its casting was diverted at the last moment to Duke Ercole d'Este of Ferrara, who urgently needed it for making cannons. When Leonardo moved to the employment of Cesare Borgia in 1502 it was once again his considerable talents as a surveyor which made him

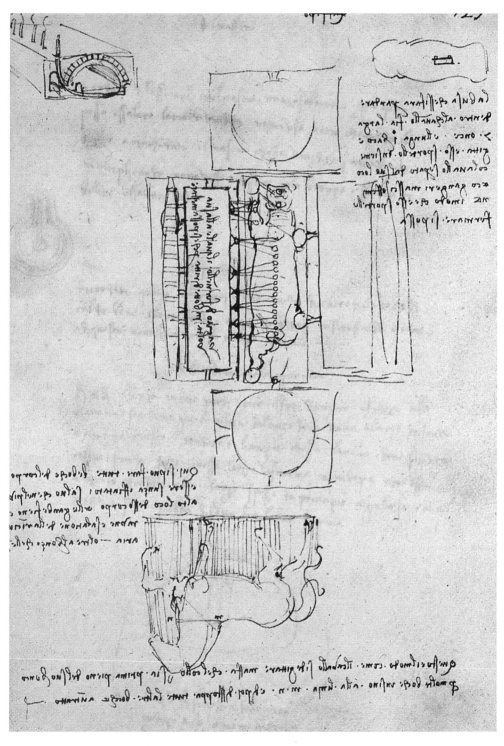

5. Design for a casting pit for the Sforza bronze horse by Leonardo da Vinci

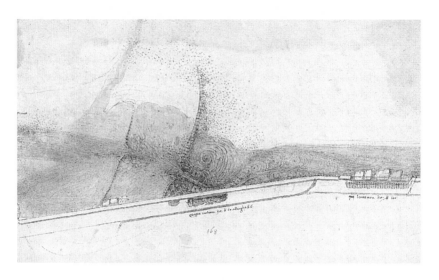

6. Leonardo's abortive plan for diverting the River Arno

an attractive hiring proposition. He inspected the fortifications of all the Borgia possessions, including the recently regained Imola (a strategic territory which had belonged to Cesare's father Pope Alexander VI), and conceived a number of drainage and dredging schemes. Back in Florence, working for the current rulers, the Soderini, in 1503, Leonardo embarked on his most ambitious hydraulics project – to divert the River Arno so as to give Florence direct water access to the sea (the scheme failed spectacularly).

The artists most highly in demand with noble employers in the period around 1500 were those with drafting, engineering and architectural talents as well as creative and aesthetic flair. Leonardo's services and those of his rival, the painter and sculptor Michelangelo Buonarroti, were competed for by patrons with military ambitions or grandiose building projects in mind. Their talents in the purely decorative arts were an added bonus. In 1506 Michelangelo was invited to Istanbul by Mehmed II's son Bayezid, to design and build a bridge over the Golden Horn. Unlike his father Mehmed, Bayezid was not interested in Michelangelo's artistic talents, since he disapproved in general of representational art, but he did set considerable store by the skills which were later to win Michelangelo the commission for the renovation of the façade of the church of San Lorenzo for the Medici in Florence (in preference to Leonardo). Although both were approached by the Ottomans, neither Leonardo nor Michelangelo actually travelled to Istanbul. (In 1519 Tomaso di Tolfo wrote to Michelangelo on behalf of Bayezid's son Selim, attempting to persuade him to visit Turkey, or at least to send a first-class painter in his place.)

Cultural exchanges between prominent patrons, facilitated by artistically and intellectually gifted individuals, were the arteries along which Renaissance art and specialist knowledge flowed. The new learning circulated among the rich and privileged, from London to Moscow, as one of the many conspicuous ways in which they advertised their magnificence to one another. Transactions might

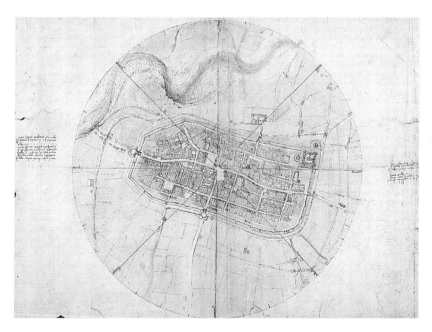

7. A technical surveying drawing of the island of Imola by Leonardo da Vinci

8. Drawing of a military machine from
Valturio's *De re militari*

take place on the basis of friendship or alliance sought (as in that between the Lord of Rimini and the Ottoman Sultan); they might also represent more provocative gestures. Shortly after his overtures to Mehmed, Sigismondo Malatesta presented another copy of Valturio's *On Military Matters* to his political enemy Federigo da Montefeltro in Urbino, presumably thereby exciting Federigo's book-collecting envy (because Sigismondo had access to such superb intellectual expertise and artistic talent) while at the same time asserting his own military superiority (since Valturio's treatise compared Sigismondo favourably to Alexander the Great). At least in the former respect the gift hit its mark: many of the carved reliefs depicting military incidents with which Federigo had his palace at Urbino decorated in the 1470s were based on Valturio's designs.

It was Michelangelo's proud boast that he had always worked in great households, for noble patrons: 'I was never the kind of painter or sculptor who sets up a shop for that purpose.' It was important to the status-conscious artist–engineer that he was not paid for his work as 'piecework' (like a small tradesman), but was rewarded with a stipend. Within the household he then 'served' its head in whatever capacities were required of him (from mounting the stage machinery for entertainments to copying maps of the fortifications). For an exceptionally beautiful piece of artistic work he might receive gifts (of the kind exchanged between those of comparable rank) from his patron in recognition and gratitude. Belonging to a great Court or house thus meant, for Michelangelo, that his social status had shifted from that of a tradesman to that of a gentleman in service. (Nevertheless, at table in the great house the artist–engineers sat with tailors, musicians and other members of the salaried household.

Those who rose in this way precipitately from artisan status into the entourages of the heads of great houses because of their prestige-related talents nevertheless worked strictly to order – however original the composition of a letter or a painting, it was understood to be the patron's product, and it was his (or her) enduring name which the work circulated and preserved for posterity. A fine piece of commemorative art like the medal of Leonello d'Este in bronze with which in the 1440s Pisanello marked Leonello's marriage to Maria of Aragon bears the legend 'Leonello d'Este, Marquis of Ferrara', while the inscription on its obverse reads, 'the work of Pisanello the painter'. But patrons who regarded their art as more directly a matter of perpetuating their fame were not prepared to permit their artists that privilege (ancient Roman medals were, in any case, unsigned). Sigismondo Malatesta had medals of himself and his mistress Isotta buried in the foundations of his buildings for posterity. On most of the medals which Matteo de' Pasti produced for him the artist's name is missing – sometimes apparently having been erased from the design just before the medal was cast.

One of the most prominent among those who sought lasting fame in their collections of rare and beautiful books was Pope Nicholas V, who in the 1450s (according to his successor, Pius II) created 'a most ornate library of old and new codices' in Rome,

9. Pisanello, portrait medal
of Leonello d'Este

'in which he assembled about three thousand volumes'. Nicholas
used his position (and his wealth) as head of the Western Church
to build up a magnificent collection of Greek and Latin manuscripts,
including copies of works hitherto entirely unknown in the West.
Conceived as a definitive collection of exemplary copies of all key
ancient and contemporary works, it subsequently formed the basis
for the great public Vatican Library. As the first Vatican librarian,
Bartolomeo Platina, wrote around 1480, to appreciate Nicholas's
personal dedication to assembling his fine collection 'one has only
to look at the inventory of the papal library so marvellously
increased by his industry and generosity'.

The private passions of other individual popes, like Paul II's
penchant for precious gemstones and cameos, might have enhanced
the general magnificence of the Roman Catholic Church, but rare
books, once made available to the company of experts in the ancient
languages who comprised the papal secretariat, made a substantial
contribution to its reputation for intellectual authority and erudition. Nicholas's enthusiasm led to a sustained programme of
transcribing and above all translating the works of antiquity which
lastingly affected developments in Western intellectual thought. The

Vatican achieved something of a propaganda coup by ostentatiously appropriating and making its own the resources of the new intellectual movement triggered by the recovery of the heritage of ancient Greek and Roman writings.

The key figures in this process were the specialists in Greek within the Vatican. Latin was the language in which Church business was conducted in Rome, and the advisers and secretaries brought from all over Europe to fill the posts in the papal office (the Curia) were all skilled Latinists, who produced the huge volume of papal correspondence with the international Church in increasingly elegant classical Latin. But since the early years of the fifteenth century there had also been a significant Greek presence in the papal Curia. The long-term attempts at reconciliation between the Roman Church and the Greek Church in Byzantium, made increasingly urgent by the strong Ottoman presence just east of Constantinople, required officials in the Curia who were equally competent in Greek. After the Council of Florence in 1438, as we saw in Chapter 1, a number of Byzantine Greeks committed to the union of the Greek Orthodox and Roman Churches joined the papal Curia in this capacity, among them Isidore of Kiev, Bessarion and the talented Cretan linguist George of Trebizond (Trapezuntius).

When Nicholas V became pope in 1447 he eagerly exploited the scholarly resources now to hand in his secretariat, and launched an intensive programme of translating the major classical texts from Greek into Latin, using the Vatican team of in-house specialists. A significant body of material was thereby made available for study by Latinists which had hitherto been unstudied in western Europe, though for the most part continuously attended to by Greek and Arabic speakers in eastern Europe. In addition to a predictably wide range of Biblical commentaries and other theological works, Trapezuntius rendered into serviceable Latin a number of important secular scientific texts, including all Aristotle's works on animals (*On the History of Animals, Of the Parts of Animals* and *On Reproduction in Animals*).

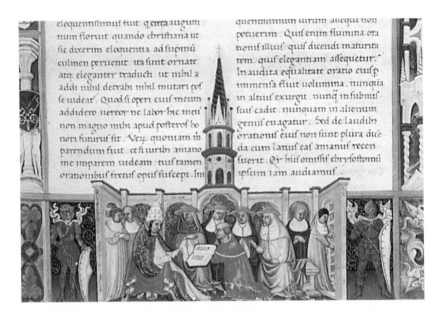

10. Trapezuntius presenting his translation of Chrysostom's *Commentary on the Gospel of St Matthew* to Pope Nicholas V. The bearded cardinal is Bessarion

The sheer bulk of the translations Trapezuntius, Bessarion, Theodore Gaza and other Greek specialists carried out in the papal office and the speed at which they produced it (in beautifully hand-written and illustrated copies suitable for the Pope's precious library) was nothing short of phenomenal. The papal secretariat became something like a translating sweatshop – Trapezuntius complained that the Pope 'would not allow us to relax or take our ease, even after so many and such arduous labours' on his behalf. It is hardly surprising that papal propagandists used this surge of scholarly productivity as the basis for a public claim to a new era in the authority and learning of the Roman Church. It was, after all, the new experts in classical Greek and Latin themselves who were professionally responsible for writing all papal letters and documents.

In an elegant piece of rhetorical sleight-of-hand, Nicholas's aspiration to make his library a complete collection of exemplary copies of the works required for Christian scholarship (a goal reminiscent of the one Vespasiano da Bisticci had set when establishing the blueprint of Federigo da Montefeltro's collection) was transformed into something more ideologically ambitious. Rome would be the guardian of Christian orthodoxy, the Pope the custodian of both the Greek and Roman intellectual traditions. Although Cardinal Bessarion never actually became pope, he (and his Greek-centred scholarly activities) became a symbol of the shift in the true Church's dominion from east to west. The idea of a transfer of dominion (*translatio imperii*) to a new, Western, unified Church became even stronger after the fall of Constantinople. From then on the group of scholars round Bessarion dedicated themselves to the task of preserving and interpreting the pagan and Christian heritage of the Hellenic world. This, the Church at Rome proclaimed, was to be the Golden Age of the Christian Church.

The everyday reality of the Vatican project, however, was less grandiose. Between March and December 1451, directly instructed by Nicholas V, Georgius Trapezuntius undertook a new translation of the ancient astronomer Ptolemy's important work of mathematical astronomy, the *Almagest*. The *Almagest* contained a comprehensive treatment of planetary theory, eclipses and the fixed stars, and was the basis for all sophisticated work on astronomy until well into the seventeenth century (when the work of Tycho Brahe and Johann Kepler finally superseded it). The Latin translation available in the West was an extremely literal one, made from an Arabic text in the twelfth century. For his translation Trapezuntius had access both to Nicholas's manuscripts and to those in Cardinal Bessarion's equally magnificent collection.

Although, as we saw, Ptolemy's *Geography* enjoyed a considerable vogue among book collectors because of the beauty of the maps that went with it, it was the *Almagest* which was the key text for calculating the movements of the heavens. All navigation and long-distance travel depended upon chart and compass readings derived mathematically from it. Trapezuntius had, apparently, always had a personal interest in astronomy. Now, he not only produced a new translation as instructed, but, at the same time, composed a lengthy original commentary on the text.

The unsolicited commentary immediately caused problems for Trapezuntius. The opinions he expressed with characteristic forcefulness did not conform with those of other distinguished members of the Pope's team of advisers. Having consulted his experts, including Bessarion, Nicholas V declined the *Almagest* commentary, whereupon Trapezuntius withdrew his dedication to him of the translation. Trapezuntius then took both translation and commentary, and left Rome for the Court of Alfonso of Aragon, King of Naples, in search of alternative patronage. In Naples he continued to work on his commentary, and rededicated both commentary and translation to Alfonso. Meanwhile, under Bessarion's direction a series of Vatican-sponsored mathematicians and astronomers (including ultimately Regiomontanus) produced detailed attacks on Trapezuntius' *Commentary*, designed to cast doubt on his competence in astronomy.

Trapezuntius' misfortune was to hold specialist views which came into conflict with the views of other members of the Pope's team of experts and which thus could not be expected to suit his patron. Pope Nicholas aspired to spearhead a collection of authoritative texts and translations of the great works of antiquity, and commentaries upon them – dissension among his advisers was hardly compatible with such a goal. The *Almagest* was, in any case, not merely a difficult, but also a theologically sensitive text. On its complex mathematical calculations depended the case for a geocentric universe (a world in which all heavenly bodies including the sun rotated around the earth). Trapezuntius had broken the first rule of patronage – retention as an adviser depended upon the trained individual providing the services demanded by the patron. Independent opinion was irrelevant and potentially, as in this case, damaging to the patron–adviser relationship. No patron was inclined to risk having his name attached to a contentious point of view, which might be countered and demolished, damaging (rather than enhancing) the patron's reputation and prestige. There is no evidence that Alfonso of Aragon was any more delighted than the Pope at receiving the dedication of Trapezuntius' *Almagest*, although his general tendency to support those opposed to papal authority might have made Trapezuntius' heterodoxy attractive to him (he had previously taken under his personal patronage another rebel from the Vatican secretariat, the brilliant linguist Lorenzo Valla).

In 1465, still determined to gain the recognition for his *Almagest* commentary which he felt it deserved, Trapezuntius took advantage of the competition for cultural prestige between Rome and Istanbul as centres of the civilized world. Pope Paul II sent him to Istanbul to 'gain information on the situation in Greece and in the Ottoman territories' (in other words, on an intelligence-gathering mission for the Vatican), and Trapezuntius took the opportunity to rededicate his *Almagest* translation and commentary to the Ottoman Sultan, Mehmed II, who was known to have an interest in ancient Greek texts, in particular those on astronomy and geography. Mehmed's image-makers were keen to advertise how the Conqueror of Constantinople was consciously moulding his imperial dominion on an informed understanding of the classical tradition:

His Highness the Sultan used to read the philosophical works translated into the Arabic language from Persian and Greek, and discuss the subjects of which they treated with the scholars of his court. Having read the works of the renowned Geographer Ptolemy and perused the diagrams which explained these studies scientifically, the Sultan found these maps to be in disarray and difficult to construe. Therefore he charged the philosopher Amirutzes with the task of drawing a new, clearer and more comprehensible map. Amirutzes accepted with pleasure, and worked with meticulous care. After spending the summer months in study and research, he arranged the sections in scientific order. He marked the rivers, islands, mountains, cities and other features. He laid down rules for distance and scale, and having completed his studies he presented the Sultan and those engaged in scholarship and science with a work of great benefit. Amirutzes wrote the names of the regions and cities in arabic script, and for this purpose engaged the help of his son, who was master of both Arabic and Greek.

The Greek scholar, and prominent member of Mehmed's entourage, Georgius Amirutzes (also from Trebizond) was Trapezuntius' host while he waited for an audience with Sultan. It was he who proposed to Trapezuntius that he should translate the introduction to his Ptolemy commentary from Latin into Greek, and offer it and his Latin *Almagest* to Mehmed. Although Trapezuntius failed to meet the Sultan himself, this attempt at Ottoman patronage apparently fared somewhat better than those in Italy. Trapezuntius was well received by the Sultan's ministers, given lavish gifts and for several years thereafter harboured the hope of an appointment in the Sultan's learned entourage.

When Baldassare Castiglione wrote his nostalgic recreation of life at the Court of Urbino, *The Book of the Courtier*, in 1528, Federigo da Montefeltro had been dead for forty-five years. Castiglione's fiction transformed the grandiose extravagance of Federigo's palace and library, and the entourage which designed and sustained them, into potent symbols of a lasting dynastic fame which his ailing son Guidobaldo could not personally sustain. Amid the enduring monuments to Federigo, Castiglione has Guidobaldo's wife, Elizabetta Gonzaga, presiding over a sequence of leisurely discussions in which the artists and scholars retained in the household took part in virtuoso displays of quick wittedness, mental agility and good manners, so as to set the noble family in its best light.

The basic skills of the trained individuals with expertise in the fine art and literature of classical antiquity were those of the professional secretary and amanuensis. It was for their ability to write letters for the members of the family in exquisite Latin, to compose a flattering speech for a special occasion, to provide appropriate classical references round which to design a theatrical spectacle for celebrating a memorable event that they were retained in great households. The versatility which enabled Matteo de' Pasti to turn his hand to artistic design and execution in every kind of medium, or Roberto Valturio to pen both a technical military treatise and an elegant Latin letter, were of the essence. In the time when they were not engaged on specific projects they were, no doubt, expected to furnish witty ripostes and general entertainment of the kind Castiglione represented. The important and the banal went hand in hand as part of the same undertaking to serve the patron as and when required.

The occasions on which the household scholar–secretary was called upon to provide elegant compositions in prose or in verse, celebrating his employer's family and enhancing their international reputation for cultivation and splendour, might be of greater significance to the prince in question than to the world at large – the employer was, after all, paying for the compositions. Ludovico Sforza commissioned his resident humanist and poet to write verses on the death of his favourite falcon. In 1512, Isabella d'Este called for tributes upon the death of her beloved lap-dog, Aura. Since Isabella was a notable commissioner of works of art, commemorative elegies, sonnets, epitaphs and epigrams in Latin and Italian poured into Mantua from humanists all over Italy.

For any prominent figure involved in national or international public life, however, there were serious benefits to be gained by employing those with a literary interest in ancient texts and the associated skills in Latin and Greek composition. A humanistic literary training in the use of formal languages was of huge benefit to royal ministers, civil servants, secretaries, ambassadors and all those involved in the conduct of international diplomatic business.

When Catherine of Aragon arrived in England to marry Henry VII's eldest son, Prince Arthur, he welcomed her in English and she replied in Spanish. Formal speeches were then exchanged by the ecclesiastical attendants of both parties in Latin. Faced with the diversity of vernaculars spoken by the various great houses of Europe, an increasingly elegant Latin was used whenever exchanges were required – in writing or in person – between them. Beyond Europe, to the east, Greek sometimes served the equivalent function – the entourages of the Ottoman and Egyptian Mamluk sultans contained highly qualified Greek scholars for their international correspondence. In the struggles between the Archduke Ferdinand of Austria and the Ottoman Sultan Suleiman for possession of Hungary in the 1530s and 1540s, diplomatic correspondence was exchanged between the two powers in Latin.

Not all prominent political figures felt the need to be competent in the language of diplomacy themselves, preferring to be well supported by professional linguistic experts. In 1526, Edward Lee, English Ambassador to Spain, reported that 'The Emperor, Charles V, hath no pleasure to speak Latin, although he understand; and I can speak no French, nor well understand it.' Charles was himself a prime example of the complexity of the language issue in the Renaissance. He was born in Flanders and raised at the Burgundian Court, whose spoken language was French (though his grandfather Maximilian was a native German speaker). When he became emperor in 1519, however, he marked his commitment to his Spanish territories by deciding to make Spanish his public political language, thus establishing Spanish, by implication, as the dominant vernacular in Europe. In dedicating to Charles his *Education of a Christian Prince* in 1516, Erasmus advised him to learn the languages of his dominions. In 1543, Charles, in his turn, instructed his son Philip to master Latin (as he had singularly failed to do himself):

> For you see how many lordships you must rule over, how different they are from one another, how far apart, and how separated they are by differences of language. And you, as their ruler, must understand those who live therein, and be understood by

them. To this end, nothing is more essential than a good command of the Latin tongue. For this reason I entreat you to learn it.

Those in scholarly service had to be prepared not just to discourse eloquently in Latin, but also to dispute, bargain, interrogate and generally master any public situation. Diplomatic dispatches were written in Latin, and vital vernacular correspondence translated. Thomas More, who as a young linguistic scholar delighted in performing in formal Latin declamations, supposedly first came to Henry VIII's attention when he helped a papal representative argue his case in Latin, following English seizure of a papal ship – 'he could report to the ambassador in Latin all the reasons and arguments by both sides alleged'. Many of the greatest Renaissance diplomats were first and foremost outstanding Latinists – including Niccolò Machiavelli, Francesco Guicciardini and Baldassare Castiglione (all of whom published elegant treatises, of lasting importance, on civil and diplomatic debating).

The best of these became 'resident ambassadors', posted abroad for significant periods of time, with their own supporting staffs of secretaries and advisers, largely at their own expense. (Although notionally paid a modest stipend, distance and the hazards of transmitting money meant that this frequently failed to materialize.) By the beginning of the sixteenth century all the great powers kept resident ambassadors at each other's Courts, and many great houses kept their own representative in those of their neighbours or allies.

The resident ambassador in his turn employed a confidential secretary, who had charge of the ciphers, kept the files and took down the dispatches from dictation. He selected his whole household staff, which would include a number of those capable of gathering information locally, in the local vernacular, and he paid them personally. This little coterie of educated and skilled individuals operated under conditions of obsessive secrecy, and with fierce loyalty to the state to which it was answerable. As the eminent

11. *The Repatriation of the English Ambassadors* from Vittore Carpaccio's series
The Story of St Ursula

Italian Latinist and diplomat Ermolao Barbaro wrote in 1490: 'The first duty of an ambassador is always to do, say, advise and think what contributes most to sustaining and increasing the status of his place of origin.'

The ambassador's task was effectively that of a political intelligence officer – his diplomatic instructions required him to report frequently and minutely everything of possible political importance. By the beginning of the sixteenth century the diplomatic dispatches sent home packed with information had been standardized in form throughout Europe. Immediately after the greeting, the ambassador was expected to note, first, official correspondence recently received, usually including pieces acknowledged in his last dispatch, and second, the date of that last dispatch, of which either a summary or a copy was enclosed. Then followed the body of the letter, supported by transcripts of relevant documents. Then, before the formal close, came the place and date of the dispatch, often with the exact hour of sending so that the speed of the courier could be noted. At the very bottom of the sheet the ambassador signed. Resident ambassadors supplemented their dispatches with lengthier papers (reports and 'relations').

Eustache Chapuys (from Savoy) was sent to London as resident Spanish ambassador in 1529, and remained there, with two short intervals, for nearly sixteen years. He arrived at a moment when Anglo-Spanish diplomatic relations had reached a complete impasse, as a result of Charles V's categorical opposition to Henry VIII's determination to divorce his Queen, Catherine of Aragon, Charles's aunt. Whereas his predecessor had relied heavily on information passed directly from Catherine of Aragon herself, or via her household, or finally from prominent figures like Thomas Wolsey on the King's Privy Council who were in receipt of pensions from Charles as 'sweeteners', all these routes were now closed.

In this critical and politically sensitive atmosphere, Chapuys set about building an alternative intelligence network. He enlarged the embassy staff (getting into debt to do so). He took into his service several of Catherine's English, Welsh and Spanish former servants, including her Spanish gentleman usher, Montoya, who had served more than twenty years in England and whom Chapuys made one of his principal secretaries. He recruited half a dozen young English-speaking gentlemen from Flanders and Burgundy, and sent them to Court to gather information on his behalf. In addition to Montoya he appointed two secretaries who spoke good English, and provided each of them with individual English contacts. Finally, he engaged a Flemish personal servant, who accompanied him everywhere and whose carefully concealed linguistic talents enabled him to glean information when counsellors talked English freely in Chapuys' presence.

After the royal divorce had been finalized in 1533, Chapuys extended his intelligence network, hiring five or six full-time agents, who in their turn paid small sums to innkeepers and servants for information. For over a year one of Anne Boleyn's maids reported regularly to one of these agents. London merchants from The

Netherlands kept Chapuys informed about the movement of money, arms and English agents in and out of Antwerp, and also helped in transmitting his dispatches and handling his funds. He regularly entertained German merchants and Italian bankers, referring frequently in his dispatches to 'the merchants who visit me daily'.

Chapuys' situation was unusual, but the emphasis he placed on gathering information by all means possible was not. The combined influences of the printing press and improved communications produced an information boom of bewildering proportions. The most distinctive characteristic of the activities, not just of Renaissance diplomats, but of all the knowledge-facilitators in household service, was the collecting, evaluating, sifting and condensing into manageable instruction documents of licit and illicit information from every possible source.

By the second half of the sixteenth century the highly educated in-house secretary had become an all-purpose 'intelligencer' – someone specifically retained to absorb and process the increasingly unmanageable flow of information on all manner of subjects which might be considered relevant to the well-informed public figure. The household office of private secretary became, in effect, the forerunner of the parliamentary secretary or civil servant, researching topics, preparing documents and writing the speeches his master delivered on key public occasions. In 1581, in his educational textbook *Positions*, the Englishman Richard Mulcaster proposed that the busy public figure should employ a suitably qualified individual in the role of professional reader:

> For *readers* of yeares, of sufficiencie, of continuance, methinke I durst enter into some combat that it were beyonde all crie profitable, and necessarie, to haue whom to follow, and of whom to learn how to direct our studies.... They that haue bene acquainted with cunning *readers* any where will subscribe to this I know.
>
> Priuate studie tied to one booke led by one braine ... cannot

compare for iudiciall learning with the benefit of hearing one, nay of repeating to one vpon interrogatories after reading, to trie his iudgement, his keeping, and remembrance: which one hath red, and digested all the best bookes, or at the least the best bookes in that kinde, whereof he maketh profession. . . . Whose seruice, for the benefit that comes from them will saue their whole hire in very bookes, which the student shall not so much neede, when his *reader* is his librarie. . . . And therefore that great sufficiencie doth still call for great recompence to be tyed a stake for it all ones life time.

In this capacity as private reader–facilitator, the Cambridge-educated scholar Gabriel Harvey read Livy's *Decades* (in an edition of the text already flanked by the scholarly commentaries of two notable Livy specialists, Velcurio and Glareanus) with, and on behalf of, the Elizabethan courtier Sir Philip Sidney, late in 1576:

The courtier Philip Sidney and I had privately discussed these three books of Livy, scrutinizing them as far as we could from all points of view, applying a political analysis, just before his embassy to the Emperor Rudolf II. He went to offer him congratulations in the Queen's name just after Rudolf had been made Emperor. Our consideration was chiefly directed at the forms of states, the conditions of persons, and the qualities of actions. We paid little attention to the annotations of Glareanus and others.

As they went along, Harvey annotated the margins of his copy of Livy with modern parallels to the events described in the text, and cross-references to a number of modern works on political theory and military tactics – Niccolò Machiavelli's *Discourses*, Bodin's *Republic*, Lipsius, Sansovino. All these were rather radical, somewhat contentious texts, appropriate choices of supplementary reading material for an aspiring front-line politician like Sidney.

Armed now with a Livy personalized for him with a marginal commentary for his own specific use, he could then reread the text with its purpose-written comments alone or with his professional reader at his side. In this way the budding professional politician was provided with a short-cut route to the most up-to-date thinking on political tactics, and primed for the public occasions on which he could thereafter demonstrate his personal expertise and erudition. Ably briefed by trained scholars hired for the purpose, Renaissance performers on the public political stage were able at least to appear abreast of the rapidly expanding new fields of political thought, modern warfare and international law.

This kind of instruction for office began early in noble households. Among the most inevitably formative relationships between the new-style literary and linguistic experts and the households that employed them were those established in tutoring the great lord's children. In the fifteenth century, Guarino Veronese's tutoring of the d'Este children, and Vittorino da Feltre's tutoring of both the Gonzaga children and Federigo da Montefeltro, laid the groundwork for the assiduous use made by the courts of Ferrara, Mantua and Urbino of humanistically inspired literature, art and architecture to promote their lineages to international prominence. The fact that the programmes these gifted teachers devised for their noble pupils in Latin and Greek literature and culture were reassuringly similar was significant, since advantageous marriages were regularly arranged between members of these three distinguished families. The humanist education Guarino and da Feltre provided produced a whole set of common points of reference for their pupils, which in turn engendered an 'Italian' ambience, for which artists and authors could readily work.

The literary and appreciative skills taught by such humanists were regarded as at once fundamental and by and large ornamental – enhancing the manners and civil graces of their charges. Hence noble girls were educated alongside their brothers. And hence the interest in the antique which these teachers inspired in their youthful charges was further disseminated via the prestigious marriages these young women made. It is Elizabetta Gonzaga, rather than her husband Guidobaldo da Montefeltro, who presides in Guicciardini's imaginative reconstruction of urbane life at the Court of Urbino around 1510, just as Isabella d'Este had presided over the courtly debates imagined in Angelo Decembrio's earlier nostalgic version of the Court of Leonello d'Este.

In the 1540s, the English King Henry VIII's cherished son Edward was tutored by Richard Cox and John Cheke, two of the most distinguished humanists and Greek specialists produced by the University of Cambridge in the sixteenth century (a third, Roger Ascham, tutored Edward's sister, later Elizabeth I). Their first goal was to make him a competent Latinist. In 1544 Cox reported of his seven-year-old charge's progress:

> He hath overcome and utterly conquered a great number of the captains of ignorance. The eight parts of speech he hath made them his subjects and servants, and can decline any manner of Latin noune and conjugate a verb perfectly unless it be an anomaly. These parts thus beaten down and conquered, he beginneth to build them up again and frame them after his purpose with due order of construction, like as the King's majesty framed up Boulogne when he had beaten it down. He understandeth and can frame well his three concords of grammar and hath made already forty or fifty pretty Latin pieces and can answer well-favouredly to the parts, and is now ready to begin Cato, some proper and profitable fables of Aesop's, and other wholesome and godly lessons that shall be devised for him. Every day in the mass time he readeth a portion of Solomon's proverbs for the exercise of his reading, wherein he delighteth much and learneth there how good it is to give ear unto discipline, to fear God, to keep God's commandments, to beware of strange and wanton women, to be obedient to father and mother, to be thankful to them that telleth him his faults. etc.

By the age of ten, Edward was using Erasmus' manual for elegant Latin composition, the *On Copiousness*, and the standard textbook of graded exercises for speaking and writing according to the rules of classical rhetoric, and had begun Greek; by twelve he was writing formal speeches (orations) on set classical themes, in both Latin and Greek. On the theme 'Love produces obedience more effectively than fear', for instance, Edward composed the outline:

Begin with an introduction stating how useful this proposition is. Develop by stating my own feelings on the topic. Confirm the statement using love of women. Fear deters one from wrong-doing, but does not encourage one to do good. A range of classical examples. Debate [he lists headings for and against].

At the end of a full development of his theme, however, he abandoned his outline and ended with a modern example, closer to home:

But why pursue remote and ancient examples, when we have plenty to hand locally? Did not love achieve more for Henry VII, winning the hearts of the populace, than fear constrained them under that most cruel tyrant Richard III? When there is a struggle over who is to rule, do we not always see that the populace is spontaneously drawn to the one they love most, and repelled by the one they most fear? For the one happens voluntarily, the other under duress. Whence it clearly follows that love is a greater and stronger cause of obedience than fear.

Edward signed this exercise, 'Eduardus Rex' ('King Edward') – for in the midst of all this schoolwork he had succeeded Henry VIII as King Edward VI of England (in 1547). We may imagine that these classroom humanistic drills, placing ancient and modern examples side by side, and bringing them to bear on pressing contemporary matters (like the disputed English succession), stayed with him when he engaged during his brief reign in policy-making with his circle of ministers and secretaries.

The plan of Prince Edward's education owed a good deal to the humanist advisers who surrounded his father, among them the talented Greek scholar Thomas More. When More devised a best-selling fictional account of an ideal commonwealth, *Utopia*, published in 1516, his description of the direct impact of ancient Greek learning on the nobility of the perfect state was an idealized version of what those who served the young Henry VIII genuinely hoped for.

More's ideal of the intellectual educating his noble patrons by means of the learning of ancient Greece was far-fetched only in that it posited a Court whose learned advisers were Greek specialists rather than Latinists. In the 1520s, the Court of Henry VIII, in which More served, and where ultimately he became Lord Chancellor, had a high reputation throughout Europe for its commitment to the new erudite Latin learning. Like Prince Edward, Henry's daughters received a classical education from the cream of the new humanist intellectuals. When she in turn came to the English throne, Elizabeth I made much of the linguistic and compositional skills she had acquired as a girl, and liked nothing more than to perform in Latin (an elegant speech, or a graceful response to an ambassador) on important public occasions.

When Henry decided to divorce his Spanish Queen, Catherine of Aragon, he had a formidable team of trained experts on hand to provide him with the learned evidence that his marriage to his deceased brother's widow had not been valid under Church law. The close intellectual friendship between Thomas More, John Colet, Cuthbert Tunstall and the Low Countries scholar Erasmus had contributed, in the early decades of the sixteenth century, to establishing the English Court's solid reputation across Europe as committed to scholarship and the new humanistic studies. The English Court's reputation as a haven for the new learning and its associated independence of mind was politically helpful in Henry's

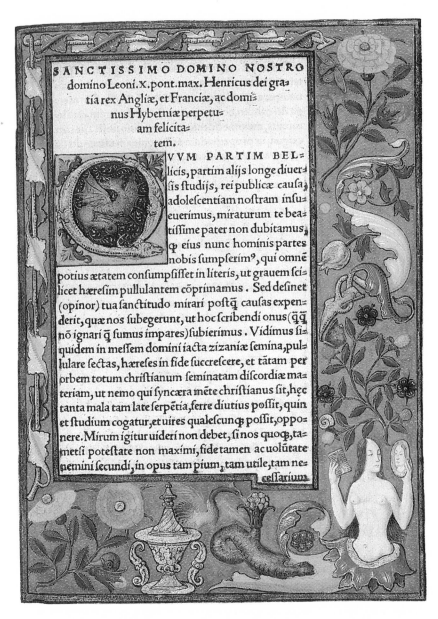

SANCTISSIMO DOMINO NOSTRO
domino Leoni.X.pont.max. Henricus dei gra=
tia rex Angliæ, et Franciæ, ac domi=
nus Hyberniæ perpetu=
am felicita=
tem.

VVM PARTIM BEL=
licis, partim alijs longe diuer=
sis studijs, rei publicæ causa,
adolescentiam nostram insu=
euerimus, miraturum te bea=
tissime pater non dubitamus,
qp eius nunc hominis partes
nobis sumpserim⁹, qui omnē
potius ætatem consumpsisset in literis, ut grauem sci=
licet hæresim pullulantem cōprimamus . Sed desinet
(opinor) tua sanctitudo mirari postq̃ causas expen=
derit, quæ nos subegerunt, ut hoc scribendi onus(q̃q̃
nō ignari q̃ sumus impares)subierimus . Vidimus si=
quidem in messem domini iacta zizaniæ semina, pul=
lulare sectas, hæreses in fide succrescere, et tātam per
orbem totum christianum seminatam discordiæ ma=
teriam, ut nemo qui syncæra mēte christianus sit, hęc
tanta mala tam late serpētia, ferre diutius possit, quin
et studium cogatur, et uires qualescunqp possit, oppo=
nere. Mirum igitur uideri non debet, si nos quoqp, ta=
metsi potestate non maximi, fide tamen ac uolūtate
nemini secundi, in opus tam pium, tam utile, tam ne=
cessarium

12 . Henry VIII's *Vindication of the Seven Sacraments, against Martin Luther,* illuminated for presentation to Pope Leo X

bid to achieve a more central and powerful position in European politics, in spite of his comparative lack of prominence in the international arena. In the interests of this image-making, in 1521, a team of scholars, probably led by Thomas More, had assisted the King in writing (or, more precisely, had 'ghosted') *The Vindication of the Seven Sacraments*, a well-researched and learned reply to Martin Luther's attack on the temporal powers of the Catholic Church, which was published with Henry's name on the title page. This competent (if unexciting) little work was widely distributed, and went through numerous printed editions, a testimony to the usefulness of the printing press for propaganda for the great powers, as well as for subversion. Thirty copies were sent to Rome, including a richly illuminated one for Pope Leo X himself. Leo X reputedly read and admired the work (and bestowed on its author the title 'Defender of the Faith'). When, following his divorce, Henry severed England's links with the Church at Rome altogether, his ministers were able to make the rift more intellectually respectable by referring to his acknowledged doctrinal competence in Church affairs.

Henry's divorce – the King's 'Great Matter' – was handled with the help of a 'research' team of experts with particular skills in textual scholarship – the very ones who had so competently manufactured Henry's *Vindication of the Seven Sacraments*. The case for Henry's divorce was put together by a team of expert 'readers' led by Thomas More and Edward Fox (Bishop of Hereford), which worked under the King's personal patronage. In 1530, these specialist advisers produced their official 'opinion', which was later translated out of Latin into English (possibly by Thomas Cranmer) under the title *The Determinations of the Most Famous Universities of Italy and France*. A short account of the negative ruling on the divorce offered by the continental theologians was followed by a treatise assembling a large body of textual evidence supporting the King's claim that the original dispensation from the Pope enabling him to marry Catherine of Aragon had been ill founded and contrary to canon law. Hence, the opinion concluded, Henry was fully entitled to set aside Catherine in favour of Anne Boleyn.

The material for Henry's favourable expert opinion was assembled by his household facilitators in exactly the fashion to be expected of trained humanistic text scholars working to a patron's brief. Alongside the case for the divorce, the same sort of scholarly effort was also harnessed to supporting arguments for the Henrican settlement itself – the definitive break with the authority of the Pope in Rome, in favour of the authority of the King in all Church matters. The efforts of a vast number of individuals taken on as advisers to this project survive in the form of anonymous tracts, annotated by Court officials, contributing to the argument.

For the royal divorce case, the procedure the researchers adopted was systematically to comb all relevant books and records for authoritative material which could be addressed to the case. They then collated it, and laid it out effectively to support the case they had been appointed to argue, in elegantly composed treatises of their own. Evidence of this process survives in the Royal Library in the British Museum in London in the form of a manuscript inventory of books found in Lincolnshire monastic houses around 1530. The list contains around a hundred titles, thirty-six of which are marked with a cross. The crosses indicate that a volume has a direct bearing on the divorce issue. In the copy of William of Malmesbury's *On the Deeds of the English Clergy* (a text marked on the list), which is in the British Library, the text has been marked in the margin where it deals with such subjects as Church councils, the authority of bishops, the authority of the Pope and the question of consanguinity in marriage. All those titles marked are to be found ten years later either in the King's 'upper library' at Westminster Palace, at Hampton Court or at Greenwich. In other words, all those works surveyed in Lincolnshire which could have been considered to contain material relevant to the King's Great Matter were acquired and transferred into the King's library – available for close consultation and transcription by the King's facilitators.

After he had finally achieved his divorce, and married Anne Boleyn in 1533, just in time for her to give birth to another daughter, the King always considered that his in-house experts had outclassed and outperformed both the official Church lawyers and the scholars of the Universities of Oxford and Cambridge. The curriculum reforms of the Universities under the direction of Thomas Cromwell replaced the entire study of Church law with a liberal, humanistic programme of study, of the kind the King's own close advisers in his Great Matter had received. As for the monasteries, whose precious books had provided Henry's advisers with their doctrinal ammunition, the assembling of books in the King's library had established a damaging precedent. The Privy Purse Expenses for the years of the divorce proceedings record substantial payments to various clerics (the priors of Sempringham and Spalding, the abbots of Ramsay, Gloucester, St Augustine's Canterbury and Evesham), for bringing books relevant to the matter into the King's library. Having discovered that they could market sought-after items from their libraries for large sums, the monasteries appear to have continued dispersing their collections for cash. John Bale claimed that the monastery libraries had been decimated well before Henry dissolved the monastic houses, the books and manuscripts 'sent over sea to the book binders, not in small numbers, but at times whole ships full, to the wondering of foreign nations'.

Throughout the divorce discussions Henry himself participated as a highly educated, concerned person, with a serious interest in the details of theology. His copies of a number of relevant works survive, including an influential work on the power of the Pope, Erasmus' commentaries on the New Testament, and a collection of Lutheran tracts in French. Henry's marginal annotations show him reading alertly, marking and cross-referencing passages relevant to his challenge to the Pope's authority.

But mounting an argument of the sophistication and thoroughness required for international theological debate demanded more than opinion framed on the basis of even an educated monarch's personal study. It depended on Henry's being properly briefed with appropriate views on public occasions. The image which had been successfully and widely circulated throughout Europe with the distribution of Henry's *Vindication of the Seven Sacraments* was reinforced in audiences with visiting ambassadors carefully scripted by the King's advisers. In 1529 he told Charles V's ambassador that Luther was right in demanding that the Pope and the Sacred College should revert to apostolic purity and abandon the struggles for secular power in which they had become involved. The evidence having been meticulously assembled by the King's advisers, Cardinal Wolsey let it be known that on the basis of his own close reading of scripture Henry himself had voiced personal doubts about the legitimacy of his marriage to Catherine of Aragon long before the divorce was mooted.

The success of Henry VIII's scholarly advisers and privy (private) counsellors in putting together the arguments he needed, to order, was a heroic moment for the new learning in England. In general, however, the eloquence and skills in negotiating imparted by the humanist training were less certain of success in an arena in which the financial outlay on such expertise by every great power was considerable. In July 1529, in the midst of the divorce discussions, Thomas More, Cuthbert Tunstall, William Knight (royal secretary) and John Hackett (English Ambassador in the Low Countries) were the English representatives at the signing of the Treaty of Cambrai, between the Habsburg Emperor, Charles V, and the Valois King, François I of France. Knight was a Doctor of Laws and one-time Fellow of New College, Oxford. He, More and Tunstall were the all-round scholar–diplomats of the English negotiators; Hackett was a technical specialist – an expert in commerce, finance and shipping disputes.

Charles V and François I met at Cambrai to negotiate, in general, the cessation of long-term hostilities between them and, in particular, the release of François' sons (the Dauphin François and Henri, Duke of Orleans) held as hostages in Spain since 1526. England was officially allied to France (England and France had together formally declared war on Charles in January 1528); Pope Clement VII was Charles's most powerful ally. Although in this line-up Henry's Great Matter was obviously significant (Catherine was Charles V's close relative, while Henry was in direct conflict with the Pope), the English diplomats were told that this was not to be an issue, but would be left to 'justice'.

English interests were tangential to the central objectives of the negotiations. The Englishmen came to Cambrai with demands for a renewed commercial treaty between England and the Low Countries (hence the presence of Hackett) and for repayment of the Emperor's longstanding and substantial financial debts to Henry VIII (some of them contracted by the previous Habsburg Emperor, Maximilian). They succeeded in obtaining the trade treaty, which was ratified in the cathedral at Cambrai on 5 August. For the rest, however, they were no match for the Emperor's negotiators.

The transcripts of the subsequent proceedings record inter-minable discussion of the imperial debts to the English kings, and also discussions surrounding the return of a jewel held by the English as security against a financial loan, the Fleur de Lys (a pendant in the form of a large gold lily set with pearls and precious stones), pledged to Henry VII by the Emperor Maximilian. In spite of the eloquence of the English, they were largely outmanoeuvred by the Habsburg and Valois ambassadorial teams. More and Tunstall came away with an agreement which proved generally unsatisfac-tory to the English Crown. The debts due to England had been whittled down from an estimated 290,000 écus to 185,000, and responsibility for them transferred to France, as part of François's financial payments for the return of the royal hostages. After elab-orate inspections and valuations, in the end the jewel was returned to Charles V without additional payment, nor did Charles have to pay the 500,000 écus damages incurred by his breaking a formal undertaking to marry Henry's daughter Mary. In this setting More and Tunstall's talents can be seen in proper perspective – oratory

and debating skills were essential in Renaissance diplomatic negotiations, but military might and political muscle were still the
deciding factors. It would not do to forget, however, that the capacity
of the great powers to manipulate tax revenues and play the financial markets, on which the settlement of the enormous debt
questions depended, was also crucial. By 1 July 1530, François had
assembled the 1,200,000 écus required for the release of his sons
by a combination of 'gifts' from the revenues of his nobility, town
grants, hearth tax and private loans. By November 1532, he had
also entirely paid off Charles's English debt.

According to More's son-in-law, William Roper, More once told
him that he would be content to be put in a sack and thrown into
the River Thames if he had lived to see three things achieved:
perpetual peace between Christian kings, the extermination of
heresy and a 'good conclusion' to the King's divorce. More, key
adviser and architect of the learned argument for the admissibility
in law, and before God, of the divorce from Catherine of Aragon,
could not in the end bring himself to endorse the case he had himself
helped to construct. His decision to dissociate himself from his royal
employer's public position led to his political disgrace, and eventually to his execution. In modern terms, his stand was a courageous
one, consistent with his learning, his personal integrity and his high
moral standards. But as Hythlodaeus stated plainly in *Utopia*, for
the learned adviser to a prince to offer advice counter to the prince's
stated principles and beliefs was unthinkable – a breach of the professional understanding between them, and an act of political suicide.

Many of the other highly educated advisers in Henry VIII's
entourage found it prudent to adjust their scholarly views to match
the line taken by the King after 1533, and, like Thomas Starkey and
Richard Moryson, to swear loyalty to him as head of Church and
state, backing up their oath with scholarly publications supporting
the Anglican cause. In the entourage of Henry VIII's political adver-
sary, the Emperor Charles V, there were pragmatists prepared to go
further to accommodate their princely employer. In the commercial

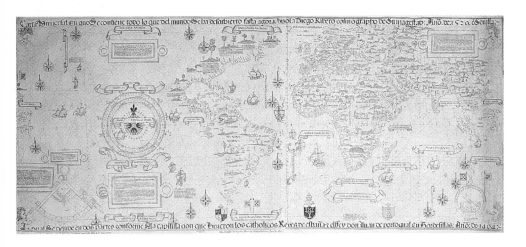

13. Diogo Ribeiro's world map

and territorial struggles among the great trading powers which followed the early voyages of discovery they were, on occasion, prepared to redraw the contours of the map.

Diogo Ribeiro's 1529 world map is outstanding both for its beauty and for the precision of its cartographic information. It is, for instance, one of the first world maps to represent accurately the east–west slant of the Mediterranean, and the angle of the Italian peninsula. The map records a vast amount of fresh information provided by successive voyages of discovery after 1492 – the contours of Africa, the southernmost tip of South America, India, the proliferation of islands of Indonesia and the coast of China. Glaringly anomalous amid all this accuracy is Ribeiro's positioning of the Moluccas, or spice islands (labelled Gilolo on his map), which have been marked significantly too far to the east. Since Ribeiro's map formed a key part of a 1529 trade settlement between Spain and Portugal specifically concerned with trade with the Moluccas Islands, this mistake is curious. In fact, Ribeiro's mislocation of the Moluccas was deliberate – a bending of the truth to suit the political purposes of Charles V, whose professional cartographic adviser Ribeiro was, and for whom the world map had been drawn.

A formidable team of cartographic experts supported each side in the negotiations between Charles V and the Portuguese King,

John III, when they attempted to settle their competing claims to trading rights to the spice-rich Moluccas – negotiations which began in 1524 and were concluded by the Treaty of Saragossa in 1529. The presence of an impressive array of map-making experts as advisers at these important diplomatic negotiations was not accidental – the issue of trade rights was a specifically cartographic matter. In 1493, following Columbus' Spanish-financed voyage westwards which had successfully (as he thought) reached the spice markets of the Orient by circumnavigating the globe, Spain and Portugal – the two most powerful commercial competitors in the oriental spice markets – had agreed under the Treaty of Tordesillas to a line of demarcation on the map 370 leagues west of the Cape Verde Islands (off Brazil). West of this line was designated the Spanish sphere of influence, and all markets opened up within this half of the map were automatically to be deemed Spanish possessions. East of the Tordesillas Line, all such new markets would be Portuguese. In terms of the known world (and the navigable routes around it) in 1493, the Portuguese acquired monopoly trading rights to the coast of Brazil and to the west coast of Africa; Spain acquired those rights to the 'new world' reached by Columbus. Conceptually, all travel westwards from the Tordesillas Line would yield Spanish markets, all those eastwards Portuguese ones.

Ferdinand Magellan's Spanish-backed voyage south-westwards in 1519, which successfully reached the known spice islands by a westwards (Spanish) route, threatened a commercial and diplomatic crisis. By this time Vasco da Gama (for the Portuguese) had reached the same islands (and the same potentially lucrative markets) by the eastwards sea-route round the Cape of Good Hope. It was clearly not enough to designate spheres of interests by westward and eastward movement from the Tordesillas Line – a corresponding line of demarcation was necessary on the other side of the globe, extending the Tordesillas Line through the poles and thereby dividing the sphere accurately into two hemispheres.

The key members of both teams of advisers at Saragossa had all been involved in producing the maps for Magellan (and therefore the Spanish) in 1519 – Diogo Ribeiro sat on Charles V's side of the table, Pedro Reinel and his son Jorge on the Portuguese side, although Charles V had written to the Reinels offering them a salary twice what they were currently receiving if they would join the Spanish delegation. Under the terms of the ensuing settlement, the Reinel maps (which showed the Moluccas well within the Portuguese sphere of influence) were discarded, while a version of the fudged Ribeiro map became an attachment to the settlement itself, providing the 'hard evidence' of exactly where the continuation of the Tordesillas Line ran:

> In order that it may be known where the said line falls, a model map shall at once be made on which the said line shall be drawn in the manner aforesaid, and it will thus be agreed to as a declaration of the point and place through which the line passes. This map shall be signed by the said Charles V, Lord Emperor and King of Castile, and by the said Lord King of Portugal, and sealed with their seals. In the same manner, and in accordance with the said model map, the said line shall be drawn on all the navigation charts whereby the subjects and natives of the kingdoms shall navigate. In order to make the said model map, three persons shall be named by each of the said lord kings to make the said map upon oath, and they shall make the said line in conformity to what has been said above. When the map has thus been made, the said Lord Emperor and King of Castile and the said Lord and King of Portugal shall sign it with their names, and shall order it to be sealed with the seals of their arms; and marine charts shall be made from it, in order that the subjects and natives of the said lord kings may navigate by them so long as the said Lord King of Castile shall not redeem and buy back the said right.

Thus acting as an expert adviser to a powerful and influential figure might on occasion involve the highly trained individual in 'cooking the books'. With regard to the Moluccas Islands, the Treaty of Saragossa admitted as much in its very rubric: on the map as authorized by Spain, the Moluccas would remain in the location agreed for as long as the Treaty held:

> This map shall also designate the spot in which the said vassals of the said Emperor and King of Castile shall situate and locate Molucca, which during the time of this contract shall be regarded as situated in such place.

SIX

A CULTURE OF
COMMODITIES

IN 1515, BY SECURING the double marriage of his granddaughter Maria and his grandson Ferdinand to the son and daughter of the King of Hungary, the Emperor Maximilian put the final piece of the dynastic jigsaw-puzzle in place and so made the Habsburgs the most powerful force in Renaissance Europe. As part of the contractual arrangements for the double marriage, Maximilian signed a pact of mutual succession with the King of Hungary and Bohemia, Vladislav II, Jagiellon, under which they agreed that, if the marriage of Maria of Habsburg and Ludwig Jagiellon should fail to produce a male heir, Maximilian's grandson Ferdinand (married to Anna Jagiellon) would inherit the throne of Bohemia and Hungary. If, on the other hand, Ferdinand and Anna's marriage produced no heir, the Jagiellons would inherit the Austrian monarchy.

As with every other political manoeuvre of his twenty-five highly successful years of imperial rule, Maximilian achieved this bold and (as it turned out) highly advantageous political move by spending extravagantly on every stage of the arrangements, from buying the necessary agreement on contracts to lavish parades at the ceremonial ratification. As usual, that impressive outlay of cash was made possible by large-scale loans from his personal banker in Augsburg, Jakob Fugger, known as 'the Rich'.

In May 1515, Maximilian wrote at length to his Council at Innsbruck, informing them that the marriage agreements were on the point of formal completion, but that considerable financial outlay would be required in order to mark the solemnizing of the marriage contracts (and their dependent political clauses) with appropriate

CLEOPHAS FRATER · CARNALIS · IO=
SEPHI · MARITI DIVAE VIRG · MARIAE
I
JACOBVS · MINOR EPVS · MARIA CLEOPHAE SORO
HIEROSOLIMITANVS · VIRG · MAR PVTATIVA MA
TERTERA · D · N
III
JOSEPH JVSTVS
II
SIMON ZELOTES CONSO=
BRINVS DNI NRI

1. Bernard Striegel, *The Family of Maximilian I and Mary of Burgundy*

2. Lucas van Leyden,
Portrait of Maximilian I

splendour, thereby ensuring that none of the parties baulked at any of the details at the last minute:

> We have therefore concluded that a meeting with our brothers, the King of Hungary and the King of Poland, should take place, and that in particular the King of Hungary's daughter should be formally delivered into our hands.
>
> Now we have reason to think, in fact, we have knowledge, that our two brothers will come to us with great array of followers, and with much regalia and other luxuries, making an imposing sight. It is therefore fitting that we too prepare ourselves for their arrival and our meeting, with an imposing array, with princes and other high personages, together with luxurious and expensive jewels and equipment. Furthermore, we must necessarily entertain our royal brothers and their children, as well as the

high personages whom they bring with them, using royal regalia, silver plate, and other tokens of honour, when the meeting takes place in our city of Vienna. As you may well imagine, we require for this a considerable sum of money.

We have arranged for 1000 horses with harness and equipment, and 1000 unequipped, together with our costly jewels and articles of luxury. We have summoned certain high princes and other people of rank, and are entirely prepared, as soon as negotiations are completed, to move immediately towards Vienna with suitable ceremony, to await the arrival of our brothers.

Inevitably, Maximilian continued, the expenses incurred by these essential shows of magnificence had already well exceeded what remained in the imperial coffers. He had no doubt, however, that his Council would agree to the loan arrangements he had had to make:

To achieve all this, we have made a financial deal with our counsellor, Jakob Fugger, through two letters, which we herewith forward to you.

You well know and realize how important this whole matter is to us, and what good benefit may come out of it for us and our children, as well as our lands and people. And for these reasons, we request you to accept the proposed loan with the above-mentioned Fugger, and to sign the above-named contract and letter according to the manner of our treasury, and to affix the seal; and to send it back to us immediately by postal courier, and not to refuse it nor delay with it. For in the gracious trust which we repose in you, we have counted upon this in our financial plans, and have arranged our affairs and departure accordingly, and have so planned for us and our family, and have also sent word to the princes and arranged with them that so soon as our negotiator writes that the main agreement with the two kings and the fact of our meeting have been concluded, we are to act immediately. But we cannot do this unless the loan from the Fuggers is carried through.

By October, true to form, Maximilian found himself unable to make the repayments on this and his other outstanding debts to the Fuggers – indeed, he actually needed a further cash loan. The two representatives he sent to Augsburg to negotiate with Jakob Fugger reported back to him on 2 October from that city. On the first day of discussions they had dealt with the matter of an immediate repayment of 12,000 gulden:

> We, with utmost zeal, opened negotiations with Jakob Fugger concerning an extension of time on the three points or articles, and first on behalf of the repayment of 12,000 gulden which is due. To this he gave us a detailed answer, namely that he had extended loans to Your Majesty for some time past, and in this year he had given to the smelting works at Rattemberg, Schwarz silver and copper, and to Your Majesty's treasury and other ways had furnished such large sums of money that the total amounted to 300,000 Rhenish gulden. Practically all this remains as yet unpaid to him. He also had not expected that Your Majesty would so soon seek a further loan, in view of the obedient loan which he had recently made on the trip to Vienna, with great difficulty and cost, to Your Imperial Majesty.

Jakob Fugger would only go so far as to say that he might be prepared to defer the repayment, if he in his turn was allowed to postpone repayment of 10,000 gulden he owed Maximilian's Council at Innsbruck, which was due in December. The following day the negotiators raised the matter of a further outstanding 58,000 gulden due from Maximilian. On this sum Fugger would not budge. If he once agreed to renegotiate, or accept delay of repayments, on contracts already arranged and concluded it might damage his credit, which in turn would undermine the financial creditworthiness of

3. M. Schwarz, *Jacob Fugger in his Office*

Maximilian's Council (since it needed constantly to rely on Fugger guarantees).

On their final visit, therefore, the negotiators raised their third item for discussion (as instructed). Setting aside the question of repayments, they offered Jakob Fugger extended long-term rights to the profits from Maximilian's German silver and copper mines in exchange for a further substantial loan. Fugger quickly pointed out that Maximilian had already given him rights to the silver for eight years, and to the copper for four years, as settlement on a previous sum advanced to the Emperor – rights beyond that were purely notional (and, furthermore, the price of silver had dropped by half since that agreement had been reached). A further loan was out of the question, and he proposed the names of other Augsburg merchants who might be prepared to consider the matter (the negotiators already had instructions to approach the Höchstetters if Fugger would not agree to further loans). In the end, however, Maximilian put further pressure on Jakob Fugger, and the money he needed was advanced, against an extension of the Fuggers' rights to all profits from the Schwarz copper mines until 1523.

In 1526, Suleiman the Magnificent, the Ottoman Sultan, whose empire by now extended from Syria to Bosnia, attacked Hungary. At the Battle of Mohács, Suleiman's 100,000 disciplined men and 300 cannons routed the poorly equipped Hungarian army, and King Ludwig was killed, leaving Hungary without an heir. After a further appropriate outlay of cash to smooth the way, Maximilian's agreement of 1515 was implemented, and Ferdinand, already Archduke of Austria, became King of Bohemia and Hungary. The strategic marriage alliance, with its associated heavy borrowing from the Fuggers (giving the merchant bankers yet more control over vital European raw materials), had paid off. The influence of the bankers, however, was felt (or at least acknowledged) even on the battlefield. Shortly before the Battle of Mohács King Ludwig tried to raise money from Anton and Raymond Fugger, now in charge of the firm, to pay the expenses of his army, but the loan was refused.

When news of the outcome of the battle was received in Antwerp in September 1526, the English resident Ambassador to the Low Countries, John Hackett, wrote in his dispatches home:

> Tonight, after psalm time, spoke with the factor [agent] of the Fuggers, who told me that, by letters from Duytchlande, they hear that the Turk has defeated the Hungarians, and that the King is dead. He was sure that if the King had had 150,000 ducats more he would have destroyed his enemies.

The Augsburg merchant banker Jakob Fugger's close involvement with the fortunes of the Habsburgs began in 1487, when he advanced over 20,000 ducats to Sigismund, Archduke of the Tyrol, and received as security control of the most productive of the Schwarz silver mines and the revenues of the whole province of the Tyrol. The following year the Fuggers lent a further 150,000 ducats to the Archduke, and assumed the management of silver production in its entirety. When Maximilian took over the government of the Tyrol in 1490 he inherited the Archduke's financial commitments (that is to say, his enormous outstanding debts). Over the next five years Maximilian borrowed yet further from the Fuggers to pay his own military expenditure, securing the loans with improved terms on the Schwarz mining profits.

It was the Fuggers' increasing involvement in and domination of the mining of key metals that enabled Jakob Fugger to build up his massive assets. In both Austria and Hungary, the monarch claimed the monopoly of casting and minting silver coin, and the whole silver output went into the production of coins (trading in silver was forbidden). Under the concession in silver mining granted against loans by Maximilian to the Fuggers, from the proceeds of each silver mark minted (whose price was fixed at 16 florins or ducats), 50 per cent went to the Fuggers, 32 per cent to the small contractors working the mines, and 18 per cent to Maximilian. On the basis of this extremely lucrative arrangement, the Fuggers

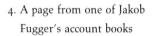

4. A page from one of Jakob
Fugger's account books

quickly accumulated enough capital to buy out the small contractors, and were then in a position to increase output and improve
purity by investing in new technological equipment. Subterranean
water in the shafts was a constant problem, and the Fuggers backed
research and development in drainage equipment and methods; they
also employed skilled, waged labour to work the mines. In return
for their investment in improving the mining facilities, and their
productivity, they further increased their percentage of the profits
on sales.

By 1508 Jakob Fugger's financial interests were spread all over
Europe, with investments in textiles, pepper and real estate, as well
as in silver and copper. His ready access to currency at locations
right across the scattered territories over which the Habsburgs ruled
effectively put him in control of Maximilian's international financial transactions. Money due to Maximilian from the vassal states
under his control could only be moved slowly and with difficulty

from Rome, Florence and Antwerp to Maximilian's German coffers. Jakob Fugger could get the money to Augsburg in as little as a fortnight by means of bills of exchange – the Fugger agent in Antwerp received the money due in exchange for a written credit note, which could be taken at speed to Germany, and exchanged for cash in Augsburg against Fugger assets there.

Silver mining made the Fuggers enormously rich, but it was copper which consolidated that wealth. Copper was a strategic material because it was used in armaments manufacture, a crucial component in making bronze from iron for the barrels of cannon and small arms. From the second half of the fifteenth century, the demand for copper for military use increased steadily, both inside Europe and beyond. Habsburg–Ottoman military struggles for the possession of Hungary had as their root cause the desire for ready access to the Hungarian copper mines. Venetian access to copper and gun founders was an important factor in successive Ottoman sultans' readiness to sign trade agreements with them.

Copper was equally important for the spice trade. Both the Venetians and the Ottomans used copper to pay for spices. The organized trade from India to Suez, Suez to Alexandria, Alexandria to Venice and beyond, designed to capitalize on European demand for Asian spices, could be satisfied only through a corresponding eastward flow of some form of acceptable payment. One of the commonest forms was copper. Copper was a commodity which could be substituted for money because of the consistently high demand for it in Egypt and India. The major sources were the Fugger-controlled copper mines of Germany and Hungary, and the copper mines of Anatolia, controlled by the Ottoman Sultan. Once the Portuguese became major operators in the spice trade, using the dangerous direct sea-route round the coast of Africa, the demand for copper increased still further.

The Portuguese trading agent and chronicler Duarte Barbosa, describing his experiences in the Indian Ocean region, emphasized the importance of copper there:

Here they sell a quintal of copper for 20 cruzados and upwards. It is used in the interior of India, and in the kingdom of Gujarat. They coin it into money; and make thereof also cauldrons for boiling rice. The Portuguese bring copper here, as well as much more which comes from the Ottomans via Mecca.

Copper was as acceptable as silver as payment for oriental spices and other luxuries. From the 1490s the Fuggers began to acquire financial interests in the copper mines of Banská Bystrica, in Hungary, against their loans to Maximilian, and by direct investment (they also increased their hold over the copper industry by astutely marrying into the only other competitor, the Hungarian Thurzo family, who had a capital stake in the copper mines). By the early decades of the sixteenth century they had established a virtual monopoly in copper – as we saw, in the course of his discussions with Maximilian over deferred payment of loans in 1515, Jakob Fugger mentioned that he was holding back 300,000 gulden worth of copper from the market so as to raise the price. Between 1526 and 1529 the Fuggers exported almost 3000 tonnes of copper, enabling them to realize a net profit of more than a million ducats.

The Fuggers' speculation in the precious-metals markets across Europe made them unimaginably rich. Their activities had a major impact on the economic fortunes of entire territories. The kings of Hungary were unable to compete with the Habsburgs on the sixteenth-century international political scene, in spite of the exceptionally rich natural resources in metals found in their territories, because throughout the period the Fuggers were systematically shifting the profits from the Hungarian mines back to Germany.

Charles V inherited his grandfather Maximilian's byzantine financial arrangements (and his personal bankers, the Fuggers) along with the Habsburg Empire which they had enabled him to assemble, and he continued Maximilian's strategy of using large outlays of cash to 'buy' political arrangements which might contribute to the Empire's stability. So, in the bargaining with the King of Portugal over trading rights in the spice islands in 1529, no sooner had the Emperor Charles V's cartographers at Saragossa spuriously established that the Moluccas Islands lay within the Spanish sphere of influence on the map than they immediately relinquished that claim, and accepted hard currency to the tune of 350,000 ducats instead. The cash settlement was far more valuable to Charles, beset, in established Habsburg fashion, by enormous debts to his bankers, than monopoly trading rights on the other side of the world.

The final agreement drawn up under the Treaty of Saragossa therefore specified that even though, according to the maps attached, the islands of the Moluccas were technically Spanish, they were to be deemed Portuguese until further notice. Both parties were well satisfied with the outcome – the Portuguese retained their monopoly commercial rights in the region, and Charles V achieved an injection of capital vital for the control of his extended territories in Europe.

Unlike the financially over-committed Habsburgs, the King of Portugal (whose international prestige depended on his country's domination of the spice trade) was prepared to put capital investment into navigational gambles. Vasco da Gama's and Pedro Alvarez Cabral's voyages were investment opportunities based on the outstanding seamanship of the Portuguese. Using their leading position in navigation to find a sea-route to India, the Portuguese set out calculatedly to control and monopolize Indian Ocean commerce for themselves. Their objective was to exclude both the Muslim merchants who currently dominated trading there, and European competitors, notably Venice and Spain. A sea-route would bypass the heavy mark-up on prices in terms of levies, transport charges, local taxes and customs duties incurred in overland travel through largely Muslim territories, and the resulting lower prices of pepper and other spices would draw European commerce to Lisbon, and away from Venice and Genoa.

When Vasco da Gama successfully navigated the dangerous waters of the Cape of Good Hope in May 1498 and arrived on the west coast of India, the port of Calicut was the acknowledged centre of a thriving international trade which included the Europeans (who came overland via the countries of the Ottoman Empire) and Muslim and Jewish merchants from North Africa, Turkey, Persia and Egypt. From Aden and Hormuz, Arab merchants carried luxury Ottoman and Mamluk goods – copper, mercury, vermilion, coral, saffron, carpets, porcelain, tin, coloured velvets, gold, silver, raisins, opium, madder, horses and textiles – to Calicut for the purchase of merchandise from India and the islands further to the east – pepper, ginger, cinnamon, cardamons, myrobalans, tamarind, canafistula, amber, aloe-wood, cloves, nutmeg, mace, sandalwood, cottons and coconuts. Italian merchants, in their turn, collected Ottoman and Indian Ocean goods from Alexandria, Beirut, Cairo and Antioch, and distributed them throughout Europe.

The Portuguese took this established market by surprise, exactly as the King of Portugal had intended when he sponsored the voyage. They were a new kind of 'outsider' dealer in the region, commercial travellers, who traded from their ships, rather than establishing a local agent to learn the local customs and practices. It was characteristic of the enterprise that the gifts da Gama had brought from Lisbon for the Prince of Calicut (the Samorin) ('twelve pieces of lambel, four scarlet hoods, six hats, four strings of coral, a case containing six wash-hand basins, a case of sugar, two casks of oil and two of honey') were pronounced by the resident European agents to be ill-judged, insulting trifles ('the poorest merchant from Mecca gave more').

The new Portuguese entrepreneurism had an immediate impact on international spice prices, which fell sharply. News of the successful voyage shattered commercial confidence in Venice, which until then had dominated the traffic in spices from the ports of Alexandria and Istanbul, at the end of the overland route from the East. In 1501 Girolamo Priuli in Venice reported the news of the successful arrival back in Lisbon of Portuguese ships from Calicut:

On the ninth of this month letters came from Lisbon, sent on August 1st. And through letters from Genoa and Lyon and other parts it is learned that the ships which were expected here loaded from spices are in Portugal.

Three of the said ships came from Calicut. This news was considered very bad for the city of Venice. Today, with this new voyage by the King of Portugal, all the spices which came by way of Cairo will be controlled in Portugal, because of the ships which will go to India, to Calicut, and other places to take them. And truly the Venetian merchants are in dismay, believing that the Portuguese voyages will ruin them.

He assessed the effect on the spice markets precisely:

Now that this new route is found, the King of Portugal will bring all the spices to Lisbon. And there is no doubt that the Hungarians, Germans, Flemish and French, who formerly came to Venice to spend their money on spices, will all turn towards Lisbon, for it is nearer to them, and easier to reach.

Furthermore, spices via this route will be better priced. The spices which come to Venice pass through all of Syria and the territories of the Ottoman Sultan. In each place they pay very large duties, and similarly, in the Venetian state they pay intolerable duties, levies and excise duty. The mark-up for transit through the countries of the Sultan and Venice is so great that whatever the spices cost in Calicut in ducats, the price in Venice has to be multiplied sixty or a hundred times. So, having found an alternative route, the King of Portugal will be able to sell at a much better price than the Venetian merchants can.

In fact, in 1501, in spite of the gifts (this time appropriately lavish) and courteous letters he carried from the King of Portugal, Cabral failed to persuade the Hindu Prince of Calicut to grant monopoly trading rights to King Manuel and to expel the 5000 or more Muslim families resident in Calicut. A year later, however, relentless bombardment by heavily armed fighting ships had more success, bringing peaceful trading in the region permanently to an end.

By 1504, just as Priuli predicted, the German Fuggers had negotiated their way into the emerging Portuguese pepper trade, and had set up a pepper-processing plant in Lisbon. The Fuggers guaranteed to supply 1,000,000 kilograms of copper every year to the King of Portugal to be carried as cargo to the Indian Ocean. In return they were given preferential rights over purchasing and distributing the pepper which arrived back in Lisbon. In 1505, in the interests of securing the Portuguese sea-route pepper-trade, a group of German merchants including the Fuggers invested 6000 ducats in fitting out, and equipping with cargo, a fleet of ships to sail round the Cape of Good Hope to the west coast of India under the command of Francisco da Almeida, the newly appointed Portuguese commander of the fleet in the Indian Ocean. The Portuguese Crown also put substantial sums into the offensive side of the enterprise, arming the ships heavily, and drawing up an ambitious strategic military plan with royal backing which included capturing and fortifying strategic locations along the east African coast, and if possible seizing Ceylon and the key port of Malacca. King Manuel justified the heavy financial outlay on his side of the venture, 'because it seems to us that nothing could be more important than to close up the mouth of the Red Sea, so that no more spices can ever be carried to the territory of the Mamluk Sultan, and everyone in India will lose the illusion of being able to trade with anyone except us'.

The 1505 expedition was a success for everyone concerned. With the spices with which the Portuguese ships returned laden, the German merchants obtained a 175 per cent profit on their original investment. The Portuguese established an aggressive policy which eventually drove the Muslim merchants out of the markets of the Indian Ocean, and enabled them to monopolize the sea traffic in spices and other Eastern luxuries between the Orient and Europe.

As they tightened their monopoly, however, the German merchants became concerned about Portugal's increasing hold over direct access to the spice trade, which gave them control of international prices for pepper, cloves and cinnamon.

In 1516, the Fugger agent in Lisbon, Cristóbal de Haro, withdrew from Portugal to Spain, in protest against the Portuguese spice cartel. In Seville he set about putting together a financial package, with the backing of the Spanish Crown, to sponsor an initiative south-westwards, round the globe to the spice islands. Such an enterprise was a direct commercial and political challenge to the Portuguese. If successful, it would establish a Spanish-controlled trade-route to the East. Pragmatically, by approaching Malacca from the east, it avoided Portugal's gunships in the Indian Ocean, which had established a system of trading permits; under this system only ships furnished with a Portuguese *cartaze* could safely navigate in its waters. By 1519, de Haro had the necessary financial backing, and the experienced Portuguese navigator Ferdinand Magellan had undertaken to lead the armada of ships.

Magellan's 1519 expedition, then, whose discoveries, as we saw, caused such international political upheavals, was dispatched with very specific commercial ends in mind. It was heavily funded by German merchants, and carried a German-financed cargo, flying under the Spanish flag. The first account to be circulated of the outcome of the voyage, written by Maximilian Transylvanus, a relative of de Haro, and published in Cologne in January 1523 (*Concerning the Islands of the Moluccas*), stressed the commercial initiative behind Magellan's voyage:

> Four years ago, Ferdinand Magellan, a distinguished Portuguese who had for many years sailed about the eastern Seas as admiral of the Portuguese fleet, having quarrelled with his king who he considered had acted ungratefully towards him, went into partnership with Christopher Haro, brother of my father-in-law, of Lisbon, who had through his agents for many years carried on

trade with those eastern countries and more recently with the Chinese, so that he was well acquainted with these matters (he also had been ill-used by the King of Portugal, and had returned to his native country, Spain). Together they pointed out to the Emperor Charles V that it was not yet clearly ascertained whether the spice port of Malacca was within the boundaries of the Portuguese or the Spanish, because hitherto its longitude had not been definitely known. It was, however, undoubtedly fact that the territories to the East of Malacca were within the Spanish limits. They asserted also that it was absolutely certain that the islands called the Moluccas, in which all sorts of spices grow, and from which they were brought to Malacca, lay in the Spanish division, and that it would be possible to sail westwards to them and bring the spices at less trouble and expense from their native soil to Spain.

This printed travelogue circulated widely within the financial community of Augsburg, popularly celebrating a successful piece of German entrepreneurship. Transylvanus was clear that the sole aim of Magellan's voyage had been to 'search for the islands in which spices grow', and that de Haro's financial backing (that is, Fugger-banking backing) had importantly underpinned the entire project. In Bartolomé de Las Casas' published account, Magellan put the commercially competitive aspect of the venture high on his own agenda:

Magellan brought with him [to Seville] a well-painted globe showing the entire world, and thereon traced the course he proposed to take, save that the Strait was purposely left out so that nobody could anticipate him. According to what an Italian named Pigafetta of Vincenza, who went on that voyage of discovery with Magellan, wrote in a letter, Magellan was perfectly certain to find the Strait because he had seen on a nautical chart made by one Martin Behaim, a great pilot and

5. Antonio Giovanni di Varese, *Portrait of Ferdinand Magellan*

cosmographer, in the treasury of the King of Portugal, the Strait depicted just as he found it. And, because the said Strait was within the boundaries of the sovereigns of Spain, he therefore had to move and offer his services to the King of Spain to discover a new route to the said islands of Molucca and the rest.

Magellan's voyage was a political triumph, in spite of the fact that he himself died in the course of it. It brought the Portuguese to the negotiating table, and secured Charles V a substantial financial windfall. In commercial terms, however, the route to the Indian Ocean westwards through the Magellan Strait proved too long, too dangerous and too expensive to represent a serious alternative either to the traditional eastwards overland route or to that around the coast of Africa. The Portuguese largely retained their hold on the spice markets and therefore, in spite of their early involvement in the discovery of Brazil, ignored opportunities for exploration and investment westwards, across the Atlantic Ocean. So, too, did the no less navigationally expert Ottomans, who, like the Portuguese, saw the expanding oriental markets in spices and other exotic luxury goods as lucrative enough to provide limitless possibilities for enrichment. The westwards opportunities were left to the Spanish, consolidating what in 1492 Columbus had called 'the enterprise of the Indies', but which now became 'the enterprise of the Americas'.

The globe which Magellan used to 'sell' his projected voyage to the Spanish had been made by Martin Behaim in 1492. It had been commissioned in 1490 by the city fathers of Nuremberg and produced as a piece of German commercial sponsorship, part of a plan to extend German trading involvement along the west coast of Africa.

Martin Behaim claimed to have acquired his technical skills as a cartographer from the distinguished Nuremberg astronomer and mathematician Regiomontanus himself – a strong recommendation. In 1490, he was approached by Georg Holzschuher, a wealthy

Nuremberg merchant, to construct a terrestrial globe on behalf of the city's merchant community. The globe was to be copiously annotated, with inscriptions detailing the commodities and the nature of the business opportunities at various key commercial locations in the world. The long legend against the spice islands, for instance, carefully itemized the cumulative customs duties incurred by the spice trade. It gave a meticulous account of the nature of the duties currently payable at each exchange point in the long chain of transactions preceding the spices' arrival in Europe:

> Item, be it known that spices pass through several hands in the islands of oriental India before they reach our country.
>
> 1. First, the inhabitants of the island called Java Major buy them in the other islands where they are collected by their neighbours, and sell them in their own island.
> 2. Secondly, those from the island Seilan, where St. Thomas is buried, buy the spices in Java and bring them to their own island.
> 3. Thirdly, in the island Ceylon or Seilan they are once more unloaded, charged with Customs duty, and sold to the merchants of the island Aurea Chersonesus, where they are again unladen.
> 4. Fourthly, the merchants of the island Taprobana buy the spices there, and pay the Customs duties, and take them to their island.
> 5. Fifthly, the Mohammedan heathen of Aden go there, buy the spices, pay the Customs and take them to their country.
> 6. Sixthly, those of Cairo buy them, and carry them over the sea, and further overland.
> 7. Seventhly, those of Venice and others buy them.
> 8. Eighthly, they are again sold in Venice to the Germans, and customs are paid.
> 9. Ninthly, at Frankfurt, Bruges and other places.
> 10. Tenthly, in England and France.

6. Terrestrial globe made by Martin Behaim, 1492: a commercial undertaking for a consortium of Nuremberg merchants. The globe was copiously annotated with inscriptions detailing the commodities and the nature of the business opportunities at various key commercial locations in the world

11. Eleventh, thus at last they reach the hands of the retail traders.

12. Twelfthly, those who use the spices buy them of the retail dealers, and let the high customs duties profits be borne in mind which are levied twelve times upon the spices, the former amounting on each occasion to one pound out of every ten. From this it is to be understood that very great quantities must grow in the East and it need not be wondered that they are worth with us as much as gold.

Armed with Behaim's cartographically precise globe, with its functional commercial annotations, the Nuremberg merchants set out to raise the backing for an expedition westwards, in search of an alternative access route to the coveted spice islands. In 1492, they approached the German Emperor Maximilian. Their attempt to interest him in a business proposition, however, got nowhere – it was neither Maximilian's temperament nor part of his financial power-broking tactics to speculate in trade. But he did pass the proposal on to the Portuguese King (well known for his interest in commercial exploration), forwarding it with a letter of recommendation from one of his own technical advisers: 'At your pleasure you may secure for this voyage a companion sent by our King Maximilian, namely, D. Martin Behaim, and many other expert mariners, who would start from the Azore Islands, and boldly cross the sea, with their cylinder, the quadrant, astrolabe and other instruments.'

In this case, however, the Portuguese King was equally luke-warm about the project, premised as it was on the commercial desirability of westwards exploration. All Portuguese navigational initiatives and all resources were targeted on exploration along the coast of Africa in the quest for a direct sea-route eastwards to the spice islands. Fourteen-ninety-two was, indeed, the very year that the Genoese adventurer Christopher Columbus – another former employee of the Portuguese – set out on his successful westwards voyage of discovery under the Spanish flag, having also failed to get Portuguese backing. It was not until Magellan used the same globe, and the same commercial arguments, to Maximilian's grandson in 1519 that Behaim's carefully constructed piece of technology achieved its intended purpose.

Commerce and new technology were inextricably bound together in Behaim's globe. In fact, in making the globe for the Germans, Behaim had been involved in a substantial piece of commercial and industrial espionage. In their accounts of Magellan's triumphant voyage, Pigafetti and Las Casas had stated that, in setting out southwestwards, Magellan knew he would find a viable route because he had seen a nautical chart in the treasury of the King of Portugal which showed it. Behaim was indeed employed by King John II of Portugal in the 1480s, as a member of his elite team of mathematicians and navigators working on the mathematics of navigation. Although he had claimed to be a mathematician by profession when he was hired, and to have been trained by the renowned Regiomontanus, his previous career had been as a successful cloth merchant. For anyone involved in the textile trade, the information he acquired in Lisbon about trade-routes and new business opportunities to the East was commercially invaluable.

In Lisbon Martin Behaim worked on detailed maps incorporating the findings of the Portuguese voyages of exploration around the coast of Africa – maps which were kept under conditions of the utmost secrecy and security. The maps were politically sensitive, since they were the vital means of safe access to the newly discovered territories; they were also commercially valuable, for the new trade-routes they recorded. Only those in the most trusted inner circle in Lisbon had access to them. In making the globe for his home town, Behaim incorporated the cartographical information he had access to in Lisbon – the most highly classified and inaccessible cartographical information currently available.

Behaim was not the only member of the Lisbon team to export top-secret cartographical information. In 1485, Columbus, having failed to interest King John in his own projected voyage westwards to India (probably on the basis of advice to which Behaim contributed), left Lisbon for Spain. His brother, Bartholomeo, however, a highly skilled cartographer in the Genoese style, stayed on in the map workshop of King John II, where he was part of the group of technicians putting together a detailed world map which combined the information from Nicholas Germanus' Ptolemy maps (the best traditional maps available), with the additional information about coastlines and distances based on actual voyages, taken from Portuguese mariners' charts. This large map (180 cm by 120 cm), continually added to by new discoveries, including those of Cão and Dias, was one of Portugal's most closely guarded state secrets. By the beginning of 1489, Columbus, waiting for a decision from the King and Queen of Spain, was running short of money, and Bartholomeo prepared to join him in Spain to help his project. Before he left Lisbon, however, he copied a number of Portuguese maps from the secret archive, including the large world map (which he transferred on to eleven sheets of paper, because paper was lighter, and easier to conceal, than parchment). The Columbus brothers sold Bartholomeo's valuable stolen maps in Italy for substantial sums, thereby dispersing vital information hitherto held only by the Portuguese.

In Seville, their financial circumstances alleviated by their map sales, the two brothers reassembled the world map, and modified it to incorporate material not yet entered at the time of Bartholomeo's departure. Crucially, this additional information suggested that, once the Cape of Good Hope had been rounded, a significant mass of land remained still to be navigated around before ships could gain access to the Indian Ocean. Although factually incorrect, the Columbus brothers' map, thus modified, apparently offered strong concrete support for the argument that a westwards route to the Indies was a viable alternative option. On the strength of comparison of the Columbuses' map (with its exaggerated coastline of Africa) with their own Ptolemaic maps (on which calculation errors significantly

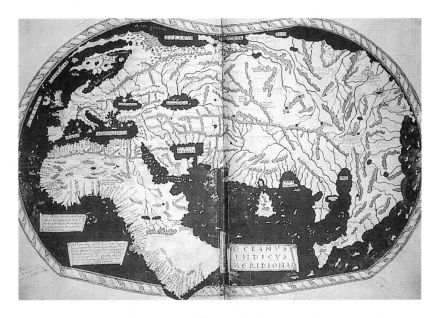

7. Henricus Martellus' 1489 world map which suggests that once the Cape
of Good Hope has been rounded there is a significant mass of land still to be
navigated before reaching the Indian Ocean. The map exaggerates the land mass

reduced the width of the Atlantic Ocean) the Spanish monarchs
Ferdinand and Isabella finally agreed to finance the venture in 1492.

In the race for the eastern spice markets, maps, globes and astronomical instruments were the vital new technology which could give
one group of commercial interests the edge. The Renaissance map
was a scientific instrument – a piece of equipment whose accuracy
allowed the user to travel where he could not travel before. Both
Columbus' and Magellan's landmark voyages took advantage of
access to stolen maps, which gave detailed information closely
protected by the King of Portugal about coastlines, routes and
distances (the King, however, was too preoccupied with the African
route to be overly concerned). The Venetian cartographer Giovanni
Contarini's planisphere of 1506 (the first printed map accurately to
depict Africa in the aftermath of da Gama's voyage) held out to the

ordinary reader in its dedication a similar promise of a new world
to be discovered with the aid of the map:

> The world and all its seas on a flat map.
> Lo! Giovanni Matteo Contarini,
> Famed in the Ptolemaean art, has compiled and marked it out.
> Whither away? Stay, traveller, and behold new nations and a
>   new-found world.

In addition to the payment for the maps and charts for the
Magellan voyage, Diogo Ribeiro received 4 gold ducats for making
four astrolabes, and 8 silver reals for 'a large, self-damping magnetic
needle', which he prepared. When the Portuguese seized the
remnants of the expedition as they limped home in 1522 they
impounded 'two planispheres belonging to Magellan and made by
Pedro Reinel, and other charts for the navigation to India', twenty-
three charts made by an Italian cartographer for the Portuguese
sorting house in India (the Casa da India), six pairs of dividers, seven
astrolabes (one of brass), twenty-one wooden quadrants, thirty-five
magnetized needles for compasses, and eighteen half-hour glasses
for keeping time. All this technical equipment was part of the initial
financial investment in the enterprise by the voyage's German
merchant backers.

Those with the training to design and make the scientific instruments needed for commerce (and for warfare) had one foot firmly
in the world of patronage and new learning, and the other in the
entrepreneurial and increasingly expansionist merchant houses
and navigation companies, where their technical services were in
demand from the backers of speculative voyages looking for new
sources of marketable commodities. In England in the 1530s, the
German artist, draughtsman and designer Hans Holbein painted
the portraits of Henry VIII's royal household, having been introduced to the King by Thomas More, whose patron Henry was,
and to whom his close friend Erasmus wrote a personal letter of

8. Renaissance astrolabe made by Georg Hartmann

9. Hans Holbein, *Portrait of Nicolaus Kratzer* surrounded by scientific instruments

introduction for Holbein. Outside the Court, Holbein also painted the portraits of another body of wealthy clients in London – the Company of German Merchants. Among them was Nicolaus Kratzer, who in addition to his trading activities was a specialist maker of navigational and astronomical instruments, and held the title at Henry VIII's Court of 'King's astronomer'.

Kratzer and Holbein were similarly placed in relation to their royal patron. Both possessed unusual technical skills (Holbein as a draughtsman, Kratzer as a cartographer and instrument-maker) with which they could earn a good living from those members of the German merchant community rich enough to purchase their services. Those same skills gave both of them access to Court patronage, Holbein as portraitist, Kratzer as astrologer and decorative map-maker. In 1527 the two men collaborated with John Rastell and another of the King's painters, the Italian Vincenzo Volpe, in organizing festivities at Greenwich to celebrate the formal conclusion of peace between François I and Henry VIII. The spectacle included two large-scale panoramas painted by Holbein – one showing the town of Thérouanne under siege by the English in 1513, with 'the very manner of every man's camp cunningly wrought'. The second was a ceiling, designed by Kratzer and executed by Holbein, 'with the whole earth surrounded with the sea, like a very Map or Chart', with all the names of the principal countries legibly marked. There is no evidence of the King's making more serious use of his German experts – the splendid astronomical clock designed by Kratzer which survives at Hampton Court was explicitly commissioned in 1541 so that Henry would know the times of high and low tide at London Bridge, in order to time the departure of the royal barge. The expertise which in the merchant community formed the basis for commercial expansion and personal prosperity was used as a source of entertainment and curiosities by the patron.

In Holbein's great painting of 1533, *The Ambassadors*, the artist painted Behaim's terrestrial globe and one of the latest astronomical globes (made, like Behaim's in Nuremberg, by the instrument-maker Johann Schöner), executed meticulously, down to the smallest detail – testimony to the artist's brilliance as a draughtsman. He had borrowed the Schöner globe from its owner, another German merchant resident in London, and the surrounding astronomical instruments (and possibly the globe) were lent by Kratzer. For the French resident Ambassador Jean de Dinteville who commissioned the double portrait of himself and the French ambassador at large, Georges de Selve, however, these items in the painting were mere curiosities and ornaments (suggesting the urbanity of the sitters). It was the faces of the distinguished sitters, and the occasion of their meeting, that Holbein was to record for posterity. By contrast, when Holbein had painted the portrait of Nicolaus Kratzer in 1528, he had shown his sitter at work, in his capacity as a skilled technical craftsman, constructing one of the very instruments which decorated the de Dinteville commission. In the Kratzer portrait the instruments were transformed from mere decoration to become part of the painting's subject. The picture stood as a tribute to the precision and technical competence of the scholar–technician who made a polyhedral portable brass dial, with a built-in compass, for Cardinal Wolsey and two important stone dials for the University of Oxford.

Those with the money and influence to acquire rare and exotic commodities collected avidly whatever was considered covetable, from astrolabes to exotic items like 'unicorn horn' (which figured in Cardinal Francesco Gonzaga's collection of rare objects). By the mid-sixteenth century it was enough to list the range of commodities collected by a public figure to indicate his cultivation. In 1560 the Pope's Ambassador in Poland, Bernard Bongiovanni, described with admiration the collections of Sigismund Augustus Jagiellon, King of Poland (in other respects, not much to write home about as a royal presence in Europe):

The king has remarkable items in his personal estate. Among other things he owns, in Vilnius, the capital of the Grand-Duchy

10. Johann Schöner's 1533 celestial globe

of Lithuania, a hundred and eighty large calibre cannons and a great number of smaller ones, wonderfully worked.

The king also owns twenty suits of armour to his measure, four of which are of exceptional beauty, especially the one which is decorated with finely chiselled scenes and incrusted with silver, representing all the victories won by his ancestors over the Muscovites; it costs 6 thousand crowns. On other armours are engraved other victories.

His Majesty dresses modestly, but has clothes of different kinds, in the Hungarian and Italian fashion, of brocade and of silk, clothes for the summer and others for winter, lined with sable, wolf, lynx, black fox, the value of which exceeds 80 thousand gold crowns.

The king takes extreme delight in jewels, and he showed them to me one day in secret, for he does not want the Poles to know that he has spent so much to buy them. There is in his chamber a large table, almost as big as the room itself, on which stand sixteen jewel cases two spans long and a span and a half wide, filled with jewels. Four cases having belonged to his Mother are worth 200 thousand crowns and were brought from Naples. Four others were bought by his Majesty for 500 thousand gold crowns. They contain: a clasp from Charles V, which is worth 30 thousand gold crowns, and his diamond-studded medal big as a gold ducat, having on one side the eagle with the arms of Spain, on the other, Charles V's personal motto: two columns bearing the inscription 'plus ultra'. There are, besides, many square and pointed rubies and emeralds. The other eight cases are very old, one of them containing a bonnet full of emeralds, rubies and diamonds which are worth 300 thousand gold crowns. I saw, finally, many jewels which I did not expect to find, and with which neither those of Venice which I have likewise seen nor those of the papacy can be compared.

Without counting the silverware used by His Majesty and by the Queens, there are in the treasure 5 thousand pounds of silverware entirely gilded, which is not used. There are likewise many fine pieces of which His Majesty is passionately fond, to mention only fountains, clocks the height of a man adorned with statues, organs and other instruments, a globe bearing all the celestial signs, bowls and vases decorated with all sorts of divine, terrestrial and sea creatures. And as for the rest, it consists of golden goblets which the bishops, the voivodes, the castellans, the starostas and the officers presented as gifts when they were appointed by the king.

The king, finally, owns thirty saddles and trappings of such splendour that it is impossible to see elsewhere more sumptuous; that some are made of pure gold and silver is not surprising since they belong to a prince, but that they should at the same time be decorated with such fine, delicate and precious ornaments no one could believe who had not seen them.

His Majesty has at his disposal persons versed in each art: for the jewels and the work in gems, Messire Giacomo of Verona; for the casting of cannons, a few Frenchmen; for sculpture, a Venetian; for instrument-making, an incomparable Hungarian; for the training of horses, Messire Prosper Anadono, a Neapolitan, and so in all the skills.

The collection also included 132 pieces of decorative fabric 'acquired in Turkey on the occasion of his marriage', and a large collection of tapestries. And just as Henry VIII 'collected' Kratzer the astronomer and Holbein the painter, Sigismund 'collected' Giacomo of Verona. Nor were the household experts the only animate objects in the great collectors' collections.

Some of the 'treasures' which wealthy Renaissance men pursued, purchased and coveted in the collections of others were expertly bred rather than creatively manufactured. In both East and West, princes collected exotic animals and birds in their private zoos. Many of them were as passionate about their hounds and purebred horses as about their illuminated books. Francesco Gonzaga II of Mantua

11. Ippolito Andreasi, elevation drawing for the Sala dei Cavalli at the Palazzo
del Te, Mantua

collected and raced Arab and Persian horses, and was as expert about
these as his wife Isabella d'Este was about her collection of antiques.
'We understand horses and arms better than engraved gems,' he
once acknowledged. In 1492, he sent his personal ambassador, Alexis
Becagut, to negotiate the purchase of horses directly with Bayezid
II in Istanbul, taking with him extravagant gifts, including a portrait
of Francesco Gonzaga himself. One of Francesco's financiers,
Silvestro da Lucca, presented him with a beautifully illuminated
manuscript book on vellum, produced at his own expense, containing
thirty-five miniatures of the Marquis's prize-winning racehorses,
with details of their names and prizes. On the title page it showed
Il Dainosauro, which had won the gold sash at Ferrara, Florence and
Mantua. According to da Lucca, Francesco had mentioned several
times that he would like to have an illustrated record of his Barbary
racehorses, and a list of the prizes they had taken.

The Gonzagas were, in fact, officially mad about horses. In his summer palace, the Palazzo del Te, Federigo Gonzaga II, Francesco's son, had portraits of his favourite horses incorporated in the *trompe l'œil* fresco decoration of one of the ceremonial receiving rooms. In the Ducal Palace in central Mantua, the great dining room was also decorated with portraits of horses – this time concealed behind *trompe l'œil* curtains, which appeared to have blown aside to reveal a hoof and fetlock here, an ear and neck there. Guests at dinner could try to identify the horses from these glimpses, presumably earning their host's approval by doing so successfully.

Arab and Persian purebred horses were vigorously traded between Hormuz and Goa, first by the Muslim merchants and later by the Portuguese, to exploit a large market throughout India. In 1514, King Vira Narasimha Raya of Vijayanagar signed an agreement with the Portuguese to pay 30,000 cruzados annually for his supply of horses. In November 1514 Alfonso de Albuquerque wrote to the King of Portugal asking for authorization to send 2000 Arab and Persian horses from Goa (which the Portuguese now controlled) to the King of Daquem.

The sturdy, small-headed horses, bedecked with saddles and harnesses of the utmost splendour, which feature prominently in Renaissance frescos are an intrinsic part of the display of riches by the powerful. Nothing the European nobility could lay on in the way of extravagant parade of their horses, however, could match the displays of the Ottoman Sultan, who acquired one perfect pure-bred horse in tribute for every ten shipped through Istanbul. In 1544 an attendant to the French Ambassador described the splendid sight of Suleiman the Magnificent's horses lining the court through which the ambassadors passed on their way to pay their respects to the Sultan:

On either side were the horses, of which some carried horsemen, and were very richly harnessed. We did not see a single one of these horses (which numbered about 200) which did not have

12. Francesco del Cossa, detail of horse racing from the fresco of St George in the
Palazo Schifanoia in Ferrara

reins and stirrups of pure gold or silver. Most had on their fore-
head a plate of gold or silver in the shape of a rose, into which
was set a ruby or a turquoise. They had bridles in the Turkish
fashion, embroidered with gold and with crimson silk, scattered
with turquoises. Each of these horses had a halter in the shape
of a gold or silver chain, of an estimated value of 500 ducats.
They had little turkish saddles, all golden, with three palms of
gold brocade or embroidered velvet on the crupper, with rows
of buttons dangling on either side, made of gold thread or of
crimson silk. The horses were very handsome turkish or barbary
ones, of black, dark brown, bay, grey, dappled or white, and each
of which would cost at least 200 ducats.

The admiration of the French ambassadorial party for such a display
of the finest horses and their precious accoutrements was unabashed.

For the Sultan (as for other heads of state), gaining respect by such displays was a serious part of the process of establishing political might in the eyes of the world by demonstrating effortless access to dazzlingly valuable belongings – animal, vegetable and mineral.

Prominent political figures exercised considerable ingenuity in ways of broadcasting their power and prestige in the days before the existence of mass media and press releases. In 1515 the Nuremberg workshop of Albrecht Dürer completed a major commission for the Emperor Maximilian – a huge triumphal arch, after the manner of those erected in Rome in antiquity to celebrate the triumphs in battle of the Roman emperors. But Maximilian's Arch was never meant to be built: it was produced as a set of 174 woodcut blocks, and printed in an edition of 700 copies, to be dispatched to all corners of the world. Along with the Arch went a companion set of woodcuts representing a triumphal procession, headed by Maximilian, wearing the Crown of Charlemagne and carried in an elaborately ornate triumphal chariot (eight woodcut sheets long). Thus whoever owned a copy of the two sets of woodcuts could assemble the Arch and Procession to create a media 'Triumph of Maximilian'. Only the block-cutter Hieronymus Andreae was actually paid for this magnificent piece of imperial propaganda (rather late, in 1526). Dürer himself complained in a letter to Nuremberg's Ambassador to the Imperial Court at Innsbruck, asking him to 'point out to His Imperial Majesty that I have served him three years at my own expense' (without success – he remained unpaid).

When Ludovico Sforza seized power from his nephew Giangaleazzo in 1482 he financed a printed edition of Giovanni Simonetta's Latin biography of his father Francesco Sforza and had it widely distributed, as part of an orchestrated cultural programme of justification for his own right to rule. The published paean to the Sforza dynasty was a public statement of Sforza power, like the uncompleted project for a giant bronze statue of his father seated in despotic splendour on a rearing horse, the ornate tomb to

13. Albrecht Dürer, Triumphal Arch for Maximilian I, assembled from
174 individual printed sheets

14. Giovan Pietro Birago, *Portrait of Ludovico Sforza and his nephew Giangaleazzo* on the frontispiece to Giovanni Simonetta's *Sforziada*

15. Marble façade of the Certosa Palace, Pavia

Giangaleazzo Visconti (a Sforza ancestor), and the ostentatious marble façade for the Certosa Palace at Pavia.

One of Erhard Radholt's early publishing ventures, when he set up his publishing house in Venice in 1476, was a narrative account of the military campaigns of Doge Pietro Mocenigo, who had recently died, written by Coriolano Cipico (Caepio), who had fought beside the Doge at the sack of Smyrna. The book celebrated Mocenigo's exploits on the battlefield one by one, emphasizing his part in restoring the prestige of Venice after its disastrous defeat at Negroponte in 1470. The Doge's family were already planning a grandiose monument to his achievements when the book appeared. The necessary contract had been drawn up with the Dominicans of S. Giovanni e Paolo: Pietro Lombardo had been hired as sculptor, and was resident in the Palazzo Mocenigo. Cipico's book offered a programme of themes he needed for the monument – the hero of

Cipico's epic was translated into monumental sculpture, each episode from the book furnishing a theme for a panel or a carving on the tomb. The tomb, however, was seen only by those local to Venice. The printed account circulated Mocenigo's name and exploits all over Europe.

Wealthy patrons regarded printed artefacts (woodcuts and books) much as they did the portrait medal – as a convenient vehicle for mass-producing and circulating their enduring fame. They acknowledged (and rewarded financially) elaborately complimentary prefaces to themselves in printed books, which offered the work to them as an unsolicited gift, as a specially selected, worthy recipient. If a payment or pension was awarded on the basis of such a celebratory dedication (as authors always hoped), it was material acknowledgement that the distribution of the book contributed to the patron's as well as the author's renown. The only pension paid to Erasmus of Rotterdam regularly was that given to him by the English

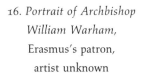

16. Portrait of Archbishop William Warham, Erasmus's patron, artist unknown

Archbishop William Warham, to whom he had dedicated his monumental edition of the *Letters of St Jerome* in 1516. Jerome's *Letters* was a work of enormous significance, and sold almost as widely as Erasmus' new Latin translation of the New Testament. Erasmus included multiple dedications to the Archbishop (at the beginning of each book), and there is no doubt that this piece of flattery really did circulate Warham's name and reputation throughout Europe. Both François I and Charles V apparently took note of the vast numbers of volumes dedicated to them and extolling their virtues, to the extent that they were prepared to protect their authors from the censors, or from attempts to plagiarize their works.

By contrast, as we saw in Chapter 3, the printed book was identified by the German merchants from the very outset as a consumer commodity with enormous commercial prospects and the potential

17. Claus van Dormale, *Portrait of Charles V* on an ornate leather binding from his library

18. A view of Constantinople, from Hartmann Schedel, *Nuremberg Chronicle*

for mass marketing. Although Venice remained for some time the centre of book-production, a significant proportion of the investment there in publishing houses like those of Nicolas Jenson and Aldus Manutius was German. From the very beginning of printing, book-distribution followed the same routes, with the same remarkable efficiency, as other consumer goods. In striking contrast to today, a new book published in Rome in 1500 was available to readers in the Low Countries and in England within a matter of weeks. The printed book's capacity both to make money and to spread information widely, quickly and efficiently was acknowledged by Anton Koberger, the most successful financial entrepreneur in Nuremberg, when he managed the production of Hartmann Schedel's *Nuremberg Chronicle* in 1493. The book was a fully illustrated history of the world, structured so as to give particular prominence to the city of Nuremberg – a piece of commercial propaganda, as well as (so it turned out) a remarkably good seller. Its woodcuts were constantly reproduced, and for the next century provided memorable visual images of exotic distant locations which readers were unlikely ever to see themselves.

Exploitation of the printed book by entrepreneurial Germans to disseminate technical knowledge followed logically from their confidence in its potential for wide, cheap, efficient distribution. Around 1470, the brilliant mathematician Regiomontanus recognized that the group of colleagues and patrons with access to the newly rediscovered and translated masterpieces of Greek mathematics in manuscript was too small to be able to make the crucial breakthroughs in a new Greek-based mathematics. To make them available to as wide an audience as possible, so that as many technically competent people as possible could set about developing the new technologies he knew would follow, he naturally turned to printing.

In 1470 Regiomontanus left Buda and returned to his native Nuremberg, home of German business investment, where he gained the backing of a local businessman to set up his own publishing house. As well as publishing clear, accurate texts (with well-produced diagrams) of the major discoveries in astronomy and mathematics, he also issued mathematical and navigational tables, technical treatises and advertisements for scientific instruments – in other words, his press functioned as a specialist scientific publishing house. After his premature death in 1476, the mathematical works promised in an 'advance publications' list shortly before were issued by his co-worker Erhard Radholt. Radholt moved the press to Venice (where skilled printshop labour was easier to come by), but the investment remained predominantly German, as did the press's steady commitment to applied scientific, technical and mathematical texts. Columbus took Regiomontanus' printed tables and his epitome of the *Almagest* with him on his 1492 voyage, along with his navigational instruments and maps. Nicolaus Copernicus used tables printed by Regiomontanus and by Radholt; and his own *Of the Revolutions of the Celestial Spheres* – the work which proved mathematically that the earth revolved around the sun – was published by Johannes Petreius' Nuremberg press, which was directly inspired by the international success of that of Regiomontanus.

In 1473, at the age of fourteen, Jakob Fugger was sent by his father to the German business house in Venice, the Fondaco dei Tedeschi, where the family held a warehouse, to learn 'Italian accounting' – commercial reckoning with Arabic numerals, and double-entry bookkeeping. Within a generation, however, the printed book had made such trips largely unnecessary – an explosion in publication of manuals of technical commercial expertise ('how to' books for merchants) had made it possible for merchants to learn their trade closer to home. Manuals by outstanding mathematicians (including the brilliant contemporary of Leonardo da Vinci, Luca Pacioli, and Thomas More's colleague Cuthbert Tunstall in London) set out a whole range of techniques in practical, applied mathematics systematically for the first time.

These textbooks were, from the outset, clearly focused on the local and specific, practical details of Renaissance trade. The author of the first book of commercial arithmetic published in Portugal in 1519 advised his readers in his dedication: 'I am printing this arithmetic because it is a thing so necessary in Portugal for transactions with the merchants of India, Persia, Arabia, Ethiopia, and other places discovered by us.' He had in mind the need to know how to reckon and account in Indo-Arabic numbers, rather than in Roman numerals, for transactions with regions used to dealing with Muslim merchants. But he was also referring to the particular methods for calculating proportional allocation of profits, percentage interest due and money exchange which enabled merchants to operate efficiently and accurately wherever they traded. Luca Pacioli wrote his *Compendium of Arithmetic, Geometry and Proportion* (1494) in Italian because 'if written in Latin ordinary peole could not understand it'. Pacioli brought together bookkeeping and business arithmetic with geometry, musical harmonics and perspective, in a compilation which bridged commerce and the arts. He expounded the mysteries of double-entry bookkeeping for merchants, but he also emphasized the importance of the study of Euclidean geometry for surveyors and architects.

The earliest printed commercial arithmetic, the *Libro de Abacho*, published in Venice in 1478, is packed with vivid examples of contemporary mercantile practice and the kinds of commercial problems that merchants are regularly required to solve. The simplest examples are taken from the exotic end of the commodity market, and give us an idea of the imaginative landscape of the would-be merchant (though one suspects that the average reckoner was more likely to be calculating lengths of broadcloth than of damask):

> If 1 yard of crimson is worth 5 ducats, what will 85 yards be worth?
> If 1 pound and ½ of saffron is worth 20 ducats and ⅓, what will 1 ounce and ¼ be worth?
> If 1000 pounds of pepper are worth 80 ducats, 16 grossi and ¼, what will 9917 pounds and ½ be worth?

Further on come worked examples of 'alligation' or the converting of silver coin of different levels of purity into a homogeneous currency:

> A merchant has 40 marks of silver, alloyed at 6 ounces and ½ per mark. He has 56 marks of another kind containing 5 ounces of fineness per mark. He wishes to make these into coin containing 4 ounces and ½ of fine silver per mark. Required to know the amount in the mixture, and how much brass he must add.
> [Answer: he will end up with 120 marks; and 24 marks' worth of brass will need to be added to bring the 96 up to 120]

Finally, the most complex calculations concern the fair allocation of profits from business partnerships embarked upon by partners with unequal levels of investment, invested at different times:

> Two merchants, Sebastiano and Jacomo, have invested their money for gain in a partnership. Sebastiano put in 350 ducats on the first day of January 1472, and Jacomo 500 ducats, 14 grossi

on the first day of July 1472; and on the first day of January 1474 they found they had gained 622 ducats. Required is the share of each.

First the reader is instructed to reduce the amount invested to a common unit, grossi (1 ducat = 24 grossi). Then each share is multiplied by the time invested in months and the shares added:

Sebastiano, 8400 × 24 = 201600
Jacomo, 12014 × 18 = 216252
201600 + 216252 = 417852

The 'rule of three' must then be applied to determine Sebastiano's share of the profit. The 'rule of three', 'merchant's rule' or 'golden rule' was regarded as the fundamental piece of mathematics for reckoning in commerce – in modern terms it was a simple calculation of proportion, made more difficult by the absence of a suitable notation:

201600:417852 = x:622 (where x = Sebastian's share of the profit)

$$x = \frac{201600 \times 622}{417852}$$

= 300.95 ducats

Jacomo's share, equivalently calculated, is found to be 321.05 ducats (and as a check the two sums are added to see that their total equals the realized profit of 622 ducats. (Actually the calculations are rather more extended because the *Libro de Abacho* does not use decimals, and converts remainders into 'pizoli'.)

The *Libro de Abacho* taught the basics. For the kind of business conducted by the Fuggers, however, very high levels of education and training were required for the voluminous correspondence, and prolific accounting, which supported the business empire. Like the great houses of the nobility, the wealthy merchant bankers in trade employed their in-house secretaries, accountants and advisers, trained in the new classically based learning and languages. It is not surprising that the printed books on the voyages of discovery sat side by side on the library shelf with the new mathematics and Latin and Greek literature, and that ambitious, educated young men were as eager to be employed in commerce as in stately homes. In Florence in the 1490s, the philosopher Pico della Mirandola owned a world map, a book on the Levant, Marco Polo's voyages (a Renaissance best-seller) and Berlinghieri's *Geography*. Leonardo da Vinci owned a world map and the travels of Mandeville.

Books, knowledge and commerce naturally went hand in hand. The Fuggers themselves were keen book-collectors, accumulating books as avidly as they did all the other types of information which might oil the wheels of business. By the middle of the sixteenth century Ulrich Fugger's library at Augsburg contained over 10,000 books and manuscripts. His collection of printed books included every major work of antiquity dealing with Asia, and a whole range of printed books on the Americas. In the race to possess the exotic goods made available by the voyages of discovery, both backers and explorers turned to the new book learning to justify the moral acceptability of their commercial ventures.

Among the volumes which Columbus owned was a little book called *Summula Confessionis*, by the Dominican friar Antoninus Florentius, published in Venice in 1474. The *Confessionale* (as it was popularly known) was a handy pocket-sized guide to personal piety and behaviour, which went through over a hundred printed editions before 1500.

The second part of this work was dedicated to methods of questioning individuals on the morality of their conduct with reference to their occupations, enabling the individual to confess his shortcomings in day-to-day affairs. Merchants and traders got a long chapter to themselves. The life of the merchant–adventurer was, according to the *Confessionale*, packed with opportunities for every kind of sin. At the head of the list, the first sin discussed was the sin of conducting trade with the Ottoman Sultan without papal licence. There followed a whole host of others: bartering worthless objects for precious ones (examples given are the exchange of wool or cotton for silks or spices), price-rigging, short-changing, false weighing, fraudulent quality control or no quality control at all, connivance with thieves, insider trading, excessive profit, trading on feast days, lying in the making of marriage contracts, and usury (taking interest on loans, which was forbidden by the Church, on Biblical authority). The pursuit of wealth, either for its own sake or as a major career objective, was singled out for blame. A slightly larger tolerance was extended to those who took great risks in the course of their trading. Those who carried their goods for trade across large expanses of land or sea were mentioned specifically as deserving special indulgence – since they exposed themselves to great danger, they were permitted a proportionately greater financial reward without becoming vulnerable to the charge of greed.

In the eyes of the Church, those who engaged in trade or commercial adventure were peculiarly prone to corruption. Prominent merchants took care to phrase their financial transactions in such a way as to avoid charges of immoral activity as far as possible. When Jakob Fugger wrote to Charles V, in April 1523, reproaching him for attempting to renege on the massive sums advanced to him to secure his election as Holy Roman Emperor, he emphasized that personal advancement had played no part in the deal:

> Your Imperial Majesty doubtless knows how I and my kinsmen have ever hitherto been disposed to serve the House of Austria in all loyalty to the furtherance of its well-being and prosperity; wherefore, in order to be pleasing to Your Majesty's Grandsire, the late Emperor Maximilian, and to gain for Your Majesty the Roman Crown, we have held ourselves bounden to engage

ourselves towards divers princes who placed their Trust and Reliance upon myself and perchance on No Man besides. We have, moreover, advanced to Your Majesty's Agents for the same end a Great Sum of Money, of which we ourselves have had to raise a large part from our Friends. It is well known that your Imperial Majesty could not have gained the Roman Crown save with mine aid, and I can prove the same by the writings of Your Majesty's Agents given by their own hands. In this matter I have not studied mine own Profit. For had I left the House of Austria and had been minded to further France, I had obtained much money and property, such as was then offered to me. How grave a Disadvantage had in this case accrued to Your Majesty and the House of Austria, Your Majesty's Royal Mind well knoweth.

It did not help the merchants that their commitment to keeping trade-routes open frequently involved them in activities which were technically 'against the national interest', particularly when a country was at war. In March 1501, at the height of the Ottoman–Venetian war, Venetian ships were at Beirut and Alexandria loading spices (Venice having temporarily allied itself to the Egyptian Mamluks). The ships at Alexandria loaded 2570 colli or loads of spices; and those at Beirut took on 3200 loads. Concerned by the possibility of an Ottoman attack on the convoy, Venice sent an escort of five to eight light galleys to accompany the Beirut galley convoy to Crete, where it stopped to take on supplies. When it left Crete, the convoy's captain, Marin da Molin, sailed past Zonchio, which was under siege by the Ottoman naval commander Kemal Reis, without offering any assistance. By definition, the convoy's task was to deliver its merchandise safely to Venice. Da Molin's decision not to risk his sailors and cargo to defend his countrymen reflected a strong mercantile motivation to preserve commercial activity, regardless of the international political situation.

1. Detail from a grammar book showing the young Maximilian Sforza at his lessons in a less than orderly classroom

2. Detail of illumination from Henry VIII's *Vindication of the Seven Sacraments against Martin Luther*: the illumination is added by hand over a woodcut frontispiece

3. Detail from Roberto Valturio, *On Military Matters*: lavishly illustrated with diagrams and drawings of military machinery

4. *Above left:* Vittore Carpaccio, detail from *The Story of St Ursula, The Repatriation of the English Ambassadors*

5. *Above right:* Detail from Henricus Martellus' world map

6. *Above:* Hans Holbein, detail from *Portrait of Nicolaus Kratzer*, showing the same scientific instruments which appear in Holbein's later painting, *The Ambassadors*

7. *Right:* Detail of Johann Schöner's celestial globe

8. *Above:* Frescos of horses in the Salone Cavalli, in the Palazzo del Te, Mantua: the Gonzagas were officially mad about horses

9. *Left:* Detail from a late fourteenth-century book illumination, showing money lenders about their business

10. *Right:* Jewel-encrusted
ceremonial helmet, Istanbul:
the wealth of the Ottoman Court
attracted many European artists
and goldsmiths in search of
lucrative commissions

11. *Below:* Detail from Mecmu^ca-i
Menazil, miniature map of
Istanbul: Mehmed II embarked
on a programme of building to
rival that of Venice as a statement
of the wealth and power of the
Ottomans

12. *The Review of the Troops at Barcelona*, detail showing Charles V on horseback: when ordering *The Conquest of Tunis* tapestries, Maria of Hungary stipulated that they should be 'rich or richer throughout in gold thread or silver thread than the tapestries depicting the poem of *Vertumnus and Pomona*'

13. Map of the Mediterranean Basin, first tapestry in *The Conquest of Tunis* series: the written instructions inform the onlooker that they are standing in North Africa looking back towards Spain

14. *Above:* The salon of Sultan Murad III in the harem, designed by Sinan Bey,
Topkapi Palace, Istanbul

15. *Below left:* Gold and enamel portrait medal of Isabella d'Este, set with precious stones:
Isabella gave copies of this medal to favoured acquaintances

16. *Below right:* Onyx cameo of Ptolemaic royal couple, 3rd century BC, from
Isabella d'Este's collection

17. Hans Holbein, *The Ambassadors*: prestige and power are represented by the accumulation of valuable goods, and by the sumptuous dress and nonchalantly self-centred pose of the sitters

On the other hand, by the beginning of the sixteenth century the opinion was being voiced that the merchant's was a noble profession, since it achieved prosperity for nations without war and aggression. This was predictably the view taken by Tomé Pires, in his survey of new-world trading opportunities, the *Suma Oriental*, written around 1515. Pires had traded along the coast of Africa and in the Indian Ocean, and recognized the impact these activities were bound to have on every aspect of life in Europe. For him, the merchants were the new nobility, and their conduct correspondingly above censure or blame:

> Trading in merchandise is so necessary that without it the world would not go on. It is this that ennobles kingdoms and makes their peoples great, that ennobles cities, that brings war and peace. Pope Paul II was originally a merchant and he was not ashamed of the time he spent in trade. Nowadays it is carried on throughout the world, and particularly in these [oriental] parts it is held in such high esteem that the great lords here do not do anything else but trade.

The topic which most clearly brought out the dilemma of commerce – how to behave morally in the eyes of the Church while making a healthy profit – was that of usury, or interest-taking on loans. The orthodox view was clear – the lender risked nothing in making surplus cash available to others, and therefore was entitled only to collect his capital when it fell due at a date agreed between borrower and lender: 'The usurer never adventureth or hazardeth the losse of his principall: for he wil have all sufficient securitie for the repaiment and restoring of it backe againe to himselfe.'

The moral difficulty did not arise where interest could be regarded as profit earned by participation in a complicated series of transactions over time. The participants in the kinds of partnership the Treviso arithmetic envisaged, who put up money for a venture in which they ran the risk of losing all or part of their investment, were no usurers, and their gain was not usury but interest, under the title of *periculum sortis* ('the danger of chance'). Someone who lent money which he could otherwise have used profitably in industry or commerce was permitted reasonable compensation for his opportunity lost, under the title of 'lost opportunity for gain'. If the lender incurred additional expenses from the loan, such as the cost of transporting the coins, keeping the accounts, professional fees for drawing up the contract, and insurance premiums, he too had a right to compensation. If the borrower defaulted on repayment, interest could be collected from the date the sum fell due, for the inconvenience to the lender. Profit could also be made lawfully on bills of exchange, because of the slight but real risk of loss of part or all of the money advanced and the uncertain amount of any possible gain, due to fluctuations in foreign-exchange rates.

On 15 July 1515, Johann Eck, professor at the University of Ingolstadt in Germany, conducted a public debate (or disputation) on the subject of usury, in which he argued the moral acceptability of a healthy rate of interest on all loans. According to at least one contemporary account, Eck won a resounding victory against his opponents. His dazzling argument in support of current commercial practice was given wide publicity, his victory being represented as a triumph for all the new German universities. Heinrich Bebel, the first professor of poetry and rhetoric at the University of Tübingen, where Eck had taken his first degree, composed a poem in his honour:

> Our Eck returns, fellow students, rejoice!
> Cry out in delight, you who join me in loving him!
> Rejoice you moderns, followers of Occam the logician,
> With his return, safe and sound from the soil of Italy,
> Not without praise, not without men's honour and esteem,
> Eck gives you back your worldly pleasures.

The source of the admiration for Eck was an ingenious three-tiered arrangement of contracts he had devised for loans. The first contract set up a simple partnership; the second transformed the partnership into a risk-carrying commercial investment, anticipating a profit; under the third contract, the borrower 'sold' the investment opportunity back to the lender, for a guaranteed profit (represented as healthily smaller than the profit anticipated from the imaginary speculation). This formula conveniently let the Church off the hook. It accepted the view that the Bible prohibited all money-lending with interest, but recast the contractual arrangements so that any loan whatsoever could be represented as an investment opportunity of the kind on which it was considered morally acceptable to take 'profit'. This was indeed the sort of solution which allowed the Catholic Church to reconcile itself to current commercial practices, and removed the whiff of sinfulness which hung over everyday merchant practice.

Eck first proposed this solution to the moral difficulties of usury in Tübingen in 1514, and his intervention attracted the immediate attention of the German mercantile community. When the Church authorities in Ingolstadt refused Eck permission, later in 1514, to debate the issue further at the University there, representatives of the Fugger bank intervened to try to persuade them to give him a hearing. His trip to Bologna in 1515, to promote his views on the international stage, was entirely funded by Jakob Fugger – the event, effectively, staged, to give the widest airing possible to a position eminently in the interests of the commercial community.

As what he called an 'afterthought' in his 1515 debate, Eck added a set of arguments justifying the sale of indulgences as a source of Church profit. Two years later, Martin Luther broadcast his compelling theological arguments condemning the 'marketing' of salvation by an overly commercial Church, using the same university debating procedure which had allowed Eck so effectively to promote Fugger interests. The ninety-five points for debate which Luther posted at Wittenberg in 1517 were, indeed, a response to the increasingly powerful arguments being mounted on behalf of the Church, with the heavy backing of the bankers, for the moral accept- ability of the dedicated pursuit of financial gain. Luther's solution – to dissociate the Church entirely from business and commerce – removed the final restraint of moral scruple from commercial practice, giving it free rein to develop its practices outside the moral frame. Business operations became a matter for secular control; the new Reformed Church offered a rigorous programme of personal piety and observance to take care of the merchant's spiritual salvation.

· SEVEN ·

MAPPING THE HEAVENS

IN THE AUTUMN OF 1520 the artist Albrecht Dürer joined an official delegation from his home town of Nuremberg, and attended the coronation in the Palace of Charlemagne at Aachen of the Habsburg Emperor Charles V. On the way home, in Cologne, he did some shopping, keeping a careful record of his expenses, as usual:

> I have bought a tract of Luther's for 5 weisspfennigs. And I spent another weisspfennig for the Condemnation of Luther (that pious man). Also 1 weisspfennig for a rosary. Also 1 weisspfennig for

1. Woodcut portrait of Martin Luther, prefixed to the Strasbourg edition of his *Sermons*

a belt. Also 1 weisspfennig for 1 pfund of candles. I have charged 1 gulden for expenses. I had to give my large oxhorn to Herr Leonard Groland and to Herr Hans Ebner I had to give my big cedarwood rosary (because they would accept no reimbursement for expenses incurred on the journey). I gave 6 weisspfennigs for a pair of shoes. I gave 2 weisspfennigs for a little death's head. I spent 1 weisspfennig for beer and bread.

For the price of a pair of shoes, Dürer acquired the latest instalments in the developing drama of the radical monk Martin Luther's confrontation with the Pope. The printing press meant that Dürer, like thousands of other ordinary German men and women, experienced the Reformation not as a remote quarrel between members of the clergy, but at first hand. It made it possible for him to participate immediately, and comparatively inexpensively, in an international crisis within the Catholic Church as it took shape. Dürer himself had turned to the new technology of printing in his own work as an artist, because he recognized that woodcuts could reach more people, and make him a steadier income, than paintings for rich patrons. Luther, likewise, from the very outset of the controversy, printed his indictments of Church hypocrisy and greed, and used the book-distribution network to circulate them throughout Europe.

2. Albrecht Dürer, *The Fall of Icarus*: Dürer had turned to the new technology of printing because woodcuts could reach more people than paintings

It was another product of the printing press, the papal indulgence, which precipitated Martin Luther's quarrel with the Pope. Indulgences were among the first pieces of commercial manufacturing carried out by the printing press. These single-sheet printed pages contained an official assurance from the Pope that the purchaser (whose name was entered in the space provided) was granted remission from the spiritual penalties for their sins – sometimes the indulgence even included a promise that the penalties for as yet uncommitted future sins were remitted in advance. They became a significant source of income for the Catholic Church at the beginning of the sixteenth century, and were marketed with increasing energy by a clergy for whom raising money for the Church had become a legitimate activity. The indulgence functioned as something between a tax and a commodity. The clergy urged all their parishioners to purchase, thereby raising a levy from them; the individual 'bought'

3. The thriving trade in indulgences at the beginning of the sixteenth century

salvation – an intangible asset, whose efficacy depended on their trust in the Pope and his Church in Rome.

The funds raised by indulgence sales were used for major Church building projects, to pay the papal military forces and to supplement clerical stipends and salaries. Of the cover-price of any indulgence, under region-by-region arrangements, part went to the papal coffers in Rome and part to local interests, to fund Church-related activities. As the Pope's most prominent international tax-gatherers, as well as the foremost marketing company in Europe, the German Fugger bankers were quick to recognize the obvious commercial possibilities of indulgences, and became overall managers of the Church's indulgence business. They collected the takings, and converted the money raised by indulgence sales at locations across Europe into currency appropriate for the Pope's activities elsewhere, delivering it as required. Their own profit was derived from a combination of a percentage of the sale-price of each individual indulgence (from a minimum of 5 per cent) and the commission they took on the currency changing necessary to remit the takings to the Pope. Fugger involvement in almost every European capital enterprise which required substantial funding – from mining to masonry – meant that the bankers also advised on suitable funding packages to be assembled for major undertakings like church-building from mixtures of loans and indulgence sales.

Military expenses and large-scale building projects were major consumers of papal funds raised in this way. In March 1517, Pope Leo X issued an indulgence to finance the reconstruction of St Peter's basilica in Rome – a building project embarked on by his predecessor, Pope Julius II (who had raised the initial funds with another indulgence, the proceeds being applied also to military expenditure against the Ottomans in Hungary). The rebuilding of St Peter's involved some of the greatest Renaissance artists of the day, including both Michelangelo and Raphael, and produced one of the architectural triumphs of the Renaissance. Because of the grandiose nature of the project and the urgent need to raise enormous sums for it, the indulgence was designed with particular extravagance – purchasers and their relatives were forgiven every conceivable sin they had committed, or might commit, and exempted from all suffering in Purgatory, advancing immediately to Heaven. The St Peter's indulgences were sold with especial enthusiasm in Germany, accompanied by charismatic preaching insisting on their efficacy, because under an agreement between the Pope and the local clergy (of which most Germans including Luther were unaware) half of the proceeds from the sale of these indulgences in Germany was to go towards paying the huge debts of the young Archbishop of Mainz. The Archbishop owed the Pope fees for his various German benefices amounting to around 26,000 ducats, and he had borrowed a further 29,000 ducats from the Fuggers.

On 31 October 1517, Martin Luther wrote directly to Albrecht of Mainz, to protest about the St Peter's indulgence:

> With your Electoral Highness's consent, the Papal Indulgence for the rebuilding of St Peter's in Rome is being carried through the land. I do not complain so much at the loud cry of the preacher of Indulgences (who I have not heard), but rather I regret the false meaning which the simple folk attach to it, the poor souls believing that when they have purchased such letters they have secured their salvation, also, that the moment the money jingles in the box souls are delivered from purgatory, and that all sins will be forgiven through a letter of Indulgence.

The ninety-five statements of opposition to papal practices which Luther proposed for public debate in Wittenberg in the same year, and which according to tradition he nailed to the doors of the church at Wittenberg, singled out for special condemnation the Catholic Church's exploitation for financial gain of the ordinary Christian's trust in papal authority. The Catholic Church's direct and, as Luther saw it, deeply inappropriate involvement in the world of commerce and luxury goods triggered the Lutheran Reformation.

4. Leo X's Bull denouncing Martin
Luther and his followers

In June 1520, Pope Leo X responded to Luther's public attacks on Church practices with a public condemnation of his religious opinions in a papal bull (an authorized announcement), drafted and delivered to Germany by Johann Eck (who five years earlier had defended the Fuggers' commercial interests in his public debate on usury and interest rates). So much public interest in Luther and his challenge to the Pope had been generated by this time that a number of presses printed and circulated copies of the 'Exsurge Domine' Bull. Some of these, like the one edited for the press by the Lutheran sympathizer Ulrich von Hutten, already carried critical responses to the Pope's pronouncements. In his preface, von Hutten accused the Pope of wanting to suppress Christian truth and German liberty, and in a postscript he exhorted Leo X to stop interfering with Luther and his followers. Luther himself issued some of his most provocative pamphlets in 1520. The 5 weisspfennig work which Dürer bought in Cologne was probably the *Appeal to the Christian Nobility of the German Nation Respecting the Reformation of the Christian Estate* – a rousing work in German, addressed to members of the Imperial Diet, which became an instant best-seller.

Dürer was already a convinced supporter of Luther when he bought the latest publications in his cause hot from the press. A list in Dürer's handwriting of sixteen of Luther's early pamphlets survives, all of them dating from the years 1518 to 1520. They include Luther's pamphlet against indulgences (Wittenberg, 1518); the sermon on indulgences and Grace (Wittenberg, 1518); the sermon on the 'Exsurge Domine' Bull (Leipzig, 1520); one of the two early pamphlets on the Ten Commandments (1518); two sermons on penitence; a tract on three kinds of sin; tracts on confession and on receiving the sacrament, on the meaning of Christ's passion; on marriage (Leipzig, 1519); a sermon preached in Leipzig (1519); the explanation of the meaning of the Lord's Prayer (Leipzig, 1518); Luther's translation of the Seven Penitential Psalms (Leipzig, 1518); an explanation of Psalm 109, addressed to Jerome Ebner; and Luther's public debate against Johann Eck at Leipzig (1519).

Earlier in 1520, Duke Frederick the Wise, Elector of Saxony, for whom Dürer had carried out a number of commissions, and who was also Luther's protector, had himself sent the artist one of Luther's works as a gift. Dürer wrote to George Spalatin, court chaplain and secretary to Duke Frederick, thanking him enthusiastically:

> Most worthy dear sir! I have already sent you my thanks in a brief letter after having read only your note. Only afterward, when the little bag that held the book was turned inside out, did I find your real letter, from which I learned that it was my gracious lord himself who sent me Luther's little book. If God helps me to come to Dr Martin Luther, then I will draw his portrait with care and engrave it in copper for a lasting remembrance of this Christian man. And I beg your worthiness to send

5. Lucas Cranach,
*Portrait of Frederick
the Wise, Elector
of Saxony*

me for my money anything new that Dr Martin may write in German.

Dürer never got to draw Luther's portrait, nor even to meet him – his own commitment to Luther's dissenting religious position and his admiration for the man were destined to continue to be based only upon a print acquaintance with the reformer. In the years 1517 to 1526 alone, around 2000 printed editions of Luther's sermons and books appeared, not counting the flood of popular pamphlets, broadsides and single-sheet woodcuts from Lutheran sympathizers. Dürer could saturate himself in the intensity of Luther's thought without leaving his study.

The extraordinary personal fervour of Dürer's commitment to Luther's cause, as recorded in his own diary, is eloquent testimony to the power and vividness of the early printed word. On 17 May 1521, a false rumour reached Dürer that Luther had been arrested and imprisoned, following his condemnation as a heretic by the Imperial Council meeting (or Diet) of the Emperor Charles V, at Worms. In fact Luther had been taken into protective custody by the Elector of Saxony, Frederick, but it was many months before this became clear and his whereabouts became known. Rumours spread like wildfire: Luther had been arrested; he had been imprisoned; he had been murdered. On 17 May, a distraught Albrecht Dürer wrote:

On Friday before Whitsunday in the year 1521 the news came to me in Antwerp that Martin Luther had been treacherously taken prisoner. For he had trusted Charles V's herald Caspar Sturm with the Imperial safe-conduct which guaranteed him immunity. And whether he is still alive, or whether they have murdered him, which I know not, he has suffered this for the sake of Christian truth and because he rebuked the unchristian Papacy, which strives with its heavy load of human laws against the redemption of Christ.

And if we have lost this man who has written more clearly than any that has lived, and to whom Thou hast given such a spirit of the Gospel, we pray Thee, O Heavenly father, that Thou wouldst again give Thy Holy Spirit to another, that he may gather Thy church anew everywhere together, that we may again live united and in a Christian manner, and so, by our good works, all unbelievers as Turks, Heathen, and Calicuts, may of themselves, turn to us and embrace the Christian faith.

May every man who reads Dr Martin Luther's books see how clear and transparent his teaching is when he sets forth the Holy Gospel.

O God, if Luther is dead, who will henceforth deliver the Holy Gospel to us with such clearness? Ach, God, what might he not still have written for us in ten or twenty years?

At the Diet of Worms in 1521, the Emperor Charles V, having heard Luther's passionate plea for his support for his religious views, pronounced him a heretic:

You know that I am descended from the most Christian emperors of the noble German nation, from the Catholic kings of Spain, the archduke of Austria and the dukes of Burgundy. To the honour of God, the strengthening of the faith, and the salvation of souls, they all have remained up to death faithful sons of the Church and have always been defenders of the Catholic faith, the sacred rituals, decrees, ordinances and holy customs. For this reason I am determined to support everything that these predecessors and I myself have kept, up to the present.

Having heard the obstinate answer which Luther gave yester-day, 18 April, in the presence of us all, I declare to you that I regret having so long delayed to proceed against this Luther and his false doctrine and I am no longer willing to hear him speak more. I am determined to proceed against him as a notorious heretic.

The Diet of Worms, which condemned the activities of Martin Luther and outlawed him in all Charles's territories, brought together delegates from all over the imperial territories (with the Pope's representatives in attendance) to settle a number of pressing policy issues. In that capacity the Diet also heard a formal complaint brought by an Augsburg merchant, Bartholomew Rem, against the powerful Höchstetter firm of merchant bankers. Rem claimed that he was entitled to 33,000 florins as his share of the profits derived from a commercial partnership in which he had invested the sum of 900 florins, over a period of six years. According to the Höchstetters, Rem was entitled only to 26,000 florins. Both sides obstinately refused to give way. Neither the attempt at conciliation by the city council in Augsburg nor even the personal intervention of Jakob Fugger himself (as senior banker locally) managed to bring about a satisfactory outcome to the affair.

The discussion of Rem's case at Worms unleashed a public outcry against the activities of the big German merchant-banking firms, and in particular against their monopolies in key commodities like silver, copper, lead, alum, leather, wax, cereal crops and wine. It was claimed that the exclusive holdings in essential raw materials by large firms like the Höchstetters and the Fuggers had driven up prices and was threatening the livelihoods of smaller family companies like Rem's. Rem's own case got no further at the Diet – he refused to relinquish goods belonging to the Höchstetters which he had seized in lieu of the profits he claimed he was owed, and was thrown into prison. But Charles V established a further Diet of his Imperial Council at Nuremberg, to look more closely into the practices of the big commercial companies. This new Diet was to conduct a survey of public feeling by putting three questions to the principal towns of the German Empire. Were the large commercial companies prejudicial to the public interest? Should all the commercial companies be disbanded, or their activities merely limited? How could this limitation be achieved and the abuses by the commercial companies suppressed?

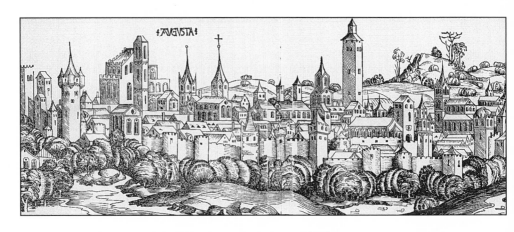

6. View of Augsburg from Hartmann Schedel, *Nuremberg Chronicle*

Of the German cities which made representation to the 1522 Diet of Nuremberg, only Augsburg – home of the Fuggers and the Welsers – considered that the operations of the big merchant-banking companies were not prejudicial to the public interest. In a long reply, that city defended unlimited commercial activity by the big companies, rejecting any intervention by the state. Instead of responding directly to the first question (Were the large commercial companies prejudicial to the public interest?), the Augsburg city council reported on the related question of whether commerce itself was useful or harmful in general. In all the states and cities where commerce was conducted, they submitted, the population profited, and not simply the burghers, but also the peasants and artisans. Customs duties, levies and other taxes increased the revenues of princes and governments. When commercial activity was interrupted by war, 'it is the man in the street who complains most loudly'. The report singled out Venice as the prime example of a city whose wealth and international prominence derived directly from her trading activities. The shift of the pepper trade from Venice to Lisbon, following the Portuguese discovery of a sea-route to the Indian Ocean, had, the Augsburg council argued, done the city of Venice as much damage as ten years of wars against the Habsburg Emperor. All the most important powers in Europe owed their power to the wealth brought in by trade – 'that is what commerce means to a city'.

On the basis of the evidence submitted by the major German trading centres, the Diet of Nuremberg established a table showing price inflation in the spice trade over the period 1515 to 1522. Among its findings were the following:

1 pound of Aquila saffron	1516	2 florins	27 kreuzers
	1522	4 florins	0 kreuzers
1 pound of cloves	1513	1 florin	27 kreuzers
	1522	2 florins	0 kreuzers
1 pound of cinnamon	1517	2 florins	24 kreuzers
	1519	2 florins	45 kreuzers
1 pound of nutmeg	1519	0 florins	27 kreuzers
	1522	3 florins	28 kreuzers
1 pound of pepper	1518	0 florins	18 kreuzers
	1521	0 florins	33 kreuzers
1 quintal of sugar loaf	1515	12 florins	
	1518	20 florins	

As these figures submitted by the various German trading centres clearly showed, prices of these kinds of luxury imports from the East had almost doubled over little more than five years. But the Augsburg delegation remained unconvinced that restricting the activities of the major German merchant bankers would improve the situation. Of the estimated 36,000 quintals of pepper imported by the German merchants from Portugal, less than a twentieth was consumed locally – the remainder was sold on at a profit, contributing to the wealth of the Emperor and his Empire (as well as that of the merchants themselves). The Portuguese would, in any case, do business only on monopoly terms – if no German merchant could play this role, the trade would be lost to one of the countries with readier access to Portugal. Limitation of the big commercial companies would, the Augsburg report concluded, do untold, irreversible harm to German business, leading to its ruin, 'for business cannot operate properly under any constraints whatsoever'.

Augsburg's stand on commerce, like its prosperity itself, was controlled by its influential merchant families, above all the Fuggers and Welsers. Fifteen-twenty-two was the year in which Magellan's triumphant discovery of an alternative route to the pepper trade was celebrated in Augsburg as its very own triumph – finally breaking the Portuguese cartel. The spokesman for the Augsburg position on commercial companies was Bartholomew Welser's brother-in-law, the distinguished jurist Conrad Peutinger, clerk to the city council. It was his meticulously researched arguments which lay behind the Augsburg submission, and which were used subsequently to draw up an alternative proposal, to counter the majority decision of the Nuremberg Diet that severe restrictions should immediately be introduced against the monopolizing companies.

The Diet's proposal that no company should be allowed to hold more than 50,000 florins in capital was unthinkable for a firm like the Fuggers, with assets of several millions, and twenty or more commercial outlets in the major commercial centres throughout Europe: at the time this proposal was under consideration, the Fugger agency in Antwerp alone was holding more than 100,000 florins' worth of copper in its reserves. In 1523 Jakob Fugger finally intervened with the Emperor, writing a letter in which he recalled Charles V's financial obligations to the Fugger firm, and the inevitable impact which regulation of the merchant-banking firms would have on imperial funds. At a third Diet in Nuremberg in 1524, in spite of continued pressure from most of the participating delegates, the whole matter was handed over to the Emperor, who duly scrapped all restrictions as being against the national interest. On the basis of a document prepared by Conrad Peutinger, the Emperor formally declared that 'the activities of the merchant bankers has never contributed to price inflation'.

The third Nuremberg Diet, in 1524, was held at the height of the Lutheran controversy. While the authorities of the Catholic Church and the secular authorities debated the powers of the commercial companies, they also discussed their policies with regard

7. The printer and instrument-maker Johann Schöner

to the proponents of Church reform. Nuremberg's position as a thriving centre for international commercial trade, with wealthy individuals willing to invest in new business ventures, including scholarly and scientific publishing, had turned it into something of a centre for new technology. It was well known internationally for the manufacture of the new instruments associated with navigation and the oriental trade-routes – maps, compasses, astrolabes, globes and scientific books. So while the chief spokesman or *nuncio* for the Pope, Cardinal Campeggio, was in Nuremberg for the Diet, he took the opportunity to order the latest mathematical books and globes to the value of about 20 florins from the printer and instrument-maker Johann Schöner. When it came to settling his account at the end of his visit, however, Cardinal Campeggio refused to pay for his purchases, on the grounds that Schöner was a known Lutheran, and as the Pope's representative he could not do business with heretics.

¶ Hęc opera fient in oppido Nuremberga Germanię ductu Ioannis de Monteregio.

ALIENA.

¶ Theoricę nouę planetarum Georgii Purbachii astronomi celebratissimi: cum figurationibus oportunis.

Marci Manlii astronomica. ¶ Hęc duo explicita sunt.

Cosmographia Ptolemęi noua traductioę. Nā uetula ista Iacobi Angeli Florētini quę uulgo habetur uiciosa ē: interpte ipso (bona ueia dictū fuerit) neqȝ liguę gręcę satis neqȝ matheāticę noticiam tenente. Qua i re summis arbitris fidem haberi fas erit: Theodoro Gaze clarissimo uiro ac gręcę latine cp dodctissimo: & Paulo Florentino gręcarū quidem haud ignaro: in mathematicis aūt plurimū excellenti.

Magna compositio Ptolemęi: quā uulgo uocāt Almaiestū noua traductione.

Euclidis elemēta cum anaphoricis Hypsiclis editione Campani euulsis tamen plerisȝ mendis: quę pprio etiā idicabūtur cō mentariolo.

Theonis alexandrini clarissimi mathematici commentaria in Almaiestum.

Procli sufformationes astronomicę.

Quadriptitum Ptolemęi & Centum fructus eiusdē noua tra ductione.

Iulius Firmicus quantus reperitur.

Leopoldus de Austria. & si qui alii pdictores astrologici illustratione digni uidebuntur. Nam Antonii quoqȝ de Montulmo quis fragmenta in usum multipliciem exponentur.

Archimedis geometrę acutissimi epa de sphęra & cylindro. De circuli dimensione. De conalibus & sphęralibus. De lineis spiralibus. De ęquipōderātibus. De quadratura parabolę. De ba renȝ numero. Cum cōmētariis Eutocii ascalonitę i tria opera ex pdictis: scilicet de sphęra & cylindro. de dimensione circuli. de equipōderātibus. Traductio est Iacobi cremonēsis: sed nō nusȝ emendata.

Perspectiua Vitelonis. opus ingens ac nobile.

Perspectiua Ptolemęi.

Musica Ptolemęi cum expositione Porbyrii.

Menelai sphęrica noua editione.

Theodosii sphęrica. item de habitationibus. de diebus & noctibus noua traductione.

Apollonii pergensis conica. Item Sereni cylindrica.

Heronis inuenta spiritualia. Opus mechanicū mirę uolptatis.

Elementa arithmetica Iordani. Data eiusdem arithmetica.

Quadriptitū numerorū. Opus uariis scatens argutiis.

Problemata mechanica Aristotelis.

Hygini Astronomia cum deformatione imaginū cęlestium.

¶ Facta pterea est arbor rhetoricę tullianę speciosa imagine. Et fiet descriptio totius habitabilis notę quam uulgo appellant Mappam mundi. Cęterū Germanię particularis tabula: itē Italię: Hispanię: Gallię uniuersę: Gręcięqȝ. Sed & suas cuiqȝ historias ex auctoribus plurimis cursim colligere statutū est: quę uidelicet ad montes: quę ad maria: ad lacus amnes qȝ ac alia particularia loca spectare uidebuntur.

OPIFICIS

tentata. quę essent ne pdenda an non: pudor ingenuus & respublica litteraria diu iter se disceptauere. Ratio audendum censuit.

¶ Kalendarium nouū quo promūt coniuctiones uerę atqȝ oppositiones lumiarium. item qȝ eclipses eorūdē figuratę. Aoca luminarium uera quotidie. borarū tam ęquinoctialium q̄ temporalium discrimia duplici instrumento ad quasuis habitati ones. ac alia pluria scitu iucūdissima.

Ephemerides quas uulgo uocāt Almanach ad trigintaduos annos futuros. ubi quotidie intueberis ueros motus oim planetarū capitisqȝ draconis lunaris: una cū aspectibus lunę ad solem & planetas. boris etiam aspectuū eorundem haud friuole adnotatis. neqȝ planetarū inter se aspectibus pretermissis. In frontibus paginarum posita sunt indicia latitudinū. Eclipses denisqȝ luminarium si quę futurę sunt locis suis effigurantur.

¶ Hęc duo opera iam prope absoluta sunt.

¶ Commentaria magna in Cosmographiā Ptolemęi: ubi exponitur fabrica usus qȝ instrumēti Meteoroscopii: quo Ptolemęus ipse uniuersos ferme numeros toti operis sui elicuit. Fal so eni quispiā crediderit tot lōgitudinum latitudinum qȝ nu meros per supernorum obseruationes inotuisse. Pręterea de scriptio sphęrę armillaris una cū tota habitabili i plano ita di lucidatur ut plerisqȝ omnes discere q̄ant. quam nemo antebac latine intellexit uicio traductoris obstante.

Commentariolū singulare contra traductionem Iacobi Angeli Florentini. quod ad arbitros mittetur.

Theonis alexandrini defensio i sex uoluminibȝ cōtra Georgiū Trapezuntiū. ubi plane quis deprehendet friuola eius esse cō mētaria i Almaiestū. traductionē qȝ ipsam operis ptolemaici uicio non carere.

Commentariolum quo cōmonstrantur placita Campani ex editione elementorum geometricorum reiicienda.

De quinqȝ corporibus ęquilateris quę uulgo regularia nūcupātur: quę uidelicet eorum locū impleant corporalē & quę nō. contra commentatore Aristotelis Auerroem.

Cōmētaria i libros Archimedis eos qui Eutocii expositiōe carēt.

De quadratura circuli. contra Nicolaum Cusensem.

De directionibus. contra Archidiaconum parmensem.

De distinctione domiciliorū cęli. contra Campanū & Ioannem Gazulū ragusinū: cuius & alia de boris temporalibus decreta ibidem retractantur.

De motu octauę sphęrę. contra Tebith suos qȝ sectatores.

De instauratione kalendarii ecclesię.

Breuiarium Almaiesti.

De triangulis omnimodis quiqȝ uolumina.

Problemata astronomica ad Almaiestum totum spectantia.

De Cometę magnitudie remotioę qȝ a tra. de loco eiȝ uero & cęt.

Problemata geometrica oi moda. Opus fructuosę iucūditatis.

Ludus pānoniēsis. quę alias uocare libuit Tabulas directionū.

Tabula magna pmi mobilis cū usu multiplici ratōnibȝ qȝ certis.

Radii uisorii multorum generū cū usibus suis.

De pōderibȝ et aquęductibȝ cū figurationibȝ istrumētoȝ ad eas res necessariorum.

De speculis ustoriis atqȝ aliis multorū generū usufqȝ stupendi.

¶ In officina fabrili Astrarium in continuo tractatu est. Opus plane pro miraculo spectandum. Fiunt & alia instrumenta astronomica ad obseruationes cęlestium. item qȝ alia ad usum uulga rem quotidianum. quorum nomina longum est recitare.

¶ Postremo omnium artem illam mirificam litterarum formatricem monimentis stabilibus mā dare decretum est. (deus bone faueas) qua re explicita si mox obdormierit opifex, mors acerba non erit: quom tantum munus posteris in hereditate reliquerit: quo ipsi se ab inopia librorum ppetuo poterunt uindicare.

8. Regiomontanus' trade catalogue of forthcoming scientific titles

Johann Schöner was another member of the intellectual circle of Dürer's patron and friend Willibald Pirckheimer. Among the instruments he is known to have constructed were three important engraved metal globes incorporating the cartographical discoveries from Magellan's voyage. He was an outstanding mathematician and astronomer in his own right, and in 1526, on the advice of the educationalist and close associate of Luther, Philip Melanchthon, he was nominated to the chair of mathematics at the New Gymnasium at Nuremberg. His printing press specialized in technical scientific, astronomical and mathematical works – inspired, like other Nuremberg presses, by the great example of their fellow townsman Regiomontanus a generation earlier. The Schöner press produced editions of many of the works which Regiomontanus had promised to the public, in the widely publicized advertisement of 'forthcoming works' which he had issued shortly before his premature death in 1476. These included both obscure works by the ancient geometers and their commentators and works by Regiomontanus himself. Schöner also published his own star tables and calendars, based on his astronomical observations.

The extraordinary impact of scientific publishing out of Nuremberg on the development of mathematics and astronomy can be judged by the library of the Professor of Mathematics at the University of Tübingen, Johann Scheubel, who willed his books and instruments to the University when he died in 1570. The hundred-odd books, published in the 1540s and 1550s, which he owned included eleven of the titles which Regiomontanus had identified in his 'schedule' as key texts shortly before his death, including the works of the ancient geometer Archimedes, Regiomontanus' own plane and spherical trigonometry treatise, *On Triangles*, his astronomical tables and his treatise on the use of astronomical instruments, and *New Planetary Theory* by his teacher and collaborator Peuerbach (this became the standard text on planetary motion until the end of the sixteenth century). He also owned several Arabic commentaries on Ptolemy's *Almagest* in Latin translation. Well over a quarter of these titles were from Nuremberg presses, and the majority of these from the press of Johannes Petreius. On the basis of a collection like Scheubel's, a competent mathematician was equipped to make the intellectual leap from simple critical assessment of the Greek geometers to fundamental advances in mathematics, astronomy and navigation.

When the young mathematician Georgius Joachim Rheticus set off from Nuremberg to visit the astronomer Nicolaus Copernicus in Frauenburg in Poland in the spring of 1539, he took with him as a gift a collection of German-printed books on mathematics and astronomy. Rheticus had been given leave of absence from the new, progressive university at Wittenberg in 1538 to visit a number of distinguished German mathematicians, and had spent some time working with Johann Schöner in Nuremberg. From Schöner Rheticus learned of the existence of the Polish mathematician and astronomer Nicolaus Copernicus (then in his sixties), who was rumoured to have devised an entirely revolutionary theory of planetary motion. Before he left to learn more about the new astronomy from its source, Schöner took Rheticus to meet another Nuremberg printer, Johannes Petreius, to discuss the possibility of publishing Copernicus' work. The two scholar–publishers, Petreius and Schöner, were undoubtedly responsible for putting together the package of important mathematical books which Rheticus took with him. The German-published works they chose advertised the scholarliness and sophistication of northern scientific publishing, as well as offering the latest specialist mathematical works for Copernicus' private library.

This gift package included the first printed editions of the Greek originals of Euclid's *Elements* (together with the latest Latin translations), the ancient geometer Proclus' *Commentary on Euclid, Book I*, and the German mathematician and instrument-maker Peter Apian's *Book on Sines*. But the most important volume presented to Copernicus by Rheticus was Regiomontanus' innovative trigonometrical work, *On Triangles*, which had been published for the first time in 1533 by Johann Schöner's Nuremberg press.

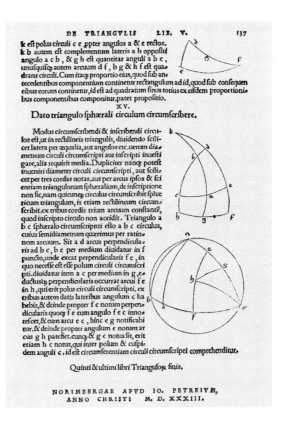

9. A page from
Regiomontanus'
innovative
On Triangles

Regiomontanus' little work was of crucial significance for both astronomers and navigators. It built on the foundations of the Greek geometers Euclid, Pappus and Archimedes to establish a series of important theorems in spherical trigonometry – the mathematics required, for instance, in surveying or astronomy to calculate location and distance by taking bearings on two remote points, so as to make allowance for the curvature of the earth. *On Triangles* provided Copernicus with additional mathematical support for the validity of his new model for the movement of the planetary system – the revolutionary model which replaced the earth by the sun as the centre of the system, requiring the assumption that the earth, like all the other planets, rotated in the heavens.

10. Astrolabe made
by Regiomontanus

Like every other astronomer of the period, Copernicus had already been using Regiomontanus' *Epitome* of Ptolemy's *Almagest* – the abbreviated and closely commented version of Ptolemy's work on planetary motion produced by Regiomontanus in collaboration with his own Nuremberg mentor Peuerbach. Copernicus had also relied upon their *Tables of Eclipses*. Having worked through the copy of Regiomontanus' *On Triangles* which Rheticus had brought him, Copernicus modified his presentation of the theorems in spherical trigonometry which provided the preamble to the detailed mathematical reasoning in his *On the Revolutions of the Celestial Spheres* – the mathematical justification of circular orbits for all the planets (including the earth) with the sun as the fixed centre. To

11. Nicolaus Copernicus' autograph manuscript of his *On the Revolution of the Celestial Spheres,* inserting his transcriptions of Regiomontanus

effect this modification in his almost completed handwritten text, which Rheticus was waiting to take off to Nuremberg for publication, Copernicus inserted two additional sheets of paper into the manuscript, between the sheets now numbered 23 and 26, and there transcribed Regiomontanus' proofs. Sixty years after his death, Regiomontanus' trigonometry put the final touches to the sun-centred Copernican system, which was finally to dislodge the Ptolemaic earth-centred system and usher in the scientific revolution.

At Frauenberg, on 23 September 1539, Rheticus finished writing his *First Report*, summarizing the revolutionary discoveries of Copernican astronomy, which was subsequently published in Gdansk. The *First Report* was written in the form of a personal letter from Rheticus to the man who had aroused his interest in Copernican astronomy, Johann Schöner:

To the illustrious Johann Schöner, as to his own revered father, G. Joachim Rheticus sends his greetings.

On May 14th I wrote you a letter from Posen in which I informed you that I had undertaken a journey to Prussia, and I promised to declare, as soon as I could, whether the actuality answered to report and to my own expectation. However, I have been able to devote scarcely ten weeks to mastering the astronomical work of the learned man to whom I have repaired. Nevertheless, to fulfil my promises at last and gratify your desires, I shall set forth, as briefly and clearly as I can, the opinions of my teacher on the topics which I have studied.

First of all I wish you to be convinced, most learned Schöner, that this man whose work I am now treating is in every field of knowledge and in mastery of astronomy not inferior to Regiomontanus. I rather compare him with Ptolemy, not because I consider Regiomontanus inferior to Ptolemy, but because my teacher shares with Ptolemy the good fortune of completing, with the aid of divine kindness, the reconstruction of astronomy which he began, while Regiomontanus – alas, cruel fate – departed this life before he had time to erect his columns.

The full text of Copernicus' *On the Revolutions of the Celestial Spheres* was eventually published in 1543, seen through Petreius' press by Rheticus. The printed version of Copernicus' epoch-making demonstration that the sun was at the centre of the planetary system, and that the earth revolved around it, along with all the other planets, finally made the theory public – to the horror of the Catholic Church, which immediately denounced it as heretical. Rheticus himself went on to become a distinguished mathematician, whose work

12. Giorgione's imaginary meeting of Regiomontanus (left), Ptolemy (centre) and Aristotle (right) – the fathers of astronomy

13. A detail from Albrecht Dürer, *Martyrdom of the Ten Thousand Christians,* showing Willibald Pirckheimer standing on the left of the artist

on trigonometry (in particular the computation of trigonometrical tables in his own *On Triangles*) earned him an independent place in the history of mathematics.

Rheticus was a convinced Lutheran; Copernicus was a canon of the Catholic Church. While individual Catholic officials like Campeggio scandalously exploited the volatile religious situation to their own advantage, the mathematicians ignored their spiritual differences in pursuit of scientific truth. But, although scholars genuinely believed that their technical arguments in specialist fields were immune to sectarian division, the Lutheran controversy did inevitably have an impact on their lives and careers. In 1534, when the Augsburg city council officially joined the Reformation, the lawyer Conrad Peutinger, who on behalf of the Augsburg merchants had steadfastly argued the case for commercial freedom, the legitimacy of taking interest in business undertakings and the desirability of big monopoly firms in international trade, was forced to resign his post as clerk to the council, a post he had held for thirty-seven years. His secular convictions regarding commerce were seen as committing him to the spiritual position of the Catholic Church.

Although Dürer never managed to meet his hero Luther, his patron and friend Willibald Pirckheimer entertained Luther on several occasions. Pirckheimer, who came from a wealthy Nuremberg merchant family, served on the Nuremberg city council and acted as patron to a wide range of artists and scholars. He was himself a Greek scholar (his parents had sent him to Italy as a youth, to acquire a humanistic education), and published translations of the works of the classical authors Xenophon, Plutarch and Plato into Latin. On his handsome annual unearned income of 750 florins he entertained local and visiting scholars in his comfortable city home, which became renowned as a scholarly salon. His network of connections was responsible for the introduction of a number of northern artists and scholars to one another – Conrad Peutinger introduced Pirckheimer to Erasmus of Rotterdam in 1514, and Pirckheimer subsequently introduced Erasmus to Dürer, who drew Erasmus' portrait, but could not forgive him for failing to speak out on Luther's behalf.

On Pirckheimer's international network, scholars and merchants constantly rubbed shoulders. Erasmus' close friend Pieter Gilles was chief secretary to the city council of Antwerp. In 1517 he provided a letter of introduction for the astronomer and instrument-maker Nicolaus Kratzer to take to Erasmus, then in Louvain:

Pieter Gilles to Erasmus of Rotterdam, Antwerp, 18 January 1517.

I felt it my duty to write to you, since Nicolaus Kratzer, who is an expert in astronomy, was leaving for your part of the world. He has with him several astrolabes and spheres to be sold there. He is bringing you a Greek book sent by the prior of St Agnes;

I took responsibility for the book, and gave the courier a receipt signed by me. The printer Thierry Martens told me of your warm and friendly reception by the theologians at Louvain, which gave me great pleasure. I hear that the god-parent of my daughter, Cuthbert Tunstall, has left. I am sorry for your sake, for I know that he was more congenial to your way of life than most people here. In Paris I bought some books – Suetonius, with Flavius Vopiscus, Spartianus and many others, printed some time ago in Italy. If you would like them to be sent to you, let me know as soon as you can, and I will see they are dispatched post-haste. My wife, who is now a mother, and my father send their best greetings. Farewell, and count me your friend, as I, you well know, am yours.

By the end of 1517, Kratzer was in England, having taken with him a manuscript on dials (instruments for calculating time) as a gift for Henry VIII. It may be that, like Holbein, Kratzer travelled to England with a letter of introduction from Erasmus to his close friend at the English Court, Thomas More. He divided his time there (as we saw in Chapter 6) between using his specialist technical skills to make scientific instruments and maps for patrons associated with the English Court, and participating in the commercial activities of the Company of German Merchants in London (in the 1520s he held a licence for importing wine and dyestuffs).

The Pirckheimer network used the connection between Pirckheimer, Pieter Gilles, Erasmus and Thomas More to help Kratzer get to England. It came into play again in 1524, when Kratzer wanted precise information about a navigational instrument which Pirckheimer had obtained, and wrote to Dürer (incidentally enquiring about the progress of the Lutheran cause, with which he, like Dürer, had sympathies):

I must write to you because you are all followers of the Gospel in Nuremberg. May God send you grace, that you may persevere to the end, for the adversaries are strong, but God is still stronger. Dear Master Albrecht, I pray you to draw for me a model of the instrument that you saw at Herr Pirckheimer's, by which distances can be measured, and of which you spoke to me at Antwerp, or that you will ask Herr Pirckheimer to send me a description of the said instrument. Also I desire to know what you ask for copies of all your prints, and if there is anything new at Nuremberg in my craft. Greet in my name Herr Pirckheimer. I hope shortly to make a map of England which is a great country and was not known to Ptolemy; Herr Pirckheimer will be glad to see it.

Since Pirckheimer was in the final stages of his translation of Ptolemy's *Geography*, the promise of a map of England was presumably extremely welcome. Dürer replied to Kratzer that Pirckheimer was having a copy of the instrument made for Kratzer himself, and would soon send it. Dürer himself wanted to know whether Kratzer was going ahead with his plan to publish a translation of Euclid. As for Luther and his struggles, Dürer preferred not to write about it in a letter.

The to-and-fro of information and expertise between the members of the intellectual circle around Willibald Pirckheimer in Nuremberg shows how closely intertwined the lives of the northern draughtsmen, cartographers, scientific publishers and instrument-makers were. They were all drawn to commercial centres where their skills could be applied in travel and trade, and they all came out of the same milieu as the budding northern reformers. They kept in touch with one another, and exchanged books and technical equipment. Since their work obliged them to travel, they were probably also involved in information-gathering for patrons – Cuthbert Tunstall proposed Nicolaus Kratzer as a useful man to collect information on Charles V's German territories and on the Lutheran controversy during a trip to Antwerp in 1520 (Dürer was also in Antwerp on that occasion, and Kratzer was present when he sketched

14. Woodcut showing scientists wielding a range of astronomical instruments, from Peter Apian, *Instrumentenbuch*

Erasmus). In 1533 when Holbein, in London, needed some scientific equipment for his painting of Jean de Dinteville and Georges de Selve, now known as *The Ambassadors*, Kratzer and other members of the Company of German Merchants obliged, lending globes and a merchant's arithmetic by Peter Apian (another German scientific publisher and instrument-maker). If technical treatises from Luca Pacioli's *Mathematical Compendium* of 1494 onwards combined pure mathematics, mathematics for surveying and commercial arithmetic in a single volume, that was because the worlds of the scholar, the technical engineer and the merchant were in practice inseparable.

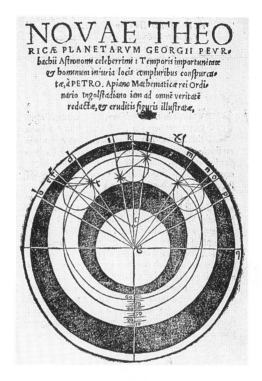

15. Frontispiece of Peter Apian, *New Planetary Theory*

One shared characteristic of all the individuals who frequented Pirckheimer's comfortable Nuremberg home was their mobility. Their work took them all over Europe, and brought them into contact with those who travelled still further, along the new trade-routes, east and west. Of all the technical equipment with which the members of this diverse group supported their professional activities, the importance to them of the printed book far outweighed all others. A striking number of the Pirckheimer circle had immediate links to publishing – not just as the authors of printed works, but as press-owners, book-distributors, editors and proof-correctors. Printed books transmitted new information between them across considerable distances in remarkably short time – their letters contain regular references to books sent, books acquired, books ordered for one another. Books were also their preferred personal gifts. In one of Erasmus' published works he dramatizes the ending to an intellectual dinner-party at which the wealthy host (like Pirckheimer) hands out parting gifts to his friends:

> *Eusebius.* Since this is the first time I've had you to dinner, I won't send you away without presents, but they'll be ones in keeping with our style. They're all worth about the same – nothing that is. There are four little books, two clocks, a small lamp, and a case with Memphian pens. This little vellum book contains Solomon's proverbs. It teaches wisdom, and is decorated with gold because gold symbolizes wisdom. This shall be given to our white-haired friend Timothy, so that, in accordance with evangelical teaching, wisdom be given to him who hath wisdom and he may have abundance.
>
> *Timothy.* Assuredly I'll endeavour to need it the less.
>
> *Eusebius.* This little book has Matthew's Gospel on vellum: worthy of a jewelled cover were it not that no bookcase or cover is dearer to it than a man's heart. This then is for you, learned Theophilus, to make you more like your name.
>
> *Theophilus.* I'll try to see that you won't regret your gift.
>
> *Eusebius.* Here are Paul's Epistles, which you, Eulalius, who are always quoting Paul, like to carry about with you. You wouldn't have him in your mouth unless he were in your heart. After this he'll be more readily in your hands and eyes too.
>
> *Eulalius.* This is to give counsel, not a gift. No gift is more precious than good counsel.

The circulation of printed books was the vital blood-supply to the Renaissance growth and dissemination of knowledge. Some indication of the order of magnitude of the impact of the printing press may be gathered from the fact that already by 1500 over 25,000 separate titles had been published in Germany alone, excluding broadsheets and pamphlets.

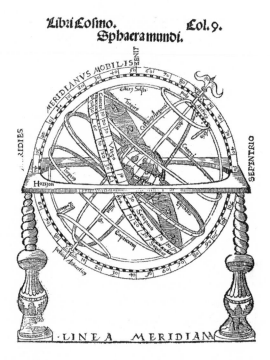

16. Peter Apian's
Sphaeramundi

Among the books which Rheticus presented to Copernicus was a mathematical work of Peter Apian's. In the same volume, printed for the first time, was a work on astronomy by the twelfth-century Spanish Muslim mathematician, Jabir ibn Aflah (or Geber, as he was latinized), in Gerard of Cremona's Latin translation. Geber's work was highly critical of the Ptolemaic system – the Arabic title translated as 'Treatise for the Reform of the *Almagest*' – although the author proposed no alternative system. Just as the Lutheran schism within the Christian Church did not prevent learned Catholics from collaborating with Lutheran sympathizers, neither did the permanent state of tension between the empires of Charles V and the Ottomans interfere with scientific exchange between the Christian and Islamic intellectual traditions. Once again, it was the printing press which made the consequent significant advances in navigation and astronomy possible.

The constructive dialogue between Christian and Islamic scientists and mathematicians which print allowed had its origins in an earlier, more deliberate attempt to bring Eastern and Western traditions together. From the 1440s there had been those, like Gemisthus Plethon, who believed that out of the turmoil of contemporary Churches and creeds would emerge a 'fundamental theology' ('prisca theologia'), or unified religion, which would bring the Eastern Orthodox, Roman Catholic, Muslim and Jewish religions together in something resembling ancient Greek philosophy. The Academy which Cosimo de' Medici funded in Florence was dedicated to the study of the Greek philosopher Plato as part of such an enterprise.

The papal secretary Georgius Trapezuntius, who like Plethon and Bessarion was an exile from the Eastern Church, was in Naples when he heard the news that Constantinople had fallen to the Ottoman forces of Mehmed II on 29 May 1453. The news had reached Venice on 29 June. On 30 June, the Venetian Senate sent a courier to Rome. Pope Nicholas V received the letter on 8 July. On 13 July Cardinal Bessarion wrote urgently to all the principal cities in Italy, relaying the news to them, and urging them to rally to the Pope's call for a crusade to recover Constantinople for Christendom (a rallying cry to which the republics and principalities of Italy failed to respond).

For Trapezuntius, Islam's conquest of the ancient capital of Christendom marked a turning point in world history. His response was to address to Mehmed the Conqueror an impassioned plea to use his imperial might to unite Christianity and Islam in a single faith. If God had delivered up Constantinople, it was in order to unite the whole of mankind in one religion. In *On the Truth of the Christian Faith* he set out to inform Mehmed of the close similarities which already existed between Christianity and Islam, similarities which would make it possible to bring them together. In his introduction he set out his hopes for Mehmed's religious leadership:

May God direct my words, and make me worthy, sinner that I am, I who believe in one God, to see all the races of men united in a single confession and faith, by the intervention of your power, and to see you become the King and Master of all, from one end of the earth to the other.

You know, O golden Sovereign and true Sultan, that the human race is divided into three parties: the Hebrews, the Christians and the Muslims. The Hebrews are few and scattered. The Christian peoples are many and great, they have great influence, and are wise and good. The Islamic peoples are very great and admirable. If someone were to bring together the Christians and the Muslims, in one single faith and confession, he would be, I swear by heaven and earth, glorified by all mankind, on earth and in heaven, and promoted to the ranks of the angels. This work, O admirable Sovereign, none other than you can accomplish.

Trapezuntius' justification for identifying Mehmed II as the imperial world leader was, quite simply, that he was the ruler who had demonstrated that he had the secular might to effect world domination. In 1451, Trapezuntius had flirted with the idea that Alfonso of Aragon, King of Naples, might be such a ruler because of his military exploits, and he later considered Matthias Corvinus, King of Hungary, for the same reason. Although only a small number of the émigrés from the East may have believed with Trapezuntius that the world was about to see the coming together of the world faiths under a single, all-powerful leader, many more anticipated long-term cultural co-operation between Christians and Muslims. Already Bessarion and other scholars had brought unknown treasures to the West in the form of Greek and Arabic manuscripts of works long lost, or never known at all. Crucial works for navigation and astronomy, like Ptolemy's *Almagest*, which had been transmitted to the West in the middle ages via Arabic translations of the original Greek, were now retrieved from Greek originals. When Trapezuntius translated the *Almagest* for Nicholas V he was able to take advantage both of Greek manuscripts never consulted before and of the extensive tradition of Arabic commentary on Ptolemy with which he had been familiar before he came to the West. It was probably these obscure commentaries which led him to produce his *Commentary* in a form which, as we saw in Chapter 5, was too unfamiliar to be acceptable to his patron.

It was the greater accessibility of Arabic astronomical works which took Regiomontanus to Buda in the 1460s. The library of Matthias Corvinus, King of Hungary, which with 2500 books was almost unrivalled in Europe, had benefited from books seized in successful military operations against the Ottomans. By the time Regiomontanus left Buda for Nuremberg, the library also contained considerable numbers of illuminated copies of original works combining oriental and occidental intellectual traditions, including works by Regiomontanus and Trapezuntius. When Suleiman the Magnificent took Buda in his turn, in 1526, and occupied the Palace, he gained possession of large numbers of the books in the library and took them back to Istanbul.

By the beginning of the sixteenth century, the idea of a single world power, and one world faith, had evaporated. The Lutheran reformers believed that the mighty Islamic Empire on Europe's borders was sent from God as a lesson to Christianity to mend its ways. Luther wrote to Melanchthon:

> I get quite excited when I think of the Turks and Mahomed, and of the diabolical fury which they vent on our bodies and souls. But at such times I shall pray fervently till he who dwells in heaven shall hear my petition. I see you are much distressed at the sight of those cowled monks who seem quite at home. But it is our fate to be spectators of the fierce onslaughts of these two realms and remain steadfast; and this onslaught is a sign and harbinger of our redemption.

By that time, however, the printing press had ensured that the collaboration between the two intellectual traditions would continue.

Pope Leo X's Ambassador to the 1522 Diet of Nuremberg was Francesco Chieregato, sent to Germany to try to effect some sort of compromise between the German Lutherans and the Catholic Church. Chieregato had originally served the Gonzagas in Mantua, and was a longstanding member of Isabella d'Este's entourage. Erasmus was delighted when he heard that it was he who had been sent by Rome, since Chieregato was a personal friend and a known moderate. In January 1523, he wrote to Chieregato from Basle, recommending Pirckheimer to him, as a Nuremberg moderate on the Lutheran side. The situation, however, had developed beyond such informal initiatives. In the same month, Chieregato wrote to Isabella d'Este from Nuremberg, expressing his dismay that 'Luther's doctrine has already so many roots in the earth that a thousand persons could not pull it up; certainly I alone cannot.'

Moving on in his report to Isabella of events in Nuremberg to more engaging topics, Chieregato then turned to the city's other great talking point – Magellan's successful Nuremberg-backed voyage westwards to the spice islands. Chieregato gave Isabella d'Este a synopsis of Antonio Pigafetti's account of the journey (and promised to send Pigafetti himself – once in his own service – to Mantua to tell her more):

> First of all, they sailed southwards to those islands in the Oceanic Sea which are called Terra Ferma, and round the point, over the Sea of Sur towards the west. Then, turning to the north and east, they found themselves in the great gulf, near the Spice Islands, and sailed through the Persian and Arabian Seas, by the Cape of Good Hope, into the Ethiopian Sea and across the Atlantic, until they reached the Canary Islands, and returned to their own land by the opposite way, having gained not only great riches, but what is worth more – an immortal reputation. For surely this has thrown all the deeds of the Argonauts into the shade. Here we have read a long account of the expedition, which the Emperor Charles has sent to the Archduke Ferdinand, who

has kindly shown it to me, and has also given me some of the spices which they brought back from those parts, with boughs and leaves of the trees from which they came. Charles has also sent the Archduke a painted map of the journey, and a bird which is very beautiful, which the kings of those countries bear with them when they go into battle, and say they cannot die so long as it is at their side.

For Chieregato and Isabella d'Este, the East, with its exotic trade in spices and oriental luxuries, lay beyond the boundaries of Christendom's religious discord, and offered welcome distraction from the growing conflict at home.

When Vasco da Gama reached the Indian Ocean and landed at Calicut in 1498, the Spanish-speaking Muslim merchant sent to greet him asked, 'What brought you hither?' Da Gama's answer was precise: 'Christians and spices.' The Portuguese had been led by the tales told by earlier returning travellers to expect that they could enter into close alliance with the supposed Christian King of the East and negotiate with him preferential terms for direct trade with Lisbon. But the stories which had come back to Europe of Christian worship in Calicut had been mistaken (as, indeed, some of da Gama's crew were mistaken when they worshipped in Hindu temples, believing them to be the temples of Indian Christianity). Having failed to find their Christian brothers, the Portuguese settled for an alternative strategy. Since there were only 'infidels' in the region, they were entitled to seize the trade they desired by force, in the name of Christendom. After the Samorin of Calicut had refused successive demands that he expel the resident Muslim merchants, and hand over all trading rights to the Portuguese, Vasco da Gama returned to the Malabar coast in 1502 with a fleet of fifteen well-equipped warships to claim them by force.

To a large extent, the Portuguese assertion that merchants in the Indian Ocean were not bound by Christian law, because there were

17. Group portrait of Reformers. From left to right: Johann Forster,
Georg Spalatin, Martin Luther, Johann Bugenhagen, Erasmus, Justus Jonas,
Caspar Cruciger and Philip Melanchthon

no other Christians in the region, was part of the make-believe world
in which religious ideology justified deeds. In part, though, it was
symptomatic of an increasingly prevailing sense that the machinery
of accountancy and business lay outside the scope of traditional
morality. The liberal-minded Willibald Pirckheimer gradually lost
sympathy with the Lutheran cause as the movement became increasingly radical. By 1525, when Nuremberg declared for Luther, he
was sceptical, and he became an outright opponent when Nuremberg
dissolved its convents, of one of which his sister Caritas was Mother
Superior. Whereas in Germany moderation gave way to religious
radicalism, in England, where the reformation of the Church had

begun as a political expedient to justify Henry VIII's divorce, the subsequent legal reforms were in many ways more moderate.

During the German discussions in the 1520s of the legitimacy or illegitimacy of the customary practices of commerce, according to the teachings of scripture and the Church, the moderates among the reformers conceded the need for secular commercial use of prohibited machinery such as interest on loans. Luther's close collaborator, Philip Melanchthon, for instance, considered that secular magistrates could allow interest on loans, on the grounds that it was an essential part of business practice and harmed no one. In a public disputation on the topic, he contended that the 'law of Christ' was not necessarily to be taken as the basis for the organization of secular society, allowing the magistrates the right to rule in accordance with civil law. Christians, however, did not have to borrow or lend, no matter what the secular ruler allowed.

18. Money lenders and their
borrowers

The thrust of such arguments was to separate spiritual belief from secular business practice, allowing the individual to act in his best commercial interests and leave the matter of Christian morality to be settled elsewhere (in his private religious observance). In his published Wittenberg sermons of 1522, Luther himself conceded that the Christian must obey the civil powers, including those aspects of civil law which allowed practices frowned upon in scripture, as long as no harm was caused by them. Only if the civil powers attempted to interfere with the individual's sincere religious convictions was the Christian entitled to rebel against his prince:

> If then your prince or temporal lord commands you to hold with the Pope, to believe this or that, or commands you to give up certain books, you should say, It does not befit Lucifer to sit by the side of God. Dear lord, I owe you obedience with life and goods; command me within the limits of your power on earth, and I will obey. But if you command me to believe, and to put away books, I will not obey; for in this case you are a tyrant and overreach yourself, and command where you have neither right nor power.

In 1545 Henry VIII's government in England introduced a new statute on usury. Abandoning the old prohibition of usury under any circumstances (as dictated by scripture), they replaced it with a more moderate, pragmatic piece of legislation. Acknowledging that covert usury was going on at punitive rates of interest, the new statute made lending at up to 10 per cent interest legal. Anyone lending at a higher rate than 10 per cent, however, was to be faced with triple forfeiture of the principal.

The 1545 Henrican usury statute entirely omitted any reference to God and divine law, taking its authority from King and Parliament alone. Since under religious law lending for interest of almost any kind was entirely forbidden, this was not altogether surprising. The outcome was, however, that England had enacted an openly secular

19. Miniature Ottoman map of Istanbul

piece of legislation concerning commerce, apparently recognizing that the control of such operations was in future to be the business of the Prince's secular law alone. Absolutely no reference was made in the new statute to the jurisdiction of the Church courts.

The 1545 statute on usury was repealed by Edward VI. From the outset devout members of the English Parliament had been appalled by its 'ungodliness'. In 1549 Robert Crowly exclaimed against the statute in an address to Parliament, deploring the separation of the secular and spiritual arms of the law:

> Alas, that ever any Christian assemblie should bee so voyde of Gods Holy Spirit that thei shoulde alowe for lawfull any thyng that Gods Worde forbideth. Be not abashed (most worthy counsellors) to call this act against usury into question agayne. Scan the wordes of the Psalmist: 'He that hath not given his money unto usury, and hath not taken giftes and rewardes against the innocent'.

In practice usury legislation did little to control what was, after all, an essential part of commercial practice. But the fact that the same Parliament of Henry VIII which passed the 1545 statute also formally acknowledged that the civil powers of the King were paramount in all affairs of the English state is significant. England's Reformation recognized the separation of civil business from faith, which elsewhere in Europe remained implicitly linked for another century.

In February 1570, Pope Pius V finally expelled Queen Elizabeth I of England from the Catholic Church, by issuing a papal bull which declared 'Elizabeth, pretended Queen of England, and her followers, heretics'. The effect of this upon the English was to arouse a renewed sense of national isolation from the rest of Catholic Europe, and to provoke an upsurge of patriotism and loyalty, symbolized by the extraordinary number of official portraits of the Queen produced in the 1570s.

There were, however, benefits to be derived from the situation, and the English merchants were quick to seize the opportunity. Officially outlawed by the Pope, they were free to take advantage of prohibited trade with the 'infidel' market in the East. The papal edict banning the export of munitions and foodstuffs from Christendom to the Islamic territories had been enforced by many popes (the Venetians were among those who had been excommunicated as a state for breaking the embargo). In the sixteenth century, when Ottoman power was at its peak, the papal ban was rigorously enforced against those who sold a whole range of commodities which could be used as war-material by an enemy to Tripoli, Alexandria and Istanbul: grain, gunpowder, arms, horses, cotton, cotton yarn, lead, beeswax, morocco leather, sheepskins, pitch, copper, sail-cloth, sulphur. Following their excommunication, the English merchants considered themselves free to export cloth for soldiers' uniforms and metal for arms, especially the precious tin. Scrap-metal from England's Catholic churches, convents and monasteries was shipped abroad for profit – lead from the roofs of ecclesiastical buildings, old bells and broken metal statuary – flaunting the break with Rome. Queen Elizabeth, in her first letter to the Ottoman Sultan, written in 1579, pointedly called herself 'the most invincible and most mighty defender of the Christian faith against all kinds of idolatries, of all that live among the Christians, and falsely professe the Name of Christ'.

In 1577 John Hawkins exploited the situation to propose a lucrative mission eastwards, carrying a cargo of prohibited goods and making use of a trading safe-conduct negotiated by another English merchant with the Ottoman Sultan:

> The determination of a voyage, to be made by John Hawkins with the Swallow of 300 tonne and the Pelican of 120 tonne to Alexandria, Tripoli, Constantinople etc. June 1577.
> First there shall be loaded here in England these parcels of ware [items of goods] following viz.

40 tonne of Brazil dye-wood called Pernambuco	600–0–0
20 hundred weight of tin	500–0–0
40 fother of lead	400–0–0
2000 lengths ordinary blue Hampshire kersey cloth	4000–0–0
100 cloths of all sorts chosen for that country of suitable colours	1000–0–0
to be bestowed in steel	500–0–0
	7000–0–0

all the goods abovesaid which amounteth to 7000 pounds will not be sufficient to fill or load the ships, and therefore they may touch at Messina, and take in such goods as may avail in freight for Alexandria etc.

If it be found that the licence of safe conduct had from Master Cordell be sure to traffic to Constantinople, then it were good to go thither, and make sale of all the goods there, and make such employments as may turn to most gain. And that which may not be had to load the ships, it were good to touch at Candia and Zante and there to take in the rest of the ship's loading in Malmsey wine, Muscatel wine and currants.

If the licence shall be doubted, then it would be best to go directly to Alexandria and load there 50 or 60 tonne of the best and cleanest spices, and so in the return to fill the ships with Malmsey wine, Muscatel wine and currants as is aforesaid.

Of Hawkins's planned cargo, four-fifths of the total value was to be invested in dye-wood (a valuable re-export) and various types of cloth, while one-fifth was to be in tin, lead and steel. All these items, intended for the Ottoman market, were 'contraband goods'.

The Spanish ambassador in London, Bernardino de Mendoza, watched with growing concern the increasing advantage the English were gaining over the Catholic merchants in the East. In May 1582 he advised Philip II of Spain of the way the English were profiting from their punishment by the Pope:

> Two years ago the English opened up the trade, which they still continue, to the Levant, which is extremely profitable to them, as they take great quantities of tin and lead thither, which the Turk buys of them almost for its weight in gold, the tin being vitally necessary for the casting of guns and the lead for purposes of war. It is of double importance to the Turk now, in consequence of the excommunication pronounced *ipso facto* by the Pope upon any person who provides or sells to infidels such materials as these.

In January 1581 he had already warned that the English were not only sending out 'a multitude of vessels to Morocco with arms and munitions, but have now begun to trade with the Ottoman Empire, whither they take tin and other prohibited goods to the Turks'. Mendoza's concern was well-founded. In spite of their comparatively late arrival on the eastern trading scene, the English merchant companies were now in a position to pursue their trading profit, in an entirely secular commercial context, free from the operating constraints of international religious law.

· EIGHT ·

CONSPICUOUS CONSUMPTION

ON 13 MARCH 1532, the Venetian Marino Sanuto recorded in his diary that a spectacular gold helmet had been shown to him in the jewellers' district of Venice's Rialto. The helmet was surmounted by a plume in an elaborate crescent-shaped mount, at whose centre was an enormous turquoise surrounded by rubies, diamonds, pearls and emeralds (174 gems in all); its headband was studded with pointed diamonds; it had an ornately wrought neck-guard, and was secured with a buckled chin-strap. Four removable crowns encircled the helmet; each of the four crowns' twelve points was topped with an enormous pearl; in addition, the three larger crowns were each set with four diamonds, four rubies and four emeralds (the topmost, smaller crown was set with three diamonds, three rubies and two emeralds). The whole thing was valued by Sanuto at 144,400 ducats (a contemporary fortune), including the cost of the helmet's velvet-lined gilt and ebony travelling-case.

The helmet had been manufactured by a consortium of Venetian goldsmiths, to the commission of the Ottoman Sultan Suleiman's grand vizier, Ibrahim Pasha (who may have contributed some of the gems from his personal collection), and a substantial portion of the helmet's cost had been paid in advance by Suleiman's chief treasurer, Defterdar Iskender Çelebi. The Venetian intermediary was probably the prominent political and commercial figure Alvise Gritti (illegitimate son of Doge Andrea Gritti), who was a powerful merchant and gem-dealer in Istanbul. The helmet was part of a consignment of regalia, commissioned from more than one consortium. Sanuto reported that the helmet 'will be sent together with a jewel-studded saddle and saddle-cloth ordered by another partnership'.

Shortly after Sanuto admired it, the helmet-crown was dispatched from Venice to Ragusa (now Dubrovnik, on the Dalmatian coast). There it was met by a hand-picked, top-security escort sent by Ibrahim Pasha to accompany the precious object to Istanbul, where it was to be presented by him to Suleiman. Suleiman, however, had already set off on his second military campaign against Vienna (which he had failed to take in his westward push into Europe two years previously) to confront the forces of the Habsburg Emperor Charles V. The helmet-crown, with its escort, set off again and caught up with the Sultan's forces outside Vienna on 12 May 1532.

The crown was not a symbol of empire used ceremonially by Ottoman sultans (who preferred the ornamented, ornate turban). The Venetian helmet-crown was designed and commissioned specifically in order to announce to political opponents in western Europe the might and imperial status of

1. Suleiman the Magnificent's spectacular ceremonial helmet, commissioned and made in Venice

380

Suleiman. Contemporary accounts confirm that a crown matching the one Sanuto admired in Venice was paraded by Suleiman (along with other regalia of imperial power) as part of his highly choreographed triumphal procession outside the walls of Vienna in May 1532 – a progress deliberately designed by Ibrahim Pasha to emulate and outdo the triumphal progress of Charles V which had followed his coronation as Holy Roman Emperor in Bologna in 1529. The Western-orientated iconography of Suleiman's progress represented him as the second Alexander the Great, to Charles V's claimed role as the second Caesar.

The Venetian goldsmiths had fulfilled their instructions assiduously in their design for Suleiman's quadruple-crowned helmet. Their brief was to create a priceless ceremonial object whose Western connotations would be those of imperial might and a genealogy stretching back to great Eastern rulers like Alexander, and which would equally capture the imagination of its recipient, Suleiman, as an appropriate symbol of limitless power and territorial dominion.

Suleiman's helmet was meant to strike awe into the hearts of the crowned heads of Europe, and to advertise immediately and unequivocally his claim to world dominion. Western contemporaries immediately noted the helmet-crown's resemblance to the papal tiara, with its three superimposed crowns, but the Pope's 'crown' was not, of course, a helmet (and the imperial connotations of his ceremonial headgear thus less immediately militaristic and expansionist). In order to convey their message with the utmost clarity, the Venetian goldsmiths used as their creative inspiration for the elements of Suleiman's helmet-crown which most strongly connoted world dominion a highly current and widely distributed source of imperialistic imagery – the portrait medals which enthusiasts for antiquities from West to East avidly collected and displayed prominently in their cabinets. The neck-guard and chin-strap of the helmet closely imitated fifteenth-century bronze medals of Alexander the Great, which in their turn were claimed to be based on antique prototypes. The superimposed crowns on a helmet base

2. Suleiman the Magnificent wearing a ceremonial turban

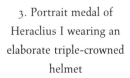

3. Portrait medal of
Heraclius I wearing an
elaborate triple-crowned
helmet

were taken from a medal of the seventh-century Byzantine Emperor
Heraclius I, originally made for the collection of the Duc de
Berry, and widely copied and circulated. The medal of Heraclius I
(an obviously appropriate precursor to Suleiman, now emperor in
Istanbul, and heir to Byzantium) carried the bust of the Emperor
over an upturned crescent, wearing an elaborate helmet with three
encircling crowns. The addition of a fourth crown readily signified
the fact that Suleiman's dominion exceeded those of the Pope and
of all his Byzantine imperial predecessors (all of whose regalia
featured a maximum of three crowns).

The 1532 Habsburg–Ottoman military campaign in Germany and
Austria was a parade of strength in which it was understood that
both the Habsburg and Ottoman emperors were reluctant to join
battle. Their vast armies were equally matched. For the first time,
Charles and his brother Ferdinand had together managed to raise
an army of equivalent numbers to the awesome might of the Muslim
forces. Suleiman's army consisted of a core of between 12,000 and
15,000 specially trained, crack troops, the janissaries, who fought on
foot and carried firearms (the unwieldy but effective iron-barrelled

arquebus), around 50,000 cavalry and a skilled corps of artillerymen and sappers for siege-warfare. Charles and Ferdinand had 10,000 men-at-arms, 20,000 light cavalry and 60,000 footsoldiers, of whom 32,000 carried pikes and 10,000 carried arquebuses. The costs of supporting these forces were enormous; those incurred by the losses of men and equipment in a significant action were unthinkable, and in this, their final major confrontation on the battlefield, the two most powerful rulers in the world studiously avoided engagement. Suleiman's parade of Ottoman magnificence outside the walls of Vienna in 1532 substituted a competition in splendour between the two emperors for direct confrontation on the battlefield.

Like many other artists and craftsmen around 1530, the consortium of goldsmiths who fulfilled the commission for Suleiman's helmet with such care may well have hoped for further lucrative work from the Sultan and his key cultural adviser, Ibrahim Pasha. According to the Italian writer Aretino, the Venetian goldsmith Luigi Caorlini was in Istanbul in 1532, looking for work, together with other, unnamed sculptors and painters. In 1533 the Low Countries draughtsman and painter Pieter Coeck van Aelst, too, spent a year in Istanbul in pursuit of lucrative commissions from the Ottoman Court.

Coeck had accepted the invitation of a firm of tapestry-weavers in Brussels to undertake a speculative commercial journey to Istanbul to try to interest Suleiman the Magnificent in commissioning tapestries and hangings. According to the contemporary German chronicler Karel van Mander, Coeck was to go to Istanbul and to make drawings of the kinds of scene used as designs for tapestries, which would then be shown as prototypes to the Sultan:

> The Van den Moeyen firm intended to establish a trade and make rich carpets and hangings for the Great Turk, and to this end they employed Pieter Coeck to paint divers things to be shewn to the Turkish Emperor. But nothing came of the plan but time spent in travelling and great loss to the speculators.

Pieter having dwelt at Constantinople about a year, and having learned the Turkish tongue, and not liking to be idle, made drawings for his own pleasure of the city and the neighbourhood from nature, and also seven pieces which have been cut in wood and printed, wherein various customs of the Turks are set forth.

Perhaps (as the chronicler van Mander suggests) the prohibitions of Islamic law made Suleiman stop short of spending money on such large-scale figurative works of art. It may simply have been that within a décor whose extravagance was traditionally Eastern, there was no appropriate place for expensive items of this particular kind. Coeck, however, did not do badly personally from the venture, according to another contemporary account:

Pieter Coeck of Aelst published some remarkable drawings of the life and manners of the Turks, which he had studied at Constantinople. There, for his rare skill in his art, he was so highly esteemed by the Emperor Suleiman, that that potentate, forgetting the law of his Koran, desired to have his portrait painted by him. By the royal bounty of Suleiman's own hand, Pieter was dismissed with honourable gifts, a ring, a jewel, horses, robes, gold, and servants, which at Bruxelles he converted into an annual pension.

On his return to The Netherlands Coeck derived further financial gain from his oriental visit by turning the drawings which had been rejected as designs for tapestries by Suleiman into a series of woodcuts, which were published in Antwerp in 1553 under the title *The Customs and Habits of the Turks*.

The venture to interest the Ottoman Emperor in narrative tapestries of contemporary events was potentially a shrewd one. Such art-objects were much in vogue among precisely the prominent European political figures against whom Suleiman (and his adviser

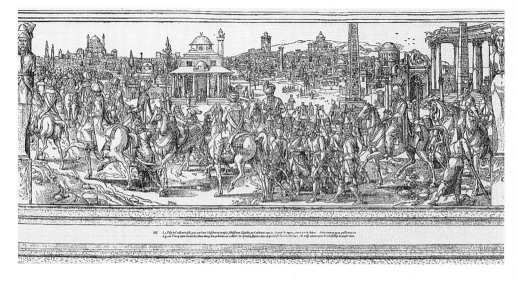

4. Pieter Coeck, *Suleiman the Magnificent in Procession,* drawn in Istanbul

Ibrahim Pasha) measured his performance in the international arena. Coeck did considerably better at obtaining tapestry commissions from European imperial clients. In his subsequent successful career as a painter and, above all, a cartoon designer for tapestry work, he carried out a number of prestigious commissions for Charles V. He produced a woodcut series depicting Charles's success, and the humiliating capture of François I, at the Battle of Pavia in 1525, and his last recorded work was on an illustrated narrative of the triumphal entry into Antwerp of Charles V's son Philip II as ruler of The Netherlands in 1549, *The Triumph at Anvers,* which was published in the same year.

In June 1535 the Emperor Charles V hired Pieter Coeck and the artist Jan Cornelisz Vermeyen from Haarlem in The Netherlands for a project along the lines of the one in which Coeck had tried to interest Suleiman. Their job would be to travel with the Emperor on his impending military campaign in North Africa and to make drawings which recorded the progress of the campaign, to be turned into tapestries celebrating the (as Charles hoped) resounding triumph of his victory.

Charles V undertook his offensive military campaign against

5. Peter Coeck, *The Capture of François I at the Battle of Pavia*

Tunis in order to bring to an end the activities of the Muslim corsair, Hayreddîn Barbarossa, who operated out of Tunis. Barbarossa, who had recently been appointed Suleiman the Magnificent's admiral of the fleet, was an outstanding naval commander, who for years had conducted a kind of organized piracy off the north coast of Africa, first on his own behalf and subsequently as an employee of the Ottomans. Barbarossa's ships intercepted the trading vessels of those who did not (like the Venetians, and more recently the French) pay regular sums to the Ottoman Sultan for safe passage from ports of the eastern Mediterranean to their European destinations, and seized their cargoes. Barbarossa also led raiding parties against the coastal ports across from Tunis. Apart from the desire to make the Mediterranean sea-lanes safer to travel in, Charles's projected campaign was politically aimed against the French King, François I. As part of a political strategy to form a power bloc capable of withstanding Charles's increasingly formidable Empire, François had

6. A. Veneziano's portrait of the Muslim corsair Hayreddîn Barbarossa

allied France with the Ottomans. The Tunis campaign was a direct challenge to the French as well as to Suleiman.

Charles V's fleet sailed for Tunis from Cagliari on 14 June, led by the imperial admiral Andrea Doria, with 400 ships and 30,000 fighting men. By late July, Tunis had fallen to Charles, Barbarossa had fled, and Charles ordered the sacking of the city – a deliberately brutal punishment for the fact that the town had refused to surrender. (The artist Paulo Giovio later became the proud owner of a painting of Barbarossa, seized in the sack of Tunis, and also of the corsair's Koran and a velvet caftan.) Symbolically the campaign was a triumph for Charles V – a decisive victory over the increasingly invulnerable Muslim forces, and a blow to the international prestige of François I, who declined to be drawn into a north African war. Actually the expedition achieved very little. Barbarossa relocated his activities elsewhere, and continued to plunder the Mediterranean, and François I retained his close links with Istanbul. In 1543, Barbarossa's fleet (newly fitted out by Suleiman at a reputed cost of a million ducats) supported François at the siege of Nice, enabling the French King to take the town from Charles's ally the Duke of Savoy, a victory which shook Europe.

The propaganda value for Charles V of a victory at Tunis, however, was clear from the moment the expedition was planned – Charles represented it as a direct attack on the 'infidel', thereby taking upon himself the role of crusading Holy Roman Emperor. Jan Vermeyen's job making detailed sketches of battle locations and troops was clearly defined – he was, in effect, Charles's personal reporter in the war zone. The new technology of the printing press meant that, on return from the field, such on-the-spot visual material provided by the war correspondent could be turned into woodcut blocks and marketed throughout Europe, broadcasting the might of the victor and the humiliation of the defeated party. After the Battle of Tunis, the Italian Agostino Veneziano published a series of woodcut prints of all those involved in the conflict – Charles V, François I, Suleiman and Barbarossa.

7. Portrait of Charles V
in stained glass from
the North transept of
Brussels Cathedral

The victory at Tunis meant a great deal to Charles personally, and he marked its significance with a spectacular commission in its honour. Plans were drawn up for a series of tapestries which would commemorate the capture of Tunis, using Vermeyen's eye-witness drawings, and a room in the imperial palace at Toledo was constructed especially to house its twelve panels. On 15 June 1546, Maria of Hungary (Charles's sister, and his regent in the Low Countries) signed a contract with Jan Vermeyen in Brussels, for full-scale cartoons from his *Conquest of Tunis* drawings:

> The said Jan Vermeyen promises that with his own hand he will make large patterns, on to good large paper, from the small ones which he showed to her Majesty, and to amend them as necessary for verisimilitude, leaving nothing out. For this purpose he will hire, at his own expense, an adequate number of skilled and

8. Second tapestry in *The Conquest of Tunis* series, showing Charles V
on horseback

suitable local painters as collaborators (whatever the cost), so that
the said patterns may be executed as well as is possible.

He will deliver the said patterns when completed for approval
by their Majesties and all their experts, one by one, one after
the other, until he has finished them all, which he promises too
perfectly, as has been said, within a year and a half. He under-
takes that all expenses, of whatever sort, arising from the said
patterns, will be entirely paid by him.

The sum agreed for these full-sized patterns was 1900 Flemish
pounds – an enormous sum. Of this, 300 pounds were paid as an
advance to Vermeyen; the rest was to be paid pattern by pattern
as they were delivered and approved. Pieter Coeck van Aelst was
presumably one of those who joined Vermeyen's team of specialist

draughtsmen to make sure that the patterns were done within the time allocated and that the designs were up to the required standard.

Meanwhile, Maria of Hungary approached Willem de Pannemaker, the leading tapestry-maker in Brussels, to agree to manufacture the twelve tapestries. The final contract with Pannemaker was drawn up on 20 February 1548, suggesting that Vermeyen had kept within the eighteen-month production time laid down in his contract. The contract stipulated that only the very finest materials were to be used for the tapestries – gold and silver thread, and the finest silk thread obtainable from Granada. Nothing but Granada silk was to be used, whether for the crimsons or any other colour:

> The warp of each of the said tapestries is to be made from the best and finest Lyon thread that is manufactured there, and if possible to make a finer selection still, whatever the cost, and similarly for all the other materials that are used.
>
> Not to economize on the said Granada silks for the said tapestries, of any colour whatsoever, which is needed. For the borders, when the pattern specifies that gold or silver thread should be used, the said gold or silver thread should be used together with a silk thread, then two other layers of silk should be applied, before getting to the fine *sayette*. And as for the figures, landscapes, trees and greenery, here also in the same way, after the gold or silver thread, two, three, four or five different silks should be used before getting to the said fine *sayette*.
>
> To account carefully for the silver and gold thread which her Majesty will provide, and to use that and no other in the said tapestry, and not to economize on silver and gold thread in any way unless absolutely necessary. For the said Pannemaker will make each of these tapestries, according to the patterns provided, as rich or richer throughout in gold thread or silver thread than the tapestry depicting the poem of Vertumnus and Pomona, which her Majesty bought from Welser, the merchant.

The Tunis tapestries were a grandiose project, whose execution was planned as meticulously as the military operation they depicted. Under the terms of the contract, Pannemaker was to subcontract the work to seven fellow master tapestry-makers – at least forty-two weavers in all were employed to work on the tapestry, and the cost of labour and materials was vast. Pannemaker himself was guaranteed an annual pension for life upon satisfactory completion of the series (which he subsequently received). He was paid a total of around 15,000 Flemish pounds, which included an advance of 6637 pounds for the silk threads.

Lavishness was a key element in the *Conquest of Tunis* commission, reiterated throughout the contract in the quality of the materials and the way they were to be used. The six *Vertumnus and Pomona* tapestries, based on a story told in the classical Latin author Ovid's *Metamorphoses,* were an exceptionally rich and magnificent series, which had also been made by the Pannemaker workshop to designs by Jan Vermeyen. The task of obtaining the expensive materials for the tapestries was closely supervised by Maria of Hungary herself. Her agent, Simon de Parenty, personally authorized the shipment of 559 pounds of Granadan silk threads in sixty-three different shades of colour to be used in Pannemaker's tapestries; another of her entourage, Louis Chaussard, was dispatched to Granada to arrange for the purchase and shipment of the thread. In a letter dated 13 January 1549, Maria also ordered de Parenty to obtain seven types of gold thread and three types of silver thread from the Antwerp financier and merchant Jakob Welser:

> Simon de Parenty, charged with keeping the accounts for the funds used on the tapestries of the conquest of Tunis by the Emperor, our Lord and brother. We order you to collect from the Antwerp merchant Jacob Welser, who has agreed to furnish it, the gold and silver thread needed for the said tapestries, at the agreed price, and to deliver it to the tapestry-maker William de Pannemaker.

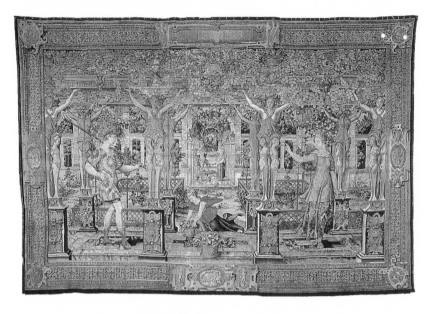

9. First tapestry in the *Vertumnus and Pomona* series

The amounts, types of thread and precise quality are specified in detail. When all the payments are included, the *Conquest of Tunis* tapestries cost, quite literally, a fortune. Like all Habsburg deals, the money was provided by obliging bankers; as the intermediary who regularly handled Maria of Hungary's tapestry purchases on behalf of Charles V, the merchant Jakob Welser presumably added the cost of the gold and silver thread to their 'tab' with him (and Simon de Parenty kept a careful account of what was owed). The Fuggers had paid the production costs for another tapestry series by Pieter Coeck van Aelst, *Los Honores*, produced in 1523 to mark Charles V's coronation three years previously. In that case, the Fugger bank had advanced all the money required for the design and execution of the tapestries (both labour and materials), and had then acted as brokers for its sale to Charles – recouping the money, one imagines, in the form of yet another promissory note from the Emperor.

Pannemaker completed the *Conquest of Tunis* series in April 1554. That summer the tapestries were packed up in Brussels under the supervision of Simon de Parenty, and Pannemaker accompanied them to London, where they arrived on 3 July. The entire series made its first public appearance at the wedding of Charles V's son Philip II of Spain to Mary Tudor, which took place in Winchester Cathedral on 25 July. Subsequently the tapestries were displayed in Antwerp and in Brussels, before they were finally hung in Philip's Toledo Palace in 1556. Several authorized copies were made – one reduced-scale series for Maria of Hungary, one complete set for one of the foremost participants in the Conquest of Tunis itself, Fernando Alvarez de Toledo, Duke of Alba.

By the time the *Conquest of Tunis* tapestry series was completed, the victory itself could no longer be regarded as the landmark moment in the imperial fortunes of Charles V. Nevertheless, as art-objects, the tapestries were masterpieces, whose lavishness and beauty of execution were appropriate to the magnificence of the

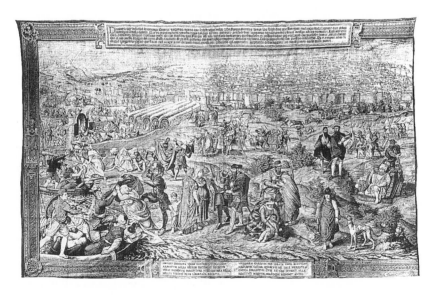

10. Tenth tapestry in *The Conquest of Tunis* series: *The Sack of Tunis*

Habsburgs. Huge, but conveniently portable, they could (and did) travel with the Habsburg retinue (which was constantly on the move, because of the sheer size of the Habsburg dominions), so that those who visited the imperial quarters could be dazzled by the tapestries' splendour, while at the same time registering the Emperor's formidable power – depicted there, panel by panel, with awesome visual realism. In England, Charles V's son Philip was a deeply unpopular choice as consort for the Queen regnant, Mary Tudor, because of the danger that on the basis of the marriage the Habsburgs might claim the country as they had so many others, and because of Charles V's personal ambition to stamp out altogether the 'heresy' of Protestantism in Europe. The *Conquest of Tunis* tapestries, proudly displayed at the cementing of the union, can have done nothing to allay English fears.

The market for tapestries on this scale was inevitably a small one – few even among the great houses of Europe had the financial means to commission these vastly expensive items (though rather more could aspire to buy copies of works designed for others, or to acquire them second-hand). Tapestry-makers had no scruples about providing their services to political rivals. In 1544, Maria of Hungary purchased a seven-piece set of the *Story of Scipio*, which had originally been commissioned by François I, Charles V's opponent in the struggles for the balance of power in Europe. The original series consisted of twenty-two scenes from the exploits and triumphs of Scipio Africanus, as recounted by the ancient Roman historian Livy. The Antwerp merchant Erasmus Schatz, from whom Charles's set was purchased, financed the manufacture of copies of the originals (made by the same workshop), which he then sold on the open market in smaller lots.

Nor could a German merchant house like the Welsers afford to restrict its involvement in large-scale tapestry-making to those commissioned for the Habsburgs. They also financed tapestries celebrating the international prestige of another of Charles V's rivals for power, this time in the newly exploited trading territories of the

11. Fifth tapestry in *The Story of Scipio* series: *The Battle of Zama*

East, the King of Portugal. In the 1520s, the Welsers paid for a magnificent series of three, entitled *The Spheres*, for King John III of Portugal, celebrating Portuguese global explorations and successes in the East. One of its panels included a meticulously executed globe of the known world, complete with the flag of Portugal, fluttering triumphant over key Portuguese conquests – Goa, Malacca and (at the very edge of the map) Java.

The King of Portugal, whose international status rested on his mariners' extraordinary feats of navigation and exploration, used the tapestry series, such as that of *The Spheres*, as a way of announcing his territorial acquisitions, while at the same time providing highly visible evidence of Portugal's magnificence. Immediately after Vasco da Gama's and Cabral's successful voyages round the Cape of Good Hope to Calicut in India, King Manuel of Portugal ordered a twenty-six-panel series of commemorative tapestries to mark the event, from the Tournai tapestry-manufacturing family of le Feire, under the supervision of Gilles le Castre. The designs incorporate a wide range of oriental exotica – from strange beasts like the camel and the giraffe to dark-skinned peoples in

12. Third tapestry in *The Spheres* series: *Earth Under the Protection of the Portuguese Monarchs in the Guise of Jupiter and Juno*

outlandish costumes. They have a curious quality, almost of disbelief, about them, since the tapestry-makers had themselves certainly never seen anything like the figures they were weaving. The tapestries could not have done better as advertisements for the sheer strangeness of the newly opened-up East and its exotic commodities.

The *Voyage to Calicut* series, which was completed in 1504, proved immensely popular – probably because of the wide range of exotic animals, plants and locations the tapestries included. To meet the demand, the manufacturers produced a number of related pieces (using similar figures and motifs), as well as copies of the original *Voyage to Calicut* series itself. In 1510 the Emperor Maximilian bought their *Savage Peoples and Animals* series, while Robert Wytfel bought a set of five pieces of *The Voyage to Calicut* for the English King, Henry VIII.

Tapestries have not endured as recognized 'works of arts' into our own period. In the fifteenth and sixteenth centuries they were a particularly ostentatious art-form, perfectly suited to the requirements of wealthy clients of the time: they combined exquisite design and workmanship with extremely labour-intensive (and therefore valuable) craft skills; they rendered any room in which they were hung instantaneously sumptuous; they kept large, ill-insulated rooms warm and draught-free; they displayed the owner's erudition (if the narrative they depicted was literary), good taste (if they simulated rural scenes of idyllic landscape) or personal prestige (if they represented some scene from his or the family's history). Furthermore, they had the advantage over frescos and paintings that they were highly portable and could readily travel with their owner on state occasions. They carried his renown along with the luggage at a marriage, on a visit to related noble families or to the Pope to pledge allegiance – carefully packed up for transit like the gems and rare books which were also taken along on such important, prestige-building trips. In the Ducal Palace at Mantua, the tapestries were moved around from room to room, according to which ones were in use for important visitors. The merchants who dealt in tapestries also ran a thriving business in short-term rentals – they hired out tapestries with all-purpose 'verdure' or landscape designs of trees, flowers, birds and small animals, which would fit in in any location, in anybody's palace.

The wall-to-wall frescos in the ducal palaces at Mantua and Ferrara were designed to resemble, as closely as possible, the much more costly tapestries which the Gonzagas and d'Estes also owned, right down to the *trompe l'œil* fabric hangings which appear to be caught back (by a tie, or as if by a gust of wind) across the painted surface, revealing the figures behind. The idea was that the warmth of tapestry could be simulated by the painted wall-surface, without the expense of gold and silver thread and costly silks (which were what drew the onlookers' admiration from the tapestry). Paint also had the advantage of being relatively cheap: Duke Borso d'Este spent 9000 ducats on a sumptuous set of Flemish tapestries and only 800 ducats on an exceptionally large fresco cycle in the Schifanoia Palace.

In 1530 the Emperor Charles V visited Federigo Gonzaga II, in Mantua, where he was entertained in the newly completed palace, the Palazzo del Te, designed by the artist and architect Giulio Romano. Federico had brought Romano to Mantua in 1524, and supported him in some style, specifically in order to embark upon an extensive building programme, to enhance Gonzaga public prominence and prestige. When the sculptor Benvenuto Cellini visited Romano he found him 'living like a lord', enjoying remarkable freedom in devising his projects and designs, and backed up by a team of skilled craftsmen and assistants, specially employed by the Gonzagas.

Giulio Romano's Palazzo del Te was constructed around existing, older buildings, as an edge-of-town retreat for Federigo and his mistress Isabella Boschetta (within convenient walking distance of the Ducal Palace). It was a building designed for recreation, and both its interior and exterior combined architectural virtuosity in the newest classicizing style with a measure of wit and light-heartedness. The elaborately frivolous interior decorations were entirely Giulio Romano's creation, although he employed his bevy of assistants to carry out the extravagant work, putting the final touches to it with his own hand. In the Room of Psyche, Romano created a breath-taking fantasy, every inch of its walls and ceiling densely covered in *trompe l'œil* frescos. The decoration showed the wedding banquet of Cupid and Psyche in meticulous detail, as a lavish, crowded bacchanal, with dozens of nude figures, apparently grouped around tables loaded with gold and silver plate. The ceiling was painted to simulate elaborately gilded and ornamented architectural features, with further mythical figures in exaggerated perspective, apparently cavorting above. The overall effect was one of theatrical splendour – a stage-set for entertaining on the grandest of scales.

On the occasion of his 1530 visit, Charles V dined alone in the just completed Room of Psyche, while Federigo himself waited in attendance on him. The Venetian Ambassador, who watched Charles V being received amid all this magnificence, reported home that 'so much gold, tapestries, paintings and fineries were there, that it was said that those palaces resembled the immensely rich ones of the Ottoman Sultan'. The Emperor was suitably impressed. As a direct consequence of the visit, with all its attendant spectacle, Charles V raised Federigo's title (and that of his heirs in perpetuity) from marquis to duke.

Federigo Gonzaga's self-conscious use of an ambitious building programme to raise his public profile proved, on this occasion, extremely successful. Building projects by public figures, in general, showed them at their most overtly ostentatious and competitive. 'There are two principal things that men do in this life,' wrote the Florentine patrician Giovanni Rucellai, 'the first is to procreate, the second is to build'. First came the perpetuation of the dynasty, second the ensuring of its lasting fame by erecting monumental buildings. Dynastic rulers kept a careful eye on each other's building projects, to make sure their own projects were in keeping with current standards of imposingness and grandeur. In 1479, Lorenzo de' Medici sent for drawings of Federigo da Montefeltro's palace at Urbino while it was going up (they were provided by the marquetry designer Baccio Pontelli, who was working on the project). Federigo Gonzaga, who was in the process of building an extension to his own ducal palace at Mantua at the time, also wanted details of the construction of Federigo da Montefeltro's palace and consulted the architect, Francesco di Giorgio. In 1489, Filippo Strozzi, head of the successful banking family, began building a lavish palace in Florence, sinking nearly 40,000 florins – almost half his estimated income for the previous ten years – in its fabric (before furnishing). Every noble house wanted to know the details of the design and construction of this piece of 'new money' grandeur; Ercole d'Este, himself an enthusiastic builder, who had built an entire new quarter in Ferrara (the 'Herculean Addition'), sent for the plans.

Since ostentatious building was an affirmation of the public significance and prestige of the builder, those families who had been catapulted to prominence by their commercial activities were quick to join in the competition. Agostino Chigi, the Pope's key financial figure from the 1490s, and the man who had taken control of the papal alum mines at Tolfa, built a spectacular villa (now called the Farnesina) just outside Rome. It was lavishly decorated by Baldassare Peruzzi (also its architect), and by Sebastiano del Piombo and Raphael, with erotic scenes from classical literature. With characteristic presumption, Chigi had his bedroom painted with scenes from the life of Alexander the Great. The Pope himself liked to retire to Chigi's villa to be entertained with appropriate sumptuousness. Architectural expenditure on this scale was the ultimate sign of a family's having 'made it'.

It could also be a way of throwing down the cultural gauntlet to political adversaries. When Charles V decided to construct a new imperial palace at Granada in 1528, he was responding to a challenge from his imperial rival, the Ottoman Sultan Suleiman. Between 1525 and 1529, under the supervision of his grand vizier Ibrahim Pasha,

Suleiman carried out a large-scale programme of new building and renovation of the Topkapı Saray in Istanbul, the palace built in the 1460s by Mehmed II. Within the perimeter wall of Mehmed's original, already magnificent palace, Suleiman built a new treasury building and a council hall, and extensively rebuilt the Chamber of Petitions, where foreign ambassadors were received. All these modifications dramatically increased the impression of awesome magnificence given to the visitor. Those who returned from Istanbul invariably described the palace in tones of awe, and its owner, as a consequence, as a formidably powerful international presence.

The Venetian Ambassador Pietro Bragadino, who came to the Topkapı in 1526 and had previously visited the Court of the Egyptian Mamluk Sultan in Cairo, found Suleiman's much more opulent and more beautiful. Some of this impression was the result of the carefully choreographed ceremonial with which movement through the various courts of the palace was conducted. In the mid-sixteenth century, Caterino Zeno described the slow progress from one of Suleiman's new buildings to the next:

> One goes to the Grand Signor's Chamber of Petitions after leaving the Council Hall from a gate at the left. First the treasurers leave and go to the gate; after them enters the one who signs the commands, then come the army judges, and then, according to their rank and order, the viziers enter the gate, where they find a large chamber well adorned with stones, covered with a beautiful ceiling, in which stands a guard of eunuchs and some of the sultan's young slaves, all richly dressed; from that chamber one passes into a very beautiful loggia, the floor of which is of diverse fine stones of many colours, with a very fine vaulted ceiling of azure and ultramarine, full of stars of pure gold, in which is a very fine fountain resembling a holy-water basin; it has most beautiful windows with iron gratings and beautiful glass panes which overlook the gardens; from this very beautiful and pleasant place one enters the Chamber of

Petitions and the presence of that Grand Signor. At its door are two eunuchs of the highest rank, and two pages.

When finally allowed, extremely briefly, to stand silently in the presence of the Sultan in the new Chamber of Petitions, at the heart of the palace, the impact of this room was overwhelming. The wooden dome of the small room was painted with azure and ultramarine, covered in stars of pure gold – it matched the ceiling of the marble-paved forecourt which visitors crossed to reach it, and echoed the colour-scheme of the paintings in the courts and vestibules through which they had passed. The room was set with glazed tiles of blue, white and turquoise, with ultramarine stars over-stencilled in gold. Globes, set with precious stones, bedecked with rich silk tassels, hung from the ceiling. The Sultan's throne was of gold, inlaid with precious stones, surmounted by a canopy whose columns were studded with pearls and gems (Suleiman was the first Ottoman sultan to give audiences seated on a Western-style throne, rather than cross-legged on cushions).

The choice of particular cushions, floor spreads, throne covers, curtains for windows and doors, and jewelled pendant globes for decoration was dictated by the status of the ambassadors who were expected on a given day. The everyday furnishings were of velvet or silk, embroidered with gold thread. For special visitors these were replaced by gold brocades, entirely covered with small pearls and gold plaques inlaid with rubies, turquoises and emeralds. In the 1550s the antiquarian Petrus Gyllius described the Chamber of Petitions as 'a little apartment built with marble, adorned with gold and silver, and sparkling with diamonds and precious stones. The Room of State is encircled with a portico, which is supported with pillars of the finest marble, the capitals and pedestals of which are all gilded.' He also mentioned the silver hood of the fireplace, enamelled latticework inlaid with rubies, emeralds and pearls.

The Topkapı Saray in Istanbul was a building of enormous political significance. Its prominent location and its opulence made it a convincing symbol of Ottoman imperial dominion, encroaching on the very borders of Christian Europe. Mehmed's new palace was begun a decade after his Islamic forces had besieged and captured the ancient centre of the medieval Christian world, in 1453. It stood in splendour at the point where Istanbul jutted out towards the sea, matching in visibility the great church of Justinian, Hagia Sophia, with its shimmering white stone and huge dome. The sheer beauty of that dome had overwhelmed Mehmed II when he first saw it (he called it 'exquisitely ornamented' on account of its profusion of interior frescos), and almost the first act of his occupation of the city was to reconsecrate Hagia Sophia as Istanbul's most important mosque. In addition to the tales told by visiting ambassadors, the Western architects and artists whose expertise Mehmed brought to Istanbul from all over Europe, to work on his new palace and to do large amounts of essential renovation work on the fabric of the Hagia Sophia, carried back to Europe their own expert estimation of the oriental magnificence of the palace and the classical perfection of the church–mosque. The great architects Filarete and Michelozzo, among many others, may both have worked for Mehmed.

When the conquering sovereigns Ferdinand and Isabella of Spain (Charles V's grandparents) entered the Islamic city of Granada, symbolic centre of the Arab presence in Spain, in triumph in 1492, one of their first acts had been to reconsecrate the Royal Mosque as a Christian place of worship. Amazed by the breathtaking oriental beauty of the Alhambra, Queen Isabella had summoned skilled *mudéjar* (Christianized Islamic) artisans from Saragossa to repair the Moorish palace, and had moved the royal household into it. As a Christianized Muslim later reminded Philip II, she thereby intended to 'preserve the rich Palace of the Alhambra as it was in the time of the Islamic Kings, so as permanently to manifest the triumph of Spain as their conquerors'. It was there that Charles V and his wife Isabella stayed on their first visit to Granada in 1526. Charles's decision to build himself a lavish palace alongside the Alhambra, on an ambitious classically inspired architectural plan,

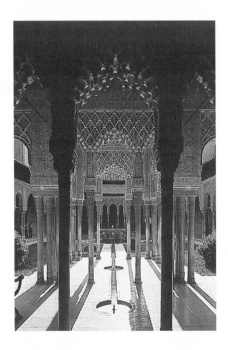

13. Courtyard of the Lions in
the Alhambra, Granada

was a statement of the Habsburgs' claim by the 1520s to an imperial power designed to match that of the Ottomans. Queen Isabella
had insisted that the Alhambra should not be altered in any way.
Charles built his palace right up against its outer wall, a 'gateway'
to the Moorish buildings, monumentally towering over them and
ostentatiously competing for aesthetic attention.

Charles V's palace at Granada, with its imposing circular central
courtyard ringed with tall marble columns, and its wealth of carving
and reliefs recalling the martial triumphs of the Habsburg dynasty,
was a worthy competitor in the power stakes with Suleiman's palace
(although the ambitiousness of the project meant that the palace
was only finally completed under Philip II). Alongside these great
imperial edifices were created matching imperial legends. Mehmed
II had organized a group of Greek and European scholars to establish a mythical, pre-Christian past for the church of Hagia Sophia
in Istanbul (barely altered for Muslim worship in the sixteenth

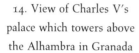

14. View of Charles V's
palace which towers above
the Alhambra in Granada

century, apart from some much needed repair work). According
to this, Mehmed's triumph at Constantinople–Istanbul, and his
consecration of the Christian Emperor Justinian's great church,
represented the impending final victory of Islam over Christianity.
At Granada, the Spanish monarchs' triumphal entry in 1492 and
their ruthless eviction of the large Jewish and Muslim populations
(the former in 1492, the latter in 1498), together with their appro-
priation of the mosque and the Alhambra, became a symbol for
Europe of a hoped-for triumph of Christianity over the awesome
might of the Islamic East – as Columbus clearly articulated, in the
apocalyptic language he used, writing to the Spanish monarchs on
the eve of his 1492 voyage (as we saw in Chapter 2):

In the year 1492, when your Highnesses had concluded their war
with the Moors who reigned in Europe, I saw your Highnesses'
banners victoriously raised on the towers of the Alhambra, the

citadel of that city, and the Moorish King come out of the city gates and kiss the hands of your Highnesses, and the prince, my Lord. And later in that same month your Highnesses decided to send me, Christopher Columbus, to see those parts of India and the princes and peoples of these lands, and consider the best means for their conversion.

Charles V's Palace at Granada was a spirited response, by the proud descendant of Ferdinand and Isabella of Spain, who regarded himself as the imperial saviour of Christendom from the threats both of the 'infidels' (Islam) and 'heresy' (Luther), to the challenge of Suleiman's investment in increased ostentation and magnificence in his Topkapı Saray in Istanbul.

Dynastic marriages were a formal part of Renaissance power politics, and the expenditure on the dowry, the trousseau and the betrothal and wedding celebrations was included in the calculations of the cost of the occasion versus the value of the contract to the families involved. When Isabella d'Este was fifteen, her mother Eleanora of Aragon had already commissioned a team of distinguished painters and sculptors, including Ercole de' Roberti, to begin making painted and gilded marriage chests, a triumphal carriage and a matrimonial bed for her wedding to Francesco Gonzaga II of Mantua in January 1491. Isabella arrived in Mantua in late 1490 with her possessions in thirteen chests, each an artistic masterpiece. Similarly gorgeous household objects were produced for her sister Beatrice's marriage to Ludovico Sforza of Milan. This was in addition to the enormous dowries Ercole d'Este had to provide in order to negotiate such prestigious marriages for his daughters.

The bride herself was, to all intents and purposes, a piece of precious dynastic property, who could be traded profitably with other, suitably distinguished families. However much the contractual arrangements were disguised at the betrothal and the wedding itself with gorgeous finery and festivities, marrying off an eligible daughter to a politically desirable partner was a serious financial undertaking. The impression that such alliances were undertaken exactly like all other types of trade in the world of commerce was enhanced by the shortage of hard currency among Europe's ruling families. In 1521 King Manuel of Portugal delivered 30,000 quintals of pepper to the Fugger merchant bankers in Antwerp – the proceeds from the sale of the pepper were to be remitted by the Fuggers to Charles V as the dowry for Charles's bride-to-be, Manuel's daughter Isabella.

Contemporary moralists anxiously drew attention to the danger of turning daughters into 'merchandise', and denounced 'dowry inflation' (as the sums attached to marriage contracts among the powerful became increasingly large), though without making any noticeable impact on the trend. Lucrezia Borgia took 100,000 ducats in cash as her dowry when she married Alfonso d'Este of Ferrara in 1502, plus about as much again in lands appropriated from the diocese of Bologna, and another 75,000 ducats' worth of jewels, plate, clothes, linen and tapestries. Her father, Pope Alexander VI (Rodrigo Borgia), also threw in a reduction (from 4000 to 100 ducats) in the annual tribute due from Ferrara to the Papacy. To symbolize this injection of capital into the Ferrara coffers, Lucrezia arrived in Ferrara from Rome in January 1502 at the head of a cortège of 700 courtiers and servants (a display of wealth also paid for by the Pope).

In addition to his complicated credit arrangements with his Fugger bankers, the Emperor Maximilian on occasion used the dowry system in dynastic alliance as an immediate source of ready money. He negotiated a spectacular financial settlement for his own second marriage to Bianca-Maria Sforza, niece of Ludovico Sforza of Milan, in 1494. The marriage was part of Ludovico Sforza's strategic planning to have himself made Duke of Milan, with hereditary rights to his heirs, a move which required the formal agreement of Maximilian. To smooth the way, Bianca-Maria's dowry was 400,000 ducats plus jewels, plate and other fineries worth a further 100,000 ducats. Ludovico Sforza also paid substantial 'sweeteners' to other powerful figures who might support (or at least decline to oppose) the endowment of his title – the King of Bohemia got 10,000 ducats.

Isabella d'Este's marriage to Francesco Gonzaga II cemented a highly desirable, powerful union between Mantua and Ferrara, and considerably enhanced Francesco's reputation (although apparently their personal relations were somewhat less successful, and for much of their marriage they lived virtually separate lives). Isabella's subsequent, highly publicized commitment to assembling an exceptional collection of gems and antiques was calculated further to enhance the public image of the Gonzagas as both powerful and cultivated. That she did so on an extremely limited budget (the Gonzagas had less disposable wealth than the d'Estes) gained her additional credit, though she constantly complained about it herself. Her sister Beatrice had married the immensely rich Ludovico Sforza, now glorying in his dukedom, but had less interest in acquiring treasures – 'would to God that we who spend willingly should have so much', Isabella commented.

Isabella's collection began conventionally enough, with gems, cameos and intaglios – portable assets of the kind her husband, and in particular his uncle, Cardinal Francesco Gonzaga, had collected. Her correspondence for the years 1490 to 1496 dealt almost exclusively with the acquisition of antique intaglios, and with commissions for engraved semi-precious stones from Venetian craftsmen. From early in 1498, however, she was writing to her agents to express her intention to broaden out her collection: 'we now want other things than cameos: rather, we are now interested in owning some figurines and heads in bronze and marble'. By the end of her life the collection contained a staggering number of precious objects: 1241 items were coins and medals, 119 were of gold, 1012 of silver, while the rest, consisting of 110 bronze medals, were mounted on twenty-two plaques in groups of five. Isabella owned a total of seventy-two vases, flasks and cups, fifty-five of which were of *pietre dure*. This included fourteen in agate and a like number in jasper. Most of them were fitted with gold covers, handles and pedestals which ran the gamut from the simple to the bizarre. Twenty-nine of the forty-six engraved gems were cameos, and three of the statuettes were of *pietre dure*. Of the remaining statues, forty-eight were in bronze and seventeen of marble, while there were thirteen portrait busts and three reliefs. In addition to the nine allegorical paintings the collection contained several watches, inlaid boxes, an astrolabe, a 'unicorn horn', several pieces of coral and 'a fish's tooth above the window, three palms long'.

All these treasures were exquisitely arranged in Isabella's two purpose-built display rooms, her *studiolo* and her *grotta*. At the same date that she began purchasing bronze figurines to occupy specified niches or sills in the *studiolo*, she also embarked on a programme of

15. Antique onyx vase from Isabella
d'Este's magnificent collection

16. Lorenzo Costa, *Allegory*, painted for Isabella d'Este who carefully specified
the programme

commissioning for it paintings by 'the most outstanding masters in
Italy'. Each artist would work to a similar scale, the direction of the
light in the picture being determined by the fall of the natural light
in the room. All the paintings were to be on canvas, and the foreground figures in each were to be the same size (a knotted piece of
silk the correct length was sent to each artist). The Gonzaga court
artist, Mantegna, produced two of the paintings, Lorenzo Costa of
Ferrara another two, and the Umbrian artist Perugino one. All were
elaborate allegories, whose programmes were carefully specified by
Isabella herself.

The *studiolo* and the *grotta* became one of the sights of Mantua,
to be shown to visiting dignitaries. Giangiorgio Trissino, one of
those given the tour of Isabella's domain, was full of admiration:

Her true liberality can be understood by the splendour of her dress, by the magnificent décor of the house, and by the beautiful – one might almost say, divine – fabrics with which the whole is adorned. There are the most delightful rooms filled with the rarest books, the most beautiful paintings, with marvellous antique and modern statues, adjoining rooms of cameos and intaglios, of portrait medals, and of the finest gems. There are so many precious and rare things, which it gives one the greatest delight, and it makes one marvel to look upon them.

Other visitors showed their admiration in a rather different fashion. After the Duke of Bourbon's entourage had been allowed to visit the *studiolo* in 1509, valuable silver objects were discovered to be missing.

In 1499 Isabella wrote to her agent in Rome, who was pursuing a possible purchase for her, 'you know how hungry we are for these antiquities'. She was never happier than when a suitor for Gonzaga favour had presented her with some fine antique object as a gift. In 1508 she told Cristoforo Chigi, who had presented her with an antique intaglio, that she had 'a continual desire for antique artefacts, which please and delight us above all else'. When she was first offered Michelangelo's sleeping cupid in 1496 she refused to buy it, on the ground that it was a modern 'fake' – only when she was informed that he was the foremost sculptor of the age did she go to elaborate (indeed unscrupulous) lengths to get hold of it. In July 1502, Isabella bought the Michelangelo statuette from Cesare Borgia, who had appropriated it from Guidobaldo da Montefeltro (its rightful owner) when he invaded Urbino in June. When Guidobaldo was reinstated in 1503, Isabella steadfastly refused to return it. It remained in her collection, occupying pride of place, alongside a genuine antique bronze cupid attributed to Praxiteles.

Isabella's singlemindedness in pursuit of an object she had set her heart on frequently verged on the unseemly, and was occasionally downright dishonest. She knowingly received stolen alabaster heads looted from the Bentivoglio Palace in Bologna. On 31 March 1515, she wrote to her husband's youngest brother Giovanni Gonzaga in Milan, to ask him to help her negotiate a purchase of important antiques from the Sforzas:

> We are extremely sad to hear of the death of Signor Galeazzo Sforza, whom we loved deeply. Nevertheless, we must accept his loss with patience, as one of the world's inevitabilities.
>
> Now we know that his brother Signor Giangaleazzo Sforza, God rest his soul, delighted in owning antiques, and had a considerable number of beautiful things, which came into the hands of Signor Galeazzo, recently deceased. And amongst the beautiful things we have heard that he had some bronze heads. And we are persuaded that the heirs of the aforesaid Signor Galeazzo will not keep the said antiques, but, as it appears, will want to realize their cash value as quickly as possible. So we ask you to approach your Master, the Duke of Milan, on our behalf (and we have also written to Count Lorenzo Strozzo about the matter), that if the esteemed heirs sell the said antiques, he will see to it that they sell to no one but us, and we will give them their money like anyone else.

Giovanni Gonzaga replied four days later, in some embarrassment:

> Concerning what Your Excellency wrote to me by the last post that she would like me to do, following the death of Signor Galeazzo Sforza, and regarding those belongings of his which you would like to be able to obtain, I have to tell you that Signor Galeazzo is still alive, and although he is extremely unwell, we have not lost all hope that he may recover.

Shortly afterwards, Giovanni wrote again. The Duke of Milan, hearing of Isabella's request, had graciously proposed to make a gift to her of such antiques as came to him from Galeazzo's will, whenever he should die. Galeazzo's condition had been improving, but now 'he is getting steadily worse, so that I believe Your Excellency will get what you want'. Isabella replied on 11 April. She was very sorry to hear that Galeazzo's condition had deteriorated, because she loved him dearly, and had been delighted to hear that he was not in fact dead. She was overwhelmed by the Duke of Milan's generosity. However, she could not resist adding a postscript:

> PS. We are extremely desirous to have these antiques, whenever Signor Galeazzo dies, therefore we ask Your Master to take on our power of attorney, to keep a careful watch on them on our behalf, and to see that they are not purloined or stolen away. And because we know that he travels a lot, and that while he is away, anything could happen, to tell the truth, we will be in a state of constant agitation until we have them here with us.

Galeazzo finally died on 14 April. Isabella sent her condolences, and shamelessly collected her antiques (valued at 1000 scudi). Three weeks later, however, she wrote to one of her agents in the Milan area: 'Count Lorenzo Strozzo was here yesterday, and told me that, in addition to the antiques which Signor Galeazzo Sforza left to the Most Illustrious Duke of Milan, there were others, which were to be sold to pay some of his servants and beneficiaries.' Between them, Lorenzo Strozzo, Giovanni Gonzaga and the agent were to get a look at the antiques and find out what the asking price was. Isabella was absolutely determined to get her hands on as many of Galeazzo's precious items as she possibly could.

The heartlessness of Isabella d'Este's death-bed antique-dealing with the Sforzas, however, pales beside her callous treatment of her own Court painter, Andrea Mantegna. In 1506, just two months before the artist's death, Isabella pressured him into selling to her an antique Roman marble bust of the Empress Faustina. Mantegna, who was in need of the money, reluctantly agreed to the sale, and asked 100 ducats – Isabella offered 25. In the end she agreed to the asking price, but the agent who collected the bust for her reported that Mantegna parted with it with such regret that he thought he would die of the loss. On occasions such as these, the passion for precious and rare possessions on the part of the very rich could take a decidedly ugly turn.

In Isabella's *studiolo* an exquisite antique cameo of a royal couple of the age of Ptolemy was exhibited alongside a gold and enamel portrait medal of herself, set with rubies, and with her name picked out in diamonds. Thus her personal fame was, by design, compared favourably with that of the kings of antiquity. Her medal was her favourite self-image, the one she presented to those who had done her special service – she regularly maintained that she preferred it to the many portraits she had to sit for.

For those who commissioned any kind of portrait of themselves, the work of art served at least three distinct functions. It satisfied the individual's desire for a likeness of themselves to pass on to their family, or to commemorate some significant occasion in their life; it was (if painted by an artist of distinction) a valuable work of art in its own right, with a 'value' which could be realized by sale if necessary; and it could, under some circumstances, circulate as an emblem of the individual's personal power and authority. Of all the portrait forms favoured by Renaissance rulers, and by the privileged wealthy who emulated their tastes, the portrait medal most readily captured all these functions symbolically and simultaneously. But, even more importantly, these conjunctions of art-object and likeness of the patron circulated – a well-achieved portrait medal, like de' Pasti's of Mehmed II or Pisanello's of Leonello d'Este, found a place in every great collector's show-case. The patron was himself (or herself) the currency of art – the portrait medal was the 'currency of fame'. Successful individuals from princes to merchants had their likenesses taken for commissioned portrait medals (which could be copied in more or less precious metals, according to the purse of the purchaser). The scholar Erasmus of Rotterdam, the city counsellor Willibald Pirckheimer and the banker Jakob Fugger all commissioned bronze portrait medals of themselves by distinguished artists, and

17. Matthes, silver portrait medal
of Willibald Pirckheimer

18. Quentin Metsys, portrait medal
of Erasmus

circulated them widely as gifts to their friends, just as did imperial rulers like Charles V.

In the letter which Sigismondo Malatesta sent to the Ottoman Emperor Mehmed II with the artist Matteo de' Pasti, Sigismondo congratulated Mehmed for wanting to obtain the services of the world's greatest painters to record his features for posterity: 'Alexander the Great, a king as glorious as yourself, made himself of great renown in this fashion.' Mehmed clearly understood the importance of circulating images of himself in the form of a valuable object, and he became one of the Renaissance's foremost patrons of medallists. Although his attempt to acquire the services of de' Pasti (a notable medallist) failed, the Venetian artist Costanzo da Ferrara, who spent a number of years in Istanbul in the 1470s, executed a profile portrait medal of a turbaned Mehmed, in two versions, and Gentile Bellini and the Paduan sculptor Bartolommeo Bellano both produced medals while working for Mehmed on building works in the 1480s.

Mehmed's enthusiasm for this form of distributing the fame of his accomplishments as the 'Conqueror' worldwide had its desired effect – in Rome in 1489, the Mantuan Ambassador compared the features of Mehmed's son Çem Sultan (who had sought refuge in the West) to Mehmed's portrait medals, and marvelled at their physical similarity. The portrait medals also served as prototypes for all later engraved and painted portraits of Mehmed. A story is told of his successor Selim I walking round one of his newly built kiosks (summer palaces), where an artist was putting the finishing touches to a fresco depicting Mehmed the Conqueror:

> A portrait painter had depicted the well-proportioned figure of the late Sultan Mehmed II. When that picture was shown to him, the sovereign said, 'He clearly wanted to portray the late Sultan Mehmed, but he has certainly not been able to capture his likeness. The deceased used to make us sit on his blessed lap in our childhood; his noble countenance is still in our memory: he was falcon-nosed. This painter has not captured his likeness at all.'

The hawk-nosed profile of Mehmed is a strong feature of the portrait medal – a more likely source of Selim's clear recollection of what his grandfather had looked like, more than thirty years after his death.

Portrait medals lent themselves, above all, to being given as personal gifts by those who had had them made. They were compact (fitting nicely into the palm of the hand), they were valuable (and could be cast in bronze, silver or gold, according to the status of the recipient), and they carried the image of the donor (generally identified by name) on one side, and some pleasing figurative image like a personal emblem or classical motif (often accompanied by some uplifting inscription) on the other.

Gift-giving was not just a spontaneous act of generosity, it was an integral part of the package of obligations and indebtednesses which accompanied any transaction of services, or any gesture of good will. In August 1509, two years after he had been contracted

19. Costanzo da Ferrara, portrait medal of Mehmed II

to do it, Albrecht Dürer completed a difficult commission – a large altarpiece for the Dominican church in Frankfurt am Main – paid for by the wealthy Frankfurt cloth merchant Jakob Heller. Heller had complained about delays in the altarpiece's execution, constantly queried the advances Dürer requested for materials, and baulked at the final asking price for the three panels. He nevertheless included personal gifts in the final settlement, and Dürer duly thanked him:

> I am glad to hear that my picture pleases you, so that my labour has not been invested in vain. I am also happy that you are content with the payment – and rightly so, for I could have got 100 florins more for it than you have given me. But I would not take it anyway, for then I should have let you down, whereas I hope to retain your friendship. My wife thanks you very much. She will wear your gift in your honour. Also my younger brother thanks you for the two florins you sent him for a *Trinkgeld* [to buy himself a drink]. I myself thank you for all the honour you have bestowed upon me.

The gift symbolically converted the commercial transaction into an exchange between friends, masking the bare mercenary payment and adding a visible display of gratitude and pleasure. A gift given also created an obligation – the recipient was expected to show his gratitude by some future favour. No doubt the Duke of Milan hoped for some future favour from the Gonzagas when he graciously presented the antiques he had inherited from Galeazzo Sforza to Isabella d'Este (and let her know that the gift items had been valued at 1000 scudi).

By the early sixteenth century, printed books made thoroughly acceptable gifts, which could conveniently be chosen to convey some special tribute to the recipient – the Roman philosopher Cicero's little Latin book *On Friendship* was a regular choice between academic colleagues. In 1514 Erasmus of Rotterdam metaphorically offered his latest literary work to his close friend Pieter Gilles as a gift, with a dedication which stressed the special significance of books exchanged between intimates:

> Friends of the commonplace and homespun sort, my open-hearted Pieter, have their idea of relationship, like their whole lives, attached to material things. And if ever they have to face a separation, they favour a frequent exchange of rings, knives, caps, and other tokens of the kind, for fear that their affection may cool when contact between them is interrupted or that it may actually die away with the passage of time. But you and I, whose idea of friendship rests wholly in a meeting of minds and the enjoyment of studies in common, may greet one another from time to time with presents for the mind, and keepsakes of a literary description. And so I send you a gift – no common gift, for you are no common friend, but many jewels in one small book.

For the rich and powerful, lavish gift-giving was part of a highly codified way of establishing networks of personal indebtedness, which could be called in in times of need. Queen Elizabeth I of England kept careful accounts of the value of the gifts her courtiers gave her at New Year, and the value of the items with which she had reciprocated (in general, slightly less costly). When Piero de' Medici chose the Adoration of the Magi as the theme for the frescos with which he commissioned Benozzo Gozzoli to adorn the walls of the chapel in the Medici Palace, he was choosing a representation of the giving of precious objects as an acceptable part of worship. The exoticism of this particular gift exchange, furthermore, allowed the artist to paint (and the Medici to enjoy) lovingly rendered images of gifts of oriental splendour, of the kind customarily offered to visitors by the Ottoman sultans, and brought home by their ambassadors.

The Renaissance prince's conspicuous consumption of fine art-objects was a complicated, calculated and functional affair – a combination of pleasure and investment, shrewdly judged so as to maximize the public impact of his resources, while retaining the possibility of surrendering individual objects as pledges against cash loans if these became necessary. Isabella d'Este's collection was, for all her talk of 'passionate love' of all things antique, a thoroughly marketable collection of items, as was Lorenzo de' Medici's, the library of Matthias Corvinus, King of Hungary, or the jewels and silverware of Sigismund, King of Poland. As they glittered on display in their purpose-built *studioli*, they also functioned as valuable assets, and as collateral in financial deals.

Occasionally, however, this convenient and civilized arrangement broke down, to reveal the financial calculations lurking behind the surface beauty. In February 1488, five years after the death of Francesco Gonzaga, the Italian Cardinal famed for his collection of valuable art-objects, Matthias Corvinus, King of Hungary, learned that the Cardinal's magnificent collection of medals and cameos might still be on the market. From Buda, his wife Beatrice of Aragon wrote to her sister Eleanora of Aragon, wife of Ercole d'Este, Duke of Ferrara, to ask what she could find out about the matter. Like

Corvinus, Eleanora and Ercole were connoisseurs and collectors of fine objects. In this case, however, Eleanora was particularly well placed for access to information on the assets and general financial position of the Gonzagas, since she was on the point of contracting a marriage between her daughter, Isabella d'Este, and the Marquis of Mantua, Francesco Gonzaga II.

In April Eleanora informed her sister of the extent of Cardinal Gonzaga's posthumous debts, adding that what remained of the medal and cameo collection was in the possession of the Medici bank:

> I have looked into the matter of the portrait medals and the cameos, and I have discovered that the most reverend Cardinal of Mantua did have a large collection of medals in silver and other metals. At the time of his death, however, he left a large number of debts, the largest of them to his personal servants, who took the silver medals in settlement, while the others were dispersed, so that none now remains.
>
> The very reverend Cardinal also had a large number of remarkable and very beautiful cameos, which were retained by Lorenzo and Cosimo de' Medici against a loan of four thousand ducats, for the settling of his legacies and other things which he had instructed on his deathbed. He left enormous debts – valued at between fourteen and eighteen thousand ducats, and they have to be settled within the next eight months.

In October, following personal discussions with a number of intermediaries, Eleanora told her sister that Lorenzo de' Medici was interested in striking a deal with the King of Hungary, but that he no longer held the cameos personally. They were now lodged with the Medici bank's agent in Rome and, although Eleanora had tried to interest the Rome branch in opening negotiations, she was not making any progress. The exquisite and rare art-objects, coveted by all and sundry ever since the Cardinal had assembled them and set them in their silver trays, were tied up as pledges in a complicated chain of financial transactions from which they could no longer be extricated. Corvinus' attempt to restore the cameos to the connoisseurs of the antique got no further.

This was not, however, the end of the story of attempts to get the Cardinal's coveted cameos back in some great collector's display case. Ten years later it was the Cardinal's nephew, Francesco Gonzaga II himself, who was trying to redeem the cameos, this time by paying off the longstanding family debt against which they had been secured – 3500 ducats plus 674 ducats of accumulated interest. On this occasion the money was to come from Milan – part of a 15,000 ducat pension due to Francesco from Ludovico Sforza.

The Sforzas were popularly believed to be fabulously wealthy and (unlike many of their peers) to have no trouble laying their hands on ready money when necessary. Ludovico Sforza did, apparently, operate a superior financial administration and accounting system. He readily acknowledged his debt to Francesco, but he too, surprisingly, turned out to have trouble raising the cash. In 1494, when he was distributing large sums to smooth the path of the proposed marriage between his niece Bianca-Maria and the Habsburg Emperor Maximilian, he had to resort to borrowing from his finance officers. He wrote to his Deputies of Finance from Piacenza:

> We need five thousand ducats right away. Please find them and have them sent to us here without delay. If they are not to hand out of our own funds at such short notice, please club together and raise the money between you yourselves, without a moment lost (borrowing it if necessary). And see to it that one way or another we have the cash tomorrow.

By 1498 even the Deputies of Finance could not keep Ludovico Sforza financially afloat. Before Ludovico could find the 5000 ducats he owed Francesco Gonzaga, Milan was invaded by the French, the Sforzas fell and the cameos once more reverted to the bankers.

By the late 1490s, Francesco Gonzaga's wife Isabella d'Este was well embarked on her collection of antiques. Ludovico Sforza was her brother-in-law – his wife, Isabella's younger sister Beatrice, had died giving birth to Ludovico's second son in 1497. This final attempt at retrieving the Cardinal's cameos was thus very much a family affair – a family of enthusiasts for paintings and statues, gems and curios, seeking to consolidate still further the reputation for 'civilization' which lavish expenditure on such collections brought with it (expenditure which was sometimes outrageous, and frequently beyond their actual means in terms of ready funds).

Waiting impatiently for news of the proposed deal in Rome, the exasperated agent for the Medici bank, Tornabuoni, wrote a final letter to his junior in Mantua, who had been kicking his heels there for months while the Marquis tried to get together the necessary cash for the purchase. Tornabuoni warned that there were plenty of other people out there willing to raise the money for such a wonderful purchase: 'I tell you, that there are jewels around, diamonds, *balasci*, and such-like, but you will never in the whole wide world find anything like these cameos. And although the price is high, I don't doubt they are worth much more – they cost Pope Paul II a fortune.'

Almost thirty years after the young Cardinal Francesco Gonzaga had engineered his prestige and renown in Rome by means of his fabulous expenditure on rare antique gems and cameos – strategically sharing his passion for them with Pope Paul – the Cardinal's collection still served to elevate his memory and clerical reputation. But the objects of beauty over which he and the Pope had pored together languished in a Roman bank-vault. Purchased deliberately as assets which could conveniently be used, when necessary, as financial guarantees, these exquisite and important cameos had become permanently trapped in the world of finance, rather than that of culture – forever currency instead of art.

EPILOGUE

HANS HOLBEIN'S almost lifesize painting now known as *The Ambassadors* hangs in the National Gallery in London. It was painted by the German artist during the spring of 1533 for Jean de Dinteville, resident Ambassador of the King of France, François I, at the Court of King Henry VIII in London. Jean de Dinteville had only recently taken up the post, in early February of that year. He replaced the previous ambassador shortly after Henry's secret marriage to Anne Boleyn, while Henry was still notionally seeking the approval of the Pope for his divorce from his previous Queen, Catherine of Aragon. The double portrait shows Jean de Dinteville with his friend, the French envoy Georges de Selve, who visited England, briefly, on secret ambassadorial business from the French King in April–May 1533. The painting left England when de Dinteville returned to France in November 1533, and hung for many years in his château at Polisy, next to an allegorical painting (also specially commissioned) of de Dinteville and his brother François, Bishop of Auxerre, who was the French King's Ambassador to Rome during the same period.

Some of the issues associated with Jean de Dinteville's ambassadorial mission in England are precisely figured in the painting in the conjunctions of objects painted on the lower shelf of the piece of furniture on which he leans. The foreshortened, uncased lute (its discarded case lies under the table on de Dinteville's side) with its prominently broken string is still recognizably an emblem of broken harmony, or discord. Beneath its neck lies an open hymn-book. The book is Johann Walther's Wittenberg edition of Lutheran hymns, in which we can clearly read the opening verse in German of

1. Detail of Hans Holbein, *The Ambassadors*, showing hymn book, accounting manual, musical instruments and terrestrial globe

Luther's 'Come Holy Ghost' ('Kom Heiliger Geyst') on the left, and 'Man wilt thou live blessedly' ('Mensch wiltu leben seliglich'), with the music for tenor voice. The discord symbolized by the broken lute-string is specified by the hymn-book to be that between the Catholic and Lutheran churches (but also between the Pope's party and that of the Lutheran-sympathizing Anne Boleyn). Since Jean de Dinteville and his brother were actively engaged in brokering a political agreement between the Pope and Henry, in spite of Anne Boleyn's known Lutheran Church sympathies, and in spite of the fact that by remarrying in advance of papal consent to his divorce from Catherine of Aragon Henry risked excommunication, this seems an appropriate theme for de Dinteville's painting. The collection of harmonizing flutes under the hymn-book lie alongside the lute, ready for use (should the mission have proved successful), but currently in their case.

On the left of this lower shelf is a terrestrial globe, so meticulously represented that it can be readily identified as Behaim's, and a German merchant-accounting book, held open by a surveyor's square. A pair of compasses spans the table between globe and lute. The markings on this globe continue the theme of discord – this time territorial. The globe is tipped away from the viewer, so that the names on it (for instance, 'AFRICA') are upside-down. However, significant names have been written so that the viewer reads them right way up. Thus all names within Europe are marked legibly, and a number of further names important to de Dinteville's own diplomatic career have been added (including that of de Dinteville's home town of Polisy). Strikingly, over in the new world, 'Brazil' ('Brisilici R.') is written legibly and right way up for the viewer, and complements the clearly drawn 'Line of division between Spain and Portugal' ('Linea Divisionis Castellanorum et Portugallenum') – the line agreed under the 1494 Treaty of Tordesillas, which designated all new-world territory to the east of it as belonging to Portugal, all that to the west as belonging to Spain. It was this line which under the Treaty of Saragossa of 1529 had been extended round to the other side of the globe (thus the side not visible if the viewer is to be able to see Europe and the Mediterranean), to decide the ownership of the spice islands, the Moluccas. The globe, with its demarcation line, represents visually the contemporary contest between the major European powers for ownership of commercially valuable territories – Brazil to the west, and the unseen Moluccas to the east.

As the hymn-book sits alongside the lute, so, in front of the Nuremberg globe, lies the German astronomer Peter Apian's arithmetic book, *A New and Well-Grounded Instruction in All Merchant's Arithmetic*. Books for reckoning up profit and loss and maps recording routes and trading rights belonged together as part of the expanding markets of the first half of the sixteenth century. Peter Apian's was particularly resonant as a symbol of commercial learning, since his geometrical, astronomical and navigational publications were a crucial part of the innovative work in these areas which was expanding commercial possibilities around the globe. Martin Behaim's globe, which had originally been commissioned by

Nuremberg merchants, to try to open up trade routes that would break the Portuguese cartel dominating the spice trade, and which had played such a vital part in the voyages of discovery, stands both for international navigation and for international trade.

On the upper shelf of the table between de Dinteville and de Selve is a celestial globe, a collection of scientific, astronomical instruments and a closed book. This globe, too, can be identified. It was made by Johann Schöner in 1532/3 – the most up-to-date celestial globe available, by the man whose innovation in commercially directed science was to extend to his key role as facilitator for the publication of Copernicus' *On the Revolutions of the Celestial Spheres* in 1543. Instrument-maker, scientific publisher and Lutheran, Schöner, like Apian, straddled the worlds of science, religious politics and commerce.

At the visual centre of Holbein's *The Ambassadors*, an array of instruments and apparatus for mastering the heavens and gaining precise knowledge of time and place, for navigating the globe and mapping and recording geographical findings claim the viewer's attention. The arrangement of instruments lies directly between the eye-level of the two sitters, and their carefully posed, rested hands (de Dinteville's left, de Selve's right). These scientific instruments appear in an earlier Holbein portrait of the German merchant and astronomer-in-residence to Henry VIII Nicolaus Kratzer. Recent X-rays of the painting taken during cleaning show that this section was inserted as a pre-existing composition by the artist. It was therefore in all likelihood painted five years earlier, as a still-life study while Holbein was painting his portrait of Kratzer. The cylinder dial is set for the equinox, and the celestial globe is very roughly set for the autumnal equinox, with the sign of Scorpio rising. The future Queen Elizabeth was born on 7 September 1533, a few days from the equinox. On the pillar dial immediately alongside the globe Holbein has painted the shadows so that the date shown is Good Friday, 11 April 1533, the date on which Anne Boleyn was accorded full royal honours.

2. Detail of *The Ambassadors*, showing scientific instruments, celestial globe and Turkish rug

The Ottoman rug which covers the upper shelf of the table in Holbein's *The Ambassadors*, and links the resting arms (and perhaps the political intrigues) of de Dinteville and de Selve, reminds us that the power to be reckoned with in the 1530s, other than the Habsburgs, was the Turks. It also reminds us what coveted items Ottoman commodities were in the circles in which Holbein and de Dinteville moved, worthy to be lovingly represented in a painting which celebrated the worldly success of the sitters. Holbein's representation of the rug is as carefully precise as that of his globes and instruments – even today it allows carpet specialists to identify it as of a particularly valuable and interesting type of early oriental carpet (known to carpet specialists as a 'Holbein'), though few actual carpets from the period still survive.

Early 1533 was a fraught period of English diplomatic activity. Anne Boleyn was pregnant, and the King was not prepared to risk the 'boy' being born a bastard by delaying her recognition as his legitimate wife while the Pope procrastinated. François I was meanwhile trying to persuade Henry not to go public until he had smoothed the path of divorce and remarriage with the Medici Pope, Clement VII, though he nevertheless expressed personal support for the English King. François was to have been godfather to the baby had it been a boy.

Meanwhile in Rome, Jean de Dinteville's brother François was trying discreetly to encourage the Pope to reach a decision acceptable to the English King concerning his Great Matter. On 23 May, a week before Anne's coronation, Jean de Dinteville wrote to his brother (in a letter whose evasive phrasing clearly showed that he expected it to be intercepted and read by Henry's agents) with a veiled warning that it might be necessary for the French to intervene directly with the Pope, since things in London were coming to a head. The official announcement that Henry's marriage was legitimate was actually made in London that very day. At the end of his letter Jean de Dinteville added a personal comment on his own current state of mind:

> This country is beginning to displease me, as I wait for the expiry of my six months' term (which expires on 22 July). I was promised by the Grand Master that I would not have to stay longer than that. I pray to God that he will keep his promise. I have had a tertian fever which it took a long time to get rid of. Please put in a word for me with M. de Paris about my recall. I must tell you that I am the most melancholy-vexed and tiresome ambassador that ever was.

'If I stay here much longer I greatly fear I'll leave my skin and bones here. I have only enjoyed one week of good health in the whole time I've been here,' de Dinteville wrote a little later, still pleading for

3. Detail of *The Ambassadors,* showing the anamorphic skull: 'If I stay here much longer I greatly fear I'll leave my skin and bones here' (Jean de Dinteville)

recall. The two skulls which figure prominently in Holbein's painting seem a fair reflection of the sitter's gloomy emotional state and his constant ill-health while in London. In addition to the curiously represented skull which dominates the bottom of the canvas (and which can be correctly seen as a skull only if viewed from one pre-scribed vantage-point below and to the left of the painting), de Dinteville sports in his hat a badge or pin in the form of a death's head. The skull was a conventional 'vanitas' emblem, a humbling reminder of death even amid splendour.

Georges de Selve arrived in London shortly before the public announcement of the King's remarriage, and left before the pageantry of Anne's coronation at the beginning of June. It is possible that his 'secret business' concerned development within the Lutheran Church (of which both he and de Dinteville were moderate

4. Detail of *The Ambassadors,* showing de Dinteville's hat badge which echoes
the anamorphic skull

supporters) and was part of Anglo-French discussions of the appropriate response to the Reformation's growing hold on the German states. De Dinteville was certainly anxious that news of de Selve's visit should not be communicated to the French Grand Master (the French King's most senior minister), Anne de Montmorency, who was a strong supporter of the Catholic party in France.

However, the most sensitive arena of negotiation in which Georges de Selve was involved was located in Venice. The previous year, François I's special envoy Rincón had set out via Venice and Ragusa for Istanbul, with instructions to ask the Ottoman Sultan, Suleiman the Magnificent, to continue his expansionist wars against Charles V on the Italian front, rather than the Austrian one, in order that the French might regain Genoa and the duchy of Milan as part of the action. Throughout 1533 Rincón and the Sultan's own trusted envoy Yunus Beg were in Venice negotiating a future Franco-Ottoman political and commercial partnership. De Selve shuttled between Paris and Venice carrying dispatches on the talks (in December 1533 de Selve was appointed French resident ambassador in Venice).

Strategically, alliance with the one contender for imperial power round the Mediterranean offered the only possible hope of resistance to Charles V. François I confided in the Venetian Ambassador: 'I cannot deny that I keenly desire the Turk powerful and ready for war, not for himself, because he is an infidel and we are Christians, but to undermine the Emperor's [Charles V's] power, to force heavy expenses upon him and to reassure all other governments against so powerful an enemy.' Under these circumstances, public hostility was a cover for something approaching diplomatic

5. Marinus van Reymerswaele, *St Jerome*, which shows a 'vanitas' skull, a humbling reminder of death

cordiality behind the scenes. When François and Henry had been on the point of signing their treaty of alliance at Calais in October 1532 François had written to Jean de Dinteville's brother (six months before Jean de Dinteville sat for his portrait in London):

> To anyone who asks you about the preparations which might be taking place with a view to an understanding between the King of England and myself, you can tell them that seeing the major preparations for an invasion of the Christian territories, which the Turks are currently involved in, we want to be prepared to combine to initiate whatever is necessary as much for the good of those Christian territories, of which we are by God's will the principal leaders, as in order not to be at the mercy of the Turkish troops.

In fact, the treaty signed between Henry and François was intended to be the first stage in the assembling of an alliance which would include Suleiman. As an early-seventeenth-century treatise on ambassadors points out, it is entirely acceptable for those of differing religious persuasions to sustain cordial diplomatic and commercial relations: 'Christian Princes and Estates make no difficulties to hold their Agents and Factors with the Turkes when they haue occasion.'

The setting for *The Ambassadors* (identified by the pavement on which the two men stand) is the chapel in Westminster Abbey in which Henry VIII's new Queen, Anne Boleyn, was crowned with great pomp and ceremony at the end of May or beginning of June 1533. Jean de Dinteville played a prominent part in Anne's coronation, as the representative of the French Crown (the only major foreign power apart from Venice thus represented) in the various extravagant processions and ceremonies, and contributing lavishly to the expenses of the spectacle. Twelve of de Dinteville's servants led the procession which took Anne to the Abbey. They wore French colours – blue velvet with yellow and blue sleeves, with white plumes in their hats. Their horses had trappings of blue sarsenet, powdered with white crosses. (In December 1533, François I reimbursed his ambassador for his personal financial outlay on this occasion with a gift of 500 gold écus.) While support for the remarriage and coronation was in the interests of the French King, whose political ambition was to cement an alliance with Henry against Charles V, Henry's subjects were openly hostile to this display of French magnificence at an English royal occasion. Charles V's ambassador Chapuys reported home in his dispatches that Jean de Dinteville and his retinue, leading the coronation procession with the Archbishop of Canterbury, had been booed and insulted by the crowd along the route.

Alongside Jean de Dinteville, Georges de Selve's presence in the double portrait registers the continuing diplomatic intrigues between the competing imperial powers in and beyond Europe, and the strong connection between these and the same powers' commercial aspirations. We do not in the end know whether the exchanges of information between de Dinteville and de Selve during the latter's brief visit were concerned with wealth-creation through trading agreements or with political alliance-formation. Their private dealings are recorded in the painting as a liaison whose purpose is secret, but whose connection with power and wealth is marked by the presence of the Ottoman rug and the German artefacts, whose exquisite beauty captures the onlooker's attention at the expense of the sitters themselves. At the centre of the painting – where we might expect a Madonna, flanked by the two diplomats as her donors or saints – is a collection of valuable scientific instruments and desirable consumer objects or belongings. And hanging over de Dinteville, revealed behind the sumptuous curtains which set off the ambassadors' portraits, is an exquisitely crafted silver crucifix. The crucifix reminds us that the political and doctrinal might of the Catholic Church and its protector, the Holy Roman Emperor, waited just beyond the bounds of the painting, shaping contemporary events. But the crucifix, too, was an object of value in its own right –

concrete evidence that the Catholic Church, also, was part of the competition for riches, spices and territorial dominion which defined the European Renaissance.

HOLBEIN'S PAINTING captured for all time the way the French Ambassador wished to be remembered by posterity, but it also celebrated the very achievements to which we still attach value in the late twentieth century. The artist has lavished infinite care on the surfaces of desirable objects – objects which are of great price, are things of beauty in themselves and are also masterpieces of technological skill. Prestige and power are represented by this accumulation of valuable goods, and by the sumptuous dress and nonchalantly self-centred pose of the sitters.

But what is not represented here is as important as what is. There is nothing parochial about *The Ambassadors* – a painting of French aristocrats, executed in England by a German artist, and replete with allusions to commercial centres in Germany, Italy and Istanbul, to intellectual developments in Nuremberg, Wittenberg and London, and to political exchanges between France, England, Germany, Venice and Istanbul. It was the Renaissance which opened these international and cosmopolitan horizons, the Renaissance which kindled the desire to purchase the rare and the beautiful as a sign of individual (or family) success. The world we inhabit today, with its ruthless competitiveness, fierce consumerism, restless desire for ever wider horizons, for travel, discovery and innovation, a world hemmed in by the small-mindedness of petty nationalism and religious bigotry but refusing to bow to it, is a world which was made in the Renaissance.

BIBLIOGRAPHY

Ackerman, Phyllis, *The Rockefeller McCormick Tapestries: Three Early Sixteenth Century Tapestries* (Oxford: Oxford University Press, 1932)

Alexander, Jonathan J. G. (ed.), *The Painted Page: Italian Renaissance Book Illumination 1450–1550* (Munich: Prestel, 1994)

Ames-Lewis, Frances, *The Library and Manuscripts of Piero di Cosimo de' Medici* (New York and London: Garland, 1984)

Amico, John d', *Theory and Practice in Renaissance Textual Criticism: Beatus Rhenanus between Conjecture and History* (Berkeley: University of California Press, 1988)

Andrews, Kenneth R., *Trade, Plunder and Settlement: Maritime Enterprise and the Genesis of the British Empire 1480–1630* (Cambridge: Cambridge University Press, 1984)

Armstrong, Elizabeth, *Before Copyright: The French Book-Privilege System 1498–1526* (Cambridge: Cambridge University Press, 1990)

Armstrong, Elizabeth, *Robert Estienne Royal Printer: An Historical Study of the Elder Stephanus* (Cambridge: Cambridge University Press, 1954; rev. edn, 1986)

Ashtor, E., *Levant Trade in the Later Middle Ages* (Princeton: Princeton University Press, 1983)

Aslanapa, Oktay, *One Thousand Years of Turkish Carpets* (Istanbul: Erin, 1988)

Atasoy, Nurhan, and Julian Raby, *Iznik: The Pottery of Ottoman Turkey* (London: Alexandria Press, 1989)

Axelson, Eric (ed.), *Dias and his Successors* (Cape Town: Saayman & Weber, 1988)

Balard, Michel (ed.), *Le Marchand au moyen age, XIXe Congrès de la S.H.M.E.S (Reims, juin 1988)* (Paris: Cid Editions, 1992)

Barber, P., 'England I: Pageantry, Defense, and Government: Maps at Court to 1550', in D. Buisseret (ed.), *Monarchs, Ministers and Maps: The Emergence of Cartography as a Tool of Government in Early Modern England* (Chicago: University of Chicago Press, 1992), 26–56

Barrucand, M., and A. Bednorz, *Moorish Architecture in Andalusia* (Cologne: Taschen, 1992)

Baxandall, Michael, *Painting and Experience in Fifteenth Century Italy* (Oxford: Oxford University Press, 1972)

Bec, C., *Les Marchands Ecrivains. Affaires et humanisme à Florence, 1375–1435* (Paris and The Hague: Mouton & Co., 1967)

Bechtel, Guy, *Gutenberg et l'invention de l'imprimerie* (Paris: Fayard, 1992)

Bérenger, Jean, *A History of the Habsburg Empire 1273–1700*, trans. C. A. Simpson (London: Longman, 1994)

Biagioli, Mario, *Galileo Courtier: The Practice of Science in the Culture of Absolutism* (Chicago: Chicago University Press, 1993)

Billanovich, Giuseppe, *La tradizione del testo di Livio e le origini dell'Umanesimo*, vol. 1: *Tradizione e fortuna di Livio tra Medioevo e Umanesimo* (Padua: Antenore, 1981)

Birrell, T. A., *English Monarchs and their Books: From Henry VII to Charles II* (London: British Library, 1987)

Black, C. (ed.), *Atlas of the Renaissance* (London: Cassell, 1993)

Braudel, Fernand, *Civilisation and Capitalism 15th–18th Century*, trans. Sîan Reynolds, 3 vols (London: Collins, 1982)

Braunstein, Philippe (ed.), *Venise 1500. La puissance, la novation et la concorde: le triomphe du mythe* (Paris: Editions Autrement, 1993)

Brenner, Robert, *Merchants and Revolution: Commercial Change, Political Conflict, and London's Overseas Traders, 1550–1653* (Princeton: Princeton University Press, 1993)

Brown, Clifford, with L. Fusco and G. Corti, 'Lorenzo de' Medici and the Dispersal of the Antiquarian Collections of Cardinal Francesco Gonzaga', *Arte Lombarda* 90–1 (1989), 86–103

Brown, Malcolm C., '"Lo insaciabile desiderio nostro de cose antique": New Documents for Isabella d'Este's Collection of Antiquities', in

C. H. Clough (ed.), *Cultural Aspects of the Italian Renaissance: Essays in Honour of Paul Oskar Kristeller* (Manchester: Manchester University Press, 1976), 324–53

Brown, Patricia Fortini, *Venetian Narrative Painting in the Age of Carpaccio* (New Haven: Yale University Press, 1986)

Brummett, Palmira, *Ottoman Seapower and Levantine Diplomacy in the Age of Discovery* (Albany: State University of New York Press, 1994)

Buisseret, David (ed.), *Monarchs, Ministers and Maps: The Emergence of Cartography as a Tool of Government in Early Modern Europe* (Chicago: University of Chicago Press, 1992)

Burke, Peter, *The Italian Renaissance: Culture and Society in Italy* (rev. edn, Oxford: Polity Press, 1987)

Carley, James P., 'Books Seen by Samual Ward "in bibliotheca regia" *circa* 1614', *British Library Journal* 16 (1990), 89–98

Carley, James P., 'John Leland and the Contents of English Pre-Dissolution Libraries', *Transactions of the Cambridge Bibliographical Society* 9 (1989), 330–57

Cartwright, Julia, *Isabella d'Este, Marchioness of Mantua 1474–1539: A Study of the Renaissance*, 2 vols (London: John Murray, 1903)

Chambers, D. S., *The Imperial Age of Venice 1380–1580* (London: Thames and Hudson, 1970)

Chambers, D. S., *A Renaissance Cardinal and his Worldly Goods: The Will and Inventory of Francesco Gonzaga (1444–1483)* (London: Warburg Institute, 1992)

Chambers, D. S., and J. Martineau, *Splendours of the Gonzaga* (exhibition catalogue, London: Victoria and Albert Mueum, 1981)

Chambers, David, and Brian Pullan, *Venice: A Documentary History 1450–1630* (Oxford: Basil Blackwell, 1992)

Charrière, E., *Négociations de la France dans le Levant*, 4 vols (Paris, 1840–60)

Chastel, A., *Mythe et crise de la Renaissance* (2nd edn, Geneva: Albert Skira, 1989)

Chaudhuri, K. N., *Trade and Civilisation in the Indian Ocean: An Economic*

History from the Rise of Islam to 1750 (Cambridge: Cambridge University Press, 1985)

Chauhan, R. R. S., 'The Horse Trade in Portuguese India', *Purabhilekh-Puratatva* (Journal of the Directorate of Archives, Archeology and Museums, Panaji-Goa) 2 (1984), 14–24

Chrisman, Miriam Usher, *Lay Culture, Learned Culture: Books and Social Change in Strasbourg, 1480–1599* (New Haven: Yale University Press, 1982)

Clot, André, *Suleiman the Magnificent: The Man, his Life, his Epoch* (London: Saqi Books, 1992)

Cole, Alison, *Art of the Italian Renaissance Courts: Virtue and Magnificence* (London: Weidenfeld & Nicolson, 1995)

Coote, C. H. (ed.), *Johann Schöner, Professor of Mathematics at Nuremberg*, trans. Henry Stevens (London: Henry Stevens, 1888)

Crone, G. R. (ed.), *Voyages of Cadamosto and Other Documents on Western Africa* (London: Hakluyt Society, 1937)

Csapodi, Csaba (ed.), *Bibliotheca Corviniana: The Library of King Matthias Corvinus of Hungary* (Budapest: Kneer, 1969)

Davies, Arthur, 'Behaim, Martellus and Columbus', *Geographical Journal* 143 (1977), 451–9

Davies, Martin, *Aldus Manutius: Printer and Publisher of Renaissance Venice* (London: British Library, 1995)

Davis, Natalie Zemon, 'Beyond the Market: Books as Gifts in Sixteenth-Century France', *Transactions of the Royal Historical Society* 33 (1983), 69–88

Diffie, Bailey, and G. D. Winius (eds), *Foundations of the Portuguese Empire, 1415–1580*, 2 vols (Minneapolis: University of Minnesota, 1977)

Dunkerton, Jill, Susan Foister, Dillian Gordon and Nicholas Penny, *Giotto to Dürer: Early Renaissance Painting in the National Gallery* (New Haven and London: Yale University Press, 1991)

Ehrenberg, R., *Capital and Finance in the Age of the Renaissance: A Study of the Fuggers and their Connections* (New York: Harcourt, Brace, first pub. 1896)

Eisenstein, Elizabeth L., 'The Advent of Printing and the Problem of the Renaissance', *Past and Present* 45 (1969), 19–89

Eisenstein, Elizabeth L., *The Printing Press as an Agent of Change: Communications and Cultural Transformations in Early-Modern Europe*, 2 vols (Cambridge: Cambridge University Press, 1979)

Ettinghausen, R., 'Near Eastern Book Covers and their Influence on European Bindings', *Ars Orientalis* 3 (1959), 113–31

Evans, R. J. W., *Rudolf II and his World: A Study in Intellectual History 1576–1612* (Oxford: Clarendon Press, 1973)

Evans, R. J. W., *The Wechel Presses: Humanism and Calvinism in Central Europe 1572–1627*, *Past and Present* supplement 2 (Oxford: Oxford University Press, 1975)

Favier, Jean, *De l'or et des épices: naissance de l'homme d'affaires au moyen age* (Paris: Fayard, 1987)

Febvre, Lucien, and Henri-Jean Martin, *The Coming of the Book: The Impact of Printing 1450–1800,* trans. David Gerard (London: New Left Books, 1976; reprinted London: Verso, 1990)

Fernández-Armesto, Felipe, *Before Columbus: Exploration and Colonization from the Mediterranean to the Atlantic 1229–1492* (Philadelphia: University of Pennsylvania Press, 1987)

Fernández-Armesto, Felipe, *Columbus* (Oxford: Oxford University Press, 1991)

Fletcher, Harry George III, *New Aldine Studies: Documentary Essays on the Life and Work of Aldus Manutius* (San Francisco: Bernard M. Rosenthal, 1988)

Flint, Valerie, *The Imaginative Landscape of Christopher Columbus* (Princeton: Princeton University Press, 1992)

Francesco, Grete de, 'Silk Fabrics in Venetian Paintings', *Ciba Review* 29 (1940), 1036–48

Francesco, Grete de, 'The Venetian Silk Industry', *Ciba Review* 29 (1940), 1027–35

Francesco, Grete de, 'Venice between East and West', *Ciba Review* 29 (1940), 1018–26

Frère, Jean-Claude, *Léonarde de Vinci* (Paris: Editions Pierre Terrail, 1994)

Gairdner, James (ed.), *Letters and Papers, Foreign and Domestic, of the Reign of Henry VIII* (London: HMSO, 1880)

Gantzhorn, Volkmar, *Le Tapis chrétien oriental* (Cologne: Taschen, 1991)

Gerulaitis, Leonardus Vytautas, *Printing and Publishing in Fifteenth-Century Venice* (Chicago: American Library Association, 1976)

Gilbert, Felix, *The Pope, his Banker, and Venice* (Cambridge, Mass.: Harvard University Press, 1980)

Gilmont, J.-F., *Jean Crespin: un éditeur réformé du XVIe siècle* (Geneva: Librairie Droz, 1981)

Gingerich, Owen, 'Copernicus's De revolutionibus: An Example of Renaissance Scientific Printing', in G. P. Tyson and Sylvia S. Wagonheim (eds), *Print and Culture in the Renaissance: Essays on the Advent of Printing in Europe* (Newark: University of Delaware Press, 1986), 55–73

Giusti, Enrico, and Carlo Maccagni (eds), *Luca Pacioli e la matematica del Rinascimento* (Florence: Giunti, 1994)

Godinho, Vitórino Magalhães, *Les Découvertes. XVe–XVIe siècles: une révolution des mentalités* (Paris: Editions Autrement, 1992)

Goldthwaite, Richard A., *Wealth and the Demand for Art in Italy 1300–1600* (Baltimore: Johns Hopkins University Press, 1993)

Goodwin, G., *A History of Ottoman Architecture* (London: Thames and Hudson, 1971)

Gordan, Phyllis, and Walter Goodhart, *Two Renaissance Book Hunters: The Letters of Poggius Bracciolini to Nicolaus De Niccolis* (New York: Columbia University Press, 1974)

Grafton, Anthony, *Joseph Scaliger: A Study in the History of Classical Scholarship*, vol. 1: *Textual Criticism and Exegesis* (Oxford: Clarendon Press, 1983)

Grafton, Anthony (ed.), *Rome Reborn: The Vatican Library and Renaissance Culture* (New Haven: Yale University Press, 1993)

Grafton, Anthony, and Lisa Jardine, *From Humanism to the Humanities: Education and the Liberal Arts in Fifteenth- and Sixteenth-Century Europe* (London: Duckworth, 1986)

Griffin, Clive, *The Crombergers of Seville: The History of a Printing and Merchant Dynasty* (Oxford: Clarendon Press, 1988)

Guy, John, 'Thomas Cromwell and the Intellectual Origins of the Henrican Revolution', in Alistair Fox and John Guy, *Reassessing the Henrican Age: Humanism, Politics and Reform 1500–1550* (Oxford: Basil Blackwell, 1986), 151–78

Hall, Edwin, *The Arnolfini Betrothal: Medieval Marriage and the Enigma of Van Eyck's Double Portrait* (Berkeley: University of California Press, 1994)

Hamilton, K., and R. Langhorne, *The Practice of Diplomacy: Its Evolution, Theory and Administration* (London: Routledge, 1995)

Harvey, L. P., *Islamic Spain, 1250 to 1500* (Chicago: University of Chicago Press, 1990)

Hay, Denys, *Europe in the Fourteenth and Fifteenth Centuries* (2nd edn, London: Longman, 1989)

Hayum, Andrée, *The Issenheim Altarpiece: God's Medicine and the Painter's Vision* (Princeton: Princeton University Press, 1989)

Helms, Mary W., *Ulysses' Sail: An Ethnographic Odyssey of Power, Knowledge, and Geographical Distance* (Princeton: Princeton University Press, 1988)

Hervey, Mary F. S., *Holbein's 'Ambassadors', the Picture and the Men: An Historical Study* (London: George Bell & Sons, 1900)

Heyd, Wilhelm, *Histoire du commerce du Levant au moyen-âge* (2nd edn, Leipzig, 1886)

Higman, Francis M., *Censorship and the Sorbonne: A Bibliographical Study of Books in French Censured by the Faculty of Theology of the University of Paris, 1520–1551* (Geneva: Librairie Droz, 1979)

Hocquet, Jean-Claude, *Le sel et la fortune de Venise*, 2 vols (Lille: Université de Lille, 1978–9)

Hocquet, Jean-Claude, *Le sel et le pouvoir* (Paris, 1985)

Hollingsworth, Mary, *Patronage in Renaissance Italy from 1400 to the Early Sixteenth Century* (London: John Murray, 1994)

Holman, T. S., 'Holbein's Portraits of Steelyard Merchants', *Metropolitan Museum Journal* 13 (1979), 139–58

Holmes, George, 'Cosimo and the Popes', in Frances Ames-Lewis (ed.), *Cosimo 'il Vecchio' de' Medici, 1389–1464: Essays in Commemoration of the 600th Anniversary of Cosimo de' Medici's Birth* (Oxford: Clarendon Press, 1992), 21–31

Hooykaas, R., *G. J. Rheticus' Treatise on Holy Scripture and the Motion of the Earth with Translation, Annotations, Commentary and Additional Chapters on Ramus-Rheticus and the Development of the Problem before 1650* (Amsterdam: North-Holland, 1984)

Hope, Charles, *Titian* (London: Jupiter Books, 1980)

Horn, Hendrick J., *Jan Cornelisz Vermeyen: Painter of Charles V and his Conquest of Tunis*, 2 vols (Netherlands: Davaco, 1989)

Hughes, Barnabus, OFM (ed.), *Regiomontanus on Triangles* (Madison: University of Wisconsin Press, 1967)

Huguenin, Daniel, and Erich Lessing, *La Gloire de Venise: dix siècles de rêve et d'invention* (Paris: Editions Pierre Terrail, 1993)

Hulme, Peter, *Colonial Encounters: Europe and the Native Caribbean, 1492–1797* (London: Methuen, 1986)

Hutchison, Jane Campbell, *Albrecht Dürer: A Biography* (Princeton: Princeton University Press, 1990)

Inalcik, Halil, *The Ottoman Empire: The Classical Age 1300–1600* (London: Weidenfeld & Nicolson, 1973; paperback, Phoenix, 1994)

Ives, E. W., 'The Queen and the Painters: Anne Boleyn, Holbein and Tudor Royal Portraits', *Apollo*, July 1994, 36–45

Ives, E. W., *Anne Boleyn* (Oxford: Basil Blackwell, 1986)

Jardine, Lisa, *Erasmus, Man of Letters: The Construction of Charisma in Print* (Princeton: Princeton University Press, 1993)

Jones, Norman, *God and the Moneylenders* (Oxford: Basil Blackwell, 1989)

Kaufmann, Thomas DaCosta, *Court, Cloister and City: The Art and Culture of Central Europe 1450–1800* (London: Weidenfeld & Nicolson, 1995)

Kaufmann, Thomas DaCosta, *The Mastery of Nature: Aspects of Art, Science, and Humanism in the Renaissance* (Princeton: Princeton University Press, 1994)

Kemp, M., *Leonardo da Vinci: The Marvellous Works of Nature and Man* (London: Dent, 1981)

Kempers, Bram, *Paintings, Power and Patronage: The Rise of the Professional Artist in Renaissance Italy* (London: Allen Lane, 1992)

Kerridge, Eric, *Trade and Banking in Early Modern England* (Manchester: Manchester University Press, 1988)

Khoury, A.-Th., 'Georges de Trebizonde et l'Union Islamo-chrétienne', in *Proche-Orient Chrétien* 18–21 (Jerusalem, 1968–71), 1–110

Kirshner, J. (ed.), *Business, Banking and Economic Thought in Late Medieval and Early Modern Europe* (Chicago: University of Chicago Press, 1974)

Knecht, R. J., *Renaissance Warrior and Patron: The Reign of Francis I* (Cambridge: Cambridge University Press, 1994)

Kristeller, P. O., and F. E. Cranz (eds), *Catalogus translationum et commentariorum: Mediaeval and Renaissance Latin Translations and Commentaries*, vol. 2 (Washington, DC: Catholic University of America Press, 1971)

Lach, Donald F., *Asia in the Making of Europe*, 2 vols (Chicago: University of Chicago Press, 1965)

Landau, David, and Peter Parshall, *The Renaissance Print (1470–1550)* (New Haven: Yale University Press, 1994)

Lattis, James M., *Between Copernicus and Galileo: Christopher Clavius and the Collapse of Ptolemaic Cosmology* (Chicago: Chicago University Press, 1994)

Lemaître, Alain J., and Erich Lessing, *Florence et la Renaissance. Le Quattrocento* (Paris: Editions Pierre Terrail, 1992)

Liss, Peggy K., *Isabel the Queen, Life and Times* (Oxford: Oxford University Press, 1992)

Lowry, Martin, *The World of Aldus Manutius: Business and Scholarship in Renaissance Venice* (Oxford: Basil Blackwell, 1979)

Lowry, Martin, 'The Arrival and Use of Continental Printed Books in Yorkist England', in Pierre Aquilon and Henri-Jean Martin (eds), *Le Livre dans l'Europe de la Renaissance* (Promodis, 1988), 450–7

Lowry, Martin, 'Venetian Capital, German Technology and Renaissance Culture in the Later Fifteenth Century', *Renaissance Studies* 2 (1988), 1–13

Lowry, Martin, *Book Prices in Renaissance Venice: The Stockbook of Bernardo Giunti*, Occasional Papers 5 (Los Angeles: UCLA University Research Library, Department of Special Collections, 1991)

Lowry, Martin, *Nicholas Jenson and the Rise of Venetian Publishing in Renaissance Europe* (Oxford: Basil Blackwell, 1991)

Lowry, Martin, 'L'Imprimerie, un nouveau produit culturel', in Philippe Braunstein (ed.), *Venise 1500. La puissance, la novation et la concorde: le triomphe du mythe* (Paris: Editions Autrement, 1993), 53–71

McConica, James K., *English Humanists and Reformation Politics under Henry VIII and Edward VI* (Oxford: Clarendon Press, 1965)

Maclean, Ian, 'L'Economie du livre érudit: le cas Wechel (1572–1627)', in Pierre Aquilon and Henri-Jean Martin (eds), *Le Livre dans l'Europe de la Renaissance* (Promodis, 1988), 230–7

Malfatti, Cesare (ed.), *The Chief Victories of Charles V* (Barcelona: Sociedad Alianza)

Mark R. and Ahmet S. Çakmak, *Hagia Sophia from the Age of Justinian to the Present* (Cambridge: Cambridge University Press, 1992)

Martines, Lauro, *Power and Imagination: City-States in Renaissance Italy* (London: Allen Lane, 1980)

Mattingly, Garrett, *Renaissance Diplomacy* (Boston: Houghton Mifflin, 1955; paperback, New York: Dover, 1988)

Maxwell, William Stirling (ed.), *The Turks in 1533: A Series of Drawings Made in that Year at Constantinople by Peter Coeck of Aelst* (London and Edinburgh: 1873)

Memoirs of a Renaissance Pope: The Commentaries of Pius II, trans. F. A. Gragg (London: George Allen & Unwin, 1960)

Mercati, Giovanni, *Ultimi contributi alla storia degli umanisti, fasc. 1: Traversariana, Studi e Testi* 90 (Città del Vaticano: Biblioteca Apostolico Vaticana, 1939)

Mollat du Jourdin, Michel, and Monique de La Roncière, *Les Portulans: cartes marines du XIIIe au XVIIe siècle* (Fribourg: Office du Livre, 1984)

Monfasani, John, *George of Trebizond: A Biography and a Study of his Rhetoric and Logic* (Leiden: Brill, 1976)

Monfasani, John (ed.), *Collectanea Trapezuntiana: Texts, Documents, and Bibliographies of George of Trebizond* (Binghamton, NY: Medieval and Renaissance Texts and Studies, 1984)

Morison, Samuel Eliot, *The European Discovery of America: The Southern Voyages, AD 1492–1616* (Oxford: Oxford University Press, 1974)

Munro, John H., 'Money and Coinage of the Age of Erasmus', in *The Correspondence of Erasmus*, trans. R. A. B. Mynors and D. F. S. Thomson, annotated by Wallace K. Ferguson (Toronto: University of Toronto Press, 1974), vol. 1, 311–47

Necipoğlu, Gülru, 'Süleyman the Magnificent and the Representation of Power in the Context of Ottoman–Habsburg–Papal Rivalry', *Art Bulletin* 71 (1989), 401–27

Necipoğlu, Gülru, *Architecture, Ceremonial, and Power: The Topkapı Palace in the Fifteenth and Sixteenth Centuries* (Cambridge, Mass.: MIT Press, 1991)

Nelson, Benjamin, *The Idea of Usury* (Chicago: Chicago University Press, 1969)

Newitt, Malyn (ed.), *The First Portuguese Colonial Empire*, Exeter Studies in History (Exeter: Department of History and Archaeology, University of Exeter, 1986)

Nicolas Copernic ou la révolution astronomique (Paris: Bibliothèque Nationale, 1973)

North, John D., 'Nicolaus Kratzer – the King's Astronomer', *Studia Copernicana XVI: Science and History. Studies in Honor of Edward Rosen* (Kraków: Ossolineum, Polish Academy of Sciences Press, 1978), 205–34

Oberman, H. A., *Masters of the Reformation: The Emergence of a New Intellectual Climate in Europe*, trans. Denis Martin (Cambridge: Cambridge University Press, 1981)

Ortiz, Antonio d', Concha H. Carretero and José A. Godoy (eds), *Resplendence of the Spanish Monarchy: Renaissance Tapestries and Armor from the Patrimonio Nacional* (New York: Metropolitan Museum of Art, 1991)

Pagden, Anthony, *European Encounters with the New World: From Renaissance to Romanticism* (New Haven: Yale University Press, 1993)

Parker, John (ed.), *Merchants and Scholars: Essays in the History of Exploration and Trade* (Minneapolis: University of Minnesota Press, 1965)

Parry, J. H., *The Age of Reconnaissance: Discovery, Exploration and Settlement, 1450–1650* (Berkeley: University of California Press, 1963; London: Cardinal, 1973)

Pasini, Pier Giorgio, 'Matteo de' Pasti: Problems of Style and Chronology', in J. Graham Pollard (ed.), *Italian Medals* (Washington, DC: National Gallery of Art, 1987), 143–59

Petrucci, A., 'Biblioteca, libri, scritture nella Napoli aragonese', in G. Cavallo (ed.), *Le biblioteche nel mondo antico e medievale* (Bari, Laterza, 1988), 187–202

Pettas, William A., *The Giunti of Florence: Merchant Publishers of the Sixteenth Century* (San Francisco: Bernard M. Rosenthal, 1980)

Pike, Ruth, *Enterprise and Adventure: The Genoese in Seville and the Opening of the New World* (Ithaca: Cornell University Press, 1966)

Poliakov, Léon, *Jewish Bankers and the Holy See from the Thirteenth to the Seventeenth Century*, trans. Miriam Cochan (London: Routledge & Kegan Paul, 1977)

Pollard, J. Graham (ed.), *Italian Medals* (Washington, DC: National Gallery of Art, 1987)

Pounds, N. J. G., *An Economic History of Medieval Europe* (2nd edn, London: Longman, 1994)

Queller, Donald, *The Venetian Patriciate: Reality versus Myth* (Urbana: University of Illinois Press, 1986)

Quirino, Carlos (ed.), *First Voyage around the World by Antonio Pigafetta and De Moluccis Insulis by Maximilianus Transylvanus* (Manila, 1969)

Raby, Julian, 'East and West in Mehmed the Conqueror's Library', *Bulletin du Bibliophile* (1987), 297–321

Raby, Julian, 'Pride and Prejudice: Mehmed the Conqueror and the Italian Portrait Medal', in J. Graham Pollard (ed.), *Italian Medals* (Washington, DC: National Gallery of Art, 1987), 171–94

Ravenstein, E. G., *Martin Behaim: His Life and his Globe* (London: George Philip, 1908)

Reynolds, L. D., and N. G. Wilson, *Scribes and Scholars: A Guide to the Transmission of Greek and Latin Literature* (Oxford: Clarendon Press, 1968; 2nd edn, 1974)

Rice, Eugene F., Jr, with Anthony Grafton, *The Foundations of Early Modern Europe, 1460–1559* (2nd edn, New York: W. W. Norton, 1994)

Richards, G. R. B. (ed.), *Florentine Merchants in the Age of the Medici. Letters and Documents from the Selfridge Collection of Medici Manuscripts* (Boston, Mass.: Harvard University Press, 1932)

Rogers, J. M., and R. M. Ward, *Süleyman the Magnificent* (London: British Museum Publications, 1988)

Roover, Raymond de, 'The Effects of the Financial Measures of Charles V on Antwerp', *Revue Belge de Philologie et d'Histoire* 16 (1937), 663–77

Roover, Raymond de, *The Rise and Decline of the Medici Bank, 1397–1494* (New York: W. W. Norton, 1966)

Rose, Paul Lawrence, *The Italian Renaissance of Mathematics: Studies on Humanists and Mathematicians from Petrarch to Galileo* (Geneva: Droz, 1975)

Rosen, Edward (ed.), *Three Copernican Treatises*, 3rd edn (New York: Octagon Books, 1971)

Rosenthal, Earl E., *The Palace of Charles V in Granada* (Princeton: Princeton University Press, 1985)

Roukema, E., 'Brazil in the Cantino Map', *Imago Mundi* 17 (1963), 7–26

Rowan, Steven, 'Jurists and the Printing Press in Germany: The First Century', in G. P. Tyson and Sylvia S. Wagonheim (eds), *Print and Culture in the Renaissance: Essays on the Advent of Printing in Europe* (Newark: University of Delaware Press, 1986), 74–89

Rummel, Erika, *The Humanist–Scholastic Debate in the Renaissance and Reformation* (Cambridge, Mass.: Harvard University Press, 1995)

Runciman, Steven, *The Fall of Constantinople 1453* (Cambridge: Cambridge University Press, 1965)

Rupp, E. G., and Benjamin Drewery (eds), *Martin Luther* (London: Edward Arnold, 1970)

Russell, Jocelyne G., *Peacemaking in the Renaissance* (London: Duckworth, 1986)

Russell, Jocelyne G., *Diplomats at Work: Three Renaissance Studies* (Stroud, Glos.: Alan Sutton, 1992)

Ryckwert, Joseph, and Anna Engel, *Leon Battista Alberti* (Milan: Electa, 1994)

Scarisbrick, J. J., *Henry VIII* (Harmondsworth: Penguin, 1971)

Schama, Simon, *The Embarrassment of Riches: An Interpretation of Dutch Culture in the Golden Age* (London: Collins, 1987)

Schick, Léon, *Jacob Fugger: un grand homme d'affaires au début du XVIe siècle* (Paris: SEVPEN, 1957)

Schmitt, C. B., Quentin Skinner and E. Kessler, *The Cambridge History of Renaissance Philosophy* (Cambridge: Cambridge University Press, 1988)

Screech, Michael, 'Histoire des idées et histoire du livre: une optique personnelle et une profession de foi', in Pierre Aquilon and Henri-Jean Martin (eds), *Le Livre dans l'Europe de la Renaissance* (Promodis, 1988), 553–66

Setton, K. M., '"The Emperor John VIII Slept Here . . ."', in *Europe and the Levant in the Middle Ages and the Renaissance* (London: Variorum Reprints, 1974), 222–8

Setton, K. M., *The Papacy and the Levant (1204–1571)*, 4 vols (Philadelphia: American Philosophical Society, 1976–84), vol. 3

Shaw, Stanford J., *History of the Ottoman Empire and Modern Turkey*, vol. 1: *Empire of the Gazis – The Rise and Decline of the Ottoman Empire, 1280–1808* (Cambridge: Cambridge University Press, 1976)

Skelton, R. A. (ed.), *Antonio Pigafetta: Magellan's Voyage. A Narrative Account of the First Circumnavigation*, 2 vols (New Haven: Yale University Press, 1969)

Skelton, R. A., *Explorers' Maps* (London: Routledge, 1958)

Skilliter, S. A. (ed.), *William Harborne and the Trade with Turkey, 1578–1582* (Oxford: Clarendon Press, 1977)

Skilliter, S. A., 'The Hispano-Ottoman Armistice of 1581', in C. E. Bosworth (ed.), *Iran and Islam* (Edinburgh: Edinburgh University Press, 1971), 491–515

Spallanzani, M., *Ceramiche orientale a Firenze nel Rinascimento* (Florence: Olschki, 1978)

Starkey, David (ed.), *Henry VIII: A European Court in England* (London: Collins & Brown/National Maritime Museum, Greenwich, 1991)

Stephens, John, *The Italian Renaissance: The Origins of Intellectual and Artistic Change before the Reformation* (London: Longman, 1990)

Strieder, J., *Jacob Fugger the Rich: Merchant and Banker of Augsburg, 1459–1525* (Connecticut: Greenwood, 1984)

Surtz, Edward, and Virginia Murphy (eds), *The Divorce Tracts of Henry VIII* (Angers: Moreana, 1988)

Swetz, Frank J., *Capitalism and Arithmetic: The New Math of the 15th Century* (La Salle, Ill.: Open Court, 1987)

'Symposium on Copernicus', *Proceedings of the American Philosophical Society* 117 (1973)

Szablowski, Jerzy, *The Flemish Tapestries at Wawel Castle in Cracow: Treasures of King Sigismund Augustus Jagiello* (Antwerp: Fonds Mercator, 1972)

Thomson, W. G., *A History of Tapestry from the Earliest Times until the Present Day* (London: Hodder & Stoughton, 1906)

Thornton, Peter, *The Italian Renaissance Interior 1400–1600* (London: Weidenfeld & Nicolson, 1991)

Tracy, James (ed.), *The Rise of Merchant Empires: Long Distance Travel in the Early Modern World, 1350–1750* (Cambridge: Cambridge University Press, 1990)

Turner, A. Richard, *Inventing Leonardo* (Berkeley: University of California Press, 1990)

van Iseghem, A. F., *Biographie de Thierry Martens d'Alost, premier imprimeur de la Belgique* (Alost: Spitaels-Schuermans, 1852)

Veinstein, Gilles (ed.), *Soliman le Magnifique et son temps: actes du colloque de Paris, Galeries Nationales du Grand Palais, 7–10 mars 1990* (Paris: La Documentation Française, 1992)

Voet, L., *The Golden Compasses: A History and Evaluation of the Printing and Publishing Activities of the Officina Plantiniana at Antwerp in Two Volumes* (Amsterdam: Vangendt & Co., 1969–72)

Wackernagel, Michael, *The World of the Florentine Renaissance Artist*, trans. A. Luchs (Princeton: Princeton University Press, 1981)

Walter, Robert, *Un Grand Humaniste Alsacien et son époque: Beatus Rhenanus, citoyen de Sélastat, ami d'Erasme (1485–1547)* (Strasbourg: Oberlin, 1986)

Whightman, W. P. D., *Science and the Renaissance: An Introduction to the Study of the Emergence of the Sciences in the Sixteenth Century*, vol. 1 (Edinburgh: Oliver & Boyd, 1962)

Wilson, Michael, *A Guide to the Sainsbury Wing at the National Gallery* (London: National Gallery Publications, 1991)

Zippel, Giuseppe, 'L'allume di Tolfa e il suo commercio', in Gianni Zippel (ed.), *Storia e Cultura del Rinascimento Italiano* (Padua: Antenore, 1979), 288–391

INDEX

Numbers in *italic* refer to pages with illustrations.

REGION FROIDE

CANADA

MER DE FRANCE

MER DESPAIGNE

MER OCCIANE

LE CANCER

ENTILLES

MER DES

LE PERV

LA LIGNE

LA SONA TORRIDA

MER DV SV

RIQVE

TROPIQVE

MER AVSTRALLE

MER DE MAGELLAN

LA TERRE